D0513722

Lobbying

The Art of Political Persuasion

by Lionel Zetter

HARRIMAN HOUSE LTD

3A Penns Road
Petersfield
Hampshire
GU32 2EW
GREAT BRITAIN
Tel: +44 (0)1730 233870
Fax: +44 (0)1730 233880
Email: enquiries@harriman-house.com
Website: www.harriman-house.com

First published in Great Britain in 2008
Copyright © Harriman House Ltd
The right of Lionel Zetter to be identified as the author has been asserted
in accordance with the Copyright, Design and Patents Act 1988.

978-1-905641-69-7

Printed in Great Britain by the MPG Books Group, Bodmin and King's Lynn

---

Praise for Lobbying

"If you read only one book on lobbying, make sure it's this one. Zetter's mastery of his subject proves why the industry voted him Public Affairs Personality of the Year 2008."

– Francis Ingham, Director General & Managing Director, Public Relations Consultants Association

"The leading book on lobbying by the UK's leading expert. Lionel Zetter takes a comprehensive, in-depth approach and writes with authority and enthusiasm. Whether you're in PR, PA, in house, consultancy or a client – this is the book for you."

– Elisabeth Lewis-Jones, President, Chartered Institute of Public Relations

"Public affairs, so often misunderstood and poorly explained, has a superb champion in Lionel Zetter: he writes a brilliant analysis of lobbying that is a must read for anyone wanting to understand the industry, from the seasoned practitioner to the curious observer."

– Robbie MacDuff, Director of Public Affairs, Precise Public Affairs and Chair of the Association of Professional Political Consultants (APPC)

"This will be the new Bible for lobbyists. An indispensable guide for public affairs professionals."

– Neil Sherlock, Partner Public Affairs, KPMG

"The best book on the art of lobbying yet written."

– Iain Dale, Blogger and publisher Total Politics

"If you buy one book about lobbying make it this one."

– Jon McLeod, Chairman, UK Public Affairs, Weber Shandwick

"Lionel Zetter understands better than most the realities of lobbying and its relevance to good governance in the UK. This is an affectionate yet serious analysis by somebody who cares about the lobbying industry. It should be read by anybody who wants to understand how British politics really works ..."

– Peter Bingle, Chairman, Bell Pottinger Public Affairs

"To my knowledge this book is unique in its breadth, depth and geographical scope and I have no doubt that it will quickly become established as an essential companion for public affairs practitioners. It pulls off the unusual feat of being both practical and entertaining and, in my experience, it all rings true. It is an added bonus that Lionel Zetter's fabled network of contacts has also enabled him to pull together incisive and useful tips from senior practitioners across the lobbying business."

– Michael Burrell, Edleman

"The best definition of politics is who gets what, when, where and how. This excellent book shows you the when, where and how."

– Edmund King, President, Automobile Association

"Lionel runs the range from nuts and bolts public affairs handbook to lobbying masterclass – this will be required reading for lobbyists, clients and policymakers."

– Kevin Bell, Regional President, Fleishman Hillard UK, Africa and the Middle East

"This book is great! As someone who has almost been around as long as Lionel – it was great to have such an up-to-date take on who we are, what we actually do and why we are worth it. This book is very informed, illuminating and, I think, the ultimate guide to lobbying."

– Gill Morris, Managing Director, Connect Public Affairs

"This book covers the waterfront of what lobbying is, why we need it, who the key players are and how it all works. Lionel Zetter has combined hard facts, expert interpretation and real-world practitioner insights into a very readable whole."

– Tim Rycroft, Diageo

"Comprehensive, wide ranging and accessible...the first book to span the world of lobbying from London, Brussels and Washington to Asia."

– David Earnshaw, Chairman, Burson-Marsteller Brussels

"Zetter provides one of the most in-depth analyses of lobbying and how it works. Unlike many, he has looked beyond Brussels, Westminster and the Beltway to examine the role of lobbying in the emerging markets. But he has also done much more than just look at the mechanics of lobbying, he has provided one of the most comprehensive analyses of the legitimacy of lobbying in today's democracies. By doing that he has done a service not just for the lobbying industry, but to politicians, civil servants and political scientists alike."

– Sacha Deshmukh, Chief Executive, Mandate Communications

"Public affairs in the UK has no more diplomatic an ambassador and no more valiant a champion than Zetter."

– Jonathan Bracken, Partner and Head of Public Policy, Bircham Dyson Bell

"Rigorous and insightful...the definitive handbook for anyone interested in the craft of lobbying, from industry veteran to A-Level politics student."

– John Lehal, Managing Director, Insight Public Affairs

"Lionel Zetter has done lobbying a big favour. His excellent book explains why well-conducted lobbying is as crucial and relevant to good government today as in the earliest days of democracy. His comprehensive perspective on the modern scene, coupled with wise tips and practical advice, will be invaluable to everyone who can now learn from his experience. The descriptions of the different arts and skills required for lobbying the devolved administrations in the UK, and in Europe, the USA and Asia, make this essential reading for all concerned."

– Barney Holbeche, Chief Parliamentary Adviser, National Farmer's Union

About the author

Lionel Zetter was born in Glasgow. He was educated at American International Schools before going to Bekhamsted School and then on to the University of Sussex. He took a BA Hons in History and African and Asian Studies and an MA in Strategic Studies. He has travelled widely throughout Europe, Africa and Asia.

On the political front the author has worked in the House of Commons and the House of Lords, and also in Conservative Central Office. He has also been a Conservative association chairman, branch chairman, election agent and parliamentary candidate.

During his professional career Lionel was an associate director of the Media Information Group, and company secretary of Political Research and Communications International. He went on to become managing director of Parliamentary Monitoring Services Ltd and Political Wizard Ltd, and non-executive deputy chairman of Dod's Parliamentary Communications Ltd.

He has been chairman of the Government Affairs Group and president of the CIPR. He is a Fellow of the CIPR and the Royal Society of Arts, and a member of the National Union of Journalists. He has written, spoken and taught widely on politics and public affairs. He is now an independent public affairs consultant, vice president of PublicAffairsAsia and a director of the Enterprise Forum.

Foreword

I have worked in public affairs for more than a quarter of a century. Over the years I have been privileged to practise public affairs not just in Westminster and Whitehall but also in Edinburgh, Cardiff and on both sides of the Irish border. I have been involved in lobbying at the local government level, spent five years in Brussels and worked in Washington DC and several state capitals across the US. In all that time I have seen governments and their leaders come and go, witnessed political philosophies rise, fall and in some cases disappear altogether and, without doubt, become more grey haired and increasingly cynical. Yet, at the risk of sounding like a zealot, I have never ceased to be seduced by the siren call of democracy. I still get a kick out of the fact that the votes cast in school and village halls by individual citizens really can make a difference to how their community or country is run. Experience has convinced me – if I ever needed convincing – that Winston Churchill was right when he described democracy as 'the worst form of government except all the others that have been tried'.

Whilst political cultures and systems of government may differ – every country has its own method of developing policies and enacting legislation – the practice of public affairs is broadly the same the world over. The common thread running through every nation is its people, and basic human characteristics and motivations really are the same around the world. At its most fundamental, lobbying is about communication: persuading decision-makers to hear and understand a different perspective or point of view. How that is done must be adjusted to take account of the local political culture, but many of the concepts in this book can easily be adapted and applied in a range of jurisdictions.

Public affairs is often seen as a modern invention and that view is understandable. The twentieth century saw a move away from the concept of limited government and politicians became increasingly involved in the lives of citizens, especially around the time of momentous events, such as the Roosevelt "New Deal" which followed the depressions of the 1930s, and in the years following the second world war. Politicians and public servants now make thousands of decisions every day which affect the lives of those they serve and, inevitably, as political activity increased so did political advocacy. Yet, in reality, lobbying is as old as representative democracy itself. The right to petition for the redress of grievances was enshrined in Magna Carta and later in the English Bill of Rights, and the first amendment to the US constitution. For as long as public figures have been making decisions which affect the lives of others, the art of persuasion – for that is what lobbying is all about – has been used to influence those decisions.

It is all too easy to criticise politicians, not least because members of no other group in society so readily put themselves up to be knocked down. Yet, my experience over the years has been that, with a few notable exceptions (and I will save their names for my memoirs!) most people come into politics motivated by a genuine sense of public service. In the 24/7 media world we now inhabit, politics inevitably moves at a fast pace and politicians often have to make decisions on the basis of limited information and adopting a broad brush approach. All too often, the devil really is in the detail and, just as often, politicians do not have the time or resources to look at that detail. It is at this point that lobbying plays such a crucial role in a democracy: helping to fine-tune public policy, ensuring that decision makers are aware of all the facts and providing practical solutions to problems, not just for politicians, but also for the people they serve.

I have known Lionel Zetter, the author of this book, for as long as I have been involved in public affairs. A well known figure in the industry, he is seemingly omnipresent, yet modest enough to know that he is not omniscient. He is a practitioner of the old school, but one who has never been afraid to embrace the new ideas which abound in public affairs. It is inevitable that there will be those who disagree with some of what Lionel has to say in this book. There will always be someone who can tell you that, in a given situation, the exact opposite approach to the perceived orthodoxy worked for them. That will undoubtedly be true and is part of the fun of public affairs. As Bismarck remarked, politics is 'the art of the possible'. No one can write a prescription for public affairs and, as an experienced practitioner, Lionel has not sought nor claimed to do so.

Lionel has many friends in the lobbying sector, and public affairs in the UK has no more diplomatic an ambassador and no more valiant a champion. It would also be much duller place without him. Lionel will long be remembered in the public affairs pantheon as the man who told a parliamentary select committee that 'there is good lobbying and bad lobbying, just like there is good sex and bad sex, but I think most of us would prefer to have bad sex rather than no sex at all.' It is fervently to be hoped that his efforts in writing this work will at least contribute to reducing the level of bad lobbying!

I have no doubt that this book will prove to be a valuable addition to the growing literature in the field of public affairs and will become required reading not just for practitioners, but also for students of politics and anyone who is looking to break into or simply understand what is a fascinating and fast growing global industry. This book dispels much of the "smoke and mirrors" image of public affairs and lays bare the true essentials of the art we practise – the art of persuasion.

Jonathan Bracken
Partner and Head of Public Policy
Bircham Dyson Bell LLP

Acknowledgements

When I set out to write this book I had no idea how much work would be involved. As ever with these projects it became both a labour of love and something of an obsession.

I could not have finished this project without a great deal of help from many friends and colleagues in public affairs. Those who reviewed the whole book deserve a special mention – so huge thanks to Tim Wilson, Francis Ingham and Jon French.

A special mention is also due to Steve Atack. Without his help – and unrivalled international contacts – this project would have been a great deal harder to undertake. Special thanks also to Jonathan Bracken, who encouraged me in this enterprise and provided the book's foreword.

Others reviewed chapters and generously gave me the benefit of their knowledge and experience of lobbying particular legislatures. They were Ian Twinn (EU), David Earnshaw (also EU), John Ashford (US), Craig Hoy (Asia), John Macgill (Scotland), Rosemary Grogan (Wales), Neil Johnston (Northern Ireland) and Chris Kelsey (London).

I should also thank the many contributors of the "top tips" which leaven my leaden prose throughout the book. Those who contributed include both some of the longest-established names in the industry (in-house and consultancy based) and some of the brightest of the more recent entrants. Also, of course, some elected politicians – who have provided a valuable insight into what it is like to be on the receiving end of the art of political persuasion. To all of them I owe my thanks.

I also need to thank my family for putting up with the early risings and lost weekends which were needed to meet the publication deadlines. Special thanks are due to my son Alec, who is studying Politics and Media at UEA. He helped me enormously with the research, checked the facts, and compiled the index.

My gratitude is also due to my publishers Harriman House – and to Myles Hunt and Suzanne Anderson in particular – for their help and encouragement.

My final thanks are due to the inimitable and irrepressible Doug Smith – he taught me much of what I know about lobbying.

Contents

Preface   xxiii

Part One – Introduction To Lobbying   1

1.1   Definitions   3
1.2   History   6
1.3   Ethics And Regulation   9
1.4   Funding And Donations   19

Part Two – The Mechanics Of Lobbying   23

2.1   Rationale For Lobbying   25

  2.1.1   Threat   25
  2.1.2   Opportunity   26

2.2   Types Of Lobbying Programme   31

  2.2.1   Profile raising   31
  2.2.2   Contact programme   32
  2.2.3   Policy shaping   42
  2.2.4   Legislation changing   50

2.3   Starting A Career In Lobbying   53

  2.3.1   Academic qualifications   54
  2.3.2   Internships   54
  2.3.3   Advertisements   55
  2.3.4   Websites   55
  2.3.5   Recruitment consultancies   56

2.4   Appointing A Lobbying Consultancy   62

  2.4.1   Written proposal   62
  2.4.2   Presentation   63
  2.4.3   Contractual benchmarks   65
  2.4.4   Freelancers   66

Part Three – Tools Of Lobbying   69

3.1   Monitoring And Intelligence   71

     3.1.1   In-house monitoring   72
     3.1.2   Monitoring agencies   76
     3.1.3   Public affairs consultancy monitoring   79

3.2   Reference Titles   81

3.3   Opinion Polling   83

3.4   Relationship Management   85

3.5   Online Campaigning   88

3.6   The Media   91

Part Four – Lobbying Whitehall And Westminster   95

4.1   The Civil Service   99

     4.1.1   Whitehall   100
     4.1.2   Contacting civil servants   102
     4.1.3   Special Advisers   106
     4.1.4   Executive agencies and non-departmental public bodies   108
     4.1.5   Regulators   111

4.2   Political Parties   116

4.3   House Of Commons   119

     4.3.1   The prime minister   120
     4.3.2   The cabinet   127
     4.3.3   Ministers   133
     4.3.4   Parliamentary Private Secretaries   137
     4.3.5   Whips   138
     4.3.6   Members of Parliament   141
     4.3.7   The Queen's Speech   143
     4.3.8   Select committees   147
     4.3.9   Consultation documents   152
     4.3.10   Early Day Motions   154
     4.3.11   Business questions   156
     4.3.12   Petitions   157
     4.3.13   Oral questions   159
     4.3.14   Prime minister's questions   162

	4.3.15	Written questions	164
	4.3.16	Written Ministerial Statements	165
	4.3.17	All-Party Parliamentary Groups	166
	4.3.18	Party committees and groups	168
	4.3.19	Exhibitions	169
	4.3.20	Function rooms	170
	4.3.21	Mass lobbies	172
	4.3.22	Debates	172
	4.3.23	Legislation	175
	4.3.24	Finance	180
4.4	House Of Lords		187
	4.4.1	The cabinet	188
	4.4.2	Ministers	189
	4.4.3	Whips	189
	4.4.4	Queen's Speech	190
	4.4.5	Select committees	191
	4.4.6	Oral questions	192
	4.4.7	Written questions	194
	4.4.8	Debates	194
	4.4.9	Legislation	195

Part Five – Lobbying Other United Kingdom Institutions 203

5.1	Scottish Parliament		205
	5.1.1	Powers	207
	5.1.2	First minister	209
	5.1.3	Cabinet	211
	5.1.4	Legislation	212
	5.1.5	Committees	215
	5.1.6	Oral questions	216
	5.1.7	Written questions	218
	5.1.8	Motions	218
	5.1.9	Petitions	219
5.2	Scottish Government		221
5.3	Scotland Office		225
5.4	Scottish Affairs Select Committee		226
5.5	Scottish Grand Committee		227

5.6	National Assembly For Wales	229
	5.6.1 Powers	230
	5.6.2 First minister	231
	5.6.3 Cabinet	232
	5.6.4 Departments	234
	5.6.5 Finances	235
	5.6.6 Legislation	236
	5.6.7 Debates	237
	5.6.8 Committees	238
	5.6.9 Questions	239
	5.6.10 Petitions	240
5.7	Wales Office	241
5.8	Welsh Affairs Select Committee	242
5.9	Welsh Grand Committee	243
5.10	Northern Ireland Assembly	246
	5.10.1 Powers	247
	5.10.2 First minister and deputy first minister	248
	5.10.3 Executive committee	248
	5.10.4 Legislation	249
	5.10.5 Finance	250
	5.10.6 Debates	251
	5.10.7 Committees	251
	5.10.8 Questions	252
	5.10.9 Petitions	253
5.11	Northern Ireland Executive Departments	254
5.12	Northern Ireland Office	257
5.13	Northern Ireland Affairs Select Committee	258
5.14	Northern Ireland Grand Committee	259
5.15	Greater London Authority	262
	5.15.1 Mayor of London	263
	5.15.2 London Assembly	265
	5.15.3 Finances	266
5.16	Local Government	269
	5.16.1 Structure	269
	5.16.2 Planning	276

5.16.3   Licensing   281
5.16.4   Procurement   282

5.17   Parliamentary Commissioner For Administration
       (The Ombudsman)   284
5.18   Judiciary   285

5.18.1   Pepper v Hart   285
5.18.2   Judicial Review   286
5.18.3   Human Rights Act   288
5.18.4   European Court of Justice   289

Part Six – Lobbying The European Union   291

6.1   History And Background   293
6.2   Council Of Ministers   300

6.2.1   Presidency   301
6.2.2   Comitology   305
6.2.3   COREPER   306
6.2.4   UKREP   307

6.3   European Commission   310

6.3.1   Powers   310
6.3.2   President   312
6.3.3   College of Commissioners   314
6.3.4   Directorates-General   316
6.3.5   UK offices   319

6.4   European Parliament   322

6.4.1   President   323
6.4.2   Members of the European Parliament   324
6.4.3   Powers   326
6.4.4   Parties and political groups   327
6.4.5   Committees of the European Parliament   329
6.4.6   Intergroups   332
6.4.7   Questions   333
6.4.8   Resolutions   334
6.4.9   Petitions   334
6.4.10 Ombudsman   335
6.4.11 UK offices   336

6.5	Policy Formulation	338
	6.5.1 Drivers	338
	6.5.2 Policy Areas	340
	6.5.3 Roles of the institutions	341
	6.5.4 Documents	341
6.6	Legislative Process	343
	6.6.1 European Union law – types	344
	6.6.2 European Union law – procedures	345
6.7	Finances	349
6.8	Other European Union institutions	352
	6.8.1 European Court of Justice	352
	6.8.2 European Court of Auditors	353
	6.8.3 European Economic and Social Committees	354
	6.8.4 Committee of the Regions	354
	6.8.5 European Central Bank	355
	6.8.6 European Investment Bank	356
	6.8.7 European Union Agencies	357
6.9	Other European Institutions	359
	6.9.1 Council of Europe	359
	6.9.2 European Court of Human Rights	360

Part Seven – Lobbying In The United States Of America   363

7.1	The Constitution	365
7.2	The President	368
7.3	The Senate	371
	7.3.1 Senior positions	371
7.4	The House Of Representatives	373
	7.4.1 Senior positions	373
7.5	Committees	375
	7.5.1 Senate committees	375
	7.5.2 House of Representatives committees	376

| | 7.5.3 | Joint committees | 378 |

7.6	Legislation	379
7.7	Finances	383
7.8	Judiciary	387

| | 7.8.1 | Supreme Court | 387 |
| | 7.8.2 | Other courts | 388 |

| 7.9 | The States | 389 |
| 7.10 | Ultimate Lobbying | 392 |

Part Eight – Lobbying In Asia   399

| 8.1 | China | 406 |

	8.1.1	The Communist Party of China	406
	8.1.2	The State and Central People's Government	407
	8.1.3	The National People's Congress	407
	8.1.4	State Council	407
	8.1.5	People's Liberation Army	408
	8.1.6	The people	408

| 8.2 | Hong Kong | 410 |

	8.2.1	Chief Executive	411
	8.2.2	Executive Council	411
	8.2.3	Hong Kong Government	411
	8.2.4	Legislative Council	412
	8.2.5	The future	412

| 8.3 | India | 414 |

| | 8.3.1 | The legislative process | 415 |
| | 8.3.2 | Finances | 417 |

| 8.4 | Japan | 418 |

	8.4.1	The Diet	418
	8.4.2	House of Representatives	419
	8.4.3	House of Councillors	420
	8.4.4	The government	420
	8.4.5	The future	421

8.5	Thailand	424
	8.5.1 The National Assembly	424
8.6	Vietnam	427
8.7	Unique Challenges	430

Part Nine – Lobbying In The Middle East   433

9.1	United Arab Emirates	436

Bibliography	438
Websites	439
Index	441

Preface

If politics, as Jay Leno maintains, is show business for ugly people, then public affairs is PR for grown-ups. It is constant crisis management, with potentially huge rewards for getting it right – and major consequences for getting it wrong.

This book is aimed at three distinct groups of people. The first group is those who are considering entering the public affairs profession, but who are neither sure about what is involved nor how to go about getting their first PA job or internship. The second group is made up of PR professionals who feel that they need to know more about public affairs in order to round off their skill-set – and to be able to function more effectively in the mainstream. The final group consists of public affairs professionals who already have a great deal of experience and knowledge, but who are still keen to continue deepening and widening their expertise.

The actual term lobbying is sometimes shunned by practitioners and clients alike. The press have tried to associate the term with sleaze, and to attach negative connotations to it. Alterative terms such as public affairs and government relations are currently more popular. I feel, however, that the industry needs to reclaim the title, and I have used it as the default term through most of this book.

There are already a small number of books dealing with lobbying in the United Kingdom, some of which just cover Westminster, whilst others also cover the devolved Parliaments and Assemblies. There are a larger number of books dealing with lobbying in the European Union and a plethora of books covering the activity in the United States. A selection of these books is listed in the bibliography.

Special mention, in particular, has to be made of three books. Charles Miller's *Guide to Political Lobbying* (Politicos, 2000) was probably the first serious attempt by a senior lobbyist to cover the lobbying scene in the UK and the EU. It is a superb publication and draws heavily on Miller's policy-based school of lobbying, concentrating on the civil service and ministers.

A more recent book by Stuart Thomson and Steve John has been published by Kogan Page as part of the CIPR's Public Affairs in Practice series. It is entitled *Public Affairs in Practice – A Practical Guide to Lobbying*. It is a truly excellent book which does exactly what it says on the cover.

The final entry in my own personal role of honour goes to Conor McGrath for his book *Lobbying in Washington, London and Brussels – The Persuasive Communication of Political Issues*, published by the Edwin Mellen Press as part of their *Studies in Political Science* series. This mighty tome is meticulously researched and has a rightful place on any lobbyist's bookshelf.

Despite these three excellent books there is still a paucity of books which concentrate on the practical aspects of lobbying, and which compare and contrast the systems in Westminster, the devolved bodies, the EU, the US, Asia and the Middle East. Hence I have attempted to throw more light on the lobbying scene in the UK and worldwide.

My own experience in the world of public affairs stretches back over three decades. I have worked in the House of Commons and the House of Lords. I have worked in Conservative Central Office and been a Conservative association chairman, branch chairman, election agent and parliamentary candidate. I have been chairman of the Government Affairs Group, and president of the CIPR. I was company secretary of Political Research & Communications International (PR+CI), which was one of the UK's first specialist lobbying companies. I have also founded, and sold, companies which provided monitoring, intelligence, publishing, polling and campaigning services. I currently act as an independent public affairs consultant in Westminster, and I am a vice president of PublicAffairsAsia (which I helped to found along with colleagues Craig Hoy, Mark O'Brien and Steve Atack) and a director of the Enterprise Forum. It is this experience which I have drawn on in writing this book.

There are nine parts to this book. Part one deals with general aspects of lobbying – definitions, history, ethics, regulation and funding. It puts the rest of the book in to some kind of a context.

Part two deals with the actual mechanics of lobbying. There are sections on the rationale for lobbying – why organisations actually make the decision to lobby. There is also an overview of the various types of lobbying programme. There is some guidance on how to embark upon a career in lobbying, and how to go about appointing a lobbying company.

The third part of the book deals with the tools which any lobbyist – in-house or in-consultancy – needs to have at his or her disposal. This part covers monitoring and intelligence, polling, relationship management, online campaigning, coalition building – and when and how to use the media.

The next section of the book covers lobbying in Westminster and Whitehall. It covers the Whitehall civil service, and also the political parties, the House of Commons, and the House of Lords. It is in many respects the core of the book.

In part five the focus moves slightly wider afield and encompasses the lobbying scene in the other institutions within the UK. This includes the Scottish Parliament, the Welsh and Northern Ireland Assemblies, the Greater London Authority, local government (and its various associations), regulators and the judiciary.

The various institutions of the European Union are covered in part six. The three main institutions are the European Commission, the European Parliament and the Council of Ministers. However there are also sections on other EU (and some extra-EU) bodies, and some advice on how to use national civil servants and politicians in the EU context.

In part seven we turn to the home of lobbying – the United States. This section covers the Senate and the House of Representatives, and also goes down to state level. It is important to look at how the lobbying industry has developed in the US, even if you are unlikely to find yourself lobbying in that arena. The Americans not only invented lobbying, but they have developed many of the techniques which are now being adopted in the United Kingdom and the European Union.

The penultimate chapter deals with the fast growing market of public affairs in Asia. This massive continent is home to the world's biggest democracy in India and the world's most populace nation in China. The public affairs industry is booming throughout the region – but most especially in the Association of Southeast Asian Nations (ASEAN) countries, Japan, China and India. The industry in Asia employs both public affairs veterans from the UK and the US, locally employed lawyers, and former civil servants and politicians. As with so many industries Asia has much to learn from America and Europe, and we have much to learn from them.

Finally, chapter nine touches on the Middle East. This region has not to date been a fruitful one for lobbyists, partly because of a lack of Western-style liberal democracies. However, there is enormous wealth in the region, and the United Arab Emirates is leading the way by opening up to Western companies and Western investment. PR is firmly established in Dubai, and public affairs will undoubtedly not be far behind.

Just a word on gender definition. I fully acknowledge the contribution which female lobbyists and politicians have made to their respective scenes, and I have tried to be gender neutral throughout this book. However, where a post (such as US president) has never been filled by a female, I have used the shorthand "he".

Inevitably this book – reflecting my own experience – has a Westminster bias. I have tried, however, to do justice to the devolved bodies which have emerged and grown in stature over the last decade. I have also, I hope, reflected the global impact which the evolving European Union has had on world politics. Finally, I have offered due deference to the United States as a military, economic and lobbying super-power, and looked to Asia, which will play an increasingly important role in the decades to come.

As I have stated in the acknowledgements section of this book I have had tremendous help in putting all of the sections together. Any mistakes, however (and there will inevitably be some) are all down to me and me alone.

Part One –
Introduction To Lobbying

1.1 Definitions

It is important at this early stage in the book to try to arrive at a definition of lobbying. No definitive definition has ever been agreed upon. To my mind a simple and straightforward definition would be that lobbying is the process of seeking to influence government and its institutions by informing the public policy agenda. It is also, of course, the art of political persuasion.

The public policy agenda does not just consist of the legislature and the civil service. A full-spectrum campaign may also need to seek to influence executive agencies, Quangos, regulators, local government and the media. These are the groups which dictate the public policy agenda, and it is the process of seeking to inform and influence them which we refer to as lobbying.

Attempts to influence the public policy agenda can take place at various stages of the process, and for a variety of reasons. The rationale for lobbying will often dictate the timing of the campaign, and the resources devoted to it. If the campaign is about dictating pure policy the odds are that involvement will be initiated at the very earliest stage of the process, and the lobbying may be undertaken by academics, think-tanks or in-house lobbyists. If it is about changing a bill which is already underway then there is a bigger chance that professional multi-client lobbying consultancies will be drafted in.

Good lobbying usually means getting involved at the very earliest stages of policy formulation. This can mean getting think tanks to champion your ideas, or it can mean feeding in to the policy reviews which all of the major political parties undertake between elections. Alternatively, it can mean using the media to alter the public perception towards an issue, thereby indirectly influencing the party officials and politicians who want to get elected or stay elected.

Author's top tip

There are few golden rules in lobbying. One of them, however, is that the earlier you get involved in the process the greater your chance of success. Early involvement also keeps the costs down. Feeding your views in to a middle-ranking civil servant at an early stage is almost cost-free and can save the substantial sums involved in retaining a lobbying consultancy to "fire-fight" at a later stage.

When journalists talk about lobbying they are usually referring to multi-client lobbying consultancies. They also usually frame their comments in a negative fashion. This is partly because some lobbyists have behaved inappropriately in the past, and these usually minor scandals are retrieved from the morgues and given a fresh airing every time a journalist pens a piece on the subject. It may also be because journalists feel that only they should have a direct influence on the public policy agenda, and they may be jealous of the influence which lobbyists can and do exert.

There are some 75 multi-client lobbying consultancies in the UK. Approximately two-thirds of these belong to the Association of Professional Political Consultants (APPC), and others belong to the Public Relations Consultants Association (PRCA). Many of the individuals within those consultancies also belong to the Chartered Institute of Public Relations (CIPR), and its sectoral group the Government Affairs Group (GAG). All of these bodies operate codes of conduct, the stipulations of which will be dealt with later in this book.

There is a division even within the small world of multi-client lobbying consultancies. Some of these – mainly the smaller ones – solely undertake lobbying. Others are the public affairs divisions of larger public relations firms. These, in turn, may be subsidiaries of advertising agencies – many of whom are in turn owned by American parent companies. There does seem to be an evolutionary process at work here, with specialist public affairs companies being set up by one individual, or two or three lobbying partners. These are then either subsumed into a larger lobbying consultancy or acquired by a public relations consultancy which wants to set up a public affairs division. After a few years the process is often reversed, with the key lobbyists breaking away to start their own independent consultancies all over again.

Lobbyist-turned-academic Karl Milner estimates that there are between 600 and 700 lobbyists working in consultancies in the UK. These individuals have often come in to the consultancies through having worked in the civil service or one of the two Houses of Parliament. Alternatively, they may have worked for one of the political parties, either at headquarters or at local level. They are attracted to multi-client lobbying consultancies because they get the opportunity to work on a wide range of clients and campaigns, and the training and experience gained is therefore very good. In the past consultancy-based lobbyists also earned the highest pay in the industry, although this is no longer necessarily the case.

As well as a revolving door between Parliament and the civil service, and lobbying consultancies, there is also a revolving door between consultancies and in-house teams. Large firms and organisations have realised that it is sometimes cheaper to poach the account executive from the consultancy and have them work full-time in-house for them. They do, however, often still retain consultancies either at a lower fee level or on an *ad hoc* basis as the need arises.

Quoting American academics Karl Milner calculates that there is a ratio of 4 to 1 between in-house and in-consultancy practitioners. That would put the total number of lobbyists working in the UK at some 3500 to 4000. These are not just divided between in-consultancy and in-house, there is also a sub-division within the in-house contingent. This is between those who work for commercial concerns (the "corporates"), and those who work for not-for-profit organisations. These latter organisations can be charities, pressure groups, trade unions, trade associations or professional bodies.

Since the term lobbyist has been saddled with negative connotations by the media, in-house practitioners in particular have adopted alternative job descriptions – from public affairs executive to parliamentary officer, to government relations executive. For the purpose of this book I prefer to stick to the shorthand of lobbyist and lobbying – partly for the sake of brevity, and partly as an attempt to reclaim the term from its negative connotations.

Contributor's top tip

Public affairs should be about delivering solutions. The most targeted and well-argued case will fail if you do not provide a workable way forward. Certainly you need to understand the needs of your audience and know who to talk to but too many campaigns simply reflect the desire to moan and criticise policy rather than offering a constructive alternative. You (in-house) or your client (consultants) are meant to be the experts and if you cannot solve the problem why should anyone be expected to work it out for you? The solution may be relatively simple, requiring just an alteration in behaviour, or more complex, requiring legislation. It is only once that you understand this that you can start to build your campaign – identifying audiences, messages, potential alliances etc.

You can make as much noise as you want to, but when the politician or civil servant asks "how can we solve this problem?" you have to have an answer that is realistic and which can be delivered.

Dr Stuart Thomson, Public Affairs Consultant, Bircham Dyson Bell

1.2 History

Lobbying has been going on since time immemorial, and there is certainly a case for saying that lobbying is one of the world's oldest professions. Whenever an individual, or group of individuals, wields power over society, there will be other individuals or groups of individuals who will have tried to persuade them to exercise that power in a particular way. Lobbying is both natural and inevitable.

The forums of both Greece and Rome were frequented by ancient lobbyists, who would seek to influence both senators and plebs for or against the issues of the day. The courts of kings and princes were thronged with courtiers, and those courtiers were the lobbyists of their day. If the barons had not lobbied King John, he would not have signed the Magna Carta at Runnymede, and democracy in Britain might have evolved very differently.

The actual origins of lobbying as a term and as a structured business – as opposed to a reflexive activity – are disputed. What is beyond dispute is that those origins lie either in Westminster or Washington.

One version puts the origins of the term in Washington in the 1860s. Those seeking to influence President Ulysses S Grant would congregate in the lobby of the Willard Hotel and try to attract the great man's attention in order to raise specific areas of concern with him. Legend has it that after a while President Grant tired of their attentions and referred to them scornfully as lobbyists.

In fact the actual activity of lobbying in the United States predates the Willard Hotel and President Grant. It is a matter of public record that in 1792 (just three years after the US federal constitution was adopted) William Hull was retained by Virginian veterans of the Continental Army to lobby for additional compensation in recognition of their services during the American revolutionary war.

In the nineteenth century lobbying in Washington had evolved to the point where it was recognisably the precursor of today's industry. Senators and Representatives were not only entertained by lobbyists, they were also extensively briefed and counter-briefed on the issues of the day. Contacts were facilitated, speeches drafted, and training was provided for those who were to appear before Congressional committees.

By the start of the twentieth century the lobbying in Washington had developed still further. New media such as radio were embraced, as were new technologies such as the telegraph. This enabled the US lobbying industry to start engaging in the kind of grassroots campaigning which is still at the heart of the US lobbying industry today.

In 1928 the Senate tried to enact a bill which would have required lobbyists to register with the secretary of the Senate and the clerk of the House of Representatives. However, the House blocked this bill, and it was not until 1946 that Congress passed the Federal Regulation of Lobbying Act. This required any person or organisation who tried to 'influence, directly or indirectly, the passage or defeat of any legislation by the Congress of the United States' to register their details (including salaries and expenses) with officials of both Houses of Congress.

So it would seem that the United States has the strongest claim to be regarded as the birthplace of the lobbying industry. However, with respect to the actual term lobbying, there is also a school of thought which claims that it originated in Westminster, referring to either the Members' Lobby or the Central Lobby of the Palace of Westminster. Since this was rebuilt in 1854 it is possible that this claim is valid and the lobby referred to was at Westminster and not the Willard Hotel.

Wherever the term originated, there is no doubt that that organised commercial lobbying originated in the US rather than the UK. In fact the first recognised UK lobbyist was Commander Christopher Powell, who did not set up shop until just before the second world war. Commander Powell's firm, Watney and Powell, was bought in the 1960s by another ex-military man, former Royal Marine Commando Professor Tim Traverse-Healy OBE.

Traverse-Healy traces the true origins of the lobbying industry in the UK to the landslide victory which Labour won in 1945. Clement Attlee set about transforming the UK political scene, setting up the National Health Service and seeking to nationalise whole swathes of British industry. It was the Labour government's attempt to nationalise the British sugar industry which prompted the launch of what Traverse-Healy refers to as the UK's first political public relations campaign – with its Mr Cube figurehead successfully fending off the government's nationalisation ambitions.

The Labour victory in 1945 firmly established that party as the alternative government in the United Kingdom. If the Conservatives were not the government, then it would be formed by Labour and not the Liberals, who were in long-term decline. This persuaded big business in the UK to organise in order to defend itself against future nationalisation plans, and against higher taxes and tighter regulation. The result was the formation of such bodies as the Economic League and Aims of Industry – and the emergence of a recognisable lobbying industry in the United Kingdom.

During the 1960s and most of the 1970s lobbying in the UK was largely discrete and below the radar. The arrival of Margaret Thatcher in 1979 seems to have been the signal for the lobbying industry to emerge from the shadows, and to openly parade its contacts with and influence on the apparatus of government. Firms such as Ian Greer Associates and PR+CI (where the author worked in the early 1980s) emphasised their strong connections with the Conservative government. Others, such as Gifford Jeger Weeks (GJW), made much of their multiparty connections. Either way, the industry was plainly prospering, and the prospect of open-ended and exponential growth beckoned.

This all came to a shuddering halt in 1994 when the *Guardian* published a series of allegations which rocked the Conservative government and ultimately led to the demise of Ian Greer Associates. Mr Greer had openly supported Conservative candidates at election time – which broke no parliamentary rules. He had also admitted paying MPs commission for the introduction of new business. The Guardian stories however, related not to backbench MPs, but to government ministers. Harrods owner Mohamed al Fayed told the *Guardian* that he used IGA to effectively hire government ministers, and Tim Smith and Neil Hamilton resigned. John Major's government never fully shook off the taint of sleaze from this point.

Further dubious practices were exposed by *The Sunday Times*, who mounted a "cash for questions" sting which netted two Conservative backbenchers. The lobbying industry reacted by setting up the APPC, and the government announced the establishment of the Nolan Committee on Standards in Public Life.

1.3 Ethics And Regulation

The lobbying industry often finds itself in a no-win position. Either lobbyists have little or no influence – in which case why should anyone retain them? Or they do have influence, in which case the press – and some sections of the public – think that this is an unwarranted distortion of the democratic process.

The answer to this apparent conundrum is two-fold. It is always worth making the point that lobbying has always gone on, it is an entirely natural activity, and it is better that it takes place in an open and structured environment rather than operating in secret. Most lobbyists agree that they need to be open and transparent in their attempts to inform and influence the public policy agenda, and that they must be accountable and answerable to somebody other than the press.

The lobbying industry must also emphasise that its activities are actually beneficial to the body politic and to democracy at large. There are at least two sides to every argument, and as in a court of law it is only right that both parties should have access to professional representation which will ensure that their side of the argument is put across in a coherent and cogent fashion.

It is also the case that the lobbying industry goes some way towards redressing the huge inbuilt advantage which the government of the day has. The government has the civil service at its disposal, and ministers usually have their own Special Advisers (SPADs). Lobbyists supply government backbench MPs and opposition front and backbenchers with detailed briefs and arguments which prevent the government from having a free run with its policies and legislation.

It is also undoubtedly true that the lobbying industry helps Parliament to produce better legislation. At a time when bills are more strictly timetabled than ever, lobbyists help redress the huge advantages which governments have both by their access to the civil service and their majority position in the House of Commons. Whether it is by responding to consultation documents, or by providing MPs and peers with detailed arguments or carefully drafted amendments, final Acts of Parliament undoubtedly emerge as better pieces of legislation as a result of the input of lobbyists.

So there is a strong argument for saying that lobbying is not just legitimate, it is also laudable. That is not to say that lobbying is above reproach, or that all lobbyists invariably behave in an ethical fashion. But then neither do all lawyers, accountants, doctors, journalists nor politicians.

It is the fact that not all lobbyists behave impeccably at all times which has led to a number of damaging stories in the *Guardian*, *The Times*, *The Sunday Times* and the *Observer*. We saw in the previous section how John Major set up the Committee on Standards in Public Life, and how the lobbying industry set up the APPC.

There are four bodies which are involved in the self-regulation of the lobbying industry in the UK. They are the Chartered Institute of Public Relations (CIPR), the Government Affairs Group (GAG), the Association of Professional Political Consultants (APPC) and the Public Relations Consultants' Association (PRCA). Full details of their codes of conduct are carried on their websites, but here is a brief description of their backgrounds and their characteristics.

The CIPR was founded in 1957, and it received its Royal Charter in 2006. The Royal Charter requires its members to always act in a way which contributes to the public good, whilst the code of conduct requires members to 'maintain the highest standards of professional endeavour, integrity, confidentiality, financial propriety and personal conduct.' All potential transgressions of this code are referred initially to the CIPR's Professional Practices Committee, and if no satisfactory solution is reached cases are then passed on to the Disciplinary Committee. This committee can fine, suspend or expel members.

Most Government Affairs Group members are also members of the parent body, the CIPR. As such they are bound by the CIPR's code of conduct. However, GAG has its own code of conduct, which deals with integrity, transparency, confidentiality, undue influence and conflicts of interest.

The PRCA was set up in 1969 and represents some 150 of the larger consultancies in the United Kingdom. Its members are mainly in public relations, but many of them also have a public affairs division. There is a PRCA code of conduct aimed specifically at lobbyists, which covers much the same ground as the CIPR and GAG codes.

The APPC was set up in 1994, specifically as a result of the furore surrounding the allegations made by Mohamed al Fayed and the *Guardian* about the activities of Ian Greer Associates and Conservative MPs and ministers. It now has some 60 members, and a strict code of conduct. This not only contains the general requirement to behave openly and ethically, but also the requirement that all staff and clients must be listed on the APPC website, and that no member company can employ an MP, peer, MEP, MSP or Northern

Ireland, or Greater London Assembly member. It also bans its members from holding parliamentary security passes.

It is on these three stipulations that the APPC has found itself in occasional disagreement with the CIPR and GAG. Some lobbying companies and individual lobbyists – including lobbying lawyers – feel that they must have the option of not always disclosing all of their clients. This can be because the client's issues are commercially sensitive, as with the case of a takeover. Or it can be that disclosure is prohibited, as may be the case where the firm is regulated by the Law Society. Or it can simply be the case that the consultancy is retained for advice as opposed to advocacy.

The second stipulation of not employing politicians is perhaps less controversial. Most legislatures prohibit members from being involved in lobbying, so the issue does not generally arise. The exception is the House of Lords. Currently peers are not paid a salary, they merely receive modest "allowances". Many therefore have to hold down a job outside of the House of Lords, and some half a dozen do so by working in public relations of public affairs. The APPC forbids its members from employing these peers, but the CIPR and GAG feel that until such time as peers are paid a proper salary it is unreasonable to deprive them of their livelihood.

There is again some disagreement on the question of passes. Some MPs and peers provide lobbyists who work for not-for-profit organisations, charities, pressure groups and trade unions with passes – and their jobs are virtually identical to lobbyists who work for companies. In Brussels lobbyists have always been able to hold security passes, provided they undergo security checks and obey a code of conduct.

To date the lobbying industry in the UK is self-regulated. This regulation is undertaken by the bodies already covered, by the press (which takes a lively interest in its activities), and to a degree by Parliament (which has a slightly ambivalent relationship with the industry).

Contributor's top tip

Ethics and accountability have never been more important – especially for public bodies. So make sure you can prove you have the highest standards by belonging to one (or more!) of the bodies that regulate public affairs work – the PRCA, the CIPR and the APPC. They have rigorous Codes of Conduct which will reassure the people who you are approaching for a meeting. Make a virtue of your membership – it may get you in the door where non-members are excluded.

Francis Ingham, Director General, PRCA

The Westminster Parliament is also a self-regulatory body. Whilst the government of the day – assuming it has a working majority – can nearly always get its legislation through, it is Parliament itself which decides on its standing orders and (at the time of writing) the remuneration of its members.

Ministers and MPs keep a close eye on each other's activities. There is a *Register of Members' Interests* published in hard copy form at the beginning of each new parliament under the authority of the Committee on Standards and Privileges. It is then updated regularly throughout the parliament and published on the Parliament website.

All employment outside of Parliament must be registered, as must all substantial gifts and all overseas trips paid for by a third party. The purpose of the *Register* is to:

> *'provide information of any pecuniary interest or other material benefit which a Member receives which might reasonably be thought by others to influence his or her actions, speeches or votes in Parliament, or actions taken in the capacity of a Member of Parliament.'*

The thresholds for registration are one percent of an MP's salary for gifts or hospitality, 10% for rental income, or 100% for property or shares. At the time of writing MPs earn just over £60,000 a year, so the percentages apply to that figure.

Contributor's top tip

I believe that there are three key attributes for successful public affairs.

1. Accessibility – politicians need to feel that they can always reach their company contact when they need too.

2. Candour – tell politicians more, not less (whilst also remembering to provide a one page summary) and do so in a timely manner. In transmitting messages to the political world it is the responsibility of all of us in the industry to understand, appreciate and comply with the demands placed on those in public life.

3. Finally, always remember that the first role of a politician is to represent their constituents.

Simon Astley, Director Parliamentary Relations, BAE Systems plc

Since 2002 peers who are not on leave of absence have to provide details of all relevant outside interests. The definition of relevant is:

'whether the interest might reasonably be thought by the public to affect the way in which a member of the House of Lords discharges his or her parliamentary duties.'

Again the *Register* is published initially as hard copy, but then updated regularly on the Parliament website.

Ministers also have to register all perks, gifts and benefits in the *Register of Members' Interests*. Their activities are, however, also subject to the strictures of the Ministerial Code. The Ministerial Code was first published in 1992, as a result of the scandals which rocked the Major government in that year. The main stipulations of the Ministerial Code are:

'Ministers must not knowingly mislead Parliament and the public and should correct any inadvertent errors at the earliest opportunity. They must be as open as possible with Parliament and the public, withholding information only when disclosure would not be in the public interest, which should be decided in accordance with established parliamentary convention, the law, and any relevant Government Code of Practice.'

The Code was tightened up by Tony Blair in 2007. The main innovation of the 2007 reform was the appointment of an Independent Adviser who could be asked by the prime minister to investigate allegations of ministerial impropriety. Allegations of breaches of the Ministerial Code are often used by the opposition parties – and the press – to try and bring about the downfall of a minister.

Special Advisers (SPADs) are quasi civil servants appointed under article 3 of the Civil Service Order in Council of 1995. Their role is to provide ministers with confidential advice, free from the constraints placed upon civil servants. This means that they can offer party political advice, and also advise ministers on their relations with the media over and above the "unspun" services provided by government press officers. The main stipulations in the SPAD Code of Conduct are:

'Special Advisers should conduct themselves with integrity and honesty. They should not deceive or knowingly mislead Parliament or the public. They should not misuse their official position or information acquired in the course of their official duties to further their private interests or the private interests of others. They should not receive benefits of any kind which might reasonably be seen as compromising their personal judgment or integrity. They should not, without authority, disclose official information which has been communicated in confidence in Government or received in confidence from others.'

Which leads us neatly onto the Civil Service Code. Civil servants are supposed to be politically neutral. They are supposed to act in the interests of the country, and of the government of the day. They are not allowed to help ministers with specifically party political matters.

Generally speaking this rule is strictly observed. Some civil servants who work closely with a minister may find the need to be strictly neutral difficult to observe. These include a minister's private office (where civil servants often spend more time with a minister than with their own family), and a minister's permanent secretary and director of communications. On the whole the British civil service has an enviable and well-deserved reputation for impartiality and efficiency, and corruption is almost unheard of.

The Civil Service Code was introduced in 1996, and revised in 1999 to take account of devolution. Its preamble states that:

'The constitutional and practical role of the civil service is, with integrity, honesty, impartiality and objectivity, to assist the duly constituted Government of the United Kingdom, the Scottish Executive or the National Assembly for Wales constituted in accordance with the Scotland and Government of Wales Acts 1998, whatever their political complexion, in formulating their policies, carrying out decisions and in administering public services for which they are responsible.'

It should also be noted that the Cabinet Office has published a detailed code on the dealings between civil servants and lobbyists. The code draws heavily on the work of the Nolan Committee. It can be found on the Cabinet Office website, but the key paragraph is:

'The government's approach, reflecting the approach of the Nolan Committee, is not to ban contacts between civil servants and lobbyists but to insist that wherever and whenever they take place they should be conducted in accordance with the Civil Service Code, and the principles of public life set out by the Nolan Committee. This means that civil servants can meet lobbyists, formally and informally, where this is justified by the needs of government.'

All politicians and civil servants in the UK are now expected to abide by the Nolan Committee's "Seven Principles of Standards in Public Life". These are detailed on the Committee's website, but in summary they stipulate that elected politicians and civil servants alike should act with selflessness, integrity, objectivity, accountability, openness and honesty, and that they should offer leadership. All of the codes outlined above draw on those seven principles.

There have been a number of inquiries into lobbying over the last two decades. The first was the original Nolan Inquiry, which the author gave evidence to in 1995. This recommended the appointment of a Parliamentary Commissioner for Standards, a recommendation which was accepted and acted upon. It also recommended the setting up of a register of lobbyists – a recommendation which was not acted upon.

There have also been two Commons select committee inquiries into lobbying in recent history. In 1991 the Select Committee on Members' Interests recommended the setting up of the Register of Members' Interests. The committee decided, however, not to recommend a public register of lobbyists. This decision was based on the view that everyone had the right to lobby Parliament and government. The committee also expressed fears that such a register might create the impression that registered lobbyists had some kind of a monopoly on influencing public policy.

In 2007 the Commons Public Administration Select Committee launched an inquiry into lobbying. This was prompted by a Labour backbencher, John Grogan, who had run a campaign criticising the activities of some lobbyists. He particularly objected to the fact that not all lobbying consultancies had chosen to join the APPC, and he tabled an Early Day Motion suggesting that only APPC consultancies should be retained by government-funded bodies. The author submitted written evidence to that inquiry in late 2007 in his capacity as president of the CIPR, and also gave oral evidence in 2008.

Washington has the most closely regulated system governing lobbying anywhere in the world. As well as the immediate post second world war legislation, there has more recently been the 1995 Lobbying Disclosure Act. This was further tightened in 1996, when a penalty of up to five years in prison was introduced for any lobbyist who did not adhere to the draconian registration and disclosures regime.

Despite this fearsome regulatory regime both American politics and American lobbyists do still on occasion behave in an inappropriate fashion. The Abramoff scandal dwarfs anything which has been seen in the UK, with Jack Abramoff currently serving a five year prison sentence for offences which shocked even colleagues and competitors on "K Street". The explanation for this and previous scandals is the nature of US politics. Because the US system allows advertising during elections, and because Representatives have to be re-elected every two years, there is a constant need for high-level fundraising. It is also the case that "pork barrel" politics are a feature of US political life, and the ability to earmark funding for particular projects and particular localities makes the stakes in lobbying very high. The rewards for a successful campaign are commensurately generous.

In Brussels a sensible compromise has been struck between the self-regulatory regime in the UK, and the ultra regulatory regime in Washington. Initial attempts to regulate the industry go back as far as 1991, when the first European Parliament recommendations were drawn up. However, the *rapporteur's* recommendations were not adopted by the European Parliament – possibly because they were linked with a proposed register of MEPs' external sources of income. The European Commission in any event concluded at that stage that there was no rationale for regulating lobbyists.

Despite this a number of lobbying associations were formed, all with their own codes of conduct. These included the European Public Affairs Consultancies Association (EPACA), the Society of European Affairs

Professionals (SEAP) and the European Association of Political Consultants (EAPC). These voluntary codes were fairly basic, covering matters such as not bribing MEPs or officials and being transparent about the clients they were representing.

They were, however, picked up by the European Parliament. From 1999 the Parliament issued lobbyists with security passes in return for basic promises of good behaviour. These passes showed who the pass-holder worked for, and they were of a distinctive shape and colour in order to easily identify the pass-holder as a lobbyist. The parliament's *Quaestors* issue annual (renewable) passes in return for lobbyists signing up to a code of conduct. They have to:

- State the interests they represent in any dealings with MEPs and their staff.

- Refrain from any activity designed to obtain information dishonestly.

- Not circulate for profit to third parties documents obtained from the Parliament.

- Not claim any formal relationship with the Parliament.

- Obtain the permission of an MEP before engaging a member of his or her staff in any capacity.

- Comply with the rules associated with employing former members of an MEP's staff.

- Comply with the rules for employing former MEPs.

The European Parliament, European Commission and the Council of Ministers are now reviewing the arrangements for regulating lobbyists and controlling their access. Estonian Commissioner Siim Kallas unveiled his long-awaited European Transparency Initiative, which contained proposals to introduce a voluntary register of lobbyists. In return for taking part in this voluntary initiative, lobbyists are offered not just security passes, but also priority access to consultation processes. The voluntary scheme has now been launched, but it seems almost inevitable that it will move in time from being voluntary to being compulsory.

So between Washington, Brussels and Westminster we have the three main models for regulating lobbying. In Washington the regime is demanding and mandatory. In Brussels the system is currently voluntary, and carries carrots as well as sticks. In Westminster, at least for the moment, regulation and registration are left in the hands of the industry's own bodies.

Whatever the regulatory regime, it is undoubtedly the case that it takes two parties to create a proper sleaze scandal. Somebody has to offer an inducement in the first place, but unless that inducement is accepted, there can be no corruption. Both lobbyists and politicians or civil service have to behave improperly in order for a corrupt transaction to be consummated.

In lobbying, as in any other walk of life or line of business, it is more about common sense than rules. The vast majority of people know nearly all of the time when they are doing something wrong. It is as much about peer pressure as anything else, and there is a need for the kind of climate to be created where unethical behaviour becomes regarded as unacceptable.

Author's top tip

If in doubt, use the tabloid test. If you (or your client) are thinking about saying or doing something and you are not sure about the ethics, ask yourself how you would feel if your words or actions resulted in a front page story in a national newspaper. If that prospect makes you nervous, or if you think that it would damage your reputation or your business, do not do it.

Contributor's top tip

Tell the truth, the whole truth and nothing but the truth. Because if you do not, sooner or later it will come back to haunt you.

Hopefully, fibbing is finally out of fashion. And politicians of all hues have proved that massaging the stats, sexing-up the text and other kinds of over-spinning can land you in real trouble. But in the era of increasing transparency, the Freedom of Information Act and an investigative/invasive media, even sins of omission can bring about your downfall.

People in power do not make decisions in a vacuum. They react to argument and they respond to the climate of opinion. So make sure your clients' cases are well presented in all the arenas of Westminster and Whitehall that matter to them. Then back that up by winning over key stakeholders, opinion formers and third-party endorsers, as well as cultivating a profile when necessary in the media. Fully integrated campaigns are simply more effective.

Simon Buckby, Managing Director, Champollion

1.4 Funding And Donations

Politicians and political parties always need money. They need it to keep their headquarters and local offices ticking over between elections, and they especially need it at election time.

Having said that, there is a vast difference between the funds that need to be raised in the US and in the UK. Congressmen need to get re-elected every two years, and the pressure to fund-raise is relentless. They need to raise thousands of dollars every week if they are going to have any chance of being successful in the next cycle.

Under Westminster electoral rules there are limits as to what can be spent at local and national level. A candidate fighting a constituency can only spend around £8000-9000 (depending on the number of electors registered in the constituency) once the election has been called. They can, however, currently spend as much as they like between elections – although there are moves to change that situation.

Currently party headquarters are more restricted by resources than regulations. The Conservatives and the Labour Party would typically spend some £25m on a general election campaign, with the Lib Dems spending approximately £3.5m. This money goes on staff, literature, mail shots and (most expensively) newspaper and poster advertising. Between elections the party headquarters spend from £10m-15m a year for the two main parties, with the Lib Dems spending perhaps a tenth of that amount.

So although the sums needed in the UK are modest compared with those in the US, parties still need to raise funds. Membership subscriptions cover just a fraction of the money needed. The Conservative Party currently claims to have approximately 275,000 members, Labour approximately 200,000, and the Lib Dems approximately 75,000. Their subscriptions and local fundraising activities cannot even pay for the peacetime needs of the parties, never mind filling their election war chests.

The funding deficits are made up by donations from trade unions (in the case of Labour) and wealthy benefactors (in the case of all three main parties). The parties also look to lobbyists to provide some funding directly, or to encourage their clients to contribute money.

The rules about making donations to political parties or to individual donations are laid down in the Political Parties, Elections and Referendums

Act 2000 (PPERA). This established the Electoral Commission, whose job it is to oversee all aspects of electoral law. Under PPERA no foreign donations can now be accepted, and all donations of £1000 or more at local level or £5000 or more at national level, must be reported to the Electoral Commission.

Warning!

Donations of over £200 from impermissible donors (overseas residents etc) not only have to be returned, but they also have to be declared even if they are returned. Check the source and permissibility of any donation before either accepting it or passing it on to a political party.

Provided an individual or company is UK registered it is perfectly legal for them to make a donation to political parties. The problem is that they will be identified as a donor, and that may not be a good political move, or it may be bad for the donor's reputation. Nevertheless many businesses and business people make such open public donations every year – especially in the run-up to a general election.

One fairly low key way of donating to a political party is to help to sponsor a front-benchers private office. It should be emphasised, however, that this has to be declared in the same way as a cash donation. The previously used system of having "blind trusts" (which enabled anonymous donations to be made) is no longer permissible.

Lobbying consultancies do swell the coffers of the political parties, although it is unusual for them to do so in the form of a straight donation. Consultancies are often asked to take tables at party fund-raisers, and many of them see this as a good way to entertain their clients and curry favour with the political parties simultaneously. Other perfectly legitimate activities include sponsoring a party policy launch, or sponsoring or advertising in a leaflet or handbook.

Party conferences represent an excellent opportunity for lobbyists to channel either their own or their clients' money into party coffers. Exhibition stands can be booked at anything from £5000 to £50,000. It is possible to sponsor fringe meetings and receptions, or to advertise in the conference centre. Again, there are usually gala dinners involving the party leader and other senior figures. It is possible to either sponsor the whole event, or to take a table. All of these are legitimate activities, which is just as well because again they need to be declared.

Author's top tip

One method of assisting a political party indirectly in a form which is non-declarable is to sponsor a think tank – or at least one of their reports. Think tanks are nearly all registered charities, so in theory at least they are not party political. However, nearly all think tanks are closely aligned with one political party or another. For instance the IPPR and Demos are closely aligned with the Labour party, whilst the Adam Smith Institute and the Institute of Economic Affairs are closely aligned with the Conservatives. What is more, some think tanks are closely associated with individual politicians – sometimes even the party leader. So, Margaret Thatcher was closely linked to the Centre for Policy Studies, whilst Gordon Brown is known to be very close to the Smith Institute (not to be confused with the Adam Smith Institute). So by sponsoring a report by one of these think tanks, it is possible to positively influence the thinking of political parties and politicians without having to register a donation.

Part Two –
The Mechanics Of
Lobbying

2.1 Rationale For Lobbying

Lobbying industries exist wherever there are democratic governments which are open to external advice and influence. In well-established liberal democracies such as the United Kingdom and the United States lobbying industries have thrived. In Brussels, as the elected European Parliament has continued to acquire more power, the lobbying industry has grown commensurately.

It has to be acknowledged that some people doubt the necessity for lobbying. These doubters can be journalists who resent the fact that lobbyists challenge their monopoly on informing and influencing politicians. Or, of course, they can be politicians who genuinely feel that they – and they alone – should have a monopoly on policy formulation and law making. We have, however, dealt with the ethical rationale for lobbying in a previous section.

What we now need to establish is the pragmatic rationale for lobbying. Why do companies, charities, trade associations, trade unions, pressure groups and professional bodies lobby government? The answer is very simple: governments represent either a threat or an opportunity to those organisations.

2.1.1 Threat

Let us deal with the threat aspect first. Every year the UK government passes some 20-30 major pieces of legislation. It also issues over 2000 Statutory Instruments, bringing into force powers granted to ministers in earlier Acts of Parliament. Any one of these Acts of Parliament or Statutory Instruments could have a dramatic effect on the activities of any one of the types of organisation listed above. That effect could be not just dramatic, but terminal. The government can put you out of business overnight.

The most obvious way in which a government could have a negative impact on a company or organisation is to ban their products or their activities. If you were a manufacturer of handguns, or you owned a shop which sold handguns, or you ran a pistol firing range, then the government effectively put you out of business with its Firearms (Amendment) Act 1997. A lobby was mounted against this legislation, but such was the strength of public feeling post-Dunblane that it was never going to succeed. In the event the Act has done nothing to help keep illegal handguns off the streets, and there has in fact been a dramatic increase in the ownership and use of illegal handguns.

Following an off-the-cuff pledge by Tony Blair on Newsnight his government tried to ban hunting with dogs. However, there was no public appetite for a complete ban, and after a successful lobbying campaign by the Countryside Alliance and others a compromise was reached whereby hunts could still operate - but it became an offence to deliberately allow hounds to kill foxes or stags. There has been minimal enforcement of this legislation, and hunts throughout England are thriving. Moreover, the Conservatives have pledged to reverse the ban when they next form a government.

The government does not have to impose an outright ban on your business or activity in order to have a substantial negative effect upon it. Smoking is not illegal in the United Kingdom, nor indeed anywhere else. What is more, the government accrues huge amounts of money by imposing swingeing taxes on tobacco. At the same time the government has legislated to ban cigarette advertising, and to ban smoking in enclosed public places. Local authorities have tried to extend the smoking ban to include open spaces under their control, and it is not totally inconceivable that in a few years time smoking in homes will be banned. The tobacco industry in the US and Europe is fighting a rearguard action, whilst developing its markets in South America, Africa, the Middle East and Asia. Meanwhile, smokers feel increasingly isolated for pursuing a habit, which whilst undoubtedly unhealthy, is still legal.

Another area where the government seems to be ambivalent is alcohol. Again, the government accrues huge amounts of revenue from alcohol excise duty – and Scotch whisky in particular is an enormous export. The current Labour government has also substantially relaxed the licensing laws in England and Wales, hoping to generate a continental café-style drinking culture. At the same time the government inveighs against binge drinking, and accuses pubs and off-licences of not doing enough to discourage under-age drinking. Currently there are voluntary agreements in place with the industry not to use advertising which is aimed primarily at young people, and increasingly health warnings appear on advertisements and labels. The industry is aware, however, that this voluntary structure may not survive forever and that the threat of legislation is never far away.

2.1.2 Opportunity

So the government can severely curtail – or even put a permanent stop to – your organisation's principle activity. It can also, of course, give an enormous boost to that activity.

Taking the example we used earlier, the government has, through legislation and policy, brought about a steady decline in the number of smokers in the UK. This is bad news for the cigarette companies but it has brought about an explosion in the market for nicotine replacement patches, inhalers, lozenges and gums. Bad news for one industry can be counter-balanced by good news for another. And, of course, it is not just alternative businesses which stand to benefit: by being seen to have driven government policy, anti-smoking pressure groups and cancer charities have done what their members wanted them to do, and have also boosted their own credibility and funding at the same time. Ultimately, of course, if a pressure group is totally successful it will put itself out of business, but such a complete public policy triumph is rare.

Pressure groups are, in some respects, the ultimate lobbyists. They exist solely to pressurise governments and to distort or dictate the public policy agenda. Whether they are environmental pressure groups, animal welfare pressure groups, or pressure groups formed to promote the interests of sufferers from a particular illness or disability, their whole efforts and energy are focused purely on shifting the government's position. They seek to make the government act in a way in which their members would approve because they gather and retain members, and keep funds coming in, only in so far as they can demonstrate progress towards achieving their stated objectives.

Charities are also pressure groups, but they often have dual functions. One is to persuade the government to change its policy in a way which is advantageous to its members and supporters. They also, however, often have the function of providing advice and support to their members, and of seeking a cure for whatever condition they may suffer from. Their lobbying activities are restrained by charity law, and the Charity Commission oversees their activities in this regard.

Trade unions attempt – quite legitimately – to increase the wages and pensions of their members, and to improve their working conditions. This means persuading the government to allocate a fractionally greater share of the national wealth pot to their members than was previously the case. Usually this involves quiet bargaining and negotiations behind the scenes. If this is not successful some unions mount public hearts and minds campaigns to get the weight of public opinion behind their demands. Failing that, of course, there is always the option of industrial action – a crude but sometimes successful form of lobbying.

Professional bodies also lobby constantly, and they are often very successful in their efforts. Some, such as the British Medical Association (BMA) and the

Law Society, have the dual advantage of very large memberships who are also both articulate and disciplined. When the former mounts a campaign on health, or the latter on the law, governments certainly listen – and often accept their arguments.

Smaller professional bodies are also active lobbyists, often trying to cement their positions as the arbiters or regulators of their particular specialist area. Although they may have the expertise bodies representing specialised professions such as physiotherapy or optometry inevitably have less clout than larger organisations. Their focused campaigns and their persistence can, however, often mean that they achieve their desired results.

Another positive incentive to lobby is the fact that the government takes in some 40% of the nations GDP in the form of direct and indirect taxes. This is then disbursed in one form or another – and represents a huge pot of wealth which some organisations are able to dip in to.

As has been said, trade unions, which can have millions of members and huge fighting funds, hold great sway over governments – particularly Labour governments. However, the business alternatives also have enormous clout – particularly over Conservative governments. No government of whatever hue wants to fall out with the Confederation of British Industry (CBI), or the Institute of Directors (IoD). All of the main parties routinely send their most senior frontbenchers to their conferences, and they are routinely consulted – and listened to – in all aspects of policy affecting industry or commerce.

Increasingly other bodies such as the Federation of Small Businesses (FSB) are also forcing their way into the reckoning. Although they are often on the same side, and wish to influence government policy to move in the same direction, there are occasions when the objectives of the CBI and the FSB are diametrically opposed. When that happens, it is a battle between the CBI's billions of pounds and the FSB's hundreds of thousands of members for the government's ear.

The government can also be a very direct source of funding for business. It spends some £600bn a year, making it by far the biggest customer in the country. It also underwrites a substantial proportion of British business's exports through the Export Credits Guarantee Department (ECGD).

For several important British industries the government is far and away the biggest customer. For the British defence industry (nowadays dominated by BAE Systems) the government is easily the biggest domestic customer – for obvious reasons. It also has to licence all exports, and it underwrites some of them through the ECGD. For really large contracts the UK defence industry often has to compete against US defence companies and other EU companies as well. This is where some of the fiercest – and most expensive – lobbying battles of recent years have taken place.

Again, the pharmaceutical industry is almost entirely reliant on government. The regulatory framework for research is set by government, and once new drugs have been developed they have to be approved – although there is now a strong EU dimension to this process. The pharmaceutical industry then has to persuade the National Institute for Health and Clinical Excellence (NICE) that their product represents good value for the National Health Service. Finally, of course, the government has to fund the NHS to a suitably high level so that it can afford to purchase the pharmaceutical products.

Whilst not as reliant as the defence and pharmaceutical industries on government, the government is the IT industry's biggest client. Departments such as Work and Pensions are largely driven by IT. The current government is also committed to seeing through the development of an IT system to co-ordinate patients' records and allow them to book hospital places. According to the National Audit Office (NAO) this project will cost £12 billion, and according to other sources might cost £20 billion. The current government is also committed to the national ID card scheme, which is also scheduled to consume billions of pounds of taxpayers' money.

There is always a tendering process for these giant projects. Quite often, however, they are won by consortia of various hardware and software companies, which sometimes form a subsidiary company simply to manage these projects. Once the project is underway, and the government has already invested billions of pounds in them, they frequently return to the government asking for more cash to cover unforeseen difficulties and developments. The government is then faced with the option of scrapping the project, or pumping in further resources.

Finally, of course, there are the management consultancies. Again, they are not solely reliant on government, but they do make billions of pounds out of government contracts. Sometimes these management consultants are divisions of the larger accountancy firms, sometimes they are specialist management consultants. Either way their use has mushroomed since Labour came to power in 1997.

Anyone who truly wonders why organisations lobby has really only got to listen to the chancellor's Pre-Budget Report and Budget Statement. In the space of about an hour the chancellor dispenses largesse in one direction – and grabs extra revenue from the other. There are always winners and losers in the Budget. The public is often given minor sweeteners in the form of increased tax allowances, but almost always ends up worse off when indirect taxes are taken into account.

For charities, pressure groups, trade unions, business organisations and companies the Budget always signals a need to lobby frantically on behalf of their members, supporters and shareholders. Sometimes chancellors are persuaded to change aspects of the Budget by a particularly noisy or skilful lobbying campaign – particularly one which has the media onside. Quite often, however, those lobbying just feel that they need to be seen to be making the effort, and they are just going through the motions.

So as we have seen the government occupies a uniquely powerful position at the centre of national life. It can – and does – legislate at will and on a whim. It raises and dispenses some 40% of every penny earned in the country. It is the nation's parent, and as every toddler and teenager knows, you can get what you want out of a parent through charm or tantrums – or sometimes a combination of the two.

Contributor's top tip

The five golden rules of lobbying are:

1. Communicate from your audience's perspective, not yours

2. Put emotional messages at the heart of your communications strategy

3. Use accessible, easily understood everyday ideas, words and images to readily communicate a simple, clear message

4. Do not be afraid of education and evidence

5. Have confidence in your message, and communicate that confidence

Derek Draper, Media Trainer and Psychologist

2.2 Types Of Lobbying Programmes

2.2.1 Profile raising

Some public affairs campaigns are designed simply to raise an organisation's profile. This is in effect political PR, with the objective being to boost recognition of a company or organisation amongst a key group of stakeholders.

There are a number of reasons for mounting such a campaign. Where a company or organisation is in a competitive situation *vis a vis* similarly placed rivals, and those rivals have a higher profile, there can be a rationale for seeking to redress that balance. Getting positive mentions in *Hansard* can be seen as the political equivalent of press cuttings: it might not achieve very much, but it does show that your consultants or your in-house team are doing their jobs.

A more pragmatic reason for mounting a profile raising campaign is to make sure that your organisation achieves its rightful place within the body politic. Government departments are constantly consulting with interested bodies over policy initiatives, and if politicians and civil servants are not aware of your existence you will not be part of that consultation process. Equally, if your profile is very low, they might not consider it worthwhile consulting you even if they are aware of your existence.

However, the main reason for mounting a profile raising campaign is so that politicians and civil servants are made aware of who you are and what you do. This has the practical effect that when an issue of concern actually does arise, those politicians and civil servants are already aware of who you are, and they will be better disposed towards accepting your right to enter in to the debate. It is much easier to have your say, and you are much more likely to be listened to, if your previous efforts have ensured that there is a high degree of recognition of who you are and what you represent.

Contributor's top tip

It is often very difficult for the clients of Public Affairs consultants or in-house communication functions to let go of the detail of the issue or project they are grappling with. This leads to the most common mistake made when trying to engage with Public Affairs stakeholders – lack of empathy. What is important to your audience is how the issue impacts on them and the people they care about. Shape your message and approach accordingly, do not presume too high or too low a level of understanding, and do your research. If you build your success on a contact book then you are destined to fail, but understanding of people and process is key and never dates. Never make your first contact with a stakeholder an "ask" – build relationships before you need them. Nothing is more certain to guarantee failure than a lack of empathy because it is symptomatic of a lack of respect.

Rory O'Neill, UK Managing Director, Sovereign Strategy

2.2.2 Contact programme

A contact building programme leads naturally on from a profile raising programme. It is the logical next step, and it enables organisations to cement the relationships which will arise as a natural result of such a general campaign.

Contact building is the most useful peacetime activity which an organisation can undertake. If the first time you approach a politician or official is when you need their help, you may get very short shrift. It is far better to establish contacts well ahead of the time when you actually need them.

There are three parts to any contact programme:

1. You need to research the people who will be in a position to make decisions about your organisation's objectives, or who may be inclined to be sympathetic towards them.

2. You then need to contact those individuals in order to brief them and establish a relationship.

3. Finally, you need to make sure that those contacts are kept up, and that their details are updated.

Research

No matter what your area of activity is there will be a civil servant whose job it is to know about it, and hopefully to also assist you when you need help.

Finding that civil servant is not always easy. The first port of call can often be the *Civil Service Year Book* – which despite its name is published twice a year. It has a comprehensive index, and each department is laid out in a fashion which should enable you to locate the relevant person. Failing that, there should be a general enquiry phone number that you can call to try and locate the relevant official. Dods also publish a civil service guide, and many senior officials are detailed in their DodOnline database.

Author's top tip

Civil servants change jobs frequently. They can either be promoted, moved to another department, be given new responsibilities, or they can resign or retire. However, if you have an established contact who you know has moved, phone his or her direct line and ask for them. You may well get straight through to their replacement, or the person answering that extension may transfer your call – which avoids using the sometimes slow switchboard or the general enquiry number.

Legislators are usually much easier to research – whether you are talking about MPs or peers, MEPs, MSPs, or members of the Welsh, Northern Ireland or London Assemblies. You can search the *Register of Members' Interests* to find MPs with an interest in your field of operation, or you can search the Parliament website to find those who have spoken or asked questions about your area of activity.

There are also subscription services which enable you to do complex searches for MPs with particular interests, broken down by region, party etc. I have already mentioned DodOnline, but such a service is also offered by DeHavilland. There are also some free sites over and above Parliament's own website – such as www.TheyWorkForYou.com

Here are some groupings which will provide you with the foundation for your contact programme:

- Ministers in relevant departments
- Opposition frontbench spokespersons with relevant portfolios
- The relevant select committees
- The relevant All-Party Parliamentary Groups (APPGs)
- The relevant backbench group or committee

Making contact

Having done your groundwork, you now have to put that research into effect.

In the case of a civil servant, the normal procedure would be to send them a detailed briefing which tells them who you are, and what you do. This can be as technical as you like, because they are (hopefully) fairly expert in their area of responsibility. It would then be advisable to follow up with a phone call, to check that the briefing document had been received, and to ask if they have any queries. If they do have queries, that is a good excuse to suggest a meeting – either at their office or yours.

> ### Warning!
>
> Civil servants are very wary about accepting lavish hospitality. However, once you have established a relationship with them, it is perfectly acceptable to either invite them to any reception you are hosting, or to buy them a modest lunch. If you invite them anywhere too exotic or expensive they will almost certainly refuse – and they may treat you a bit more warily in the future.

With politicians the first thing you have to realise is that you have to get past their gatekeepers. Most MPs receive over a hundred letters (and even more emails) a day. Priority is always given to constituency mail – because the number one consideration for an elected politician is to get re-elected. After that, priority will be given to the politician's major subject interest area – especially if they are a minister or frontbench spokesperson. After that would come the politician's secondary areas of interest – perhaps relating to a portfolio or select committee membership which they formerly held, or their former occupation prior to being elected.

Briefing documents for politicians need to be less technical than those for civil servants. It is also very important that the briefing includes an executive summary, preferably on one side of A4 – two at most. It is essential that you not only spell the politician's name correctly, but that you get all of his or her titles and any honours down correctly.

If you are a company, charity or other interest group it is as acceptable just to send briefings to politicians who your research has identified as having a genuine interest in your area of activity. Some public bodies, however, feel obliged to send all politicians their annual report. They may end up in the bin, but there is a statutory duty to inform Parliament which must be observed.

Whether you are sending a briefing to a civil servant or a politician it is important to abide by a few basic rules:

- Briefly describe who you are, and what you do
- Succinctly outline the problem or issue
- Be absolutely accurate in your facts, and scrupulous in the way you present them
- Always offer a solution
- Always include a "call to action".

Author's top tip

A substantial proportion of correspondence sent to politicians is filed unopened in the round metal filing cabinet – commonly known as the wastepaper bin. This is especially true where the correspondence is in a brown envelope with a printed address label. If you want to get your correspondence opened then I suggest that you use better quality white envelopes, and type (or even write) the address. Having succeeded in getting your correspondence opened, it will have more chance of actually being seen by the politicians if it is topped and tailed – preferably by a senior person within your organisation.

Contributor's top tip

Think carefully about where to target your message – and to whom. Your client's best advocate or champion may not be the most obvious person.

A managing director I knew wanted to send a letter about government policy relating to breast cancer to all female MPs, on the basis that they would all be bound to be interested in the subject, purely by virtue of their gender. A small voice from the corner of the room opined (correctly, in my view) that it was a mistake to exclude male MPs, simply for being male, when so many of them might have had personal experience of the disease through their wives, daughters, sisters or mothers.

Helen Johnson, Helen Johnson Consulting Ltd

Maintaining contact

Having identified the targets for your contact programme, and having made the initial contact, it is essential that you maintain that contact.

Meetings with civil servants are fairly easy to arrange provided you have something relevant to discuss with them. Depending on their seniority you might get between half an hour and an hour with them, and they are generally more comfortable in the environment of their own departmental buildings.

Politicians are usually very busy – and they are not really in control of their diaries. They will normally arrange to meet you at their office, or in one of the many lobbies or corridors which Westminster and the devolved Parliament and Assembly buildings possess. It is important to get straight to the point with them, because they tend to have very low boredom thresholds, and they may be called away at any minute. Also make sure that you take a briefing note of some kind with you, so that you can let them have it if the meeting is cut short.

Ministers are also obviously extremely busy. They do, however, tend to have more control over their diaries – or at least their private offices do. It is not always easy to get a meeting with a minister, but if you can persuade a supportive MP to request a meeting with a delegation, ministers nearly always agree. It is vital to field a senior team when meeting ministers – probably your chief executive and your head of public affairs should attend. If you employ lobbying consultants they should also form part of the delegation, but their role should probably be confined to that of note-taker (the minister's private secretary or assistant private secretary will also be taking a note). As observers they will also probably be able to give you a good assessment of how the meeting went. After the meeting make sure that you write to the minister, thanking him or her for their time, and briefly chronicling the discussions and any action points.

Author's top tip

Before the meeting check with the private office how much time has been allocated for the meeting. Then make sure that you only use a maximum of half the time putting your own case. You need to allow the minister time to respond, and you need to allow time for discussion. If your delegation talks for the whole of the meeting, the minister will simply thank you for coming and his or her staff will show you the door at the end of the allocated time.

If you invite a minister or backbencher out to lunch it is important to establish timings in advance. A normal lunch would be 12.45pm or 1pm until 2pm or 2.15pm. Proximity to the minister's office, the Parliament or the Assembly building is crucial. If you are lunching just one individual ask them where they would like to go. If it is small party, book a table at a good restaurant which is close to hand. In Westminster the restaurants which MPs especially like are Shepherds, The Cinnamon Club, The Atrium and Quirinale.

If you are organising an evening reception location and timing are crucial. If you can book a room in the actual Parliament or Assembly building that is ideal, because if a division is called politicians can disappear and vote and then return to pick up where they left off. Because business is usually only arranged two weeks in advance you will not be able to avoid particularly popular debates or running three line whips. It is, however possible to avoid certain days. In Westminster, Friday is useless because there is either no business at all or just private Members' business. Thursday evenings are also pretty hopeless, as most MPs travel back to their constituencies that afternoon. Mondays are also not ideal, because some MPs like to stretch out their weekends by an extra day. So that basically leaves Tuesdays and Wednesdays!

If you are holding a reception it is a good idea to try to secure a minister in a relevant portfolio to say a few words. The head of your organisation should introduce him or her, and also do the thanks – but briefly. You should have name badges for the "home team", and for other external guests, but not for parliamentarians (who will generally be wearing their passes in any event). You should also have some literature which they can take away if they are interested. It is permissible to have "goody bags" to dispense to guests, but their value should be modest, they should be easily portable, and ideally they should relate to your organisation's field of activity. A photographer is also essential, to capture images for your website or magazine.

Author's top tip

Politicians are notorious for not showing up at events which they have accepted invitations for. Do not take offence – they are very busy, and often have last-minute matters to deal with. As a rule, only about half of those who accept an invitation to turn up may actually do so. Also, some who have declined or have not replied actually do in the end turn up.

Through a sponsoring politician it is sometimes possible to mount a small exhibition within the precincts of the Parliament or Assembly building. In the case of the House of Commons, this is in the Upper Waiting Gallery at the entrance to the select committee corridor.

There is no actual fee for securing an exhibition – you just have to find a member prepared to enter the ballot until he or she is lucky enough to win. However, you will have to put on a good display, and you will have to have staff on hand to answer any queries throughout the week.

Party conferences present the best possible opportunities for maintaining contacts. Ministers and backbenchers almost all attend – even if only for a day or two. Ministers are without their civil servants (who are not allowed to attend party political events), although they are likely to have their Special Advisers (SPADs) with them. Backbenchers are generally quite relaxed, and they are often looking for a chance to get away from their constituency delegates.

At party conferences there are a number of ways to establish your presence. Traditionally taking an exhibition stand is the favoured method. It gives you a solid location and base, and you will attract the attention of passing politicians, delegates, party activists and journalists alike. They are, however, expensive. A stand will cost you anything from £5000-50,000, you will have to have a team of at last two and ideally four people to man it – and they have to be put up in hotels and fed and watered. By the time you factor in travel, a four day conference could cost you £10,000 without any problem. If you do all three main conferences, that is a serious slice of any organisation's public affairs budget.

Author's top tip

Nothing looks sadder than an unmanned stand. If you are going to the trouble and expense of organising a conference stand make sure that you take enough people to man it during conference hours. That probably means taking a team of at least four people.

Instead of having an exhibition stand some organisations organise a fringe event. These usually take place at lunchtime or early evening. The key element is the speaker. You need to get the minister or senior spokesperson for whatever field of activity you are engaged in. Sometimes it is better to form a small panel, with the senior spokesperson, somebody from your organisation, and perhaps a journalist who specialises in your field. A backbencher from a relevant committee can also be useful.

When organising a fringe event it is important to realise that you will be in direct competition with a large number of other events. You must therefore not have unrealistic expectations as to turnout – anything above 20 people is good. The main point is that you get the senior spokesperson, you exchange views with him or her, and you get some pictures and coverage – even if it is only in your specialist magazines.

There are some things which you can do to maximise turnout at your fringe event:

- Choose a subject which is topical

- Give the event a catchy title

- Try and make sure that you have a minister – or shadow minister – making the address or sitting on the panel

- Try and avoid clashing with a major event – such as the leader's speech

- Advertise in the conference fringe guide
- Have pre-printed flyers – and hand them out from your stand (if you have one) or just to passing delegates
- Offer food – preferably hot food
- Offer alcoholic drinks – champagne if you can afford it

Easier than having an exhibition stand or holding a fringe event is to organise a reception. You will still need a heavyweight speaker, but otherwise all you need to do is book a room, publicise the events (as above), and pay for the food and drink. Depending on numbers and what you are serving, this can be done for well under £5000.

Warning!

Never stay in the conference hotel. It will cost you twice as much as any other hotel, you will not get any service because all the staff will be tied up with receptions and events – and some idiot will always set off the fire alarm at 4am!

If you have gone to the expense of attending conference (paying for a pass, travel and accommodation) you should also take as much advantage as possible of other people's events. Some are invitation only, but most are happy just to have their numbers boosted. If you take along a good supply of business cards you can make some great contacts – politicians, lobbyists, exhibitors or journalists.

Author's top tip

If you are going to make the most of party conferences you need to be out and about for 18 hours a day. My tips to anyone attending conference is to wear comfortable shoes, grab food any time it is on offer, and watch your alcohol intake and drink spacers (a non-alcoholic drink between each alcoholic one). Also, if you get a chance, slip back to your hotel for a 'power nap' during some of the duller afternoon sessions!

If you meet somebody at conference get their card and follow up with a letter or email saying how great it was to meet them. Then add them to your Christmas card list, and then write to them ahead of the next year's conference saying that you hope to see them again. That is enough to keep a contact simmering until such time as you may need to get in touch with that individual over a specific issue.

Anecdote

In the 1980s and 1990s conferences were much more alcoholic affairs than they are today. During the last night of conference it was something of a tradition for hardened conference attendees to drink through the night in the conference hotel bar. At one conference in Bournemouth we were still in the bar when they began setting up for the early morning conference TV interview. A young man came in and was bibbed up whilst his make-up was applied. We did not recognise him, so one young female delegate went up, tapped him on the shoulder, and politely asked who he was. He leaned back and rather pompously announced 'I am Justin Webb.' She nodded and then turned to the assembled bar flies and asked in a very loud voice 'who the f*uck is Justin Webb?' Not unreasonably, we were all asked to leave!

Contributor's top tip

Do not listen to the "nay-sayers" – go to the party conferences! Frankly, if you do not want to go to a political conference you should be asking yourself what you are doing in public affairs.

Okay, there is the time away from home/office and the cost, if not covered by a client. But you will be mixing with senior politicians, various stakeholders, policy wonks, think-tankers, delegates and, of course, the media – the very people your clients are paying you to engage with on their behalf.

Conference tips?

- Balance a planned daily itinerary with spontaneity – you simply do not know where that breakthrough opportunity might come from and may need the freedom to explore

- Prepare a 30 second pitch spiel – short introductory chats work better than long presentations, and often lead to formal meetings subsequently

- Throw yourself into and enjoy the networking – fringes, receptions and the bars are ideal places to combine insightful political discussions with contact building, identifying new business opportunities and, of course, developing your wine-tasting skills!

Darren Caplan – Brands2Life

2.2.3 Policy shaping

In theory at least policy is what politics is all about. Politicians always say that arguments should be about policy and not personalities. In fact politics is about policy, personalities and events. Lobbyists cannot control events, although they can try and foresee them. They also cannot change politicians' personalities, although they should be aware of them and what the effect those personality traits have on outcomes. What lobbyists definitely can do, however, is help to shape policies.

Political parties

The most obvious starting point when seeking to influence the public policy agenda is with the parties themselves. Most political parties have a perceived place on the political spectrum – either left, right or centre. They do shift their positions, however, in order to maximise their support from the electorate. Most parties in the UK try and lay a claim to the centre ground, because history shows that in UK electoral terms that is where most of the votes are to be found.

Most political parties also have their shibboleths – policies or beliefs that are so rooted in their history that they are visceral and almost impossible to shift. Examples might be the Conservative's belief in free markets, Labour's attachment to the welfare state, and the Lib Dem's passion for electoral reform. On occasion the parties are prepared to compromise on even these core beliefs, although if they abandoned them completely they would no longer be the same parties.

These core beliefs influence policy across the full spectrum – they inform all of the parties' central policy commitments. Ultimately, however, political parties exist to gain – and then hold – power. If you can persuade them that a particular policy is a sure-fire vote loser, they will undoubtedly at least consider ditching or diluting it.

All of the political parties pay at least lip service to the notion that they consult their rank and file members in the formulation of policy. In the case of the Lib Dems, indeed, their annual party conference is technically the sovereign body when it comes to policy formulation.

In fact, policy is tightly controlled by the party leader, the cabinet or shadow cabinet, and elite groups within the party headquarters. They may consult widely, they may pay lip service to their party board, or the National Executive Committee (NEC), or conference – but ultimately policy is formulated by half a dozen ultra bright individuals. It is then sanctioned by the party leader – following consultation with senior colleagues. The alternative to this tight control is an incoherent and contradictory document, and electoral disaster.

When a party is in opposition it has a golden opportunity to fundamentally review its policy. It is unburdened with the responsibilities of government, and it can be radical in its thinking. It can also take a long hard look at exactly why it finds itself in opposition, and which of its policies helped to place it in that unsatisfactory position. Sometimes, as with Labour after 1979 and the Conservatives after 1997, it can take several election defeats to persuade the losing party that it has to have a root and branch overhaul of its policies, and perhaps its image.

Parties in opposition tend to be short of money, and sometimes short of ideas as well. Their confidence can also be badly shaken, and all of this puts them in a position where they are approachable and amenable to new policy ideas. Lobbyists should encourage their clients to engage with opposition parties and seek to help to shape their thinking. In the case of the Conservatives and Labour, they will almost certainly form another government at some stage. In the case of the Lib Dems, they might realistically hold the balance of power in a hung Parliament and be in a position to dictate policy in certain areas.

In the run-up to a general election there is a final opportunity to try and influence the policies and manifesto commitments of political parties. Even the governing party is in effect in limbo, until such time as it is returned to power or sentenced to opposition. Manifestoes are drafted and redrafted right up until the eve of publication: keep on pressing your policy case right up until the party's manifesto goes to print.

Contributor's top tip

In 2008, many lobbyists have woken up, or finally resigned themselves to, the importance of engagement with HM Official Opposition. In David Cameron's Conservative Party, those in the know have long understood that since 2005 there has been a shift of power away from the Conservative Research Department to the offices of shadow secretaries of state.

There is an increased need to engage with selected parliamentary candidates, especially given the size of Commons majority recent polling suggests the Conservatives will enjoy after the next general election.

Conservative Spring Forum is now an important vehicle for engagement with key Party decision-makers and opinion formers (and is, arguably, more valuable to a seasoned public affairs consultant than the national party conference).

Effective engagement means having pro-consumer, pro-competition and pro-environment solutions to offer as the Party begins its manifesto drafting. Intellectually confident and impressive frontbench teams (who draw upon a wide range of high level external advisers) have less and less time for individual meetings as more and more people wish to speak to them: so lobbyists need to make sure their clients are well briefed on Party policy developments, and are incisive and cogent in the way they make their points.

Simon Nayyar, Managing Director Public Policy, Citigate Dewe Rogerson

Consultation documents

When a party is in opposition it can afford to be radical, and it has the luxury of flexibility. When a party is in power, its room for manoeuvre is much more limited, and the process of policy formulation is much more structured. That does not mean, however, that lobbyists cannot seek to influence the policy making process. In fact, there is a formal process for engaging external groups and inviting their input.

In the past government would issue two types of consultation document. They still do issue Green and White Papers, but there is also a move towards issuing consultation documents without any indication of whether they will lead to legislation or not.

A Green Paper is an outline of government thinking in a particular policy area, and an invitation to contribute to that thinking. Green Papers represent an initial approach, without any firm indication that legislation will follow. Sometimes they are published as a result of a manifesto commitment to review policy in a specified area.

A Green Paper might be followed by a White Paper. These documents are more structured and definitive, and give a firm indication that the government intends to legislate. Sometimes governments go straight to the White Paper stage, without going through the initial Green Paper stage.

General consultation documents are becoming much more frequent under the current Labour government. They can apply to broad policy areas as well as to defined areas where specific legislation is contemplated. These are a reflection of the Third Way espoused by Tony Blair when he was prime minister, when ideology was displaced by pragmatism. For Mr Blair what mattered is what worked – and the best way to decide what is going to work is to consult frequently and widely.

Another innovation since 1997 has been the publication of draft bills. In the past government's would allow trusted organisations with a strong locus to have sight of draft bills, but they were not published or widely circulated. The innovation of doing so is a welcome one, and should lead to better legislation with fewer unexpected consequences, as it allows lobbyists and other interested parties to feed in to the process.

Third party endorsement

Sometimes your reputation alone will be enough to get your arguments listened to – or even accepted – by government. Other times your argument will be strong enough to carry the day on its own. More often, however, you will need to have your argument and your position reinforced, and there are a number of ways in which you can go about attracting that crucial third party endorsement.

One tried and trusted method is simply to research whether there are any other bodies that hold similar or identical views to your own. You can then form a temporary alliance with them, joining forces to try and influence government policy in a specific area. If the battle is likely to be a long one, there is sometimes an argument for forming some kind of an umbrella pressure group, and getting as many like-minded organisations as possible to join it.

Another method of attracting third party endorsement is to commission a think tank to research and publish a supportive pamphlet. Obviously you would have to declare the fact that you had commissioned the study, but provided the think tank in question is sufficiently respected the study will still carry weight.

There are dozens of think tanks in the United Kingdom, of varying size, viewpoint and standing. They are all registered as charities, so technically they are not allowed to be party political. They are therefore usually described as being "left leaning" (ie, aligned with the Labour Party), "right leaning" (ie, aligned with the Conservatives) or "centrist" (ie, aligned with the Lib Dems). Some of these think tanks have been enormously influential in the past – having very direct influence over policy making, especially when parties are in opposition. Before she came to power in 1979 Margaret Thatcher was especially beholden to the Centre for Policy Studies, which had been set up (partly at her behest) by Sir Keith Joseph and Alf Sherman. The IPPR helped to set the agenda for New Labour in the run-up to 1997, and today the Policy Exchange is reckoned to be performing a similar role for David Cameron's Conservative Party.

Contributor's top tip

To be successful in public affairs it is necessary to have a clear strategy from the outset. There is no point in scoring a tactical victory over government, for example by getting a minor amendment to a bill through, if you fail to meet your strategic objective and you upset ministers in the process.

Public affairs is about building relationships – not grabbing headlines. Megaphone public affairs is like megaphone diplomacy – counter-productive. Relationships with politicians and other stakeholders are the most powerful tool at the disposal of the PA practitioner.

Third party advocates can also be a crucial element in any PA campaign. Whether you are in-house or you work in a consultancy you need to have good relationships with all of your external stakeholders. Ministers and civil servants are far more likely to change their stance if they have 25 organisations lined up against them, instead of just one.

Dan Murphy, Head of External Affairs, Remploy

Before you commission a think tank to write a report it is important to feel confident that the end result will bolster your case. That is usually just a matter of choosing a think tank which occupies the appropriate position on the political spectrum and agreeing the broad parameters in advance.

Here is a selection of think tanks, arranged in alphabetical order. A simple web search will give you all the information you need to know about their political leanings – and any specialisations they may have:

- Adam Smith Institute
- Centre for Policy Studies
- Chatham House
- Compass
- Demos
- Fabian Society
- Foreign Policy Centre
- Institute for Public Policy Research
- Institute of Economic Affairs
- New Economics Foundation
- New Policy Institute
- Policy Exchange
- Policy Network
- Policy Studies Institute
- Politeia
- Progress
- Reform
- Smith Institute
- Social Market Foundation

As well as think tanks there are also a wide range of academic bodies, business schools and economic consultancies that can produce authoritative studies which can help to underpin your policy case. Before commissioning any research from these bodies – the costs can be quite considerable – it is always worth finding out if such as study has already been undertaken, so that you can quote from it.

Again, here is a selection of such bodies, listed in alphabetical order:

- Cass
- Centre for Economic and Business Research
- Deloitte
- Ernst & Young
- Henley Management College
- Institute for Fiscal Studies
- KPMG
- London Business School
- PA Consulting Group
- PricewaterhouseCoopers

Another potentially very powerful source of third party endorsement is through polling companies. Either through straightforward public opinion polls, or through focus groups, they are able to gauge opinion on specific issues, and present those opinions in a powerful and coherent form. If you can present solid polling figures showing substantial support for your policy viewpoint it can have a strong impact on government thinking. Here, again in alphabetical order, are the main polling companies in the United Kingdom:

- ComRes
- Dods Polling
- Gallup
- Gfk NOP
- ICM
- Ipsos MORI
- Opinion Leader Research
- Populus
- Rasmussen
- YouGov

Opinion polls can form the basis of press releases which are interesting enough to be taken up even by the national press. Since politicians are avid readers of newspapers, and voracious consumers of radio and television news, getting a favourable story carried by these outlets can be a good way of shaping their opinions on policy.

Contributor's top tip

Third party endorsement is useless without selecting a partner who brings credibility.

- Rule number one is to choose a "name". This does not need to be the biggest brand you can find – indeed, the largest players can sometimes lack innovation – but there is no point spending money on an outcome if nobody will be interested.

- Rule number two is to find a partner who has a creative approach to your organisation or issue. This may be harder to do with academics but it is what you pay pollsters and think tanks to do.

- Rule number three is do not go for the first quote, or the cheapest, as it can be a false economy. You usually get what you pay for.

- Rule number four is to look at the most junior person at the pitch meeting and ask whether you can work with them with confidence – they will probably be looking after you day-to-day.

- Rule number five is to develop long-term relationships with think tanks, academics and pollsters. Even if you are engaging them only briefly, they probably live, eat and breathe your issues and you will get lasting value from the friendships created by a short-term project.

Andrew Hawkins, Chief Executive, ComRes

Contributor's top tip

Often, due to news coverage of the horse-race nature of UK politics, public affairs professionals think polling is only for political parties. They could not be more wrong. Polling key populations (MPs, peers, senior civil servants, think-tanks, and media) can play a critical role in successful modern lobbying. Any lobbying plan or communication strategy should start with a benchmark poll to form a roadmap to navigate the issues and uncover support or opposition.

Next, the use of follow-up polls during the campaign should be utilised to make strategic adjustments along the way to fine-tune messages and help determine what populations need to be reached. At the conclusion of a campaign, a final poll can reveal how perceptions have changed since the benchmark poll as a result of your efforts. Be wary of the public affairs professional who says, "I do not need a poll to tell me how parliamentarians think." There are a lot of parliamentarians out there and you can drive your next lobbying campaign based on hunches and assumption, or you can drive your campaign based on reliable and valid polling data.

Matt Bricken, Dods Polling

Whilst it is not possible – in this country at least – to buy editorial coverage, it is possible to invest in a political PR programme that will generate it. Once you have commissioned your report from a think tank, academic body or management consultancy you can hopefully generate press coverage on the back of it. Newspapers, in particular, are very keen on opinion polls – whether they have been commissioned by their own paper, a rival paper or a third party. You can either just send out a press release to the relevant correspondent, or you can try and meet with them or buy them lunch. Journalists are human like anybody else, and if you invest some time and money in them you will often get a return. Once a favourable piece has been written or broadcast, you can be pretty sure that the policy makers you want to reach will be aware of it. If they are not you can always draw their attention to it.

2.2.4 Legislation changing

Perhaps the purest form of lobbying is that which is aimed directly at introducing, blocking or amending legislation. If you have failed to have your arguments accepted and your policies carried during the consultation phase, then you will have no choice but to engage directly and seek to carry the day either on the floor of the House or in committee.

In the Westminster Parliament there are some 20 to 30 government bills introduced every year. Some of these are political bills introduced as a result of a manifesto pledge, or in order to further the ruling party's philosophy. Other bills are introduced at the behest of civil servants, who feel they need further legislative powers to adequately and efficiently administer the policy areas which their department is responsible for. To give one obvious example, almost every year there is a Criminal Justice Bill, designed to introduce new categories of offences which the Home Office feels are not adequately covered by existing laws.

Quite a substantial proportion of bills introduced every year have the purpose of transposing an EU Directive into UK law. There is a certain amount of flexibility given to national governments and civil servants in the way in which they translate EU law into national law. UK civil servants and ministers have long been accused of "gold plating" EU Directives – making them more rigid and stringent than was originally intended – and tacking on additional measures which have been on their domestic agenda, but which have never been enacted.

As well as the 20-30 government bills which are introduced every year there are also upwards of a hundred private members' bills. Of these only one or two – three at most – will actually make the statute book, but they serve a useful purpose nevertheless.

Finally, there are private bills – not to be confused with private members' bills. Private bills relate to a specific body – such as a local authority, or a company. These bills have an entirely different procedure to public bills. Occasionally such bills are deemed to be "hybrid", which means that they share some of the characteristics of both private bills and public bills. The procedure for these bills is a mix between the procedure for public bills and private bills.

Even if you do not succeed in securing the amendments you want in the House of Commons there is always the prospect of getting an amendment carried in the House of Lords. Because the committee stage of bills takes place on the floor of the House (as opposed to in standing committee as is the case with the Commons) any peer can table an amendment. What is more, no government in recent years has had a majority in the Lords, and they can therefore be (and often are) defeated by a coalition of opposition parties and the non-aligned crossbenchers. Although many of these defeats are subsequently over-turned when the bill goes back to the Commons, quite a few are not. This is particularly the case where their Lordships stick to their guns, and amendments go back and forth between the two Houses in a procedure nicknamed "ping pong". If the end of a session – or even a general election – is imminent, the government will quite often not use its Commons majority to impose its will.

Even in the House of Commons it is sometimes possible to secure concessions from ministers without actually having an amendment carried.

Ever since the Pepper v Hart court case in 1993 judges have on occasion looked at the debates in *Hansard* in order to try and work out the intentions of a minister where the legislation itself is unclear. Therefore persuading a minister – usually at report stage or third reading – to rule out a particular interpretation of a clause during Commons or Lords debate means that the courts would feel perfectly entitled to rule according to that debate, rather than according to the ultimate text of the Statute.

A detailed account of how to seek to introduce, derail or amend legislation will be included in part four of this book.

2.3 Starting A Career In Lobbying

Public affairs is a booming industry. A few years ago there were just a few hundred people in the UK working in the field. Today there are up to 4000 – although not all of these will have lobbying as a primary job function. In a 2005 study lobbyist-turned-academic Karl Milner (now a senior lecturer at Leeds Business School) estimated that there were approximately 600-800 lobbyists working in consultancies. The generally accepted in-house to in-consultancy ratio is four to one, and the industry has undoubtedly grown since Milner made his calculation – hence the figure of approximately 4000.

In the early days of lobbying in the UK most people entering the industry had some kind of an established relationship or connection with the field. Very often they had a relative, or at least a close acquaintance, who worked in lobbying and were able to affect an introduction for them. Nowadays the industry is much more professional in its recruitment procedures, as it is in all other areas. However, the old maxim of "it's not what you know but who you know" still has some currency in the world of lobbying.

Contributor's top tip

'There was a young man from Tyree,

Who wanted to be an MP,

But mad for the cash,

To big business he dashed,

And lobbied for a great big fat fee.'

This limerick captures some of the most commonly held misconceptions about the profession of public affairs: that it is primarily a job for young men, that it is the realm of wannabe-politicians, that it all about money and that our services are the preserve of big business. In fact, public affairs offers a great career for anyone with an interest in solving problems through intelligent communications with other influential people. Politicians rarely make great lobbyists – we share a common interest in politics, but we engage in political discourse differently. It is about much more than money – it provides ample scope for personal and professional development working in some of the most rewarding team environments. It is definitely not the preserve of big

---

business – NGOs and charities maintain some of the most influential and best resourced lobbying operations.

James O'Keefe, Tetra Strategy

2.3.1 Academic qualifications

It has long been possible to gain a degree in politics – or even the highly regarded PPE (Politics, Philosophy and Economics), which so many senior politicians read at Oxford or Cambridge. Nowadays it is possible to get a degree in public relations, and within that broader discipline there are now growing opportunities to specialise in public affairs.

Public affairs qualifications took a giant step forward when Brunel University became the first to offer a post graduate degree in the discipline. Interestingly Brunel has opted to offer an MSc – rather than an MA – in public affairs and lobbying. Other related degrees include undergraduate and postgraduate degrees in public administration, and in political science. So universities have certainly woken up to the fact that public affairs and lobbying are now established careers, and students will opt to study the subject at both undergraduate and postgraduate levels.

As well as degree courses it is also possible to study public affairs in training workshops. Some of these are provided by professional bodies, including the Chartered Institute of Public Relations and the Public Relations Consultants Association. They are also provided by professional training firms such as Westminster Explained (which is owned by Dods, where the author was previously deputy chairman), ComRes (a polling and training company, Pinnacle (a PR training company) and Neil Stewart Associates (an events and training company).

2.3.2 Internships

Where careers are much sought after it is common practice for undergraduates to go and work as interns. This can either be entirely without payment, or for expenses only.

Up until recently many MPs would take interns – sometimes several at a time – and not pay them anything. Being able to say that you had worked for an MP – however briefly – on your CV was regarded as being so valuable that payment was deemed to be unnecessary. MPs were criticised for this arrangement though, and most now pay at least a nominal sum.

Another excellent way to pick up valuable experience as an intern is to go and work for a political party. Obviously it helps if interns are intuitively inclined towards that party's philosophy, but it is not generally a firm requirement. Working for a political party at general election time – either at headquarters or at local level, is also invaluable experience.

Finally, some of the larger public affairs companies offer internships. This can be either in the form of a holiday job, or an academic year in lieu of something like the more traditional year abroad. They generally pay a modest salary, and often interns end up returning to work for these firms full time.

2.3.3 Advertisements

Public affairs is such a tight-knit industry that many jobs are never publicly offered, but instead filled through word of mouth and personal contact.

Some lobbying jobs are, however, advertised. There is a real shortage of appropriate organs to advertise in, so many job advertisements appear in two Dods publications – the *House Magazine* (a weekly published only when Parliament is in session) and *Public Affairs News* (a monthly). Iain Dale's *Total Politics* magazine has now entered the market and can be bought at newsstands or subscribed to directly. It also has a controlled circulation covering all of the UK's elected politicians.

There are other publications such as *Parliament Brief*, and a string of titles published under the GovNet banner. These publications do, however, generally tend to carry lobby-style advertisements, rather than recruitment ads.

2.3.4 Websites

As well as advertisements in print journals some jobs are advertised on the Internet.

The website with the most lobbying jobs advertised is probably www.w4mp.com. Lobbying jobs also feature on the PubAffairs website. Although initially a social networking site, this now carries a number of commercial ads and is much visited.

The recruitment firms which specialise in lobbying jobs also nearly all have websites. It is often useful to check out these websites first before approaching the recruitment firms directly and offering to send them your CV.

2.3.5 Recruitment consultancies

There are a vast number of recruitment firms in the UK – but only a handful specialise in public affairs. Here are the main firms who place – and headhunt – the lobbyists:

- Atack – Steve Atack, International Executive Search
- Childs – Peter Childs Associates
- Electus – a division of Dods Parliamentary Communications
- Ellwood & Atfield – Search and Selection
- Hanson Search
- JFL – specialist PR and marketing recruitment
- VMA – Search and Selection

Before contacting any of these firms it is probably worth looking at their websites, and seeing what level of positions they specialise in. Both the websites and advertisements in public affairs magazines will give you a good idea of the level of seniority of the candidates they place.

The next step is either to apply for one of the advertised positions – or to email or telephone them to ask who you should send your CV to. As with any line of work it is important that your CV is well laid out – and accurate. Specialist public affairs recruitment consultants are well aware of the fact that the political parties and MPs often take on undergraduates and recent graduates as interns. They pay them very little money – and sometimes provide them with very little in the way of meaningful work. Just having worked in Parliament or for one of the political parties is a major plus – but do not try to exaggerate your seniority or the complexity of the work that you undertook. Recruitment consultants will have interviewed scores of applicants with similar experiences, and will be wise to any attempt to talk up a position.

On your CV you also need to be careful about the referees you quote – because references will be taken up. If you have worked for an MP, check with him or her that they are happy to give you a reference. Indeed, it might be a good idea to ask them for a generic reference at the time you leave. But do check with them before quoting them as a referee. MPs are busy people, and if they cannot be bothered to respond to a reference request – or they give you a discursive reference – it could seriously damage your job prospects.

If you are a political activist for any of the three main parties do not be shy about mentioning the fact. List any positions you have held within the party, and any recent campaigns you have been actively involved in. Lobbyists are retained for their knowledge of how the political system works. If you are an activist you will have acquired some of that general political knowledge – and you will have gained a particular insight in to the characters and workings of your chosen party. Just be sure that at interview – and when you have successfully landed a lobbying job – you are able to offer completely non-partisan advice to colleagues and clients.

Contributor's top tip

The four "I"s: Impact, Intelligence, Intent, Integrity: Personal qualities of the successful lobbyist.

First impression – impact – has such a high value everywhere. It is difficult to analyse and therefore difficult to teach. It is a mixture of eloquence, presence, charm, eye contact and other indefinable "somethings". Impact is an immediately recognisable quality: the ability to gain and maintain attention and its importance, in lobbying as in other walks of life, is a given.

Then there is intelligence: not just the intellect to mount argument but an expansive outlook – the instinct to view the wider theatre of business and democratic society first, in which politics is a fascinating sub-plot. Opinion is less worthy if context is uninformed.

Without a clear intent – without some obvious passion – to deliver one's message, such qualities are for nothing. If "messenger for hire" is a flashing neon sign all else is undermined.

Last, and certainly not least, there is integrity. Without this an argument might sometimes succeed, but with it, the chances are greater. Integrity is the energy of the piece.

Is it possible to succeed with just some of the above? Probably, but to a lesser extent. Our experience during 20 years contact with the practitioners is that it is the presence of all four that characterises those who get to the top, who open doors, whose word is respected and who make real change.

Peter Childs, Peter Childs Associates

Contributor's top tip

The early years of the Blair Government ushered in a period of change, the product of which has been an overall increase in the transparency and accountability of operators in this space, and in turn a dramatic increase in the need for public affairs practitioners. Planning a career in public affairs means thinking strategically. As public affairs evolves it is increasingly drawing on its sister disciplines such as media relations, corporate social responsibility, policy and stakeholder relations in order to obtain better results. Practitioners, whether they be in-house or consultancy, must have an understanding or better still some experience of these other strategies in order to achieve greater outcomes through deploying more sophisticated strategies.

It is not just the practitioners and the process of public affairs that are becoming more sophisticated and professionalised, it is also the purchasers of public affairs services. The increasing awareness from purchasers of exactly what they are buying, be that in the form of consultancy advice or in-house expertise, has also shifted significantly in recent years. As a recruiter I see this in the increasing need for experienced in-house public affairs people – it is becoming harder for professionals to cross over from other disciplines such as PR into public affairs. Public affairs is now a recognised and valued discipline within an in-house communications team. A career in public affairs can now be planned as more high profile organisations take the discipline with ever increasing seriousness. Successful public affairs professionals ultimately translate the language of the political and regulatory classes in to one a chief executive can do business with, and vice versa.

Gavin Ellwood, Ellwood and Atfield

Contributor's top tip

Ten to fifteen years ago graduates and young professionals might have fallen into public affairs and corporate communications roles, often through the "old boy network". However, nowadays there seem to be channels through which candidates are expected to progress. The sector has grown significantly, but equally job opportunities have become increasingly competitive as more candidates seek to enter this exciting profession.

Relevant experience is a huge advantage. Candidates who have worked for an MP or a political party inevitably have a head start over other applicants, as do candidates who have done some work experience for a public affairs agency or campaigning organisation. Familiarity with the workings of Westminster and Whitehall, the procedures, the terms used, the documentation are all extremely useful and will make one's CV stand out among the many that agencies receive.

An interest in politics and policy issues is essential, a degree in politics is usually a prerequisite, but experience is the all-important factor. Grassroots political involvement, whether through student politics or a local political party, will be looked upon favourably, as will a clear awareness of and interest in current affairs. However, it is also important to be able to stand back and understand political positions with which you may not agree. An element of impartiality is required by all who work within public affairs.

The ability to write well and to express oneself in a clear and concise manner is essential. One needs to be able to analyse material quickly and to draw out the points relevant to the issues at hand in a systematic, coherent way. Personal discipline and interpersonal skills are important also and often the chemistry at interview is likely to be a factor in deciding the successful applicant.

Getting started in public affairs can often be tough and persistence is advisable. Do not give up and do not be too proud to muck in as part of a team, occasionally undertaking repetitive or mundane work. At other times you may find you have far greater autonomy and responsibility and the work is exciting and requires real creativity and strategic thinking. Ultimately the trick is to join a firm which has the career structure to allow you to develop your skills and provide a path for you for the future.

Judith Dilnot, Managing Director, Electus

Contributor's top tip

Lobbyists work at the nexus between politics and business. Most entry level jobs are not advertised, so you need two networks: one of lobbyists with jobs to offer and one of politically-aware candidates who are looking for jobs or internships. Planning is everything. To break into lobbying, start building your networks when you are still a student. All the political parties have ginger groups, some of which occupy positions on the political spectrum and others focus on particular subject areas – such as Tory Green Initiative or the Socialist Environment and Resources Association. All these groups are permanently short of volunteers. Stick your hand up, and you are appointed. Write policy papers. Help run fringe events at one of the party conferences. That way you will have a valuable network of contacts in your favoured political party and a network of lobbyists trying to get close to them.

Quentin Langley, Director, PR PeopleBank Ltd

Contributor's top tip

Public affairs is now such a competitive business that to succeed you need to carefully plan your career. It is, alas, all too easy to get that decent job and then get sucked into the vortex of serious overwork and pressure which is daily life for many in the profession. You need to put time aside to review your performance – are you investing enough time in sustaining and developing your internal and external relationships, for example? How effective are you as a messenger? Are your communications clear, focused and concise? We are a communications profession after all. Are you getting enough development and training opportunity?

In today's ever more commercial public affairs industry those practitioners who are good managers and understand business process have an automatic head start over many in the industry who come from political or media worlds, important as those backgrounds can be. Do you feel you are improving your business skills year on year?

Finally, if you are a consultant, do you listen to your clients enough and do you sit down regularly and think forward about the issues they will be facing, not just in the coming months but in the years to come? If you are in-house do your colleagues in other communications disciplines within the company fully appreciate the contribution you and your team are making to the corporate common good?

In a nutshell, of course clients or the corporation's interests will always come first, but invest a little time each month in yourself and your career improvement. None of us, no matter how senior we may be, do not have scope to improve our game. That investment will, I suspect, contribute significantly to your success.

Steve Atack, Consultant, International Executive Search

2.4 Appointing A Lobbying Consultancy

As with the appointment of any kind of consultancy it is vital that from the outset you have a clear idea of what it is you want them to achieve on your behalf. You also have to be realistic about what you hope to achieve with the budget which you have available. If you are a small organisation with a modest budget you are not going to be able to hire one of the "big beasts" of the consultancy world.

Public affairs consultancies – lobbyists – are hired by a large range of organisations. It is not just big business that hires lobbyists – it is also smaller companies, charities, trade associations, trade unions, professional bodies, and government agencies. Lobbyists are hired either to change the law, to raise an organisation's political profile, to help shape the public policy agenda, or to build relationships in the anticipation that they will be needed in the future.

I have used the term hired deliberately, rather than the more frequently used term retained. That is because there are two distinct ways of engaging the services of lobbyists – you can either pay them a monthly retainer, or you can hire them for a fixed term and price to work on a specific project. In the past most organisations kept lobbyists on a monthly retainer: nowadays there is a tendency to offer project work rather than retainers.

In order to get some idea of who the specialist public affairs consultancies are, a good starting point is to contact the Chartered Institute of Public Relations, the Public Relations Consultants Association or the Association of Professional Political Consultants. You can telephone them and ask for their advice, or you can visit their websites and have a look at who their members are. *The Hollis UK PR Annual* has a section that deals with public affairs consultancies, as does *Who's Who in Public Affairs*. Many consultancies also advertise in the annual *Dod's Parliamentary Companion* and the *Vacher's Quarterly Companion*.

2.4.1 Written proposal

It is sometimes appropriate to ask lobbying consultancies to submit a brief written proposal prior to any formal presentation. Some firms will decline to do this, and others may enquire as to how many firms have been asked to submit a proposal at this stage. The maximum you should ask to submit a written proposal is six.

This written proposal should include an over-view of the consultancy itself. Details should include the ownership of the company – whether it is privately owned or it is part of a larger group – the size and experience of the staff, and an indication of the types of clients they work for. Details of any industry awards they have won might also be useful. This is not just because it shows that they are capable of producing outstanding work, but also because the awards won will give a good indication of the type of clients and they have worked for and the areas they specialise in.

Part of the written proposal should, of course, contain some ideas as to how the consultancy will help you to achieve your aims. This could take the form of an account of how they have helped a client to achieve their objectives in similar circumstances, or it could be entirely bespoke and geared to your unique circumstances. Do not expect consultancies to give you all of their ideas at this stage: they may well be worried that if they give you a complete blueprint for your campaign you will either implement it yourself, or share the ideas with whichever consultancy you ultimately appoint.

So a written proposal does not have to be that long, or that specific. It should, however, leave you with the impression that this is a consultancy worth putting through to the next round.

Author's top tip

It is often worth discussing your needs with a "matchmaking" service to ask their advice on retaining an agency. The PRCA run a PReview service, and there are also commercial firms such as creativebrief which specialise in putting potential customers in touch with agencies which are most likely to be able to meet their needs. Otherwise, 'word of mouth' is often your best bet.

2.4.2 Presentation

Whether or not you have filtered the consultancies by dint of a paper sift or not, you need to arrive at a shortlist of firms who you are going to ask to formally present in person.

Normally I would advise that you aim to interview three consultancies. Any fewer and you may narrow your choice to an unacceptable degree, any more and you risk wasting the consultancies' time, your time and the time of your colleagues. Bear in mind that some consultancies may decline to pitch for your business. They may have a conflict of interest, they may not regard the contract as being weighty enough to warrant their attention, or they might simply be too busy to pitch. So in order to arrive at your three finalists you will probably need to have four or five consultancies in mind.

Generally it is better if presentations take place in your premises rather than the consultancy's. This is partly for your convenience, but also because it is important that you are seen as the "home team" in charge of proceedings. This may not be practical – you may not have premises anywhere easily accessible or you may not have the space – in which case you should consider hiring facilities for the day, rather than going to the consultancy's offices.

Almost all consultancies will require audio-visual facilities. Most will wish to make a PowerPoint presentation as part of their pitch, and some may wish to go online. It is important not to be too swayed by these slick presentations. Very often they have been expensively produced as part of a consultancy's new business development programme, and they may be generic rather than directly applicable to your needs.

Depending on the size of the potential contract most consultancies would field a pitch team of three to five people. Their team might include the MD or CEO, an account director and an account manager – and possibly one or two juniors to make notes and operate the audio-visuals.

Author's top tip

It is important to establish who exactly would be working on your account. You need to know the level of experience and expertise you will be getting for your fee – and also whether you think you can work with that person. Beware of professional pitching teams who come in, make a phenomenal presentation, and are never seen again.

On your side it is important that you field a team of at least three – otherwise you will be at a numerical and psychological disadvantage. Obviously that should include the person who will be working most closely with the appointed consultancy. So your team should be a permutation of the managing director, finance director, communications director and head of public affairs. If there is a strong online element to the campaign you might also consider fielding your chief information officer, head of IT or webmaster.

As with any industry or profession there are certain kite marks which should offer you some reassurance about the lobbying consultancies you might be looking to appoint. There are three bodies which represent and regulate the lobbying industry. The Chartered Institute of Public Relations (CIPR) represents individual practitioners who work in-consultancy or in-house. The Public Relations Consultants Association (PRCA) represents the larger PR consultancies in the UK – some (but not all) of whom have a public affairs offering. Finally the Association of Professional Political Consultants (APPC) represents purely lobbying consultancies. All three bodies have codes of conduct and disciplinary procedures, so you do have some leverage if you hire one of their members and they fail to perform to your satisfaction. In 2007 all three bodies signed up to a generic set of principles which provide broad guidance as to standards of ethical behaviour of lobbyists. It is hoped that these generic principles will be tightened up and extended in the future.

2.4.3 Contractual benchmarks

As with any type of contract it is important that any contract for public affairs or lobbying work contains some benchmarks. This is so that you can judge the performance of the appointed consultancy over the course of the period of the contract, and so that you have some comeback if the consultancy does not perform as promised.

Here are a few benchmarks which you might consider writing in to the contract:

- Ethics: If the consultancy (or its directors) claims membership of the CIPR, PRCA or APPC you may require proof of this fact to be supplied. If the consultancy claims to operate to standards imposed by its own bespoke code of conduct you might require it to be appended to the contract.

- Staff: If at the original pitch you have been promised that particular individuals will be working on your account, you probably should work that in to the contract. At the very least you should stipulate that if an individual moves on they must be replaced by somebody with equally relevant experience.

- Reports: The contract should stipulate that you must receive regular written reports, on either a weekly or fortnightly basis. This report should include any relevant parliamentary or political monitoring which has been unearthed, plus a round-up of contacts with politicians and civil servants. They should also list any Key Performance Indicators (KPIs) which have been achieved.

- Review meetings: There should be regular face-to-face review meetings so that progress can be assessed and relationships can be refreshed. These should probably be on a monthly basis. Venues can be fixed or they can alternate between the client's offices or the consultancy's offices. They can also be held over lunch – although the client usually ends up paying for these lunches one way or another!

- Objectives: It is vital that the contract contains benchmarks and KPIs, and that the written reports and review meetings are geared to assess progress towards meeting them. Obviously the nature of these indicators must be based upon the nature of the campaign. As mentioned earlier, there are many types of campaign, and the consultancy could have been hired to raise the client's profile, establish a contact programme, shape the public policy agenda, or to change the law.

2.4.4 Freelancers

An alternative to hiring a consultancy is to retain the services of a freelance (or independent) public affairs consultant. These individuals are often senior figures with many years experience in the industry. They can provide the client with:

- Independent viewpoint: They are outsiders, and they are able to view your organisation and your public affairs programme with an objective eye.

- Close relationships: Because they do not work for a consultancy, freelancers often develop very close relationships with their clients, and demonstrate great loyalty towards them.

- Wide experience: Independent public affairs consultants have often worked in-house and in-consultancy. They may also have worked for political parties or the civil service – and many have worked in either the House of Commons or the House of Lords (or even both).

- Flexibility: Depending on how in demand they are freelancers can generally gear their commitment to clients up or down depending on the client's needs and resources.

- Value for money: Because they have low overheads and no staff their rates can be very competitive and affordable.

Part Three –
The Tools Of Lobbying

3.1 Monitoring And Intelligence

It is not possible to operate effectively or even to survive in public affairs without monitoring and intelligence. It would be like a modern jet fighter trying to operate without radar, a submarine trying to function without sonar, or even driving around London without SatNav. Without having an effective real-time knowledge of what is happening politically, you will not have any chance of influencing the public policy agenda.

The key reasons for undertaking political and parliamentary monitoring are:

- To find out what is being said about a particular topic

- To identify politicians who are active in a particular policy sphere

- To categorise politicians into supporters, opponents and neutrals

- To spot any new draft laws or regulations which will impact on you or your clients

- To create an archive of relevant political and parliamentary material which can help current or future lobbying campaigns

- To gather relevant material which they can then distribute to colleagues or to clients

- To identify an opportunity to respond when a politician has raised a particular issue

Fortunately there are a number of ways in which you can go about gathering political intelligence and undertaking your parliamentary and political monitoring.

Author's top tip

Monitoring is vital – but intelligence is crucial. If you – or your monitoring agency – can find out about a debate, a publication or an event before it is widely known, or "on the record", it could give you a very big edge. You can brief supporters – and the media – ahead of the crowd, and enhance your reputation as somebody who knows what is going on. Some intelligence ("elint"), can be gained from the Internet, but the best intelligence ("humint") is gained by being out and about and talking to people.

> ## Contributor's top tip
>
> Time spent on research is never wasted.
>
> *Robbie MacDuff, Director, Precise Public Affairs*

3.1.1 In-house monitoring

Hard copy

It is perfectly possible to do your own monitoring. The question you have to ask, however, is whether this is a cost effective use of your time?

It is still possible to do your monitoring in hard copy – if you are a confirmed technophobe. Of course before the advent of the Internet all monitoring was done using hard copy, and it is still possible to subscribe to the required documents either through Her Majesty's Stationery Office or through The Parliamentary Bookshop. It can, however, work out to be a very expensive option – and you could end up paying more for the subscriptions than you would pay for a retained basic monitoring service.

In order to undertake your own hard copy monitoring you would need to subscribe to:

- *Hansard*: House of Commons and House of Lords
- Order Paper: Showing the Business of the House of Commons, and forthcoming written and oral questions (as well as Early Day Motions)
- Lords Minute: The Upper House version of the Order Paper
- Weekly Information Bulletin: This covers the main business (in Chamber and in committee) of both Houses, including progress of legislation and publication of reports

If you are following a government or private members' bill particularly closely you will have to subscribe to the Commons standing committee *Hansard* for that bill, and also to the new and marshalled lists of amendments from both Houses.

This is how monitoring was done in the 1970s and 1980s. My strong recommendation would be to avoid trying to monitor in this way in the twenty-first century – nearly all of this information is available online free of charge.

Online

As mentioned above nearly all of the information (as opposed to intelligence) you will ever need is now available online.

The relevant websites vary considerably in their user-friendliness – and none have got particularly good search facilities. However, if you have got the time, and budgets are a problem, you can get by perfectly well doing your own monitoring online. You can also subscribe to the email alerts which most of the sites offer, or set up RSS feeds.

There are obviously dozens of websites which deal with politics and public affairs. The main ones – in terms of pure parliamentary monitoring – are:

- www.parliament.uk
- www.scottish.parliament.uk
- www.new.wales.gov.uk
- www.niassembly.gov.uk
- www.europa.eu/index_en

You will also need to keep a close eye on the official political party websites – which again have improved dramatically in recent years. The main ones are:

- www.labour.org.uk
- www.conservatives.com
- www.libdems.org.uk
- www.snp.org
- www.plaidcymru.org
- www.dup.org.uk
- www.sinnfeinassembly.com

Monitoring these websites will give you most of the information you will need in pure parliamentary monitoring terms. However, you will also need to compile a list of other sites to keep an eye of:

- Government departments
- Executive agencies
- Regulators
- Think tanks

As well as the hard monitoring information which the above sites will provide you with, there are a large range of other sites which will provide you with political intelligence. This is based not around fact, but around gossip, rumour and opinion – which are in effect the hard currency of politics.

There are dozens of these sites, but again a selection of relevant and interesting websites are:

- www.politicalbetting.com
- www.iaindale.blogspot.com
- www.order-order.com
- www.conservativehome.blogs.com
- www.labourhome.org
- www.recessmonkey.com
- www.totalpolitics.com
- www.stephentall.org.uk
- www.libdemblogs.co.uk

If you can find the time to monitor those of the above websites which are relevant to your area of operation, you should have all of the facts – and much of the intelligence – which you need to do your job. Bloggers are often prepared to run speculative stories and disclose intelligence which conventional media outlets might be reluctant to carry (for legal or reputation reasons).

Contributor's top tip

Blogs are important to anyone with a campaign to run and should form part of any public affairs related communications strategy. Most bloggers are open to receiving ideas for articles, particularly those who are relatively prolific and post several times a day. But lobbyists wishing to influence the "blogosphere" should do their research and ensure that the blogger concerned might be well disposed to their campaign before making contact.

A quick read of previous blog entries should suffice. Blogs are often seen as a threat rather than an opportunity, not just by politicians but by public affairs practitioners. This is misconceived. If you have a message to promulgate in the corridors of power, a favourable mention on my blog, Guido Fawkes (or several others) will guarantee that a sizeable number of MPs, lobby journalists and political researchers will see it. I am constantly surprised at the small number of lobbyists who understand that.

Iain Dale, blogger and publisher of Total Politics

Contributor's top tip

The last 20 years have witnessed phenomenal technological advancement and it is essential that lobbyists – whether in agency or in-house – are utilising the latest technology to their absolute maximum. We stand on the brink of web 3.0 and we need to keep pace, adapting to change and updating our approach.

Parliamentarians are finally embracing technology and recognising the benefits to representation and democracy it brings. Webcameron and the 10 Downing Street YouTube channel are thriving and most political figures now have their own blogs, which they update daily. Increasingly in the future we will see two-way dialogue between MPs and constituents taking place through new media technology in the palm of our hands.

Across the Atlantic, Barack Obama's victory in securing the Democrat nomination is in part thanks to his superb website and his efforts on social networking websites (MyBo), something we will almost certainly increasingly witness here. Obama has stated that 'there is no more powerful tool for grass-roots organising than the Internet' and he is absolutely right.

To successfully influence decision makers, lobbyists need to be fully prepared when new technology is introduced.

Amanda Stuart, Account Director, Insight Public Affairs

> ## Contributor's top tip
>
> Ok, I admit it. Lobbying is not actually the oldest game. But it can be massively enhanced by the use of the newest technology. Let us just look at three of them. Firstly, the YouTube effect. The gaffes and embarrassing moments are now played endlessly on this site. It's great for research. It's brilliant for entertainment. This video www.youtube.com/watch?v=uHVEDq6RVXc also shows the future of the next new technology. Blogs have been with us for a while, but the growth in citizen journalism means they will become more powerful. The "Bosnia video" comes from a US blog. It is funny, it is viral and it is true. Finally, research is everything. RSS (Really Simple Syndication – more here: www.whatisrss.com/) is key to this. It has been with us for five years already, but it has been slow to be applied. This powerful software is easy-to-use and it is free. When a journalist or blogger files copy, the first place it appears is the web. RSS readers allow you to receive alerts on any story posted. This can be further filtered to only see the stuff you are interested in. Do not be afraid of learning new techniques. That is what this book is all about.
>
> *Chris Lewis, CEO, Lewis Communications Ltd*

3.1.2 Monitoring agencies

Most serious organisations which operate a public affairs function also have a budget for monitoring. If they can afford to have an in-house public affairs executive, then generally speaking they can afford to pay for a monitoring service. Salaries – especially in London – tend to be high, and using an experienced and well paid person to trawl the Internet is not usually a cost-effective undertaking.

As well as saving the time of the public affairs executive – and therefore the money of their employer – monitoring agencies also have other advantages to offer. These agencies have thrived in recent years, with the implication that the services they are offering are in demand.

Although I have listed above the main websites which you would need to cover in order to be confident about picking up all of the vital material which touches on your field of operations, there are many other websites which will conceivably carry material which affects you. One of the advantages of retaining a monitoring agency is that they have the resources to monitor not dozens but hundreds of websites – and on occasion this breadth of coverage could be vital.

If you are the only public affairs person in your organisation – or you are part of a very small team – it is also possible that through holidays, sickness or other commitments you will not be able to undertake your monitoring function and something vital will be missed. Having an agency doing the work for you provides the reassurance that there will be no gaps in your coverage.

Another area where monitoring agencies can usually outperform in-house teams is in the gathering of political intelligence. They will tend to have staff from all of the main political parties, and this generally gives a degree of privileged access in to their thinking and policy development. They also tend to attend a lot of Westminster events, and to frequent the many bars and restaurants where gossip is exchanged.

Finally, monitoring agencies tend to employ people who have been in the business for many years. They have often built up an encyclopaedic knowledge of parliamentary procedures, and they usually have a great deal of experience in matters which do not strictly fall under the banner of monitoring. Being able to draw on this experience and expertise is a useful bonus and helps to justify the fees over and above the benefit of having your monitoring served to you on a plate.

Contributor's top tip

Monitoring what happens in Parliament and the wider political environment remains as essential to the public affairs industry as it always has been – knowing what the political agenda is must be vital to any company, and any advice given by public affairs companies will only be as good as the information and knowledge that they themselves have.

Monitoring in the UK has evolved in recent years – there is now so much accessible information around, far more than just Hansard and Government press releases. Monitoring is also required to be more proactive, helping spot opportunities rather than merely responding to requests. Technological advances have of course changed the face of political monitoring, but precisely because of the amount of information now available it is not advisable to rely solely on automated key word searches. At some stage human resources, specifically judgement, must be brought to bear to separate masses of semi-relevant, unfiltered information from the timely, analysed, tailored and specific monitoring that most companies require.

Using a specialist monitoring service can provide an accurate and cost-effective resource to the public affairs industry. Any respectable monitoring company provides not only the analysed information but also a professional and experienced team behind this who can deal with any enquiries and build up a greater understanding of their clients' needs.

Patrick Robathan, Randall's Parliamentary

Contributor's top tip

Information and intelligence lie at the heart of effective lobbying. Whether the objective is to raise the profile of an issue, to manage the reputation of a business or industry, or to work in collaboration to change a piece of legislation, a successful public affairs practitioner has to be supported by comprehensive, speedy and proactive monitoring that identifies and delivers only what is relevant amid a plethora of information sources. Without an understanding of what is happening in the political environment, it is impossible to influence it.

We are all subjected to torrents of information and sheer volume easily detracts from meaning. Make sure that the information you get is managed well, delivered effectively, and accessible in a format that matches your organisational structure.

The best monitoring services are the most proactive. It is incumbent upon them to ensure that the customer remains abreast of relevant developments and to seek out potentially explosive information that might be hidden away. The key to monitoring is clear communication so that the supplier quickly becomes an extension of the client's office and can be trusted to deliver exactly what is needed, with the necessary context and in the right format so that it has maximum impact.

Dan Gunner, DeHavilland

Contributor's top tip

If your political intelligence service is to work for you, you have to let them in on the way you work your aims and your aspirations. The real value of a good intelligence service is the one or two nuggets that they pick out of thin air and send to you, not because it is on an interest list, but because they understand your objectives of those of your organisation. A good service is proactive. It will not wait for you to tell them that they have an interest in something: a top-notch service will tell the client when they should be involved.

Knowing what is going on in Parliament, in politics and the wider public affairs agenda is essential to the bottom-line activities of any company operating in Britain today. How can you hope to influence the agenda if you do not know what that agenda is? How can you work with detractors and supporters if you do not know what they are saying about you?

The Internet has widened the monitoring source list to infinite proportions – far too much for most companies to handle themselves. The ease in which organisations can become active in the policy agenda means that the traditional model of monitoring being delivered by consultancies has withered. Picking the wheat from the chaff is a hard job, and it is becoming even harder in this age of information overload.

What is wheat to one person is chaff to another, and vice-versa. Your service has to understand the information from your perspective, not see it just as a commodity. Leave it to those who specialise, and do not be blinded by gadgets and gimmicks.

Bradley Rogers, Dods Monitoring

3.1.3 Public affairs consultancy monitoring

A final potential source of political and parliamentary monitoring is through a full-blown public affairs consultancy. Generally these firms charge high fees (either on retainers or on project work) and would not be attracted to the comparatively low-value field of monitoring. There are, however, reasons why most of them do offer monitoring.

Whilst some public affairs consultancies use external monitoring agencies, others perform the function in-house. They do this either because they are concerned about confidentiality, or because they feel that it is a more cost-effective solution to their monitoring needs. They also often use monitoring as a way of employing interns, or of teaching junior public affairs account executives the ropes. Whatever the rationale for doing the monitoring for their consultancy clients in-house, it does mean that they can offer the service to non-consultancy clients at marginal cost.

The other main reason why some public affairs consultancies offer political and parliamentary monitoring is that they believe – often correctly – that it will lead to more high value work. If monitoring identifies an issue which could have a serious impact on the clients' activities, it is quite possible that they will retain the public affairs consultancy to lobby on their behalf. This means that they sometimes offer monitoring as a loss leader, confident in the belief that there will be consultancy work to follow.

3.2 Reference Titles

Reference books are another essential tool for any public affairs professional. Whether they sit on your desk or on your book-shelf, you need to have access to books which you can just refer to without going online, or which you can take with you in to meetings. It is also easier to learn from books than from screens. So if you want to read-up on the biographies of politicians, or memorise the composition of a select committee or a frontbench team, having the right books to hand is extremely useful.

You do not need to spend vast sums of money building up a huge reference library – as was stated in the previous chapter, much of the information is available online in any event.

Here are some of the reference books which deal primarily with the personalities and structures of politics:

- Times Guide to the House of Commons
- Dod's Parliamentary Companion
- Almanac of British Politics
- Who's Who in Public Affairs
- PMS Guide to Interest Groups
- Hollis UK PR Annual
- Vacher's Quarterly Companion

There are also some periodicals which you probably need to subscribe to in order to keep up with the news and gossip of the industry:

- Weekly Information Bulletin
- The House Magazine
- Public Affairs News
- Total Politics
- PRWeek

In terms of procedure there are also some excellent reference books you can buy (see the bibliography for full details):

- Erskine May

- How Parliament Works

- Public Affairs in Practice

- Political Lobbying

- Lobbying in Washington, London and Brussels

You do not need to buy all of these books – some of them are similar in content. Also, you do not necessarily need to buy all of the annual publications every year – sometimes the edition after a general election will cover your needs.

Author's top tip

Before you buy some or all of these books you can obviously look at them online. However, if you have an hour to spare and you are in Westminster you can browse through all of these books either at the Westminster Bookshop on Artillery Row or The Parliamentary Bookshop on the corner of Whitehall and Bridge Street. You can then decide which books to actually buy on the basis of empirical research.

3.3 Opinion Polling

Another essential tool in any lobbyist's armoury is polling. This not only tells you (or your client) what the general public or more specific audiences are thinking – it also enables you to convey that thinking to your target audience of opinion formers.

Polling in the UK and elsewhere has become considerably more sophisticated over the years. It used to be that most polling was done face-to-face, with a researcher interviewing members of the public. Then telephone polling became more popular, and now a great deal of polling is done over the Internet. Some firms specialise in face-to-face polling, some in telephone polling and some in Internet polling, while some firms use a mixture of all three methods.

As part of this increasing sophistication and quest for ever-greater accuracy, polling companies now weight their responses. This means that they use their experience from previous polls to make up for imbalances or distortions. For instance, it used to be the case that there was a so-called "spiral of silence" amongst Conservative voters. After time it became apparent that Conservative voters were more reluctant than supporters of other parties to participate in polls – and as a result the Conservative share of the vote was consistently under-reported. This was either as a result of their more conservative attitude, or as a result of their being embarrassed to admit to voting Tory after 18 years in power (a period which saw the party become deeply unpopular). It is through methods such as weighting that polling companies have refined their techniques to the point that the margin of error is now down to 3% or less.

As well as mass polling of the general public (for a poll to have any credibility it has to include at least 1000 participants) polling companies now also use focus groups. These are small groups of members of the public carefully chosen to represent the demographic structure of the country. The advantage of using such a group is that pollsters can track with total accuracy the changing opinions of identified members of the focus groups.

Polling companies also now put together panels of people with a particular expertise or experience. They can be panels of car drivers, frequent flyers, patients, doctors, lawyers or accountants. These specialist panels are usually of more use for consumer PR or market research, but they can be of use to public affairs practitioners where a policy decision or piece of legislation impacts upon a particular group.

From a public affairs point of view panels of politicians are obviously the most relevant. Several polling companies have set up panels of 200 or more MPs and peers. Some have also set up smaller panels of MEPs, and members of the Scottish Parliament, Welsh Assembly and Northern Ireland Assembly. These highly focused (and highly influential) panels can be asked one-off questions, or a rolling series of questions to see if their perceptions are changing over time.

The questions to political panels can be policy related and very specific. Examples of these might be whether the age limit for purchasing tobacco – or alcohol – should be raised. Alternatively they can be more about perception – asking politicians which companies or charities they admire the most, or asking them to rank a given list of organisations according to the effectiveness of their lobbying activities.

Choosing which one suits your need is sometimes not easy. There is, as ever, the question of cost, but there is also the question of methodology. You need to meet with the pollsters, and if you feel that they understand what it is that you are trying to achieve, they may well be the company for you.

For more information on polling see the earlier section on Third Party Endorsement.

Author's top tip

Polls can be used in two ways. They can be used to gauge the opinion of the public so that the findings can be used to influence politicians. Alternatively, they can be used to directly gauge the opinion of politicians – and this information can then be used to influence government and the media.

3.4 Relationship Management

As with any public relation discipline, relationship management is crucial in public affairs. Whereas with mainstream PR the concentration is on building contacts and relationships with journalists, in public affairs the emphasis is on doing the same with politicians and civil servants. This makes having a relationship management system another important part of every lobbyist's "toolkit".

The politicians in your relationship management database will be those who you have met, spoken to or corresponded with as part of your lobbying activities. Obviously the scale and range of your contacts will depend on what size of organisation you are, and the nature of your issues. Public affairs consultancies would normally have far bigger relationship management databases than in-house teams and these will be broken down by client.

The type of groups which might feature on a relationship management database could include:

- Members of a select committee

- Members of an All-Party Parliamentary Group

- Politicians with a constituency connection

- Politicians from a particular region

- Politicians with a particular background (eg, lawyers or trade unionists)

- Politicians with an interest in a particular policy area (eg, health, defence or education)

Although there are many more civil servants than there are politicians, the number of civil servants on your relationship management database is likely to be very much smaller than the number of politicians. Even if your interests cut across several departments and executive agencies, there will only be a handful of public servants who will have a specific interest in or responsibility for your particular area of operation. Nevertheless they need to be entered into your database because civil servants move quite frequently. This can be because they are rotated out of a post, they get promoted, or they retire. Their movements do not tend to be as well publicised as those of politicians, so it is vital to have a system in place to keep track of them.

Author's top tip

Half way between civil servants and politicians are Special Advisers – or SPADS. They serve a vital role in acting as gatekeepers and sounding boards for ministers, and they are often more approachable than mainstream civil servants. There are about 70 SPADs, plus another dozen or so at 10 Downing Street, and they are a vital component of any contact programme.

There are a limited number of relationship management databases on the market in the UK. They are:

- DodOnline
- DeHavilland
- Augure

DodOnline is part of Dods, but it can be subscribed to independently of the monitoring package. It has biographical databases with excellent search facilities covering all of the UK's political institutions, and you can also subscribe to a separate package covering all of the EU institutions. Both the UK and EU databases have good relationship management functionality.

The databases on the DeHavilland system can only be subscribed to as part of their overall monitoring and public affairs package. The databases are comprehensive, and the functionality on the contact side is also good.

Augure is a specialist relationship management platform. Its political data is good (they buy it in from third parties), and the relationship management software is exceptionally good. As this is a highly specialised and sophisticated system the accompanying price tag can seem quite high – but it is probably the best relationship management system around anywhere in the world.

Author's top tip

Lobbyists need a good relationship management database package in order to efficiently organise their contacts. A good package also allows multiple user access – both to review the system and to update it. This is important because individuals can be away for various reasons or they may leave, in which case there needs to be a system in place which keeps those contacts alive.

Contributor's top tip

Successful public affairs teams effectively manage relationships and communications to key stakeholders.

However, when the number of issues grows in complexity the size of the stakeholder audience expands, making it difficult for a "corporate communications memory" to be stored inside people's heads, spreadsheets or shared folders.

To successfully manage these relationships, a "customer relationship management-like" system should handle contact information and the stakeholder communications. A joined-up approach is needed.

PA professionals must keep in touch with stakeholders including journalists, analysts and NGOs, allowing them to react to news and events and to drive a positive news agenda.

Barry Betts, VP Northern Europe, Augure

Contributor's top tip

Start by working out if government or politicians can help at all. The two cardinal sins are wasting your client's money and everybody's time. Then identify who you need to target. Understand the outlook, objectives and motivations of the person you are trying to persuade.

Construct and deliver your case accordingly, explaining what you want your target to do for you.

Adrian Pepper, Pepper Media

3.5 Online Campaigning

In this electronic age emails are given the same weight as letters. A recent poll by ComRes showed that there was no statistical difference in the amount of attention given to an email as that given to a letter. This makes online campaigning another useful tool for lobbyists.

The principle behind online campaigning is a simple one: a database of postcodes is linked with a database of politicians in order to put campaigners (and voters) in direct touch with their elected representatives. The online campaigning tool is inserted on to a client's website through an "I-frame", and all would-be campaigners have to do is to enter their postcode correctly.

From a politician's point of view emails are easier to respond to than letters. They can also capture email addresses – with a note of the issue which they are concerned with – for future use. Come election time, they can email the voters pointing out that they responded to earlier communications, and asking for electoral support in return.

This is a very direct – and effective – form of lobbying. It can be used to either influence the way in which politicians vote over a particular piece of legislation, or it can be used for specific projects such as boosting the signatures on an Early Day Motion.

There are currently only two online campaigning systems available in the UK:

- Advocacy Online
- Political Wizard

Online campaigning alone is unlikely to achieve results. However, as part of a co-ordinated public affairs campaign, online campaigning can be extremely effective.

Author's top tip

Make sure that every emailed message which you ask your supporters to send begins with the magic words, 'As one of your constituents'. Nothing grabs the attention of politicians like a message from a constituent and potential voter.

Contributor's top tip

Online campaigning has taken the legwork out of the classic coordinated letter writing campaign to parliamentarians. Hand signed letters and licking stamps have made way to "click here now" and "lobby your MP here" hyperlinks. Though the mediums have changed, the basic rules remain the same.

Rule 1)   Keep your message tight and to the point: parliamentarians receive a lot of correspondence and they are more likely to read and get the message in 150 words than 500.

Rule 2)   Make sure that the sender has the ability to highlight his/her connection to the constituency at the beginning. Highlighting a constituency address or constituency specific issue, even if the campaign is national in nature, will ensure that the parliamentarian takes notice. The carefully crafted message will not then find its way to the recycle bin without being read first.

Matt Bricken, Dods Political Wizard

Contributor's top tip

There has been a huge increase in the number of organisations using the Internet to engage supporters in grassroots advocacy. The most successful organisations build a longer-term strategy around four critical building blocks: engaging supporters, building lists, sustaining community and evaluating outcomes.

Engaging supporters on the Internet means picking the right issues that work in an online environment, branding issues and campaigns, using imagery to convey the issue, and using effective and efficient copy (less not more!).

Building lists is essential to longer-term success as organisations experience drop-off and campaigner fatigue. Marketing campaigns to reach new audiences will involve online PR, leveraging affiliate networks, integrating all communication (offline and online), and selectively adopting new technology to create viral activity (eg, widgets or gadgets).

Sustaining your community is the biggest problem area for most organisations. Working hard to build your lists is not useful if you cannot retain the ongoing interest of your audience. Regular and personal communication is the most effective way of sustaining your online supporters.

The Internet is still a relatively young phenomenon with lots of new ideas emerging daily! While it is critical to try new ideas, make sure that you have a good matrix in place to evaluate outcomes. If you do not know what works then you are probably wasting money and resource. Evaluate!

Graham Covington, Managing Director, AdvocacyOnline

3.6 The Media

The media is a tool like any other when it comes to lobbying campaigns. It can, however, be a double edged tool. Either the media itself can turn against you or your campaign, or the people you are trying to influence – the politicians or the civil servants – can resent the fact that you have brought the media into the equation. So, it is more often than not the tool of last resort where public affairs campaigns are concerned.

Just as civil servants almost invariably resent the fact that you have gone over their heads to their political masters, so politicians – especially ministers – can be irritated by the fact that you have chosen to make your case publicly through the media. Sometimes, however, you will have no choice. Private reassurances have not been translated into action, and you need to employ the leverage of the press. This is where lobbying becomes political public relations – a status which many PR professionals bestow upon it in any event.

Even if you initially decide not to use the media as part of your public affairs campaign, you may still be forced to do so. If your opponents in the campaign – and there are always opponents – decide to use the media, you will have no choice but to respond. If you do not have the necessary media relations skills in-house you may need to bring in some PR support – just as PR companies frequently have to draft in PA support.

Initially it may be advisable just to brief the specialists. This would include the lobby journalists who are based in and around Westminster and Whitehall, but it might also include the trade press for the sector which your campaign involves.

If this more subtle use of the media fails, then you may have to resort to standard PR techniques. A press release needs to be drafted, and issued to a wider range of relevant media. Key journalists need to be briefed either personally or over the telephone, either by the lobbyist or by the client. If the campaign has got to the point of no return, then there may even be an argument for a full-blown press conference with radio, TV, print and online media present.

Relevant media and journalists can be identified through media directories or online databases. Hard copy reference books include:

- *Hollis UK PR Annual*
- *Guardian Media Directory*

- *Editors Media Directory*
- *BRAD Media Directory*

Online resources include:

- Hollis PR Portal
- Mediadisk
- PR Newswire
- MediaHub
- Vocus

If you need to draft a press release in support of your public affairs campaign remember there are certain rules which apply:

- Come up with an attention-grabbing title – and use it in the email subject area to increase the chances that it will be opened and not just deleted
- Keep it short – ideally one side of A4 – although you can include editors notes by way of further background information
- If there is an embargo, put it at the top in bold
- Put all the relevant facts in the first paragraph so that a busy or lazy journalist does not have to read too far to gather the gist of the story
- If possible include a quote – preferably an interesting one from a well-known person
- If relevant, include a photograph – or make it clear that one is available on request
- Include contact details (including a mobile number) so that journalists can get back to you
- Try and follow up with a phone call just asking if the press release has been received, if it is of any interest, and if you can supply more information or answer any queries

Politicians and journalists – particularly lobby journalists – have a close symbiotic relationship. On occasion they irritate each other, and from time to time outright hostilities break out. Ultimately, however, both sides realise that they cannot do their jobs without this relationship continuing – and being made to work. Politicians need journalists to tell the general voting public what they have been doing, and journalists need politicians to fill those spaces which are not taken up with stories about sport and celebrities.

Author's top tip

All media is important to politicians. However, the programme that all politicians, their advisers and civil servants listen to is the early morning Today Programme on Radio 4. It sets the agenda for the day, and if you can get a three minute slot on the Today Programme it is worth dozens of column inches in the newspapers – even the heavyweight broadsheets.

Contributor's top tip

Politicians and policymakers both court and consume the media. They know how effective it can be in getting messages across to key target audiences – that is why the media relations operations of the major political parties have become ever more sophisticated and significant. And that is why the media is a key weapon in the armoury of any effective lobbyist.

Crafting lobbying campaigns with the media in mind is useful to ensure they are properly focused and carefully thought through – by definition, to be usable a story has to be newsworthy. Of course, it is not appropriate for every campaign to have a media angle, but this principle should still apply.

In a nutshell, the media puts issues on the political agenda and highlights important campaigns. A cabinet minister who reads a page lead – generated by your campaign – in the Financial Times over his breakfast cornflakes, is more likely to give that campaign serious consideration than one in the same space but without media coverage.

Jonathan French, Association of British Insurers

Contributor's top tip

Practitioners should never underestimate the importance of non-political audiences in influencing political decisions. Of course, it is important to make the case and win the argument with politicians, officials and advisers, since they will be making the critical decisions. However, they will not be making those decisions in a vacuum and it is equally important to focus your attention on the groups or forces that influence politicians' thinking. This includes consumer groups, business groups, charities and unions, but above all, the media. It is the media's ability to shine a spotlight on an issue, and to transform the way that issue is viewed, that has a significant impact on the scope political audiences believe they have to make tricky decisions.

Gidon Freeman, Lexington Communications

Contributor's top tip

Never underestimate the power of the media in lobbying. We are often inclined to think of public affairs and public relations as separate communications disciplines. After all, most practitioners define themselves as one or the other. In fact, they are joined at the hip.

Whether you are lobbying on behalf of a potentially popular cause or a marginal one, the media can be your most virulent opponent or your most powerful ally. No-one consumes the media more avidly than elected representatives, and the officials who advise MPs are correspondingly hypersensitive to what the media says about policy decisions.

As the news-conveying function of the press declines in favour of online news sources, the influence of columnists – "the commentariat" – increases. It makes sense to brief them early and thoroughly, and then to keep them in the picture. With luck they will support your cause – at the very least they will understand your point of view.

Adrian Wheeler, Agincourt Communications

Part Four –
Lobbying Whitehall And
Westminster

The democratic system in the UK has always been fluid. After Magna Carta (signed by King John in 1215) power started to ebb from the monarch to the barons, and after the English civil war (1642-1651) it moved decisively to the House of Commons.

Since the United Kingdom joined the EU on 1 January 1973 (a decision endorsed in a referendum on 6 June 1975) there has been a steady flow of power from Westminster to Brussels, Luxembourg and Strasbourg. Each successive treaty has added to the erosion of Westminster's power – from the original Treaty of Rome in 1957, to the Single European Act in 1986, the Treaty of Maastricht in 1993, the Treaty of Amsterdam in 1997, and finally the more recent Treaty of Lisbon (although at the time of writing this last treaty was in abeyance due to a "No" vote in the Irish referendum).

Within the United Kingdom there has also been a comparatively swift devolutionary process since New Labour came to power with a landslide majority in 1997. The Scottish Parliament was set up, with primary legislative powers and tax varying powers, after a substantial "Yes" vote (74.3% to 25.7% on a turnout of 60.4%) in a referendum called on 11 September 1997. The Welsh Assembly, with no tax raising powers and limited legislative powers, was also set up after a wafer thin majority (just 6721 votes on a turnout of 50.3%) in a referendum on the 18 September. The legislative powers of the Welsh Assembly were substantially enhanced by the Government of Wales Act 2006. A referendum in May 1998 gave the green light to devolution in London, and the Greater London Authority Act was passed the following year. It paved the way for an elected London Mayor, whose activities were to be overseen by the London Assembly. Finally, after years of devolution being set up and then suspended, the Northern Ireland Assembly now seems to be on a firm and permanent footing following the St Andrews' Agreement in 2007.

Local authorities in the UK have also had wide-ranging powers since the nineteenth century. These vary from the standard municipal responsibilities (such as emptying bins and managing street lighting) to more complex, expensive and strategic services (such as school age education and social services). Under the current Labour administration substantial powers have been given to Regional Development Agencies, and non-elected Regional Assemblies have been set up. Abortive attempts have also been made to set up elected Regional Assemblies in England.

In one way or another considerable powers have moved from Westminster and Whitehall to the European Union, to devolved Parliaments and Assemblies, and to local and regional authorities – and much more will be said about the

EU and these regional and local bodies later in the book. The fact is, however, that these powers have been devolved by Act of Parliament. All of these powers could – in theory at least – be constrained or removed entirely by the revocation of the relevant Acts of Parliament. That is why Westminster and Whitehall remain at the centre of the United Kingdom's democratic system – and that is also why this section sets the scene for the rest of the book.

Contributor's top tip

Denis Healey once likened running the Treasury to gardening. Lobbying can be similar, with sometimes disappointing results from the most promising conditions, and encouraging results from unlikely quarters. Spotting opportunities and then exploiting them to the full to further your cause is vital: apart from mainstream issues like health, education, and crime, Parliament and government may visit a specialist area of policy or law once in a generation or even a lifetime! In a democracy a good case certainly can be advanced, but patience is needed, and hard work. Politicians and officials must be persuaded, credible allies found, and judgments carefully made about what exactly it is that you want. These judgements should then be tempered by a hard-nosed sense of political reality. Governments like well thought-out solutions that save them trouble and which may earn them political brownie points. However, constant vigilance is needed to identify and deal with the devil that lurks in the detail!

Barney Holbeche, Head of Parliamentary Affairs, National Farmers' Union

4.1 The Civil Service

The average lifetime of a parliament since the second world war in the United Kingdom is just over four years. The civil service, however, has been running the country continuously for centuries – certainly since the Northcote-Trevelyan reforms of 1854. These reforms professionalised the civil service, ensuring that recruitment and promotion were on merit, and they in theory at least removed the danger of any politicisation of the civil service.

Not only do parliaments and governments come and go every four years or so, but ministers are rotated – or removed entirely – on a far more regular basis. It has become a tradition in recent years that prime ministers undertake fairly wide-ranging reshuffles every July, so that ministers have time to read-up on their new briefs ahead of the annual party conferences in September and early October, and ahead of the Queen's Speech in November. This reshuffle ritual is partly designed to periodically refresh a government – both in terms of substance and image. It is also, some cynics would say, designed to ensure that ministers are never in a post long enough to have to see their promises through to fruition – or to be made to bear the consequences of their mistakes.

Whatever the motivation of periodic – and frequent – reshuffles, the end result is that enormous power resides with civil servants. They are in place – and virtually "unsackable" – as governments come and go. If there is a particular secretary of state, minister of state or parliamentary under secretary who they especially dislike (or whose policy they vehemently disagree with), they know that they only need to stall them for a year or two and they will be gone. They also know that ministers are rarely in post for long enough to acquire any real expertise in the policy areas which they are supposed to be overseeing – so they are almost never in a position to challenge civil servants, who are the long-standing incumbents and the experts in a particular field.

Margaret Thatcher famously said 'civil servants advise and ministers decide'. Certainly in a parliamentary democracy that is the way things should be, and with a strong premier and a vibrant government that is usually the way it actually is. Very often, however, ministers do not have the expertise or the energy to make every decision – and they are content to let the civil service do that for them. The man in Whitehall may or may not know best – but he (and nowadays frequently she) often has the final say.

Contributor's top tip

Lobbying is ultimately the provision of accurate information whereby elected representatives can make an informed decision based on accurate advice. Therefore the information must be true and transparent.

Effective lobbying is about more than providing press cuttings and extracts from *Hansard*. I have lost count of the number of clients who are reluctant to engage with the civil service (or the European Commission), believing that MPs and MEPs should be the first point of contact, only to discover that when they do engage with officials the meetings are fruitful and effective.

Effective lobbying is often mundane but must be precise. Meet the right people and always ensure that you are informed and well briefed and that your client, who must be the spokesperson, is equally well briefed. By following this you will do the best for your clients and be able to remain what you should be – an effective adviser and consultant – not the story or the issue.

Peter Golds OBE, Senior Consultant, PPS Group

4.1.1 Whitehall

The main concentration of civil service power is centred on the Whitehall departments. Although I refer to Whitehall, many of these central departments are no longer physically located there – although they tend to be very close to hand. Whitehall was originally a palace acquired by Henry VIII from Thomas Wolsey in 1529. The building was substantially improved by Inigo Jones at the behest of James 1st when he ascended to the throne in 1603, although it eventually burnt to the ground in 1688.

Some of the great departments of state – and the great offices of state which go with them – go back centuries. These include HM Treasury, the Foreign and Commonwealth Office, the Home Office and the Ministry of Defence. However, some of these have been rebranded over the years. The current Foreign and Commonwealth Office has been simply the Foreign Office in the past, and had a lengthy spell as the Foreign and Colonial Office. The current Ministry of Defence was formerly the War Office – a belligerent-sounding title which did not suit the post-war era which has seen the United Nations formed, and armed aggression by one state against another increasingly frowned upon.

As well as re-branding to deal with changed attitudes and circumstances some re-branding has been a straightforward attempt to leave behind images of past failure. The Ministry of Agriculture, Fisheries and Food (MAFF) was scrapped following its perceived failure to deal with the Foot and Mouth and BSE crises, and its functions were merged in to the newly-formed Department of Environment, Food and Rural Affairs (DEFRA). Again, the long-established Home Office lost some of its functions to the Ministry of Justice following an assertion by John Reid, who was home secretary at the time, that it was not fit for purpose.

Sometimes new governments – or new administrations – like to "shuffle the pack" of Whitehall ministries in order to assert their authority. When Gordon Brown became prime minister in 2007 he scrapped the existing Department for Education and Skills and replaced it with a Department for Children, Schools and Families and a Department for Innovation, Universities and Skills. Equally, he turned the long-established Department for Trade & Industry into the Department for Business, Enterprise and Regulatory Reform.

Anecdote

When it was first decided that the Department for Trade & Industry had to be re-branded the alternative name which was initially rumoured to have been chosen was the Department for Productivity, Enterprise, Innovation and Skills. Fortunately somebody spotted that the acronym for this was very close to PEnIS, and the suggestion was hurriedly dropped!

Author's top tip

When dealing with civil servants it is important to understand where they are coming from. Most civil servants are not specialists – they are either gifted generalists, or administrators. The primary role of the civil servants who you will generally routinely deal with is drafting – whether that is speeches, answers to parliamentary questions, policy papers, or reports. Their principal aim in life is to keep their ministerial masters secure and happy – whilst at the same time fostering their advancement within the civil service by maintaining a reputation for quiet competence. They do not like taking risks, and they do not like publicity or politics. Conversely, that can on occasion mean that you can get your way by threatening them with the risks associated with those very same demons of publicity and politics.

Contributor's top tip

Flash tactics are often unnecessary and wasteful. In many cases it is simple and effective enough to get your brief across to the relevant official at G7 level who will be producing recommendations for the minister. They can be surprisingly receptive to an early approach from outside interests, as it can help insulate the government against any future backlash. Try to provide solutions which they can trust by being upfront about potentially awkward issues and clarifying how the exchequer would be affected. If you are blocked then take the political route through Special Advisers, the minister's office and senior MPs. If you still have no joy then there is a place for pressure tactics such as media campaigning, demonstrations and so on. These are good at giving the impression of activity to other audiences, but are less likely to produce the decision you want than a properly produced piece of evidence communicated to the right person.

Martin Koder, Lanson Communications

4.1.2 Contacting civil servants

In the twenty-first century civil servants are far more approachable than they were twenty – or even ten – years ago. In that respect they have learnt a great deal from their equivalents in Brussels. So-called euro-crats have always been approachable and they have always embraced the principles of maximum consultation and contact.

Pretty much any organisation – from the largest company to the smallest charity – will have a sponsoring department. Within that department there will be a unit covering their broad area of activity, and within that unit there will be an individual tasked with overseeing your specific area of interest or activity. The trick is in identifying that individual, and then establishing contact and building a relationship.

As ever a lot of the information you will need is either available online – or in hard copy reference books. Most government departments have reasonable websites, some including "organagrams". In terms of paid for online services, the choice is between:

- DodOnline

- DeHavilland

- *Civil Service Year Book Online*

There is slightly more choice with hard copy reference books. Relevant reference books are:

- *Civil Service Year Book*

- *Dod's Civil Service Companion*

- *Vacher's Quarterly Companion*

- *Carlton's Directory of Westminster and Whitehall*

Between these various websites, online directories and reference books you ought to be able to identify the civil servant who you should be dealing with. If not, there is a general enquiries number for every government department – although they are not always prompt or helpful. If you cannot find the individual civil servant who seems to precisely suit your needs, try calling somebody occupying a vaguely relevant position and see if they can help you. Most Whitehall departments are broken down by division and branch and identifying the relevant division and then branch within the correct department will usually lead you to the actual individual you need to deal with.

As has been stated earlier, civil servants do tend to move fairly regularly. They can be promoted, or rotated into a new and roughly equivalent position, or they can leave the civil service, or retire. If your regular contact tells you that he or she is moving on, try and find out through them who their replacement will be. Quite often they will occupy the same office or desk. They may even have the same telephone number – so always give that a try first.

In the past civil servants all had uniform grades from one to ten. Grades one and two were the permanent secretaries and assistant permanent secretaries, grades three to seven were policy officers, and grades eight to ten were administrative or clerical officers. Today this uniformity has disappeared, and there is a confusing proliferation of titles. A selection of these titles are:

- Permanent secretary (former grade 1)

- Director general or director (former assistant permanent secretary or grade 2)

- Director or head of division (former under secretary, grade 3)

- Assistant director or head (former assistant secretary, grade 5)

- Principal (former grade 7)

Author's top tip

The level of civil servant you should be aiming to deal with is assistant director, head or principal level – the old grades 5 and 7. If you try and approach a minister or a senior civil servant without having had dealings with these key grades, you will merely be "bumped" down to them, and they in turn will feel aggrieved because you have gone over their heads.

Other titles in common usage within Whitehall include:

- Divisional manager

- Team leader

- Head of unit

- Branch head

Once you have identified the key civil servant for your area of activity you can contact them by telephone, email or letter. Initially this can be just to identify yourself, or your organisation. It is usually an idea, however, to find some pretext for a face-to-face meeting. Initially this should probably be at their offices, although if a further meeting is necessary you can invite them to your offices.

Civil servants are governed by the Civil Service Code and they are not allowed to be in receipt of either gifts or lavish hospitality. You can, however, invite them to lunches or dinners where a large number of people will be present, or to drinks receptions. You can also invite them to lunch on their own – provided it is not a frequent event, and provided that the cost of the entertainment is modest. Very senior civil servants are also allowed to be in receipt of corporate hospitality.

The purpose of making contact with civil servants is to open up the channels of communication. They should want to know what your organisation is up to – not every new deal or every new appointment, but major contract wins or changes in the most senior personnel. You, in turn, want to be sure to find out when government departments issue consultation documents, Green Papers and White Papers. You might hear about it in the press or through your trade body, but it is much better to hear about it direct from the department responsible for issuing the document and collating the responses. Again, if there is an advisory body being formed – you want to be sure that somebody from your organisation is being represented on it.

For all of these reasons it is worth finding out which is your sponsoring department, and who the individual is within it who has direct responsibility for your field of activity. Once you have identified that individual make, and maintain, contact.

Some civil servants are very adept at keeping external bodies at bay, and insulating their civil servant and political masters from troublesome external influences. Favourite ploys used by civil servants to deflect external approaches include:

- *"It has already been decided/it is government policy"*: When faced with this ploy, it is a clue to go political and call their bluff.

- *Zero response*: If you do not even get an acknowledgement follow up with a phone call. If you still find you are hitting a brick wall, ask a supportive MP to table a parliamentary question.

- *"Thank you – your views will be taken into account"*: This is standard Whitehall for "whatever". Follow up with a phone call requesting a meeting.

- *"The issue you raised is not being considered at this time"*: This may be true – but follow up by asking when it will be considered.

- *"This issue is being considered at ministerial level"*: This is an open invitation to request a meeting with the minister.

Contributor's top tip

The key to all lobbying is to understand what makes your interlocutors tick. What is their motivation?

Some things change. Whitehall warriors no longer see ministers merely as a temporary political resource at their disposal. But others remain. Civil servants still cling to the pursuit of fact and detail, and the need to work things through. And they are constantly short of facts.

So you need to show with hard fact and comprehensive information that what you say is true. Preferably this hard fact will be attributable to an independent third party.

Collect, collate and present the facts as and how they are needed. Understand the negative arguments around your case, and counter them before they are put to you. Make yourself and your resource available to civil servants. Provide them with the information they need. Create an informal partnership.

The politics are secondary. Information is their drug, and they are short of it. Give them their fix, and you have a friend for life. Mislead them at your peril.

Warwick Smith, Managing Partner, College Public Policy (and former senior civil servant)

4.1.3 Special Advisers

Special Advisers (or SPADs as they are sometimes known) occupy a unique position between the civil servants and politicians. Technically they are civil servants and therefore bound by the Civil Service Code. In fact their position is so uniquely powerful that they are bound by their own Code of Conduct for Special Advisers. Like the Civil Service Code, this is drafted – and enforced – by the Cabinet Office.

Special Advisers are (generally) young, bright men and women with political ambitions of their own. Whilst they are fostering those political ambitions, it suits them to be attached to a minister – usually a cabinet minister or minister of state. There are some seventy SPADs serving individual ministers at any one time, plus perhaps another dozen or so working at 10 Downing Street in the Policy or Delivery Units.

Author's top tip

Special Advisers owe their loyalties to individual ministers. If there is a dispute between departments – and between ministers – they are often happy to be briefed with your side of the argument – and then to brief the press against the opposing minister.

In previous administrations Special Advisers were usually just that – specialists in particular areas of policy. That meant that they tended to function at a particular department, and they would often stay on to serve successive ministers. Today they tend to have more general political nous rather than policy specialities, and they tend to follow a minister from one post to another. When that minister is finally sacked the SPAD would also lose his or her job. When a general election is called, all SPAD contracts are cancelled. If a SPAD gets selected to fight a Westminster seat, they have to resign immediately. So although it is an interesting existence – and looks great on a CV – the life of a SPAD is a precarious one.

The main functions of a Special Adviser are as follows:

- To act as a political sounding board for a minister
- To act as a political gatekeeper for a minister
- To write a minister's political speeches
- To handle the political aspects of a minister's media relations
- To insulate the civil servants from party politics

Contributor's top tip

Remember the SPADs of today are the future ministers of tomorrow. SPADS of the past include David Cameron, Jack Straw, David Miliband and Andy Burnham to name a few, so today's SPADS are worth long-term investment.

SPADS sometimes seek allies against their own departments. Let them know which members of their department are briefing against them or their minister. Write direct to them seeking a quick phone call or meeting. They will often want a speech location and audience for their boss – offer a flexible time so as to fit around their diary.

Help them with policy by offering to write letters they can use with backbenchers explaining why your organisation supports what the government is doing.

Help them organize a coalition of the willing behind a policy they are pushing.

Send them press cuttings of people being supportive of government policy.

Give them story ideas or the chance to write an intro for a book/pamphlet that reaches a large group of people.

Anon – former SPAD to a senior cabinet minister

Contributor's top tip

Special Advisers succeed either by securing visible successes for their boss, or by helping their boss to avoid visible failures. Their role is spectacularly ill defined and chaotic and so, too, are their ways of working. To engage successfully with a Special Adviser you need to help them to achieve those visible successes and avoid those visible failures, whilst always being mindful of the pressures under which they operate.

Tim Rycroft, Diageo, former SPAD to the Chairman of the Conservative Party

---

4.1.4 Executive agencies and non-departmental public bodies

Margaret Thatcher was not a great admirer of the civil service. She found the UK civil service to be slow to react and difficult to manoeuvre, fitting its reputation as a Rolls-Royce. She therefore took as much power and responsibility as she could away from the main Whitehall departments and distributed it amongst bodies officially called executive agencies, but which were more widely known as Quangos (quasi-autonomous non-governmental organisations).

Under the "next steps" programme during the Thatcher and Major premierships large numbers of civil servants were moved from Whitehall Departments into executive agencies. The idea was to move them away from the dead hand of Whitehall, and to imbue them with business-like virtues of efficiency and competition. They were headed by chief executives rather than permanent secretaries, and they had budgets, targets and bonuses.

Today they are often also referred to as non-departmental public bodies. There are a wide range of "arm's length" bodies which undertake the work done by the Whitehall departments. They are categorised by the Cabinet Office as:

- Executive NDPBs

- Advisory NDPBs

- Tribunal NDPBs

- Monitoring boards of penal establishments

- Monitoring boards of immigration removal centres

- Public corporations

- Public broadcasting authority

- Central bank

- Nationalised industries

- National Health Service bodies

A full list of all of these can be found in the *Public Bodies Directory*, published by HMSO, or on the Cabinet Office website. Altogether these "arm's length" bodies are responsible for massive amounts of public expenditure, and they have huge executive powers.

Examples of some prominent and powerful NDPBs are:

- Environment Agency

- Housing Corporation

- Arts Council

- English Heritage

- Learning and Skills Council

- Disability Rights Commission

- Design Council

According to Cabinet Office figures in 2007 NDPBs were responsible for £30,837m of expenditure – and the employment of 96,456 people.

Apart from the very large sums of money, which they get from government to spend and allocate, the interesting thing about NDPBs is that they lobby government themselves, and that they are in turn lobbied by others.

Many of these bodies – especially the larger ones – have in-house government relations teams. Some of them also retain external public affairs consultancies – often at substantial fees. From time to time the press and the opposition parties criticise the fact that government-funded bodies are spending taxpayers' money to lobby the government. In fact it is entirely logical that they should do so. These bodies were created by government and Parliament, and they can be dissolved – or merged – at the whim of government. They therefore need to keep an eye on government and Parliament, and to be in a position to influence them if need be. This is also the case with funding. Government allocates most if not all of their funding, and government can – and on occasion does – turn off the tap.

Equally these NDPBs expect to be lobbied themselves. If business, a local authority, or the community need a by-pass built or an "A-road" dualled they will lobby the minister and the Department of Transport. However, the final decision will be made by the Highways Agency, and it will be the Highways Agency that commissions the actual road building. Consequently, they too must be lobbied. The same goes when a patient group wants a new pharmaceutical drug approved. They will lobby Parliament, and the secretary of state for health, but the final decision is down to NICE.

So NDPBs can be huge and powerful. They lobby government, and they expect in turn to be lobbied. Unless the trend of the last twenty-five years is dramatically reversed, lobbying NDPBs will remain very much a core activity for in-house and in-consultancy public affairs professionals.

Author's top tip

Because many of these bodies are quasi-autonomous, it is sometimes hard to exert influence over them. Ministers often deny direct responsibility for them, and parliamentary influence is two steps removed. Sometimes, however, the press can have a very direct influence – as prolonged media campaigns over the Child Support Agency and the Passport Agency testify. The former ended up being abolished, whilst the latter was pressurised into dramatically improving its level of service.

4.1.5 Regulators

Regulators are a form of Non Departmental Public Body. They have a sponsoring department, and there will be a minister with oversight responsibilities towards them. However, for obvious reasons, they are even more arms length – and more autonomous – than other types of NDPB.

The Department for Business, Enterprise and Regulatory Reform (DBERR) – which took over most of the responsibilities of the Department for Trade & Industry (DTI) – has identified the principles to which all regulations (and therefore regulators) should conform. They are that all regulations and regulators should be:

- Transparent
- Accountable
- Proportionate
- Consistent
- Targeted

Regulators can oversee fairly obscure professions and fairly minor industries. Some however, have very wide ranging remits. Examples of some of the better known regulators include:

- Financial Services Authority
- Food Standards Agency
- Office of Fair Trading
- Ofcom
- Ofwat
- Postcomm

Other bodies – such as the Charity Commission – have dual roles. They are part regulator, and part judicial body. This makes them, in effect, judge and jury.

It is advisable for lobbyists and monitoring agencies to keep a close eye on the activities of regulators. They regularly publish consultation documents, and invite responses from interested parties. It is also essential to monitor the outcomes of regulators' inquiries, so as to have a good idea of how they are interpreting their own and government regulations.

It is permissible to have informal discussions with regulators about hypothetical cases which fall within their remit. It should be made clear, however, that this is with a view to ensuring that you or your client will be staying within the letter and the spirit of the rules – not with a view to circumventing them.

Warning!

Once a regulator has announced an inquiry no informal or unsolicited approach should be made to them. The initiative lies with the regulator, and they will approach you or your client for the information they require. There is also no point in lobbying ministers or politicians – they will regard the case as being sub judice and refuse to discuss it with you.

Regulators are set up by statute and often have a semi-judicial role. Whilst it is essential to build up a relationship with them, full-on traditional lobbying is not encouraged and is not advisable.

Author's top tip

Whilst – as has been said – direct lobbying of regulators by interested parties is not advised, indirect lobbying through third parties can be extremely successful. Using grassroots opinion – boosted by the involvement of the media – can produce results. An example was the National Institute for Health and Clinical Excellence having to perform a u-turn and authorise the NHS to prescribe new drugs for combating breast cancer and Alzheimer's disease.

Contributor's top tip

Regulatory bodies tend to be fiercely protective of their independence, wanting to be seen as independent both of the industries they regulate and of government.

Lobbyists should bear this in mind when campaigning and ensure that they identify how and where the regulator's objectives might differ from both the Government's objectives and those of the industry. Do not assume that industry can either rely on enlisting the regulator's support in lobbying government, or that the regulator can be targeted with the same campaign as ministers and departmental officials.

An example of this is the recent energy retail industry's campaign to secure a Government mandate to install new generation smart meters in every home in Britain.

While all parties agree that the technology is necessary, differences in the priorities of the government, industry and the regulator have led to a difference in opinion over the implementation model.

Madeleine Hallward, Public Affairs Manager, Energy Retail Association

Contributor's top tip

The traditional perception of regulators is one of robotic officials, lacking understanding of the industries they police, and sporting a tendency to justify their own existence with unnecessary rules and red tape.

Little surprise then that some people still think the best way to deal with regulators is to shout at the top of their voice about red tape, faceless bureaucracy, and so on.

But regulators are, like any other organisation, made up of people. These people will have different levels of understanding of your particular business and related issues, and also different perspectives.

So establishing close links and gaining real understanding of the particular executives most important to you is crucial:

- Network at events. Remember to say hello and name check all your key regulatory contacts. All your key executives need to have a view to this (provided you can be sure they are on-message, of course), even if they think they are at events for B2B reasons. Meeting more representatives from a company gives the regulator a fuller picture of your organisation and its key drivers.

- Site visits. Regulators are just like any anyone else – they love a chance to get out of the office and have a change of scenery. As a useful by-product, it fleshes out their own understanding of the industries they regulate. So ask them in for a presentation and/or site visit

- Offer to conduct/provide research. The fuller picture of an industry a regulator has, the better they can oversee it and design policy that is sympathetic rather than obstructive. So if you have a point to make and are confident research will bear it out, use your own organisation's unique position within your sector to offer to provide relevant research to the regulator, by briefing them early and giving them some involvement in the design and objectives.

All the above enable you and your organisation to build a constructive relationship. Rather than meaning you cannot later criticise the regulator, it allows you to do so within the context of a well-constructed relationship. This practical involvement, coupled with an understanding of the limits of co-operation as opposed to submissiveness, makes for a sensible, practical and hopefully positive relationship with your regulator.

Ultimately there are always times when lines have to be drawn in the sand. But know what those lines are, be clear to the regulator about them, and ALWAYS make arguments evidence-based.

Tim Wilson, public affairs consultant

Contributor's top tip

Good lobbying gives an alternative solution. It should also be succinct.

Where a regulator is concerned about an issue, constructive suggestions will be more effective in moving policy. If a proposal should be stopped, clear industry data should be given to explain why.

There is a tendency to submit too much data, much of it irrelevant or clearly selective, which the usually small regulatory team have limited time to absorb.

Steve Barclay, Barclays Bank

Contributor's top tip

The concept of lobbying a regulator would have been entirely out of the question little more than a decade ago. While lobbying as an activity is now perhaps at its strongest in some of the most heavily regulated industries – health and financial services being prime examples – the concept of trying to influence the outcome of regulatory decisions and judgements would not have been possible.

An era of greater transparency and a culture of greater openness in terms of regulatory decision making has allowed considerable opportunity for public debate and therefore opportunity to create impact.

For years the "regulated" have spent the vast preponderance of time on compliance led activity – essentially ensuring the boxes are ticked. However, the growth of principles-based regulation in many sectors has meant box ticking is no longer the answer. Firms need to focus much more on influencing the outcome of regulatory policy.

Therefore my top tip is to ensure you develop strong relationships with those working at the regulator who are engaged with the development of policy and look to provide them with evidence based materials and arguments. At the same time, ensure that the main government department responsible for oversight of said regulatory body is also aware of your viewpoint. Regulatory decisions, which are essentially a matter of public policy, are usually worked out as part of dialogue between the two.

Iain Anderson, Cicero Consulting London

4.2 Political Parties

Obviously most politicians – with the exception of a handful of independents – are members of political parties. However, what we are talking about in this section is the people who work at the party headquarters – and in Parliament supporting the frontbenchers.

The party in government relies to a large degree on the civil service, government press officers, and the 70 or so Special Advisers we talked about in an earlier section. For the party in power, the main role of the headquarters staff is:

- Fundraising
- Recruiting members and candidates
- Organising the manifesto
- Fighting election campaigns

For the opposition parties, over and above the roles listed above, there are other strong calls upon the time of their headquarters and Parliament staff. They also have to:

- Handle media enquiries
- Undertake research
- Develop policies

This mismatch between the resources at the disposal of parties in government and parties in opposition means that it is much easier to lobby the latter than the former. With the governing party they have the whole of the civil service at their disposal – and a strong imperative not to be perceived as backing down or performing U-turns. Opposition parties have far fewer resources at their disposal, and they find it much easier to change their policies than governments – which have no choice but to operate in the full glare of the media spotlight.

All of this means that opposition front benches in the Commons and Lords welcome approaches by lobbyists. If the lobbyist is proposing a course of action which is anathema to the party's core beliefs, he or she will still get fairly short shrift. However, any line of questioning or any amendments to a piece of legislation which could discomfit the government is likely to be welcomed. Opposition front and back benchers are far more likely to ask questions, table Early Day Motions or try to introduce amendments to a government bill than backbenchers from the governing party. With a handful of exceptions, most opposition MPs – front and backbench – regard lobbyists as their friends.

Opposition parties are also more likely to agree to meetings with lobbyists, and to give their suggestions careful consideration. This can be important not only for day to day issues like debates, parliamentary questions and the progress of bills, but also where strategic matters such as the formulation of policy for the manifesto are concerned.

Author's top tip

Opposition parties – and politicians – are under-resourced, and they often (for obvious reasons) feel rejected and unloved. Once they return to power (or once they are convinced that they will be returning to power) their attitudes change very quickly, so the time to get to know them is when government seems like a distant prospect.

Contributor's Top Tip

Members of Parliament are busy people. I recall as a Parliamentary researcher, my key morning task was to divide up the post into (i) invitations to events, (ii) areas of personal or frontbench interest, (iii) constituency correspondence, (iv) everything else.

The post would be read by the MP in that order. In other words, "everything else" is rarely seen by the MP, even if it is personally addressed and tailored. In an electronic age, it is even more difficult for MPs to keep up with torrents of incoming communications and increased expectations from their constituents.

As a result, it is surprising how comparatively little attention is given by public affairs campaigns to the research staff who support and advise MPs – including those in the central headquarters of political parties.

This is not to over-state the importance of such support staff, as MPs will always make the final decisions and take responsibility for them. But in the small print – and most lobbying is about the small print of legislation and regulation – such specialist staff have a key role in drafting responses and policy.

A good public affairs strategy will therefore seek to inform and engage behind the scenes, as well as those who appear in the headlines.

Sheridan Westlake, Deputy Director, Conservative Research Department

4.3 House Of Commons

Over the centuries, the House of Commons has established its pre-eminence in United Kingdom politics. This pre-eminence was sealed by the English civil war of 1642-1651, and was not substantially reduced by the restoration of the monarchy in 1660. The power of the House of Lords, although substantial, is severely limited by conventions such as the Salisbury Convention, and by statutes such as the Parliament Acts of 1911 and 1949. Just as the power of the House of Lords has been severely restricted over the years, so the last monarch to refuse to sign an Act of Parliament was Queen Anne in 1707.

In recent years the House of Commons has devolved a great many of its powers. The European Union in particular has acquired extensive powers in areas as diverse as agriculture, trade and the environment. Some estimates put the percentage of legislation which originates in Brussels as high as 80%. Only areas such as taxation, education, foreign affairs and defence remain completely outside of the EU remit, and Brussels does seem to have ambitions to spread its writ into these areas as well. Every new EU treaty increases the ratchet effect, with the flow of power being very much in one direction only.

Local authorities have ever larger budgets, and they retain responsibility for the delivery of a wide range of vital services. Apart from the things which people usually rate the performance of their local authorities on – such as emptying the bins and maintaining the pavements – they have responsibility for a the delivery of a range of other services, including primary and secondary education (which is still largely delivered through Local Education Authorities) and social services. Cabinet style government has replaced the traditional structure in many local authorities, with elected cabinet members having substantial powers and claiming large salaries. Local authority chief executives and chief officers now routinely earn substantial six figure salaries – often more than their equivalents in Whitehall departments.

Elected mayors are another novelty which has been introduced by the Blair government. Although only a handful of referendums have been held to bring in this system of government, some of them, such as in Hartlepool and Middlesbrough, have been very high profile – and not without controversy. The most high profile – and powerful – elected Mayor is the Mayor of London. Ken Livingstone won in 2000 and 2004, and brought in radical schemes such as the congestion charge, using the substantial executive powers at his disposal. He has since been replaced by Boris Johnson, who has set out a very different agenda.

Other substantial devolutions of power have seen the establishing – or re-constitution – of the Scottish Parliament, which has powers to initiate legislation and to vary taxation. Devolution in Northern Ireland has been resumed through the Northern Ireland Assembly, and Assemblies have also been set up in Wales and London. These areas will be dealt with in detail later on in the book.

The fact remains, however, that all of these powers have been devolved through Acts of Parliament – and those Acts could be revoked and those devolved powers could be rescinded. In practical terms that would be very difficult to achieve, but since the House of Commons remits large sums of money to all of these bodies it has both the legal basis and the financial muscle to do so should it so desire. So, despite the growth of the European Union, and despite the increasing trend towards devolution and localism, the House of Commons remains the ultimate arbiter of the political fate of all parts of the United Kingdom.

Contributor's top tip

Never forget that we live in a pluralist political system. Labour in national government, Tories running London and most of local government, Liberal Democrats in charge in many of the big cities and holding effective balance in the House of Lords, Scottish Nationalists dominating Scotland and Plaid Cymru-Labour in a joint Welsh administration. A political lobbying strategy needs to reflect this and, for business, the growing importance of that most diverse Parliament of all – the European Parliament.

Neil Sherlock, Partner Public Affairs, KPMG

4.3.1 The prime minister

The first prime minister is generally regarded to have been Sir Robert Walpole in 1721. He was a Whig (the antecedents of the modern Liberals) and he held power for what is still a record period of time – 20 years and 314 days.

The United Kingdom has a cabinet style government with the prime minister – in theory at least – being merely *primus inter pares* (first amongst equals). In practice, the authority of prime ministers varies according to the size of their majority and the force of their personality. It also waxes and wanes according to the general political climate and the state of the opinion polls.

The prime minister has a wide range of powers – despite the first amongst equals tag. In recent years, certainly since the days of Margaret Thatcher, UK prime ministers have become increasingly presidential, trying to draw more and more powers in to an ever-burgeoning 10 Downing Street operation.

One of the main powers of a prime minister is that of patronage. At a very immediate level the prime minister can appoint – and sack – cabinet and other ministers at will. This is regarded as being a crucial element in the maintenance of party discipline, because anybody who speaks against the party line or who is deemed to be engaged in plotting can be summarily dismissed. This power also enables prime ministers to refresh their government after a particularly severe drubbing at the ballot box, or a substantial dip in the opinion polls.

The prime minister also has substantial powers to appoint life peers – although recent scandals have led to those powers being curtailed. Appointing people as life peers has long been regarded as being a good way of rewarding loyal party supporters, MPs who have lost or given up their seats, and party donors. It is also a good way of bringing outsiders with relevant experience directly into government. Recent cash for honours scandals have led to the curtailing of the powers of the prime minister to appoint peers, and the creation of the House of Lords Appointments Commission to oversee this work.

Apart from ministers and life peers, the prime minister has powers of appointment in a huge range of other areas. These include Bishops and Archbishops, the heads of MI5, MI6 and GCHQ, and (along with the chancellor of the exchequer) the Governor of the Bank of England. There is also, of course, the power to ensure that a host of other honours such as Knighthoods, CBEs, OBEs and MBEs go to individuals who have helped his or her cause. Prime ministers use these powers frequently and ruthlessly to firm up their power base, and that is why they always oppose any moves to dilute their powers of patronage.

Although the prime minister in the United Kingdom is not the head of state, he or she is widely regarded as being the *de facto* leader of the country. The prime minister has a weekly audience with the monarch, and represents the UK at the EU summits and across the world. Only at Commonwealth events does the monarch tend to be centre stage in anything other than a ceremonial way.

Prime ministers also have the power, in theory at least, to take the country to war and to order British troops into battle. In practice, prime ministers always consult the monarch over issues such as this, because the UK armed forces (technically at least) owe their allegiance to the Crown rather than to government. Also, any prime minister who goes to war without at least tacit approval of Parliament risks losing their job. Anthony Eden was brought down by Suez, and Tony Blair's departure was undoubtedly hastened by his decision to join George Bush in the invasion of Iraq. Gordon Brown has indicated that he would not take the country to war without Parliament's approval, and this may be cemented in statute.

One of the greatest powers of a prime minister is the discretion to call a general election at any time – provided it is not beyond the fifth anniversary of the last general election. This means that they can chose a time which is advantageous to them and their party – such as when they have just pulled off a successful treaty negotiation, when their opponents are going through a difficult patch, or when they are simply riding high in the opinion polls.

So prime ministers in the UK wield very substantial powers – albeit subject to the advice of the monarch, the scrutiny of Parliament, and the support of their political parties. From a lobbyist's point of view, the question is – how do you get at the prime minister to persuade him or her to exercise that power on your behalf?

Prime ministers are nowhere near as accessible as MPs or even ministers. This is because they are busier than even cabinet colleagues, and because the security threat to them is much greater. This means that if you do get a chance to meet the prime minister, you need to seize the opportunity to convey the issue you want to raise with him or her very succinctly, before aides step in to move them on.

Having said that they are relatively inaccessible, prime ministers have to get out and about, or they are accused of developing a bunker mentality. When they attend party conferences they do have security and aides with them, but they are relatively approachable. They also have to attend set-piece annual events, such as the CBI annual conference. They regularly lead delegations of business people abroad to try and "drum up" trade for UKPLC. In the UK they make factory and constituency visits – especially at election times. There can be opportunities to have a quick word, but as you will be one of many seeking to do so, it is vital that you follow up with a letter detailing the issue which you raised with him or her verbally.

You can also, of course, simply write to the prime minister at 10 Downing Street, London SW1A 2AA. However, unless you or your organisation are very eminent or extremely worthy, or you can intimate in the letter that you have actually met the prime minister and you have discussed the issue outlined in the letter with him or her, you will get a response from an official (which the PM will probably not even have read).

One recent innovation on the 10 Downing Street website is that it is possible to set up – and add your signature to – an electronic petition. Unfortunately, since it is so easy to set up a petition, the impact is very limited. At the time of writing over 30,000 petitions had been set up, from serious issues such as giving UK residency rights to Ghurkha veterans, to trivial issues such as reversing the deduction of points from Leeds United Football Club (apologies to any Leeds fans reading this). That is not to say that these petitions are necessarily a waste of time. A petition against road pricing attracted nearly 2m signatures and is widely credited with changing government policy in this area. The prime minister does send an automated email response to everybody who signs a petition on the number Ten website.

Perhaps a better – though less direct – method of influencing the prime minister is through the media. Most prime ministers are avid consumers of all forms of media – radio, TV and newspapers. Prime ministers do try, of course, to play down their addiction to the media. Legend has it that Margaret Thatcher did not read the press – she relied on a digest produced for her every morning by her press secretary Bernard Ingham. She did, however, famously phone up the Today Programme direct after hearing some highly critical comments about her handling of the Falklands war. Dave Hill – latterly Tony Blair's press secretary following the departure of Alastair Campbell – maintained that Tony Blair never listened to the Today Programme. In both cases, however, this was towards the end of their premierships, and there is a strong case for saying that their alleged disinclination to engage with the media hastened their departures from office.

So, despite what they may say, it is a pretty safe assumption that all prime ministers (unless they have retreated to the bunkers and pulled down the hatch) take the media very seriously. Whereas radio and TV have to restrain any bias, newspaper journalists, commentators and bloggers can give vent to their prejudices – although any politician would filter any comments they read from these sources through that prism. However, if the press are virtually unanimous, or organs which normally support the prime minister and his or her party are critical, then they would be advised to take notice. If you can therefore get a bandwagon going in favour of your lobby, or you can persuade the generally government-supporting press to back you, you can be pretty sure that this will filter through to the prime minister's psyche.

One other area which has a large impact on prime ministers – despite all of their denials – is opinion polls. Generally these are political polls, asking about voting intentions. All politicians embrace those polls which are favourable, and rubbish those which are not. However, they do carefully follow polls, and they are the source of endless discussion within parties.

If you can commission a poll from a respected polling company (which means being a member of the British Polling Council), with a significant sample (which means more than one thousand), which supports your lobby, it will be picked up by Number Ten and every other government department. So if you can produce a poll which says that, for instance, 85% of people are in favour of the imposition of a tax on plastic carrier bags, then that will have an impact. The party may commission its own polling on the issue, or it may wait for further polls to come out supporting the original, but they will take notice.

So far we have discussed trying to get to the prime minister directly. Usually, however, you will find yourself trying to get to the prime minister through his or her staff. 10 Downing Street is like the "TARDIS" – it is much bigger inside than it looks on the outside. This is because it has been extended a long way back towards Horse Guards Parade, and because it has sprawled sideways into number 11 and towards the Cabinet Office – to which it is now connected.

10 Downing Street is now a mini department of state. At one stage during Tony Blair's premiership it was rumoured that he was thinking about creating an actual Department of the Prime Minister. Instead, he settled for boosting the staff at 10 Downing Street, and using the Cabinet Office more. There are four main departments within the 10 Downing Street machine:

- Political Office: This mainly handles speech writing and relations with the PM's political party. It is staffed by non-career civil servants

- Private Office: This deals with the PM's relations with the official apparatus of government.

- Press Office: This is headed up by the PM's press secretary or official spokesman and handles relations with UK and overseas media.

- Policy Unit: The PM's own personal think tank

Within 10 Downing Street there are a number of key posts. The titles of the posts change, as (obviously) do the individuals holding them. Generally speaking, however, there has been, in recent years, a:

- Permanent secretary

- Director of communications

- Chief of staff

- Deputy chief of staff

- Head of strategy

- Director of government relations

- Director of political strategy

- Head of policy unit

As well as these key individuals, there will also be another 10-15 Special Advisers who will have been drafted in to offer advice on key policy areas. These are normally young, bright and politically-motivated individuals looking to establish a career in politics. Some of them are very well known (Tony Blair appointed Lord John Birt as his "blue skies" adviser), but generally they operate behind the scenes in a low-key manner.

Around a dozen bright individuals will work in the Policy Unit or the Policy Directorate. Because there are so few of them, they tend to have to work across broad policy areas – but they do tend to have specialist areas of expertise. They also tend to work closely with the Special Advisers (SPADs) attached to Whitehall Departments. It is not always easy to identify the individual with responsibility for your policy area, but if you can do so, and establish a relationship with him or her, then you will have found a route in to the very highest level of government.

Also within 10 Downing Street is the Delivery Unit – established by Tony Blair in 2001. Again this is staffed by a small cadre of highly intelligent and driven individuals who are tasked with trying to make sure that the PM's writ runs through all government departments. Its main task is delivering the priorities of the prime minister of the day, but again if you can establish a relationship with the Delivery Unit you can undoubtedly boost the chances of your objectives becoming incorporated into the government's overall strategy.

Other units within 10 Downing Street include:

- PM's Private Office

- Press Office (handling media enquiries)

- Direct Communications Unit and Strategic Communications Unit (both part of the Corporate Communications Unit)

- Government Relations Unit (dealing with relations with the Labour Party and the trade unions)

- Appointments and Honours Unit (making the PM's recommendations for honours)

- Parliamentary Section (dealing with relations between 10 Downing Street and Parliament) and the Correspondence Unit

All of these are important – but none can be lobbied in the same way that the Policy Unit or the Delivery Unit can.

Finally, all prime ministers (like any other senior minister) have a parliamentary private secretary. Generally, in fact, they have one from the House of Commons and one from the House of Lords, and they sometimes even have two in the Commons. These individuals are responsible for keeping the prime minister in touch with thinking on the backbenches. They have daily access to the prime minister, and obviously he or she trusts their judgement or they would not have been given the job. These individuals are normally easy to identify, and if you can persuade them of the strength of your case they are a very good route to the prime minister.

There is no doubt that the best route to lobbying the prime minister is through his or her secretariat at 10 Downing Street. The problem can often lie in identifying the relevant person. Because they want to insulate these very important civil servants or Special Advisers from being lobbied, their identities and responsibilities are not widely advertised. However, there are a number of sources where you can try and find this type of information:

- National and specialist press
- *Civil Service Year Book*
- *Dod's Civil Service Companion*
- *Vacher's Quarterly Companion*

Alternatively, you can try phoning Number Ten directly and asking. The Number Ten switchboard (known colloquially as "switch") is justly famed for its efficiency – and you can try them on 020 7930 4433. The odds are that they will not identify the individual you are looking for, but they just might put you through to a department which will help.

Author's top tip

If you want to invite the prime minister to an event try to give at least six months notice, personalise the letter as much as possible, emphasise the potential media interest in the event and follow up with a phone call to the Correspondence Unit.

Contributor's top tip

Politicians often need your help. The trick is to find ways to help them that also help you. Following the 2000 fuel crisis I got my then Chairman to write to the prime minister suggesting he set up an independent inquiry into the future of paying for transport. I had sounded out a senior Downing Street adviser about what might be helpful to the prime minister. This action meant that someone on the inside knew about the letter, knew it was sent with good intentions, and knew it could be useful.

Indeed the PM replied that we should set up the independent inquiry. His adviser and Department for Transport and Treasury officials were kept in the loop as the work progressed. Hence the Government felt some "ownership" for the work even though we were running it. I even had to brief the PM personally on the work and convinced him to write the foreword. Hence my tip is to sound out political advisers and civil servants prior to approaching politicians on a major issue. If you have them on side you are already winning the battle.

Edmund King, President of the Automobile Association

4.3.2 The cabinet

The cabinet consists of 22 cabinet ministers, mainly made up of the secretaries of state of the principle Whitehall departments.

The prime minister chairs cabinet meetings, which used to be held on a Thursday morning but now (under Gordon Brown's premiership) are held on a Tuesday morning. Of the 22 cabinet ministers, at least two usually come from the House of Lords – the Lords Chief Whip and the Leader of the House of Lords. In recent years the convention has also been established that other senior ministers, of minister of state rank, also attend cabinet regularly, whilst middle and junior ranking ministers may be called in on occasion when the topic to be discussed is particularly relevant to their area of responsibility.

The way in which cabinet meetings are conducted varies enormously, depending on the style and character of the prime minister. It was always said that Margaret Thatcher did not encourage debate in cabinet, and Michael Heseltine famously walked out of one cabinet meeting – and out of government – over Mrs Thatcher's refusal to have an open discussion over the future of Westland. John Major was reckoned to have been much more consensual in his approach, often going round the table seeking the views of cabinet ministers one by one. Tony Blair kept his cabinet meetings short, preferring to take decisions on the sofa in his den, overlooking the garden at 10 Downing Street. Gordon Brown is reckoned to encourage debate – but not opposition to his set views. Whatever is debated and decided in cabinet, there is a convention of collective responsibility which means that if a cabinet minister feels obliged to speak out against agreed policy in public he or she has to resign.

Occasionally the cabinet meets as a political cabinet. This is usually when vital party political issues are being discussed – such as the timing of an election, or the results of an election. On these occasions all civil servants (including the cabinet secretary – who is also usually head of the home civil service) are excluded and no minutes are taken. If the press report that a political cabinet is to held, you can be reasonably sure that a major policy announcement or event is about to occur.

Decisions are only taken at cabinet level if they are either vital to the national interest (such as a replacement for the independent nuclear deterrent) or if they cut across a number of departments which have failed to reach agreement between themselves. Cabinet is the final arbiter of these inter-departmental disputes, but every effort is made to try and resolve such issues before they reach this point.

Because cabinet only meets once a week – other than in emergency situations – much of the work of cabinet is actually done in cabinet committees, known formally as ministerial committees of the cabinet. These cabinet committees are supported by a dedicated group of civil servants known as the cabinet secretariat. They are divided between six main secretariats within the Cabinet Office covering:

- Economic and Domestic affairs
- Constitutional affairs
- Central and Machinery of Government
- European Union
- Defence and Overseas
- Intelligence and Security

The main purpose of cabinet committees is to:

- Resolve disputes between Whitehall departments
- Relieve the burden of cabinet
- Maintain the principle of collective responsibility

Most cabinet committees are permanent and deal with perennially important policy areas. These tend to have a range of subcommittees, which come and go depending on circumstances and the priorities of the prime minister of the day. For instance the Domestic Affairs Committee (known as the DA Committee), which is jointly chaired by the secretary of state for justice and the Lord Chancellor, has subcommittees dealing with:

- Borders and Migration
- Communities and Equalities
- Families, Children and Young People
- Health and Well Being
- Justice and Crime
- Local Government and the Regions
- Public Engagement and the Delivery of Service

The Economic Development Committee, known as the ED Committee, is chaired by the Chancellor of the Exchequer. It also has a range of subcommittees, which at the time of going to press were:

- Environment and Energy
- Housing, Planning and Regeneration
- Olympic and Paralympic Games
- Panel for Regulatory Accountability
- Productivity, Skills and Environment

The other big permanent cabinet committee is the National Security, International Relations and Development Committee, which is known by the acronym NSID. This is chaired by the prime minister, although some of the subcommittees are chaired by the foreign secretary or the home secretary. Its subcommittees are:

- Europe
- Overseas and Defence
- Africa
- Trade
- Protective Security and Resilience
- Tackling Extremism

Other important cabinet committees include:

- Civil Contingencies Committee
- Constitution Committee
- Legislation Committee
- Life Chances Committee
- Public Services and Public Expenditure Committee
- Security and Intelligence Services Committee

As well as setting up subcommittees to deal with highly specialised or transient issues, prime ministers also appoint *ad hoc* committees – known as miscellaneous committees. These are usually given a name and a number, and are wound up as the issues disappear or become less pressing. Examples of recent miscellaneous committees include:

- MISC 32 – Pandemic Influenza Planning
- MISC 33 – Post Office Network

It is possible to make submissions to cabinet or to cabinet Sub-committees. To a certain degree, that is what they are in place for – to gather all of the information available, to try and ensure that the Government does not make a political mistake, and to arrive at the best recommendation to cabinet or the prime minister. However, you do need to bear in mind that you are dealing with the very highest echelons of government here. If possible you should seek to access the decision-making process at a lower – departmental – level. There are also a wide range of factors which cabinet (and cabinet subcommittees and miscellaneous committees) – need to bear in mind when they meet – and that means that you also have to bear them in mind. Amongst the factors which they need to consider are:

- Economic and fiscal implications
- Regulatory impact
- Human rights and equality aspects
- Third party implications – from local government, to the devolved Parliaments and Assemblies, through to the European Union

Discussions and decisions at this level are only held and taken for the most important strategic decisions facing the country. Examples would include constitutional and electoral reform, the future structure of public services, energy sources and security, and issues affecting intelligence and military strategy. Before considering putting together a cabinet submission, you should meet with the Whitehall department or departments concerned, and also with the Cabinet Office – especially bearing in mind that ministerial cabinet subcommittees are shadowed by subcommittees made up entirely of civil servants. Above all, you should satisfy yourself that your case is robust, and will stand up to the most intense scrutiny.

External organisations are permitted to make a cabinet submission. However, the format is strictly regulated, and all submissions have to take in to account a wide range of factors. These are:

- Public expenditure
- Human rights
- Devolution
- Local government
- Equality
- Health
- E-commerce and e-government
- Regulatory impact (including a formal Regulatory Impact Assessment)

Contributor's top tip

So you have briefed a Special Adviser and your points are accepted with enthusiasm. Job done! Well maybe, but just consider this:

Will the minister agree? If so, will his departmental colleagues agree? Will his senior civil servants agree? Will the Treasury agree? Will cabinet agree? Depending on your argument, these are all potential barriers to success.

Brief the Special Adviser by all means, but also look very closely at those other tripwires in the decision-making equation – the adviser might even suggest one or two. Plot the likely course of your proposal through the government machine, identify possible points of conflict and consider the impact of a wider, carefully targeted briefing agenda.

A civil servant, for example, might have a very different agenda. So what? Well, one carefully aimed call to the Treasury or Downing Street and your proposals could be dead in the water, minister or no minister. I know – I have done it!

Keith Lockwood, Public affairs consultant (and former senior civil servant)

Contributor's top tip

At the heart of what we do is trust. We trade in whispers and that is dependant on long-term relationships and friendships. Politicians and advisers never tell us things that they should not. However, if they trust us they will tell us things that are helpful both to them and to our clients. Trust is crucial. That is why a trusted lobbyist will do well no matter which government is in power.

It is also important to remember the purpose of what we do and to be open about it. Our job is to deliver commercial advantage for our clients. We use our understanding of the political process and our network of contacts to help our clients anticipate political developments better than their competitors. That is why the main board of every major company and trade association now takes public affairs seriously. That was not always the case.

Finally, we must enjoy what we do. We are the luckiest people alive. We love politics, enjoy the company of politicians and Special Advisers and work with some of the most successful and powerful business leaders in the UK. And the end result? Better government thanks to our ability to help business to talk effectively to government. It's not a bad life, is it?

Peter Bingle, Chairman, Bell Pottinger Public Affairs

4.3.3 Ministers

Ministers are the workhorses of government. In return for an enhanced salary, a nice office and a chauffeur-driven car they are expected to work upwards of 18 hours a day for six (or even seven) days a week. The United Kingdom is unique in the work-load which it piles onto its ministers – and yet the public and the press are invariably outraged when as a consequence of this pressure they either make bad decisions or seek solace in alcohol, drugs or illicit sex.

There are roughly speaking about 115 ministers at any one time, with most being in the Commons. Prime ministers can appoint more than this, but the number who can actually receive a ministerial salary is restricted by statute. Of the total number of ministers, only about a dozen will be in the House of Lords. They therefore have to cover a wide range of subjects. However, unlike in the Commons, Whips in the Lords do speak for the government in the Lords Chamber, and this is a considerable help in spreading the burden.

There are three categories of ministers:

- Secretaries of state: These all sit in the cabinet, and they are all privy councillors (or Rt Hons). Most (but not all) head up a Whitehall department.

- Ministers of state: These are the middle ranking ministers. A few attend cabinet and are privy councillors. Larger Whitehall departments can have several ministers at this level.

- Parliamentary under-secretaries of state: This is the lowest form of (paid) ministerial life. Again, some larger Whitehall Departments will have several ministers of this rank.

The duties of a minister are many and varied – hence the huge pressures on their family and social lives. Here is just a brief round-up of some of the things they have to do on a daily or weekly basis:

- Constituency duties: Ministers (unless they are in the House of Lords) are also constituency MPs. They have to correspond with their constituents and hold surgeries just like any other MP – if they want to get re-selected and re-elected.

- Departmental duties: They must hold meetings with ministerial colleagues and civil servants, and receive delegations.

- Cabinet and cabinet committee meetings: Assuming that they are sufficiently senior to be required to attend.

- Parliamentary duties: These can range from voting in the lobbies, to attending oral questions when their department is top of the rota, to replying to an opposition debate or adjournment debate, to steering a bill through the Chamber and through committee stages.

- Overseas trips: These can be to Brussels for Council of Ministers meetings, or to other parts of the world leading a delegation.

- Red boxes: At the end of every day, and at the weekends, ministers are expected to wade their way through red boxes filled by their civil servants with papers which they need to either just read or to actually approve.

Author's top tip

Because ministers are so busy, they regard any function which they are invited to attend but not invited to address as a waste of their precious time. They are great speakers – but terrible listeners. If you invite them along to any kind of function without asking them to say a few words they may be very unhappy.

Given this pressure it is little wonder that ministers long for the recesses (especially the summer recess) when they can spend at least some time with their families and read something other than civil service briefs and policy documents. It is also little wonder that ministers – and governments – gradually run out of ideas and energy, and need to be replaced by fresh blood.

Ministers – especially senior ministers – make a great many of the important decisions in government. As we have seen the really vital decisions are taken at cabinet level, and the less important decisions are routinely taken by civil servants – albeit with ministerial oversight. However, ministers do make decisions on a daily basis.

So, given how important ministers are, and how busy they are, and the fact that that they are almost constantly surrounded by civil servants, how do you get to them? Although it is not easy, there are a number of ways in which you as a lobbyist can get through the screen and directly or indirectly influence a minister's thinking and (ultimately) decisions. You can:

- Correspond: Anybody can write to a minister, but bear in mind that your letter will be seen by a civil servant first. So make sure that you make your case fully and fairly, and outline any dealings you have already had with the minister's department.

- Meeting: Again, anybody can ask for a meeting with a minister. However, as his or her time is so precious the odds are that (unless you are representing a very large commercial interest or pressure group) you may be turned down.

- Conferences: Invite ministers to speak at your conference – and to take questions afterwards. That way you will learn more about their thinking – and they will learn more about yours.

- Constituency: Most ministers (unless they are in the Lords) are constituency MPs as well as ministers. If you can get to know them in that context, they might be more sympathetic when you want to discuss issues relating to their ministerial brief.

- Functions : Again, if you are having a reception, invite the minister to address it. The odds are he or she will stay for a few minutes afterwards, and you will have a chance to have a few words in (semi) privacy.

- Delegation: If you can persuade an MP to write to the minister asking him or her to meet a delegation, the odds are strong that this will be granted – especially if the MP making the request is a senior or respected member of the minister's own party.

- Colleagues: Ministers (if they have any sense) are always willing to listen to backbench colleagues. It is considered perfectly acceptable for ministers to be "button-holed" by parliamentary colleagues in the corridors of Westminster or in the division lobbies.

- Chamber: Again, most ministers maintain a healthy respect for the Chamber of the Commons, and many of them like to think of themselves as being good Commons men or women. If you can get your issue raised – reasonably and effectively – on the floor of the House ministers will take note.

- Media: All ministers are inveterate readers of the political press, not least because they like to read about their own political standing – and that of their colleagues. Starting from the Today Programme first thing in the morning through to Newsnight last thing at night (with several national newspapers along the way) ministers are voracious consumers of political news. If you can get your issue highlighted through the major news outlets you can be absolutely certain that ministers will notice.

- Party conferences: For three or four days every year ministers are stripped of their civil servants and open to being directly lobbied. Their security detail will deliver them to the secure zone at the conference, and their Special Adviser may accompany them to some events, but generally speaking they are on their own. Provided you are polite (and sober!) it is perfectly acceptable to raise an issue with a minister, and promise to follow it up with a detailed letter once back in the office. That letter can then start with the words "It was good to talk to you at party conference," which should ensure that it gets through the civil service screen and is actually read by the minister.

- Special Advisers: We have already covered Special Advisers (or SPADs) in the civil service section of this book – noting that they are hybrid creatures half way between permanent civil servants and transient politicians. They are often the best route to a minister, as they have their trust and their ear and (although they have their own Code of Conduct) they are less hidebound by convention than civil servants. It is possible to have off-the-record discussions with SPADs, and they will generally have a very good idea of what their ministers thinking will be on a subject. Many of them go on to be politicians (or even lobbyists) in their own right, so it is in their interests to build up and maintain a reputation for discretion and sound judgement.

Anecdote

One of my clients secured a meeting with a minister of state to discuss the need for the government to support a large-scale infrastructure project. After a fairly lengthy (probably too lengthy) explanation of the long-term benefits of the project, the client was stunned when the minister simply replied "NIMTO". Turning to me for an explanation, I had to gently explain that the minister was not enthused by the project because its benefits would not be immediately forthcoming – or, in minister speak, "Not In My Term of Office".

Contributor's top tip

Build your case before asking for support.

Too often in public affairs and political campaigning I see decision makers being pushed to support an issue before the case has been put.

They are pressurised into making a choice before they understand the issues involved, often leading to a disappointing outcome.

During election campaigns leaflets request votes for a party or a candidate months ahead of an election. The electorate are asked to make their decision before the campaign has explained why their candidate is the right choice. Once this initial decision has been made it is much more difficult to ask them to change it.

In public affairs the mistake is to ask a key decision maker to state their view at the beginning of the engagement process on a specific issue. Instead, it is important to put the case and all the reasons for supporting it before asking the decision maker to come down on one side or the other.

Mark Glover, Bellenden Public Affairs

Contributor's top tip

My top tip is "keep your eyes wide open". If escorting a senior executive to meet a politician, ensure that the executive is conscious of other issues in the politician's "in tray", treats them like another human being and yet remembers that their masters are their constituents, party Whips and their media profile. The majority of politicians I deal with are sympathetic to market challenges facing business, but on the whole they avoid major political intervention on business issues. If you want action, press the right buttons politically and work with third parties to support your case.

Katherine Bennett, Director of Communications and Government Affairs, Airbus UK

4.3.4 Parliamentary Private Secretaries

Parliamentary Private Secretaries (or PPSs) are the unpaid "bag carriers" of senior ministers. As we have already seen, the prime minister can have two (or even three) PPSs. However, a secretary of state will have just one PPS, whilst ministers of state may have to share a PPS with one or two colleagues. Parliamentary under-secretaries of state are not entitled to have a PPS, or even a share of a PPS.

PPSs are unpaid, but they are generally considered to be part of the "payroll vote" (made up of ministers and Whips) who the government can always rely on to support them in the division lobbies. This is because, although unpaid, PPSs are reckoned to subscribe to the convention of collective responsibility, and therefore have to resign if they speak or vote against government policy. Being a PPS is also regarded as being the first step on the path to a ministerial career – in effect having one foot on the first rung of the ladder.

The job of a PPS is to:

- Attend departmental meetings (including morning "prayers") with their minister, or even on occasion to represent their minister.

- To keep ministers informed as to opinion on the backbenches, so that they do not lose touch with the sentiment of parliamentary colleagues.

- To update their minister on the gossip doing the rounds of the tea room and many bars of the Palace of Westminster.

Because PPSs are the personal appointment of a minister, they can generally be regarded as being their trusted confidants. They also spend many hours with the minister, either in the department, in the House, or travelling to and from meetings. Securing a meeting with a PPS is therefore the next best thing to securing a meeting with a minister, or a Special Adviser.

4.3.5 Whips

Many ministers started their political careers in the Whips Office – in fact former Conservative prime minister Ted Heath was at one stage Chief Whip. Some like the cosy and collegiate world of the Whips Office so much that they spend their entire political careers there – although most politicians regard a period as a Whip as being a useful stepping stone to ministerial office.

In the House of Commons the governing party have a Chief Whip, a Deputy Chief Whip, a Pairing Whip, six Whips and ten assistant Whips. The official opposition has a similar set-up (although only the Chief Whip and Deputy Chief Whip are paid), as do the Lib Dems. Smaller parties do have Whips, but their task is largely to maintain the "usual channels" whereby the business arrangements of the House are agreed.

The Whips in the main parties have two distinct areas of responsibility. They will be responsible for one or two policy areas – broadly reflecting the main departments of state – and they will also be responsible for the MPs within a geographical area, often the one which they represent themselves.

There is always a Whip on duty on the front bench whenever the Commons is sitting. In the Commons, however, Whips do not speak and they play no active part in debates.

The job of a Whip is varied. They have responsibility for:

- Maintaining party discipline, and maximising the vote for their party.

- Mentoring MPs who are going through difficult periods – either personally or politically.

- Spotting talent amongst backbenchers for promotion as either Whips or ministers.

- Maintaining good working relationships between the parties.

- Warning the cabinet and the prime minister of dissent and rebellions within the ranks.

Although Whips do not take part in debates in the Commons, they are omnipresent, and always on the lookout for developments which impact on their area of geographical or subject responsibility. They will, therefore, notice if you mount a lobbying campaign through questions, debates or Early Day Motions.

Warning!

The Whips are not there to be lobbied, and they do not expect to be lobbied. The only exception is where there is a matter which directly affects their constituency. In those circumstances you can ask them to discreetly raise the issue with the relevant minister.

Anecdote

The Whips use a variety of methods to impose discipline on backbenchers – from cajolery, to bribery to (it is alleged) brute force. One famous story (probably apocryphal) involved Tory Whip Lt Colonel Sir Walter Bromley-Davenport MP. Stationed in the Cloisters to intercept backbench MPs skulking off to avoid a late vote he spotted a small figure in tails scurrying towards the exit for Westminster tube station. Grabbing the miscreant by the collar he frog-marched him towards the division lobby, only to find that he had manhandled not one of his own backbenchers, but the Belgian Ambassador.

Contributor's top tip

The law-enforcers and intelligence-gatherers of the UK parliamentary system, the Whips Offices wield immense power across the political parties.

There is an official office supported by civil servants for the government and official opposition parties, and party-staffed offices for other major parties. There are separate offices in the Commons and Lords that run on semi-autonomous lines, reporting directly to Downing Street or the Party hierarchy.

The role of the Whips Office is to report the views of backbench members to the party leadership and to enforce the line to take, fed back down after consideration of that intelligence. Attendances for every vote in the Chamber and in bill committees are monitored and measured against requests for absence. Additionally, places on select committees, foreign visits and requests for accommodation within the parliamentary precincts are also dealt with here.

The two main offices consist of a Chief Whip, Deputy Whip and Pairing Whip. Below these three senior roles there are Whips who have a regional and departmental responsibility. They are responsible for the all of the MPs within that particular region and for any business going through the House from a specific department. The Whips Office should be an integral part of a bill-related lobbying campaign, used in three distinctly separate ways:

- To report back the views of backbenchers, determined during a lobbying campaign.

- To confirm that a vote on the clauses of interest will be included in the bill as it progresses though the House.

- To confirm what form the vote will take and when (particularly if the clauses are in committee or remaining stages)

It is important to help Whips understand the strength of feeling amongst backbenchers so they can reflect these views when a line to take is being developed by senior party figures.

As we all know, the parliamentary process rarely runs smoothly: time delays, votes dropped and even debates on clauses that do not take place during a timetabled debate. The Whips Offices will have the latest real-time information on what is happening, as it happens.

The Whips Office is an essential element for any bill-related campaign, and is under-used by lobbyists – though I suspect that is about to change.

Charles Willis, Royal Pharmaceutical Society (ex government Whips Office)

4.3.6 Members of Parliament

There are currently 646 Members of Parliament (MPs). This number does, however, vary from one parliament to the next. The Boundary Commission are constantly reviewing and revising constituencies so as to make them broadly equal in the number of constituents which they represent. As the population rises – which it is currently doing – more seats have to be created.

As has been seen many MPs are either ministers or Whips for the ruling party, or frontbench spokespersons or Whips for opposing parties. Those MPs who are neither ministers, frontbench spokespersons nor Whips are known collectively as backbenchers. The main functions of backbenchers are:

- Representing their constituents
- Holding the government to account
- Serving on select and standing committees
- Joining backbench committees or All-Party Parliamentary Groups (APPGs)

For the lobbyist, ministers and frontbench spokespersons are easy to target because of their job titles and published areas of responsibility. Where backbenchers are concerned, lobbyists usually target them in terms of:

- Constituency interests
- Political interests
- Outside interests

Contributor's top tip

My tip for success in practising the art of public affairs from the viewpoint of the practitioner is to always look for the areas where there is a synergy between the client's objectives and those of the public affairs audience you are interacting with. There is little point in lobbying about a case to an audience whose interests it genuinely does not serve to take on board your client's concerns, issues or business requirements. However, if you can identify the sweet spot where both parties can work together to achieve a common goal then you can seriously achieve something.

Simon Elliott, Managing Director, FD-LLM

Contributor's top tip

While there are many different techniques that one can use, the crucial ingredient of any successful lobbying campaign is the message. Without a compelling narrative no amount of energetic lobbying will succeed. It must be a message that is based in fact (half truths will be found out), is credible (do not pretend you are something that you are patently not), resonates with your key audiences, is supported by the evidence (research is key), and is robust enough to withstand intense scrutiny and the obligatory criticism. It must also be a narrative that is able to cut through the plethora of competing messages and associated comment that are bombarding politicians, the media and the public each and every day.

Alex Bigg, Managing Director Public Affairs, Edelman

Contributor's top tip

My top tip is on how public affair professionals should use the opposition.

The first reason for dealing with the opposition is to ensure that you have established contact with and briefed the individuals who will be ministers in the event of a change of government. In any case, your discussions should help to build a small group of members with a genuine interest in your cause. Some of these may have only a transient involvement as holders of a shadow portfolio. Others may have a passionate belief in what your client wants to achieve. Your chances of mobilising politicians to do something will be enhanced if you have a solid core of really committed political supporters rather than a small army who have graced your client's drinks party.

Secondly, while government politicians can be invaluable batting for you behind the scenes, do not underestimate the value of having some political support that is willing to raise the profile of your issue, ask questions in Parliament, call debates, raise the temperature in the press. Ministers are sometimes more susceptible to embarrassment than to persuasion.

Graham Brady MP

4.3.7 The Queen's Speech

To the general public the state opening and the Queen's Speech represent the glittering pageant where the Queen progresses from Buckingham Palace down The Mall to the Palace of Westminster by coach, accompanied by the Household Cavalry. She then goes to the Royal Robing Room where she is attired in her formal regalia and dons the Imperial State Crown, before proceeding to the House of Lords. The Commons are then summoned to the Lords by Black Rod – but not before he has had the doors to the Commons Chamber slammed in his face. All of this ritual makes good television, and reminds everybody that Parliament is made up of the monarch, the House of Commons and the House of Lords.

However, for the professional politician, pundit, journalist and lobbyist the Queen's Speech marks the beginning of another parliamentary session where perennial issues will be dusted down and revisited, but also where a whole raft of new proposed government legislation will be unveiled and launched. Unless it immediately follows a general election, the Queen's Speech is generally in the first two weeks of November, following the tidying-up session known as "spill over" – which itself follows the party conference season. The Queen's Speech following a general election is normally three to four weeks after polling day, and such a session will generally run from that spring or summer through to October or November the following year. This makes for an extra-long session which provides a new government with the opportunity to introduce as much legislation flowing from its manifesto as possible.

The Queen's Speech invariably starts off with a recitation of the state visits which the Queen will be making, and the heads of state who she will be receiving in the United Kingdom. There is then a general outline of the government's over-arching priorities – usually involving maintaining a stable economy, but also reflecting a prime minister's personal priorities – such as tackling child poverty or Third World debt.

After this preamble the Queen then goes on to outline – in fairly general terms – the bills and draft bills which the government intend to introduce during the course of the forthcoming parliamentary session. As a general rule of thumb there will be 20-30 bills outlined in the Queen's Speech. If there are any less, the government will look like it has run out of ideas. If there are any more, the government risks giving the impression that it is hyperactive and overly bureaucratic. It also risks over-burdening MPs and peers, something which has a tendency to make them fractious and rebellious.

It is important to realise that the Queen's Speech introduces the government's intended legislative programme – it is not a definitive guide. Some of the bills outlined by the Queen may not be published in that session – and may indeed never see the light of day. Equally, the government can introduce bills which were not presaged in the Queen's Speech as new issues and priorities arise.

When Gordon Brown became prime minister he swept away the tradition that the contents of the Queen's Speech were never discussed in advance. In July 2007 he gave a detailed breakdown of the contents of the speech which the Queen would deliver four months later, and this process has been repeated since

Author's top tip

The Press Gallery and Lobby in the House of Commons and Lords receive an embargoed copy of the Queen's Speech about two hours before she actually delivers it. They are also provided with the Queen's Speech bundle. This contains a press release giving considerable detail on every bill to be outlined in the Speech. You can obtain these explanatory notes after the Queen's Speech from the departments sponsoring the bills in question.

After the Queen has delivered her speech and returned to Buckingham Palace both the Commons and Lords briefly suspend their sittings. They then return to appoint various officers and implement various procedural motions and introduce ancient bills not contained in the Queen's Speech (the Outlawries Bill in the Commons and the Vestries Bill in the Lords). All of this is designed to demonstrate the independence of Parliament from the monarchy.

After all of this pageantry and procedure there then follow four or five days of debates on the contents of the Queen's Speech. After a couple of light-hearted speeches by a novice and then a veteran government backbencher the leader of the opposition finally gets his or her chance to address the substance of the government's legislative programme. The prime minister then follows, and is in turn followed by the leader of the Liberal Democrats, before the debate is thrown open to backbenchers from all parties.

After the first day's general debate, the "usual channels" agree themes for the subsequent day's debates. These are grouped, so you might have defence and foreign affairs on one day, and then the economy and employment the next, and home affairs and crime on another. This enables the front benchers to prepare their big set-piece speeches, and provides backbenchers with a particular policy focus to prepare their own contributions.

For the lobbyist the debates on the Queen's Speech offer a number of opportunities. Hopefully you will not be caught unprepared by the announcement that a particular piece of legislation, which will impact on your interests or those of your client, will be introduced during that session. You will have spotted it in the governing party's general election manifesto, or will have been tipped off by civil servants you have established a working relationship with, or you will have responded to the Green and then White Paper which preceded it, or you will have spotted a trailing announcement by a minister or even the prime minister.

This being the case, you will have prepared a response welcoming – or condemning – the bill in question. If you do not know enough about the bill to either welcome or condemn it, you must try to urgently get hold of the press release accompanying the bill which will be issued by the sponsoring department.

If the bill in question is one of the government's flagship bills, you must try to issue your response on the first day of the debate on the Queen's Speech. That generally means getting it to the national press and media, and to the office of the leader of the opposition. If your bill is more specialised, you will have more time to formulate your response. Instead of dealing with the national press and the leader of the opposition, you might be briefing the trade press and the shadow secretary of state for the relevant department. You will also, of course, have the opportunity to brief backbench MPs from all sides who are likely to support your view.

That is assuming that you disagree with the provisions of the relevant bill. If, in fact, you wholeheartedly welcome it – say so. The government will be grateful for your support, and the opposition might be less inclined to criticise the contents of the bill in question. The opposition parties often lay out their positions on a bill during the Queen's Speech debate, and this can affect the way the bill is handled during its progress. So, if you broadly approve of a bill, and you have a strong *locus* or standing where its provisions are concerned, this is your chance to put down an early marker.

Finally, of course, you might approve of the broad thrust of a bill, but be concerned about certain provisions within it. Again, this is your chance to broadly welcome the bill, but to outline your specific concerns. If you can persuade the opposition parties (and even government backbenchers) to support your views and note your reservations, you will have a better chance to secure concessions during the bill's progress through both Houses of Parliament.

Contributor's top tip

Be clear what you want to achieve, be determined to achieve it.

Identify who will be making the decision that you need to influence, when they will be making it, what factors they will take into account, through what prism of personal and political prejudices they view the subject, and who in turn will influence them.

Prepare your arguments thoroughly, present your case clearly, deploy your political pressure ruthlessly. Present to the right people, in the right way, at the right time and with individually tailored messages. Follow up every lead arising, never leave your supporters abandoned and never take "no" for an answer. Always challenge constructively and sustain the campaign for as long as necessary.

Do not gloat in victory, and as a consultant never expect credit, but instead take pride in a job professionally done.

Chris Whitehouse, Managing Director, The Whitehouse Consultancy

4.3.8 Select committees

The House of Commons has used select committees since the sixteenth century. The current structure, however, dates back to 1979 when the newly-appointed Leader of the House of Commons Norman (now Lord) St John Stevas persuaded the Commons (and prime minister Margaret Thatcher) to adopt the current system of departmental committees.

Under the current system there is a select committee to shadow every Whitehall department. So if there is a Department of Culture, Media and Sport, there is also a Culture, Media and Sport select committee. If – as often happened – Whitehall departments are merged or re-named, the shadowing select committees will also be rearranged.

In the current House of Commons there are 18 departmental select committees – each one shadowing a current Whitehall department. There are also, however, four joint committees with the House of Lords (on Bill Consolidation, Human Rights, Statutory Instruments and Tax Law Rewrite), nine other committees (Environmental Audit, European Scrutiny, Modernisation, Procedure, Public Accounts, Public Administration, Regulatory Reform, Selection and Standards and Privileges), and four internal committees (Administration, Chairmen's Panel, Finance and Services, and Liaison).

For the lobbyist, however, the key select committees are the departmental ones, which at the time of writing were:

- Business and Enterprise
- Children, Schools and Families
- Communities and Local Government
- Culture Media and Sport
- Defence
- Environment, Food and Rural Affairs
- Foreign Affairs
- Health
- Home Affairs
- Innovation, Universities, Science and Skills
- International Development
- Justice
- Northern Ireland
- Scottish Affairs
- Transport
- Treasury
- Welsh Affairs
- Work and Pensions

There are 11-14 members on each select committee, and the membership is made up in rough proportion to the number of seats which political parties have in the House of Commons. Thus in the current parliament (although there is some variation) there might be 8 Labour members, 4 Conservatives, and either two Lib Dems or one Lib Dem and another member from a nationalist party.

Again, the chairmanships of committees are allocated roughly in proportion to the electoral fortunes of the parties. Thus ten of the current committees are chaired by Labour MPs, five by Conservative MPs, and three by Lib Dems. In theory both the members and chairs of select committees are appointed for the duration of a parliament. In practice, there are fairly regular changes, as members get offered frontbench jobs or simply decide that they have other priorities – such as trying to hold on to a slim majority in a marginal seat. Although select committees are supposed to be the exclusive bailiwick of backbenchers, the Whips do try to influence their membership, and the chairmanships are divvied up by the "usual channels". Governments are also very fond of trying to allocate the chairmanship of key select committees to recently demoted ministers in need of a consolation prize.

Over the years the staffing resource available to select committees has improved dramatically as their status has improved. A departmental select committee would normally have on its payroll:

- Clerk

- Second clerk

- Inquiry manager

- Media officer

- Assistant

- Secretary

Select committees would also typically have two specialist advisers. These should not be confused with the Special Advisers (or SPADs) who are the political advisers to senior ministers. These specialist advisers are genuine experts in the policy field which their select committees cover. For some highly specialised inquiries, select committees also have the power (which they do use) to appoint specialist advisers just for the duration of that inquiry. There is a large pool of well over a hundred specialist advisers who can be hired on a daily rate.

The role of departmental select committees is fairly straightforward. Formally their powers and responsibilities are spelt out in their orders of reference, which are contained in the Commons' Standing Orders. Their role is defined as being to "examine expenditure, administration and policy" of the department they are shadowing. In practice they have a huge amount of leeway, and can look at any subject which touches – however tangentially – on their policy area.

Select committees also have considerable power – backed up by the authority of the Commons. Officially these can be summed up as having the powers to "send for persons, papers and records". In other words, they can summon whoever they wish, and demand to see almost any records. However, ministers and their civil servants cannot be compelled to reveal confidential information or papers, unless the full authority of the House of Commons is brought to bear on them – something which rarely occurs.

The main strength of select committees lies, however, not in their formal powers but in their expertise, and in the non-partisan way in which they go about their work. Select committee members and chairs are supposed to put their party political allegiances to one side when they are conducting inquiries and preparing reports, and almost invariably they do so. On occasion members will insist on producing a minority report, and in those circumstances the inquiry loses much of its impact.

Select committees offer a great deal of scope for lobbyists. The usual principles of public affairs work apply: a select committee inquiry can represent either a threat or an opportunity, for either the in-house lobbyist or the consultancy client. The expertise of lobbyists comes very much to the fore when dealing with select committees. The lobbyists will (or at least should) spot the threat or the opportunity presented by a new inquiry. The lobbyists should be able to help clients present their evidence in a professional, cogent, accurate and appropriate form. And lobbyists should be able to coach their client to give the best possible oral evidence, helping them to overcome any nerves or stage fright which might otherwise set in.

Select committees are very collegiate, but the chair and the clerk do have considerable latitude in deciding – or at least suggesting – a programme for future inquiries. It is perfectly possible – and perfectly legitimate – to either write to or speak to the chair or the clerk and suggest a subject for a future inquiry. This will have to be agreed by the rest of the committee, but if your suggestion is topical and valid there is no reason why it should not be considered for inclusion in the inquiry programme.

If you or your client have been invited to submit written evidence it is essential that you stick rigidly to the guidelines for presenting the evidence – in terms of format, layout and length. However, it is perfectly acceptable to telephone the clerk (whose contact details will be on the committee's website) and ask for some pointers as what emphasis you should place on certain aspects of your written evidence.

Equally, when you submit your written evidence, you can ask for it (or certain parts of it) to remain confidential. You can also, at the time of submission, ask to be called to give oral evidence, so that you can elaborate on certain aspects of your evidence. If you are called to give evidence, it is common practice to telephone the clerk and ask to be told about the likely broad thrust of the questioning, so that you can be prepared.

If you (or your client) are called to give oral evidence here are a few pointers as to how to make sure that all goes well:

- If there is already evidence given by previous witnesses on the committee website from other contributors, be sure to review it.

- Read through your own written evidence very carefully so that you are as familiar with it as possible.

- Read up on the profiles of the chair and the members so that you will have some idea who they are and where they may be coming from.

- Arrive in plenty of time so that you are not flustered.

- If there is an evidence session before yours try and attend it so that you can comment on it if asked.

- Have a brief opening statement prepared in case you are asked if you want to give one.

- Address your responses to questions to the chair, but include the questioner in your answers through eye contact and gestures.

- Never attempt to just give one side of an argument, or you will be pulled up by the committee.

- Never knowingly mislead the committee, and if you do so inadvertently correct the mistake as quickly as possible.

Select committee inquiries and reports are respected and widely reported by the media. They therefore represent a great opportunity to highlight your case – provided you do so even-handedly and professionally. Some reports are launched with a press conference, some are debated in the Commons, and the government must respond to every report within two months. All in all, therefore, there are few better opportunities to highlight your issues.

Author's top tip

If you or your client are summoned to appear before a select committee it is not enough to read its evidence, view its website, or watch an evidence session on the Internet or television. You would be well advised to attend at least one session so that you get a really good feel for how the committee operates and where any points of tension might arise. You should also, if at all possible, have a rehearsal ahead of your appearance, with colleagues or consultants playing the role of committee members.

Contributor's top tip

The best way in which public affairs professionals can find out more about the personal views and beliefs of MPs is to establish a good personal relationship based on trust. Although some MP-sized egos might like to endlessly be told how much their opinions matter it pays to be totally honest about the purpose of contacting an MP.

Given that I represent a constituency with one of the highest localised swings in the country it will not be a surprise that I think the best way of attracting and retaining an MP's interest is to go local. Any reference to localised stats or even better an individual constituent, puts a letter or document in the "to do" pile rather than the "I will briefly look through when there is time" pile.

Finally, from my time as a member of the Public Administration Select Committee, I was impressed by those called to give evidence who wrote to me after the evidence session to follow up issues and maintain a dialogue.

David Burrowes MP

4.3.9 Consultation documents

All governments, to a greater or lesser extent, consult before they legislate. This is partly because of a desire to produce workable and effective legislation, and partly through a wish to govern through consensus. Although our parliamentary system is partisan and adversarial, governments in the UK generally like to govern with the broad consent of the population at large. Where they fail to do so, the results can be riots in the streets – as with the Poll Tax riots of 1990.

The formal consultation process usually starts with the issuing of a Green Paper. These are published by government departments and outline government thinking in a given policy area. They are sometimes debated in Parliament, and on occasion the relevant select committee may hold an inquiry.

Following on from a Green Paper a White Paper may be issued. The publication of a White Paper signals the government's intention to legislate, and interested parties are again invited to comment. A deadline by which comments must be submitted is published, and the relevant government department will invite contributions from the organisations which are on its regular circulation list.

In the past Green Papers and White Papers were literally that – they had green and white covers. Nowadays such papers have full-colour covers – and very often snappy titles. This sometimes makes it hard to discern whether it is supposed to be a Green Paper or a White Paper, and sometimes such documents are referred to as Green Papers with a white tinge – or White Papers with a green tinge!

Increasingly the convention of Green and White Papers is dispensed with, and government departments simply issue consultation documents. This enables government to keep open the option of legislating, without having any firm commitment to do so.

Another innovation used more frequently is the publication of draft bills. This procedure is generally used for complex pieces of legislation, and gives interested parties the chance to see in detail how the bill is framed. It also allows a select committee (or joint committee of both Houses) to examine the draft bill, and suggest amendments in the less partisan environment which prevails in select (as opposed to standing) committees.

For the lobbyist – whether in-house or in-consultancy – the consultation process provides great scope and tremendous opportunities to inform and influence the public policy process. The trick is to spot the opportunities early on, and to engage at every stage of the process. Lobbyists should not just contribute to the process themselves, they should also keep a very close eye out to see who else is contributing. This will enable them to identify potential allies and adversaries further down the line.

It is also acceptable to be "one-eyed" during the consultation process. Unlike contributing to a select committee inquiry, it is acceptable to simply push your case – leaving others to take the opposing view. The purpose of the consultation process is to "road test" legislation, and to subject it to a reality check. It is your job to push your agenda as hard as possible – leaving others to take the contra view.

> ## Author's top tip
>
> Every bill has a bill team consisting of a specialist draftsman and civil servants from the relevant department or departments. Find out who the bill team leader is, and feed in your comments and concerns to him or her. It is much easier to get a bill amended in draft form before it hits the cockpit of the House of Commons.

4.3.10 Early Day Motions

Early Day Motions (or EDMs) are, technically at least, motions to be debated at an early day. In fact there are now around 2000 EDMs tabled every year, and therefore it is easier to debate none of them, rather than try and choose which should be debated.

There are strict rules which apply to the tabling of EDMs. They may be tabled by any MP, although in fact only backbenchers tend to table or sign them. They must be no more than 250 words long, and must not use any unparliamentary language. They must also not refer to the Royal Family, or to matters which are *sub judice*. Finally, they must be just one sentence in length – which simply means that they are broken up by a series of semi-colons.

EDMs stay live for the full duration of the parliamentary session in which they are tabled. They have one main sponsor, and four other supporters – whose names stay on display throughout the EDM's life. Every time a new name is added during the first two weeks the EDM is re-printed in the Order Paper. After the first fortnight, the EDM is only reprinted once a week on a Thursday – assuming at least one new name has been added.

Many EDMs relate to local issues. These can be serious issues, such as the closure of a local post office or accident and emergency department. Or they can they can be trivial issues – such as the success of a local football or rugby team. These EDMs are tabled mainly so that a local MP can show his local newspaper – and through them his constituents – that he or she is aware of what is happening and he is at least going through the motions of doing something about it.

Some EDMs, however, are very serious. If a government has a majority of 60, and 30 or more of its own backbenchers sign an EDM which contradicts government policy or implies that they will vote against a particular government bill or clause within a bill, the Whips take notice. It could be that the government will shy away from this policy, knowing that defeat is a real possibility. Alternatively, ministers can meet with the disaffected backbenchers, and offer them a compromise. Very often, however, the Whips simply work their way through the signatories, offering bribes or making threats in order to get them to change their minds about voting against the government – or at least persuading them to abstain.

As has already been stated, for a backbench MP EDMs offer a tremendous opportunity to impress their electorate. The local press – and sometimes even the national press – often say that "Fred Bloggs MP has tabled a House of Commons motion criticising the government's policy on post office closure". The fact that such a motion is going nowhere, and will achieve very little, is by the by.

The same is true of EDMs initiated by lobbyists. Very often they are just a device to demonstrate to the client – or to colleagues – that something is being done, and that they have the clout to get an EDM tabled. There are, however circumstances where an EDM can be useful, and a powerful lobbying tool.

The best way to make sure that an EDM is going to have some impact is to make sure that the main sponsor – and the next four supporters – are respected MPs. As has been said, their names stay on the motion every time it is reprinted, and parliamentary colleagues will check the names of the sponsors before adding their own names. If you can get sponsors from all three of the main parties, you will get far more signatories. If you can get the signatories up beyond the 100 mark, then the Whips will take notice, and draw the EDM to the attention of the relevant minister.

In lobbying terms EDMs can also develop the character of trench warfare, with both sides of an argument throwing increasing resources into getting their side the highest number of signatures. Alternatively, opponents can table an amendment to an EDM, and try and get more signatories on the amendment than on the original motion. These "trench warfare" EDMs often reflect perennial conflicts between (for example) pro and anti abortion MPs, or pro or anti hunting MPs. They are a political trial of strength – and stamina.

Other EDMs can assume great importance where a one-off trial of strength emerges. There may be a proposed company takeover, with lobbyists for those in favour of the takeover and those opposed to it battling it out through an EDM. Where there is a major defence contract to be awarded, lobbyists for (say) the UK, European and US defence contractors may try and influence the decision of defence ministers and the Ministry of Defence by marshalling their backers and demonstrating the depth of their support.

Whether your policy issue is a hardy perennial or a one-off crisis the EDM is definitely part of the lobbyist's arsenal. It should not, however, be overused – and its importance should not be over-emphasised. An EDM demonstrates the fact that you have support – but if you do have substantial levels of support there are other parliamentary devices you can also use to aid your cause.

Author's top tip

Although EDMs are nowadays never actually debated, if you can get an MP to refer to one by its number during business questions then the full text will be "read into" the record and appear in the following day's Hansard – and the Leader of the House will have to explain why there is not time in which to debate it on the floor of the House.

4.3.11 Business questions

Every Thursday at approximately 11.30am the shadow Leader of the House asks the Leader of the House to make a statement about the forthcoming Business of the House of Commons. This is normally given in great detail for the week ahead, and in outline for the week after that. It is obviously vital for lobbyists to know as soon as possible what stages of a bill are to be progressed, and what topics are to be raised during debates – so having somebody listen in to the Business Statement is a very good idea.

Once the Leader of the House has read out the forthcoming Business the shadow Leader of the House makes a short speech – usually lambasting the Leader and the government for not announcing a debate on a series of issues which the opposition wish to highlight. The Leader of the House then responds in kind, pointing out that if the topics suggested are so important and so urgent then the opposition are at liberty to use one of their opposition days to debate it.

It is then the chance for backbenchers from all parties to quiz the Leader of the House about why certain topics are not to be debated in the next fortnight. Unless the question is framed in a particularly partisan fashion, the Leader of the House generally simply advises the questioner to apply for the ballot to raise the subject in an adjournment debate or a Westminster Hall debate.

The Speaker will generally call every MP who is in his or her place looking to question the Leader of the House – alternating from one side of the House to the other. This is a very good opportunity for backbenchers to raise issues when the House is quite full, and when the Press Gallery is also fairly full.

This is also, of course, an opportunity for lobbyist to have their issues raised. As with any other form of lobbying, it is simply a case of identifying an MP (or group of MPs) who are willing to raise a topic for you. The reason they will be willing to do so is either because they have a constituency interest in your topic, it is a matter of long-standing interest to them, or they are currently running (or helping to run) a campaign around the subject in question.

Author's top tip

If you can persuade an MP to raise your issue during Business Questions they are pretty well guaranteed to be called – unlike during Oral Questions when there are more questioners than there is time available. If you can persuade a government MP to raise your topic, they are more likely to get a sympathetic response from the Leader of the House.

4.3.12 Petitions

Parliament was receiving petitions back in the fourteenth century, and the rights of citizens to petition the House of Commons was given formal standing by a resolution adopted in 1699. During the nineteenth century tens of thousands of petitions were presented to both Houses of Parliament.

There is a very strict form of words which must be used when petitioning Parliament, and there is a Clerk of Public Petitions whose job it is to make sure those presented are in order. Petitions must be asking for something which it is in the power of the House of Commons to grant, but other than that (and the format of the preamble) there are very few restrictions on petitions. The number of signatories can be anything from a few dozen to several hundred thousand.

Once a petition has been cleared by the clerk it can simply be deposited by any MP in the green bag which hangs on the back of the Speaker's chair. The text of all such petitions are printed in the Order Paper, and thus become a matter of record.

However, MPs can also formally introduce a petition in the Commons Chamber – in which case the text will appear in *Hansard* the following day. The Speaker will call the member to present the petition either just before the adjournment debate in the evening, Mondays to Thursdays, or at the start of business on a Friday.

As well as being reprinted in the Order Paper or *Hansard*, petitions are referred to the relevant select committee – although none has so far been taken up. The government does, however, make observations on the majority of petitions which are formally presented by MPs.

In this electronic age 10 Downing Street has a facility on its website whereby anybody can set up a petition and seek to gather as many signatories as possible. Many of these petitions are trivial in nature – although if they are offensive or insulting they will be blocked. The Commons Modernisation Committee has considered the possibility of introducing electronic petitions, and it has also discussed the setting up a Select Committee of Public Petitions to deal with them and to give the act of petitioning more point.

Petitions can be a useful lobbying tool. However, to have any real effect they have to carry a very large number of signatures. Alternatively, a large number of small petitions from around the country has a similar effect as one very large petition. Widespread petition campaigns have in recent years been launched on local issues such as the situating of telephone masts and the closure of local post offices.

Author's top tip

No petition on its own – no matter how large – is likely to have a substantial impact on government thinking. As part of a concerted campaign, however, petitions are a useful lobbying tool. Using the Internet can substantially help the process of gathering signatures, even if the petition and signatures are ultimately presented in traditional hard copy format.

4.3.13 Oral questions

One of the great strengths of our democracy – and of the Westminster Parliament – is that ministers (from the prime minister downwards) have to regularly and in person respond to questions from backbench MPs of all parties, and from the opposition shadow ministers. Questions must either seek information or they must press for action. Technically they should not convey an opinion – although there is a fair amount of scope for doing so in supplementary oral questions.

Ministers are not obliged to answer questions fully, and on occasion they may deliberately withhold a significant fact which they are aware of because they have not been specifically asked about it. However, if ministers deliberately mislead Parliament, that is regarded as being an automatic resigning or sacking offence. Any inadvertent misleading of the House must be corrected at the earliest possible opportunity.

The major Whitehall departments answer questions once a month at the start of Business, Mondays through to Thursdays (there are no oral questions on a Friday). Because of the Commons' variable sitting times this means that oral questions start at just after 2.30pm on a Monday and Tuesday, 11.30am. on a Wednesday, and 10.30am on a Thursday, and last for just under an hour.

Immediately after the oral question and answer session for a department has finished questions can be tabled for the next session for that department. Thus the maximum period for tabling an oral question can be up to a month in advance. The minimum period for tabling questions is three working days before an oral question and answer session. This means that ministers – and civil servants – have a minimum of three days in which to prepare a response, whilst MPs (if they are lucky in the electronic shuffle) have a chance to table fairly topical questions.

Questions must be tabled either in writing by the MP, or via a secure electronic tabling system. Members can only table one oral question to each department answering questions that day, although quite often there are two sessions during the one hour slot. All parliamentary questions are vetted by the Table Office to ensure that they are in order. After the tabling deadline there is a shuffle which randomly puts the questions in order, and they are printed in that order in the following day's Order Paper. About 3000 parliamentary questions a year actually receive an oral answer.

Major Whitehall departments answer questions for the full hour (in practice 55 minutes), whilst smaller departments (such as Scotland, Wales or Northern Ireland) and specialist areas (such as for the Church Commissioners, the Solicitor General or the Olympics) can be for considerably less time. The notional quota for the number of oral questions tabled for each length of session is:

- 55 minutes – 20 questions
- 45 minutes – 20 questions
- 30 minutes – 15 questions
- 15 minutes – 10 questions
- 10 minutes – 8 questions

The value of the oral question to the opposition parties is the opportunity to hold ministers to account – and the opportunity to score political points. The value to the lobbyist is to raise an issue, to perhaps find out some fresh information, and possibly even to secure a concession or an endorsement.

The first thing an oral question does is to highlight an issue to a minister – and his or her civil servants. All ministers are extensively prepared by their civil servants ahead of an oral question session, so simply having a question on the Order Paper will guarantee that awareness on that issue is raised.

From the lobbyist's point of view, it is also (very occasionally) possible to get a concession out of a minister at oral question time. If the minister is not properly briefed, is not on top of his or her game, or simply succumbs to the pressure of the moment, they might just promise something which they are then bound to see through. Once something is in *Hansard* it is a matter of public record. That is why you regularly see a minister's Parliamentary Private Secretary, Special Adviser or Private Secretary desperately trying to persuade the *Hansard* editor that their minister said something different to what they actually did – or at least that they meant to say something different.

From both the opposition politician's, and the lobbyist's point of view, it is very often the supplementary question which produces the best results. Ministers – and their civil servants – have had at least three days to look at the main question as it appears on the Order Paper. And, as has been said, ministers are carefully briefed to answer those questions. In fact they usually simply read out a prepared answer.

A great deal of time is also prepared in briefing ministers for supplementary questions. The Member who asks the original question is entitled to also ask one supplementary question, and then the Speaker usually allows another two or three supplementary questions from other MPs on both sides of the House – including frontbench spokespersons if they indicate they would like to participate. Supplementary questions must be relevant to the original question, and ministers are "prepped" to answer almost any conceivable supplementary question. However, ministers are sometimes ambushed and caught out by particularly clever political supplementary questions. Equally, they can, on occasion, be caught out by a carefully crafted lobbying supplementary. Whilst no minister would ever be foolish enough to prejudge the awarding of a tender, or to promise more money for a particular project, they just might, in the heat of the moment, find themselves agreeing to visit a particular facility, or to receive a delegation from a particular interest group.

Author's top tip

If you are looking for willing support from a minister – as opposed to trying to force concessions out of him or her – try and get your question tabled by a respected government backbencher (possibly a former minister) – and suggest that they give the minister notice of their supplementary question in advance so that they can prepare a considered response.

Contributor's top tip

In politics, change is the only constant. Anticipating and understanding the dynamics of political change and positioning clients to shape the developing agenda is the art of public affairs. Working with all shades of the political spectrum is key to that work.

It is a truism that today's opposition is tomorrow's government, but the significance of a strong cross-party capability goes much wider. Not only is the opposition often the most effective way to address unwelcome legislative or regulatory proposals – not least through the detailed and often overlooked day to day work of Parliament – it is also often a fertile source of ideas and new thinking that shape the overall political debate.

> In thirty years working in UK politics and public affairs I have seen dramatic shifts in the political landscape – from the rise of Thatcherism to New Labour and now the Conservative resurgence – and taking the broad view has been the key to keeping clients one step ahead.
>
> *Kevin Bell, Fleishman-Hillard*

4.3.14 Prime minister's questions

Prime minister's questions (PMQs) are simply a turbo-charged and testosterone-fuelled version of departmental oral question sessions.

PMQs take place every Wednesday from mid-day for half an hour. This is peak time – the Press Gallery is full, and the Commons Chamber is full to overflowing – with some members sitting in the upper gallery, some sitting in the aisles, and some having to stand beyond the Bar of the House. The exchanges – especially between the prime minister and the leader of the opposition – are usually shown (in edited form) on all the main television news channels.

The main difference between PMQs and oral questions to departmental ministers is that they are, in effect, open questions. The vast majority of questions simply ask the prime minister to list his or her engagements for the day, to which the prime minister invariably replies "This morning I had a meeting with ministerial colleagues and others. In addition to my duties in this House, I shall have further such meetings later today". Once that ritual question has been asked and answered once, all further questions are open and "untrailed", and the questioner does not have to repeat the engagement question but goes straight onto his or her supplementary question.

A large proportion of the time at PMQs is taken up by the opposition frontbench. The leader of the opposition is allowed to ask six questions in all. He can either ask all six together, two groups of three, or two groups of four and two. This gives him ample scope to press the prime minister hard on either one topic, or to move swiftly from one topic to another, hoping to wrong-foot him. The leader of the Lib Dems only gets two questions, but that at least means he can follow up his original question – and have time to deliver a sound bite for radio, television and those national newspapers which still report parliamentary proceedings.

As a lobbyist you are pretty unlikely to be able to suggest one of the questions to be asked by either of the opposition leaders. There are, however, questions on the Order Paper from backbench MPs – one of whom might be prepared to raise an issue for you. Backbench MPs who are likely to be called do, however, get bombarded with requests to raise certain issues. You are only likely to succeed, therefore, if you have got a very good established relationship with that MP, or if you know for certain that they have a long-standing political or constituency interest in your policy area.

The prime minister will have been briefed on likely topics to be raised by the Conservative and Lib Dem leaders. They also invariably have a thick file which they take in with them (known as the "plastic fantastic") which has details on almost any topic likely to be raised. Normally, however, the exchanges between the PM and the opposition benches are all knockabout and political theatre.

The PM will also, of course, be briefed on every backbencher down to ask a question, and the briefing team will try to anticipate every question they are likely to ask. This briefing will be based on other questions they have asked, and on any topical constituency interest. Prime ministers often welcome the lower-key exchanges which they have with backbenchers (especially backbenchers from their own party) as a brief break from the hand-to-hand combat with opposition leaders. Therefore he or she will quite often take a conciliatory line with reasonable questions from backbenchers – even if they are from the other side of the House. It is, therefore, often possible to get the PM to publicly endorse a worthy campaign, or to agree to meet a delegation, or to write to a Member directly on a specific issue.

Author's top tip

As with an oral question to departmental minister's, if the Member who asks your question to the prime minister tips his office off in advance about the question which will be asked, you are more likely to get a considered and helpful response.

> ## Contributor's top tip
>
> The secret of achieving success in business lies in putting the customer at the heart of everything you do. Meeting their changing demands creates challenges and also creates new opportunities. Politicians are our customers. It is imperative that we understand their demands and demonstrate how, as businesses, we contribute positively, directly and openly to the greater good of society. Because it is wider society which is the politician's customer.
>
> Effective communication, clear in delivery and purpose and with a credible and resourceful message must always underpin effective customer engagement.
>
> *Richard Rumbelow, Head of Public Affairs, T-Mobile*

4.3.15 Written questions

There is a very different rationale behind questions tabled for written answer. They are not generally designed to elicit a response about broad policy areas, rather they are designed to produce a very specific – sometimes quite detailed – response on a question of fact.

There are now well over 50,000 questions for written answer tabled every year. Most written questions are ordinary questions, which are generally tabled for answer within two sitting days – although the convention is that departments try and answer them within a week. Where MPs table questions for a named day, they have to allow at least three sitting days for an answer, and there is a strict limit of tabling no more than five named day questions by any MP in any sitting day.

Members do use written questions to raise the profile of an issue, but generally they use them to find out the facts about what the government is doing in a particular policy area, or a particular geographical area – usually their constituency. A good example may be to ask one question about the national average unemployment rate – and then follow up with another question about the unemployment rate in their constituency. If the latter is greater than the former, then the MP can press the government to do something to redress the balance.

Lobbyists do not find it hard to get written questions tabled – it is simply a question of asking an MP with whom they have a good existing relationship and explaining why the information should be in the public domain. Alternatively, if they do not have such an existing relationship, it is usually just a case of asking an MP who has a long-standing interest in the topic to ask some further questions which highlight a particular aspect of the topic, or which provides more up-to-date figures.

There is, of course, a cost attached to every question which is answered – civil servants have to research them and (in theory at least) ministers have to approve the answer. The government can refuse to answer a question on the basis that it is not cost-effective to do so – this is known as the Disproportionate Cost Threshold (DCT). Currently the DCT for written answers is £700 – and there is no DCT for oral questions. In practice ministers and civil servants try to answer almost all questions – unless they are seen as being particularly vexatious.

Author's top tip

Use written answers to gain irrefutable statistics to support your campaign. If the relevant department has supplied the figures, the government cannot subsequently deny them.

4.3.16 Written Ministerial Statements

The current government introduced the innovation of the Written Ministerial Statement (WMS) to replace the previous device of the planted question. This used to be a question for written answer which would appear at the last minute on the Order Paper. It was usually tabled by a Parliamentary Private Secretary. It enabled the government to make a statement without doing so orally, and therefore without laying ministers open to cross-questioning.

There are now an average of roughly six WMSs every day. They allow the government to get an announcement on the record in a manner which is more authoritative than, say, a press release. They are sometimes a method of correcting the record, where a minister has perhaps inadvertently misled the House. They are also, on occasion, a way for the government to try and "sneak out" a major policy announcement without making an oral statement – as with the old planted questions.

Lobbyists cannot inspire ministers to make a Written Ministerial Statement. They do, however, need to keep a very sharp eye out for them. WMSs usually relate to important policy matters, and they can be issued at any time of the day, so if you do not want to be caught out you do need to monitor all WMSs carefully.

Author's top tip

If you see a Written Ministerial Statement tabled, and it directly affects you, you can telephone the parliamentary clerk in the department and ask for it to be emailed to you as soon as it is released. Alternatively, if you have a friendly journalist in the parliamentary Press Gallery, they usually get the text of WMSs slightly ahead of even MPs, and they might be prepared to let you have the gist of the statement as soon as they get it.

4.3.17 All-Party Parliamentary Groups

All-Party Parliamentary Groups (or APPGs) are quasi-official bodies set up by MPs and peers themselves – sometimes with the assistance of outside bodies. They are, however, regulated by rules established by Parliament in 1984, and their activities are overseen by the office of the Parliamentary Commissioner for Standards.

The rules governing the formation and running of APPGs are stringent. The main stipulations are:

- They must have an AGM and at least one other meeting every year.
- They must publish a summary of their purpose.
- They must publish a list of officers, which will normally include a chair, one of two vice chairs, a secretary and a treasurer
- Membership must be drawn from both Houses of Parliament, and at least one officer must be from the House of Commons
- All groups must have at least 20 members, of whom ten must come from the governing party, and at least six from the main opposition party
- Lists of officers and members must be kept up to date and filed with the office of the Parliamentary Commissioner for Standards
- Any financial sponsorship of £1000 or more must be declared

If groups meet all of these criteria they are placed on the approved list. This gives them priority for booking rooms within the Palace of Westminster, and enables them to advertise details of their meetings in the All Party Notice. It also gives them right to style themselves as an APPG. Groups which for a time fail to meet these criteria can re-apply for approved list status once their eligibility is restored.

Most APPGs have memberships which are entirely made up of members of the House of Commons and the House of Lords, although they can have a professional secretariat. However, some APPGs also have external individuals and bodies as members. They have a slightly different status, and they are known as Associate All-Party Parliamentary Groups (AAPPGs). There are about 40 groups in this category.

There are two main types of APPGs, dealing with countries and subjects respectively. All-Party country groups obviously specialise with the country concerned. Most of them are affiliated either to the Commonwealth Parliamentary Association or the Inter-Parliamentary Union. There are approximately 130 groups in this category. They arrange for speakers who are experts on the country in question to address meetings, and usually have strong links with the relevant Embassy or High Commission. They also often arrange facility visits to their countries.

All-Party subject groups cover a vast array of subjects. There are well over 300 of these APPGs, although they tend to be more transient than the country APPGs. Subjects covered range from adoption through to zoos. They can deal with heavyweight subjects such as AIDS and cancer, through to sports and pastimes such as cycling, cricket and football. Many of them relate to industries or medical conditions.

APPGs fulfil a useful purpose in Parliament. Whilst select committees can range far and wide in their inquiries, there are only a couple of dozen of them. There are – as has been shown – hundreds of APPGs, and they can develop a real expertise in their closely-defined areas. Increasingly many of them now produce reports. Although these are of variable quality, their parliamentary status does ensure that they receive a fair amount of media attention.

Lobbyists can engage with APPGs at several different levels:

- They can actually sponsor an APPG – although this has to be declared
- They can provide the secretariat for an APPG – although again this has to be declared
- They can arrange for speakers to address an APPG meeting

- They can arrange site visits for APPGs
- They can arrange for external bodies to join Associate All-Party Parliamentary Groups
- They can suggest topics for APPG reports, and assist in their compilation and distribution

Because APPGs receive little support and no funding from Parliament, they are often grateful for outside assistance. They are, therefore, an excellent entrée into the system for external companies and consultancies.

Warning!

APPGs which are thinly-veiled fronts for commercial organisations can attract extremely negative press comment. Any lobbyist – whether consultancy based or in-house – would be well advised to apply all of the rules governing APPGs stringently, and to consult the office of the Parliamentary Commissioner for Standards if in any doubt.

4.3.18 Party committees and groups

Both the Labour Party and the Conservatives have a range of committees and groups which represent backbench interests and focus on particular regions or policy areas.

The two most powerful of these bodies are the Parliamentary Labour Party (of which all MPs who receive the Labour Whip are automatically members) and the 1922 Committee (which represents Conservative backbenchers). Both have elected chairs and committees, and both meet weekly whilst parliament is in session. Their meetings are usually routine and thinly attended – it is only when there is a crisis looming that their meetings become well-attended, and in those circumstances the party leader (or the relevant frontbencher) will usually address the meeting. These meetings are supposed to be private, but details inevitably make their way to the lobby journalists who invariably hang around outside trying to gauge the temperature of the meeting and pick up snippets of gossip.

Within the two main parties there are also a series of "ginger" groups which are formed to represent MPs on one wing or the other of the party. In the Conservative Party the Bow Group represents the broad centre of the party, whilst the Conservative Way Forward represents the right. Other groups, such as the No Turning Back Group and the Cornerstone Group represent the Thatcherite rump of the party. Those on the left of the party are not as organised in terms of ginger groups, but some MPs and party members still belong to the Tory Reform Group, which is committed to the ideals of 'one nation' conservatism.

Traditionally in the Labour Party the Tribune Group has represented the left wing of the party, although the Campaign Group occupies similar ground. The Compass Group is also leftward leaning, but bills itself as a progressive force – as does Progress. The Fabian Society has a long tradition going back to the foundation of the Labour Party in the early twentieth century.

The Lib Dems have no equivalents to the Labour and Tory ginger groups. However, the "orange bookers" are a loose collection of Lib Dem MPs determined to keep the party firmly camped on the centre ground and to push the case for the free market.

Both of the main parties have a network of backbench committees which shadow the main Whitehall departments, and others which concern themselves with the nations and regions of the United Kingdom. These groups can be very influential behind the scenes. When the party is in power, they can advise ministers on backbench opinion relating to a policy or piece of legislation. When the party is in opposition, they can help to shape party policy to go in to the general election manifesto.

Author's top tip

Backbench committees are always happy to receive written briefings from external lobby groups. Once a relationship has been established, they do occasionally invite external representatives in to give a presentation, and this can have a significant effect on policy formulation.

4.3.19 Exhibitions

At any one time there are probably two or three exhibitions going on within the precincts of the Palace of Westminster. These are aimed partly at parliamentarians, but also at the many thousands of people who visit the precincts every day.

Westminster Hall is the oldest surviving part of the Palace of Westminster, and its huge floor space and vaulted ceiling never fail to impress visitors. In recent years it has become the custom to set up exhibitions in this space. They are normally set up to mark the anniversary of historic events, and recent exhibitions have included those commemorating the abolition of the slave trade, the Gunpowder Plot, and the 175th anniversary of the Great Reform Act.

Another very impressive space is the atrium in Portcullis House. However, events held there are mainly of a cultural nature – either art exhibitions or performances aimed at politicians and their staff who work in the building. Members of the public do not enter the ground floor area of Portcullis House in large numbers, and if they visit the building it is usually because they are attending a select committee hearing on the first floor.

One other venue is heavily used by politicians, their staff and visitors. This is the Upper Waiting Hall, where MPs and the public congregate to meet, or to wait for a select committee hearing to begin on the upper committee corridor. The important thing about this exhibition space from a lobbyist's point of view is that it is open to external organisations. If you can get a supportive MP to enter the ballot on your behalf, and he or she is successful in that ballot, then you can hold a small exhibition right in the heart of the Palace of Westminster. There is no actual charge for holding the event but you will have to have an exhibition to put on, and you will need to have people in attendance to discuss its purpose with politicians and visitors.

4.3.20 Function rooms

As well as being the seat of our democracy and a legislation factory the Palace of Westminster is also a vast catering organisation and entertainment venue. The staff of the Refreshment Department have to serve drinks and meals to upwards of 5000 people a day who work in the precincts or have occasion to visit them. Part of the Refreshment Department is known as Banqueting, and it is they who are responsible for organising larger catering events.

Priority for room hire and facilities is obviously given to MPs and peers, but the system allows for outside organisations to hold events within the Palace of Westminster. However, they do need to find an MP or peer to sponsor the event, make the booking, and be in attendance when it actually takes place.

There is a very wide choice of rooms and facilities which can be booked during the day and evening when Parliament is sitting – and a few which can also be booked when it is not. They can be booked for sit-down lunches and dinners, or receptions with canapés, or even for lectures or debates.

The most popular rooms which can be hired with the sponsorship of an MP or peer are:

- Dining Rooms A, B or C
- The Terrace Marquee
- The Jubilee Room
- The Cholmondeley Room
- The Churchill Room
- The Strangers' Dining Room
- The Members' Dining Room

Some of these rooms – such as the Members' Dining Room – can usually only be booked when the House is not sitting, or when attendance is likely to be light (such as on a private members' bill Friday). There is always a lot of competition for bookings, so rooms do need to be booked well in advance.

Warning!

The Administration Committee feels that it is better for the Palace of Westminster kitchens to be used, and the Refreshment Department staff employed, even at times when Members themselves have no requirement for them. However, there is a complete ban on purely commercial events being held within the precincts of the Palace of Westminster, and this is – quite rightly – very strictly enforced.

Author's top tip

Only MPs can book facilities in the House of Commons, and only peers can book facilities in the House of Lords. However, a peer who has been an MP can make bookings in either House.

4.3.21 Mass lobbies

Demonstrations in and around Parliament are now effectively outlawed. It is possible, however, to organise a mass lobby of MPs.

Very often these mass lobbies relate to factory closures or other forms of large-scale redundancies. They can also relate to industrial disputes. They are therefore often organised by the trade unions, who provide coaches to bring in dozens – or even hundreds – of their members.

Participants have to queue up and go through security like everybody else. Once inside, they can fill in the green slips asking for their constituency MP to come and meet with them. Alternatively, in a well organised mass lobby, MPs will have been warned to expect this mass influx, and will have set aside time to meet their constituents and discuss their issues. They might even have booked one of the committee rooms so that a semi-formal presentation can be made and discussions held.

Author's top tip

If you are organising a mass lobby, do not just flag it up with the relevant constituency MPs. Phone the Parliament switchboard (020 7219 3000) and ask to speak to Police Operations. Give them ample warning of your intention to bring a large number of petitioners to speak to their MPs.

4.3.22 Debates

Apart from oral questions and statements, the Commons Chamber is principally there as a forum for debate. Obviously a large proportion of these debates relate directly to the progress of legislation – but that aspect is dealt with later on. The debates we are dealing with here are the wide range of non-legislative debates.

These are the main categories on non-legislative debates which take place on the Floor of the House of Commons, or in Westminster Hall:

- Substantive motion debates: These are government-inspired debates which require approval of a specific motion – usually along the lines of "That this

House takes note of…" These usually relate to something as routine as a government response to a select committee report. However, occasionally the motion can be something as crucial as confidence in the government (and if the vote on a confidence motion is lost the government falls) or whether the United Kingdom should participate in armed conflict.

- Opposition day debates: Every session 20 days are set aside for debates on motions initiated by the opposition parties. Of these 17 are allocated to the main opposition party, and three to the second-largest opposition party. Quite often these debates are divided in two, in order to increase the range of subjects which can be covered. There is a formal motion – usually highly critical of government policy – and an amendment, both of which are voted on.

- Government adjournment motions: These debates are very similar to substantive motion debates, other than there is no motion before the House (other than "That this House do now adjourn"). The topic for debate is announced in advance and at the commencement of the debate. Once the allotted time has been used up the vote is taken and the House adjourns. Governments use this device to trail policies and sound out opinion – but also to fill the odd day when there is no substantial business to put before the House – usually because legislation is log-jammed in the House of Lords.

- End of sitting day adjournment debates: At the end of every sitting day – including Fridays – there is a half hour adjournment debate introduced by a backbencher. He or she speaks for about a quarter of an hour, and a government minister responds for a similar period of time. There is no vote, and there may only be a handful of Members in the Commons Chamber, but it gives backbenchers an opportunity to raise an issue – usually constituency-related – and have a government minister respond.

- Recess adjournment debate: Before the Commons goes into recess there is an opportunity for any backbencher to raise an issue which he or she considers has not been satisfactorily dealt with during the session. It is up to the Leader of the House (rather than individual ministers) to answer all of the points raised, but it does give backbenchers a final opportunity to get something off of their chest before the House rises.

- Westminster Hall debates: Since 1999 the grand committee room off of Westminster Hall has been set up as a parallel chamber in order for MPs to hold debates for which time cannot be found in the main chamber. These sittings are held from 9.30am-2.30pm on Tuesdays, from 9.30-11.30am and then from 2.30-5pm on Wednesdays, and also from 2.30-5.30pm on Thursdays. On Tuesdays and Wednesdays two 90 minute debates and three 30 minute debates initiated by backbenchers are held. Thursday debates are often on government motions, and there are regularly debates on key select committee reports. The ethos is far more consensual that that which prevails in the main Commons Chamber, and no divisions are held. Because of this, it is not uncommon for ministers to stray off of their brief, and either offer some small concession, or at the very last express some sympathy for the cause under debate.

From the lobbyist's point of view this range of non-legislative debates offers two distinct opportunities. On one level, as soon as a forthcoming debate is announced on a subject about which they have knowledge and expertise, they can offer to brief MPs. This offer can be extended to backbenchers on both sides of the House, and also to the opposition front benches. Briefings can either be by way of hard copy delivered by post or email, or through face-to-face meetings.

Alternatively, lobbyists can seek to prevail on backbench MPs to actually initiate a debate. The subjects of end of day adjournment debates, and most Westminster Hall debates, are decided by ballot. If you can persuade supportive MPs to enter the ballots – and to keep on entering them until they eventually win – then you will have a great platform from which to have your cause expounded.

Although they are not balloted, it is also possible on rare occasions to persuade opposition parties to use one of their precious opposition day debates (or even half of one day) to highlight your issue. You will, however, have to have an extremely persuasive case. You will have to convince them that government policy in your particular policy area is badly wrong, and that you will be able to provide them with the facts and arguments to prove that that is the case.

Author's top tip

The recess adjournment debate is an excellent opportunity to have your issue aired one last time before Parliament goes into recess. Attendance is high – because there are a great many MPs who wish to speak – and every Member who wishes to speak is called.

4.3.23 Legislation

As has already been stated, one of the main functions of the Parliament is to pass legislation. Most (but not all) legislation which ultimately becomes law is initiated by the government. All bills, whether initiated by the government or by a private Member, have to go through the same legislative stages. Well over a hundred bills are introduced every year, of which about a third (nearly all of them government bills) actually make it onto the statute book.

As has been stated earlier in this book legislation often has its origins deep in the bowels of a party research department or a think tank. There may have been a Green Paper and a White Paper, possibly even a draft bill. Once a bill actually reaches the House of Commons, however, the normal procedure and timetable is:

- First reading: This is merely a formality, with the short and long titles (and a list of its principal supporters) of the bill being read out and entered onto the record.

- Second reading: There is usually a gap of at least two weekends between first and second readings. The second reading is a broad debate on the principles of a bill, and usually takes up a whole parliamentary day. No amendments can be tabled and there will usually just be a straightforward vote on whether it should receive a second reading or not. No government bill has failed to receive a second reading in the Commons since the Shops Bill in 1986. Immediately after the vote there is almost invariably a programme order (which is also voted on) and which sets out the amount of time which will be spent on the bill in committee.

- Committee stage: This stage follows within a week or two of second reading. Almost invariably (other than with the Finance Bill or bills of constitutional importance) the committee stage in the Commons is taken in standing committee. This is composed of between 16 and 50 MPs chosen by the Committee of Selection in rough proportion to the general composition of the House of Commons. There will always be a government minister leading on the bill, and Whips from the three main parties are continuously in attendance. The chairman is appointed by the Speaker's Panel. Depending on the size and complexity of the bill, a standing committee can meet anything from just once to as many as twenty times. The job of a standing committee, in theory at least, is to go through a bill line by line, clause by clause, and schedule by schedule. In practice, time constraints – and restrictions imposed by programme orders – mean that large portions of a bill may go through without any meaningful scrutiny. It is largely at the discretion of the chairman as to which amendments are actually called, debated and voted on.

- Report stage: Once the bill has completed its committee stage it is reprinted, as amended by the standing committee. There is generally then a gap of two weekends before it reappears in the Commons Chamber for its report stage – which is technically the standing committee reporting its activities and amendments to the Commons. New amendments can be introduced at this stage, but are unlikely to be called, unless they are being introduced as a result of a government commitment to think again at committee stage. Occasionally the Speaker will allow a crucial matter to be reviewed again at report stage, even if an amendment has been introduced and defeated at the earlier stage. Usually report stage takes up one day on the floor of the Commons – although major bills can have two days devoted to them at this stage.

- Third reading: Immediately after the report stage the bill will be reprinted (if it has been further amended) and goes straight in to third reading. This is very similar to the second reading stage – a broad debate on the principle of the bill (as it now stands), followed by a final vote. The bill is then sent to the House of Lords – or back to the House of Lords if that is where it originated.

There are a great many opportunities for lobbyists to have an impact on a bill during its passage through both Houses of Parliament. As has been previously stated, the best time to amend a bill is when it is still in its consultation phase, preferably before it has even reached draft bill stage. The further a bill progresses down the legislative timetable, the harder it is to amend.

Author's top tip

If you need a bill or amendment drafted it may well be worth retaining parliamentary agents to do it for you – bad drafting stands out a mile. Many people think parliamentary agents only do private bills – in fact they are experts at all forms of legislation.

However, there are certainly opportunities to affect the ultimate form which an Act of Parliament will take. If enough backbenchers speak out against the certain provisions contained within a bill at second reading the government will certainly take notice – especially if a fair proportion of them are members of the governing party. Ministers and Whips are often prepared to accept amendments proposed by external lobbyists, provided they are convinced of the rectitude and efficacy of the proposals. The one thing they are always hugely reluctant to do is to accept amendments proposed by the opposition.

An actual government defeat in the Commons is highly unlikely – assuming that they have a working majority. However, force of logic and strength of public opinion can on occasion prompt ministers to either put down their own amendment – or promise to look at the issue again at a later stage. Any concession – or even implied concession – by government ministers can signal to the House of Lords that they have *carte blanche* to table their own amendment. If the government does not live up to promises made in debate in the Chamber or standing committee, it can also lay itself open to legal challenge, as was established in the Pepper v Hart landmark case in 1995.

Author's top tip

Backbench MPs who speak at second reading of bills are often drafted on to the standing committee. So do not wait for the actual make-up of the standing committee to be announced. Contact those who spoke immediately after the second reading debate and offer to brief them, on the assumption that they may well be drafted onto the standing committee.

The procedure described above relates to a government public bill in the House of Commons. There are various other types of bill, all of which have their own procedures:

- Ballot bills: During the Tuesday and Wednesday of the second week of each session MPs can put their names down to take part in the ballot for private members' bills which is drawn on the Thursday. The 20 MPs who come top in the Ballot have priority for introducing their own bills, with the first seven getting top priority. There are only seven Fridays set aside for private members' bill second readings, before going into the one standing committee (standing committee C) which is especially reserved for them. After that, there are a further six Fridays set aside for all of the remaining stages. Despite these hurdles, between one and three private members' bills typically get through their Commons and Lords stages each year and receive Royal Assent.

- Ten minute rule bills: After the seventh week of a session ten minute rule bills are introduced every Tuesday and Wednesday by members who have, again, been chosen by ballot. Before the main business that MP gets to speak for ten minutes on his or her "hobby-horse" subject. Any objecting MP can then also speak for ten minutes, and then if necessary there is a vote. However, the object of ten minute rule bills is not legislation, but publicity.

- Presentation bills: Any MP can introduce a bill on any day. Notice is given in the Order Paper, and the MP presents a dummy of the bill with its long and short title to the Clerk of the House. The fact that it has been presented is recorded in *Hansard*, but that is the end of the matter – there is no mechanism or facility to take the bill forward from that stage.

- Private bills: These have nothing to do with private members' bills. They are bills which only have a local or personal (as opposed to national or general) impact. Very often they are introduced by local authorities or companies to give themselves extra powers to deal with a local issue or to pursue a particular opportunity. Private bills have a unique procedure, some of which takes place in joint committees of MPs and peers. Witnesses (or petitioners) for or against them are represented by parliamentary agents.

- Hybrid bills: These bills share some of the characteristics of both public and private bills. They tend to be bills which affect one group very directly, but also have an impact on the public at large. Examples include the Channel Tunnel Bill and the Crossrail Bill.

- Delegated Legislation: This is secondary legislation under powers which have already been granted in an existing Act of Parliament. Most delegated legislation consists of Statutory Instruments, but there are a variety of other forms, including orders, regulations and codes. Some delegated legislation comes into force automatically, some is brought into force by ministers. The majority of delegated legislation is not scrutinised, but some is debated and voted upon by MPs and peers either in committee or on the floor of the House. Parliament can approve delegated legislation – or vote it down – but cannot amend it.

Although, as has been stated, there is ample opportunity to lobby in favour of or against government public bills, that is not the case with most of the other bills detailed above. Some bills (such as presentation bills) will not be going anywhere in any event, so it is generally pointless to oppose them. Private bills are very much the domain of parliamentary agents and petitioners. Delegated legislation is hard to block – because it has in theory already been pre-approved.

The exception is balloted private members' bills. It is very easy for MPs to block these, so it is therefore equally easy for lobbyists to conspire against them. By the same token, a skilled lobby can greatly increase the chances of their succeeding.

Helping to get a high priority balloted bill through all of its stages is the highlight of some lobbyist's careers – and usually results in nominations for one or other of the various industry awards. Other than actually helping to transform a bill into an Act of Parliament, however, the best lobbying opportunities lie with ten minute rule bills, presentation bills, and balloted private members' bills which are outside the top seven. They may never actually become law, but they are a valuable opportunity to highlight an issue and put it firmly on to the public policy agenda.

Author's top tip

If you have a bill already drafted, and you are in a position to contact successful MPs immediately after the result of the ballot has been announced, you could well have a chance of getting one of them to adopt your bill.

Contributor's top tip

Lobbying has to be done months in advance of the first reading. This gives you time to prepare background material, such as a written briefing of your organisation's views on the issue, and to arrange meetings with MPs and civil servants. Do not under-estimate the time required to research and educate yourself on the subject and themes - you need to put forward your case competently and confidently. Identify sympathetic MPs and approach them to represent your interests. Maintain constant contact with other stakeholders such as professional bodies or charities that share your position. They are your allies and you may need to mobilise help quickly when issuing statements. Finally, watch out for the amendments after the second reading – you need to dissect each clinically and develop arguments and counter-arguments for committee and report stages.

Top tip: observe like a doctor, think like a lawyer.

Gerald Chan, Royal College of Obstetricians and Gynaecologists

4.3.24 Finance

As well as generally holding a government to account, and scrutinising its legislation, one of the House of Commons principal functions lies in scrutinising and approving government expenditure. The House of Lords has had no significant role in scrutinising or approving the government's finances since it rejected Lloyd George's 1909 Budget. The result was the 1911 Parliament Act, restricting its power in this – and other – regards.

The government's financial agenda is dominated by three distinct cycles – the estimates cycle, the Budget cycle and the reporting cycle. None of these cycles conforms to the calendar year, the financial year or the parliamentary year. Scrutiny of government spending is undertaken by the departmental select committees (especially the Treasury Select Committee and the Committee of Public Accounts), by the House of Commons itself, and by the Comptroller and Auditor General (C&AG) and the National Audit Office (who report to Committee on Public Accounts).

The Estimates Cycle is the process of authorising public expenditure. It begins just after the start of the parliamentary year with the presentation of the Winter Supplementary Estimates in October or November. This is followed by the passing of the Consolidated Fund Act in December, and then the Spring Supplementary Estimates are presented in February. The Main Estimates are then presented in March, usually at the same time as the Budget, with the Summer Supplementary Estimates in June. There is also provision for excess votes, where the previous estimates have proved to be inadequate. Every year three days are set aside for government estimates to be debated on the floor of the House of Commons. Under his chancellorship, Gordon Brown introduced the Comprehensive Spending Review (CSR). This gave government departments budgets stretching three years ahead. The CSRs impose Public Service Agreements (PSAs) on government departments in an effort to ensure that the additional resources allocated to them actually resulted in improvements to the services provided to the public.

The Reporting Cycle ensures that information relating to how public money has been spent is made available. Its timetable is less rigid. Throughout the year select committees hold inquiries into the expenditure of their relevant government departments. Government departments publish their annual reports in spring, usually after the March Budget. The C&AG and the National Audit Office undertake a rolling programme of value-for-money inquiries, and report their finding to the Commons Public Accounts Committee. Every year the NAO's 800 staff undertake some 600 inquiries in to the full range of government-funded bodies – although local authorities fall within the remit of the Audit Commission. The C&AG decides which inquiries should be held. He is not subject to the authority of the Public Accounts Committee, and can only be sacked by a vote of both Houses of Parliament. The chairmanship of the Public Accounts Committee is invariably held by a member of the main opposition party. There is a considerable degree of independence in the bodies which scrutinise government expenditure.

The Budget Cycle is much better known to the man and woman in the street – and it provides far greater opportunities for lobbyists. The Budget Cycle deals with broader issues such as the management of the economy and the general economic outlook – but it also deals with the raising of taxation. It therefore represents either a potential threat or potential opportunity to individuals and organisations, and that is the kind of scenario where the skills of lobbyists are most frequently in demand.

The Budget Cycle usually unfolds in the following way:

- Pre-Budget Report and Statement: This is another innovation which Gordon Brown introduced as chancellor in November 1997. Initially it was billed as a sort of "Green Budget", allowing the chancellor to provide an over-view of the general economic situation and to presage taxation changes which he anticipates instituting in the spring. Increasingly, however, it has become used as a "Mini Budget" rather than a "Green Budget".

- Budget Report and Statement: This is normally made by the chancellor in March or April, on a Tuesday or Wednesday. Next to the Queen's Speech it is the biggest set-piece parliamentary event of the year. It is accompanied by the publication of the "Red Book" (a publication running to several hundred pages detailing the government tax and spending proposals) and the "Budget Bundle" (a series of press releases produced by every government department detailing how the Budget provisions affect them). Both the "Red Book" and the "Budget Bundle" can be pre-ordered from

HMSO and collected as soon as the chancellor finishes his speech (which generally lasts about an hour). An order is then passed giving the provision of the Budget immediate legal effect (subject to subsequent approval by the Commons) which is granted in a series of debates and votes spread over four or five days.

- Finance Bill – Commons: The Finance Bill is usually published in April. The Commons Treasury Select Committee immediately begins an inquiry, which it concludes in time to report back to the Commons before second reading later in the month. In May the Finance Bill goes into standing committee – but with the main provisions being taken on the floor in a committee of the Whole House. Report stage and third reading follow in June. Once returned from the House of Lords the Finance Bill must complete all of its stages and receive Royal Assent before Parliament rises for the summer recess in late July.

- Finance Bill – Lords: As has already been stated the power of the Lords to oversee the government's finances was severely restricted by the Parliament Act 1911. The Lords do, however, hold a general second reading debate on the general principles of the bill, before giving the remaining stages formal consideration and speeding the bill back to the Commons.

There are, of course, exceptions to this timetable. In times of severe economic crisis governments have been forced to introduce emergency Budgets. After a change of government following a general election it is quite common for the new administration's first Budget to be brought forward to June or July.

Before the current Labour government came to power in 1997 Treasury ministers and senior civil servants would go into self-imposed "purdah" in the weeks prior to a Budget. Not only has Budget "purdah" been consigned to the dustbin of history, but so has the previously hallowed notion of Budget secrecy. Nowadays some putative Budget proposals are widely trailed in the press, either to curry favour with a particular newspaper or to "fly a kite" and judge the reaction to the proposal.

Anecdote

Budget secrecy used to be taken so seriously that when in 1947 pipe smoking Labour Chancellor Hugh Dalton made a joking reference to tobacco duty to a journalist on his way to deliver the Budget he was forced to resign.

From the lobbyists point of view this relaxation of conventions presents great opportunities. It has always been possible to arrange meetings with Treasury ministers and senior civil servants outside of the Budget "purdah" period, but now these can – subject to availability – be arranged at shorter notice and in greater time proximity to the actual Budget.

If you do manage to secure a meeting with a Treasury minister it is important to make the most of the opportunity. Here are some suggestions for maximising the potential beneficial outcome from your meeting:

- Budget Submission: You should prepare a formal, detailed document which makes your case – but which also acknowledges any counter-arguments. A one-sided submission will be rubbished by officials and as a consequence dismissed by ministers.

- Revenue: If your proposal can be seen to be revenue neutral, this is obviously beneficial. Generally speaking Budgets are about raising revenue to spend on public services, and proposals which will have the effect of restricting that revenue are not generally welcome.

- Third party endorsement: You should also, wherever possible, go into any meeting armed with endorsements from third parties. This will mitigate any impression of special pleading on your part, and add clout to your arguments.

- Time: As with any meeting with any minister, find out in advance how much time is being made available and leave the minister at least some time to respond.

- Persistence: Even if it looks like you have succeeded in getting adverse proposals deferred from this Budget, or that you have succeeded in getting a favourable policy adopted, that is not the end of the story. You do have to keep seeking meetings and you need to keep making Budget Submissions every year, because circumstances (and ministers) change – so you just have to keep making the same case time after time.

As has been said the era of Budget secrecy has now largely passed, and chancellors do now use the media to trail announcements. That pretty well gives lobbyists *carte blanche* to respond in kind: if chancellors can float ideas in the media, you can use the media to support or knock back those ideas. After all, the whole idea of "flying kites" is to find out which way the wind is blowing – so it is down to you to puff just as hard as you can.

Just because a proposal has been announced in a Pre-Budget Statement or Budget Statement, or even if it is contained in the Finance Bill, it does not mean that it is set in stone. MPs of all sides are alert to proposals which will damage their re-election prospects, and there are opportunities for the Finance Bill to be amended at committee stage and report stage. Margaret Thatcher had to back down over petrol duty increases in 1980, and John Major was similarly forced to concede defeat over the increase on duty on domestic fuel in 1994. Gordon Brown, as chancellor, had to bring the fuel escalator to an emergency halt, and as prime minister he has had to reverse the effects of the scrapping of the 10p tax band. The one thing all of these measures had in common is that they were widely unpopular. Many minor changes are made to the Finance Bill without any serious revolt or any accompanying publicity. Amending the Finance Bill is all about making the political or economic case unarguable.

When dealing with the Treasury it is important to bear in mind that they – and the chancellor of the exchequer – hold unparalleled sway over other government departments. Only the prime minister can exert any real influence over the chancellor – and only full cabinet can over-rule the Treasury.

Author's top tip

Ideally Budget Submissions should be handed over in person during a meeting with a Treasury minister. However, any organisation can prepare a Budget Submission – and have a photograph taken as they prepare to hand it in at the Treasury's impressive new entrance in Horse Guards Parade.

Contributor's top tip

As Woody Allen said '80% of success is showing up'. The lobbyist needs to be on the spot – in Parliament, at the political event, or facing the press. The age of social networking, email and text is with us, but despite this, digital public affairs will never eclipse the value of eyeballing your target audience.

I would add a supplementary to Woody Allen's advice, and that is, 'Always assume no-one ever reads anything.' They do not, so make sure you do. Nothing beats having read a text for sparking ideas, and putting you in a position to challenge the party you are lobbying.

So it is simple really: read stuff, see people.

Jon McLeod, Chairman UK Public Affairs, Weber Shandwick

Contributor's top tip

What happens if the Budget brings a nasty surprise? This is where lobbying meets crisis management. Budgets are high profile and so are notoriously difficult to get changed. The biggest problem is time. If the Budget is announced in March the Finance Bill debates will go on until July.

Obviously you will want to lobby ministers and civil servants at the Treasury and your home department (eg, Department of Transport, if it is a transport as well as a Budget issue). If your arguments are not strong you may need to commission further research, but it will have to be done quickly.

The main parliamentary lobbying opportunities are:

• Commons Treasury Select Committee

The Treasury Select Committee will meet soon after the Budget to take written and oral evidence. If you cannot get in front of them look at who regularly attends so that you can brief them if they are sympathetic.

• Commons committee and report stage

At the committee and report stages remember to treat the opposition with care, they will be useful if you want points clarified, but any amendments they put down will almost certainly be rejected. Contrary to myth the Lords do debate the Finance Bill, but they do not vote, so if you have useful allies in the Lords you can still use them.

If you have a big problem and the Government are not listening then you will want to think about allies. Allies such as the CBI or the City of London Corporation will be crucial but it might be difficult to get them to focus on your issue.

You may consider going to the press. This is a high risk strategy but can be effective (eg, non-dom tax debate 2008). You will have to be confident your arguments are strong and that they are not simply self-interested, but are also beneficial to wider society. The more your issue is raised positively the more likely you are to garner the support of important allies and get the interest of ministers. Conversely the higher profile it is the more embarrassment will be caused by a U-turn.

Keith Johnston, Society of Trust and Estate Practitioners

Contributor's top tip

My top tip is "know your onions". There really is no mystique attached to how to be a successful lobbyist, no smoke nor mirrors – you just need to know the people, policies and processes (the 3Ps) which will influence the decision making process. This means that knowledge is the key. A good consultant must always be prepared, rehearsed and informed.

If they are, they will not only appear supremely confident, they will impress and win the confidence of others. I am a firm believer in the statement "piss poor preparation = piss poor performance" (or the 6Ps) so my top tip is, take the time to learn who's who and what's what in terms of the decision making process. The more you know the more likely you are to succeed. It's that simple!

Gill Morris, Managing Director, Connect Public Affairs

Contributor's top tip

It still amazes me how few businesses realise the value of their constituency presence. Even a cabinet minister in a safe seat, never mind a newly elected backbencher in a marginal, will do whatever they can to help local businesses, whether independent small ones or subsidiaries of major multinationals. Using local staff also says a lot about the trust that the organisation has in its people. So my simple advice is this - forget the mass mailings of corporate social responsibility reports which mostly just go straight into the socially-responsible recycling bin and forget the uniform e-mail from a junior account executive in your public affairs consultancy. Instead coach your local staff in the old-fashioned art of letter writing (or even telephoning) and get them to approach MPs, MEPs local councillors and all the other political opinion formers. It will be cheaper, probably much easier, and much more effective. However, as a former consultant myself, I must add that a consultancy is often invaluable to work out what you should be saying, to whom and when. Keep the dog, yes, but bark yourself.

Peter Luff MP, Chairman Business and Enterprise Select Committee

4.4 House Of Lords

The House of Lords (or Upper House or House of Peers) holds many attractions for the lobbyist. It is less party political and more consensual than the Commons and therefore more open to outside influences. It is also full of people who in their previous working lives – or even their current working lives, since many of them are part-timers – are experts in their fields. This again makes them more likely to be swayed by force of argument.

The government almost invariably has a majority in the House of Commons – unless it is a minority government, or part of a coalition. This is certainly not the case in the House of Lords, where no party has a built-in majority. At the time of writing the make-up of the House of Lords consists of:

- 217 Labour peers
- 201 Conservative peers
- 197 crossbench peers
- 76 Lib Dem peers
- 26 Bishops
- 2 UKIP peers
- 14 peers on leave of absence

Thus, even though Labour has the largest number of peers, it is very far short of a majority. The Lib Dems have a great deal of influence and often hold the balance of power in the Upper House – as do the very large body of crossbench peers. They are non-partisan, and they neither issue nor receive a whip. They do, however, adopt positions on certain polices and bills, and often vote largely *en bloc*. They also have a convenor – currently the Rt Hon Lord Williamson of Horton.

The House of Lords Act 1999 removed most of the hereditary peers from the Upper House. This got rid of the phenomenon of the "backwoodsmen" – peers who rarely attended the House but could be relied upon to turn out and vote (usually Conservative) on key issues. However, under a compromise reached with the Viscount Cranborne (at that time Tory leader in the Lords) 92 hereditary peers survived the "cull" and they (or their elected successors) still attend regularly and take a very active part in the proceedings of the Lords.

It is also the case that procedure is much laxer in the House of Lords. The Upper House is still largely self-governing – although since 2006 an elected

Lord Speaker has presided over its proceedings. Backbench peers have far more latitude to speak, table amendments, or introduce legislation than do backbench MPs in the House of Commons. Therefore, for the lobbyist, the House of Lords is a much easier place to get an issue aired – and it is likely to receive a fairer hearing, and a more erudite response.

Rather than go through every aspect of Lords procedure, this section of the book will simply concentrate on where procedure differs from that in the Commons – and where the Upper House presents enhanced opportunities for the lobbyist.

4.4.1 The cabinet

As has been stated earlier the number of full members of the cabinet is restricted by statute – and most places are taken by members of the House of Commons. By convention, however, at least two members of the House of Lords would sit in the cabinet as of right – with perhaps another one or two in attendance.

The office of Lord Chancellor – who was the Presiding Officer in the House of Lords prior to the creation of the post of Lord Speaker – has been downgraded, with his responsibilities split between the Lord Speaker and the secretary of state for justice. This means that the two most senior members of the House of Lords are the Leader of the House and the Chief Whip. In the current government at the time of writing the Attorney General also sits in the Lords and attends cabinet.

In previous governments senior statesmen who sat in the Lords were often members of the cabinet. They were there to offer wise counsel and to share their many years of experience of political life.

Anecdote

Margaret Thatcher relied heavily on the sage advice of the MP, home secretary, deputy prime minister (and latterly peer) William Whitelaw. She once famously opined that 'every prime minister should have a Willie'.

In the current government the representation from the Lords is more to ensure that the government does not run into unnecessary problems in what the Commons refer to as "another place". Whilst previous Conservative administrations were regularly defeated in the Lords, it is undoubtedly the case that the frequency of such defeats has escalated since 1997. This has heightened the likelihood of further reform of the House of Lords – to which all political parties are now committed.

4.4.2 Ministers

Despite the fact that there are more members of the House of Lords than the House of Commons, and the fact that the Upper House has an equal (if not greater) burden of legislative scrutiny to bear, there are substantially fewer ministers in the Lords than in the Commons.

At the time of writing there were just 14 government ministers in the House of Lords – not even enough to cover each of the main Whitehall departments. Bearing in mind that other duties may call them away for one reason or another, this means that ministers in the Lords often have to cover departments or policy areas of which they know very little. From the lobbyist's viewpoint this can be a good thing: government frontbenchers who are not experts in the areas under question may be more prepared to listen – and they may be tempted to say and offer more than a colleague in the House of Commons might.

As we will see, however, ministers in the Lords do have some support – from the Whips.

4.4.3 Whips

As has been pointed out, Whips in the House of Commons never speak in the Chamber. Their role is to maintain party discipline, to rate the performance of contributions (from both the front and back benches), and to spot up-and-coming talent suitable for promotion.

In the House of Lords their role is very different. Of course they still try and maintain discipline – although with no re-selection of re-election they have very few sanctions to deploy (other than the counter-productive withdrawal of the whip). Equally, they do try and ensure that government legislation is passed

– with as few amendments as possible. However, in the Upper House, they also reinforce government ministers, and act as frontbench spokespersons.

In the House of Lords there is one Chief Whip, one Deputy Chief Whip, and five Lords in Waiting and Baronesses in Waiting – or Whips. With the exception of the Chief Whip, all have to speak from the front benches in support of their overstretched ministerial colleagues. In some cases they have to speak to briefs prepared for them by up to five different government departments. Unlike in the Commons, it is not unusual for the government frontbench to admit to ignorance, and to promise to get back to the House with answers at a future date.

4.4.4 Queen's Speech

As we have seen, for historical reasons the monarch actually reads out his or her speech in the House of Lords – with the Commons summoned in to listen from the Bar of the House. In this respect, at least, the House of Lords has equality with (if not primacy over) the House of Commons.

Approximately half of the bills outlined in the Queen's Speech will begin their legislative journey in the House of Lords. This is so as to avoid a logjam in the middle of the session. If all bills started in the Commons, the Lords would have nothing to do at the start of the session, and be overloaded at the end of the session – and vice versa for the Commons. By dividing the bills more or less equally logjams should be avoided and the maximum time for scrutiny should – in theory at least – be preserved.

The convention is that only less political bills start their passage in the House of Lords. In fact the decisions on which bills begin where are made by the Whips of the three main parties from both Houses through the "usual channels".

As in the Commons four or five days of debate follows the Queen's Speech – and again they are grouped around broad themes. Unlike in the House of Commons, however, there is no vote at the end of the debate on the Queen's Speech in the House of Lords.

4.4.5 Select committees

The House of Lords select committee structure is radically different to the departmental structure which the House of Commons has adopted.

There are currently four main select committees in the House of Lords:

- European Union Committee
- Science and Technology Committee
- Constitution Committee
- Economic Affairs Committee

These committees can have any number of subcommittees. For instance, the European Union Committee has subcommittees on:

- Economic and Financial Affairs and International Trade
- Internal Market
- Foreign Affairs, Defence and Development Policy
- Environment and Agriculture
- Law and Institutions
- Home Affairs
- Social Policy and Consumer Affairs

The House of Lords also sets up ad hoc committees. These can be established either to look at a particular piece of legislation, or to look at a topical policy area. Quite often these policy areas have an ethical dimension. For instance in recent years select committees have been convened – and reports published – on assisted dieing (or euthanasia), abortion, animal experiments, stem cell research and the law of blasphemy. Generally these *ad hoc* committees are convened, take evidence and produce a report all during the course of a single session.

The House of Lords also has a range of committees dealing with legislation. These include committees on Delegated Powers and Regulatory Reform, Hybrid Instruments, Statutory Instruments, personal bills and private bills. These committees perform an invaluable function of closely scrutinising secondary legislation in a detailed manner, which the House of Commons does not always have time to undertake.

In order to help ensure that the Upper House functions efficiently there are also a series of House committees. These include an Administration and Works Committee, an Information Committee, a Liaison Committee, a Procedure Committee, a Refreshment Committee, a Selection Committee, a Works of Art Committee, and a Committee for Privileges.

Finally there are a range of joint committees set up with the House of Commons. Apart from APPGs (dealt with earlier) these are the only example of the two Houses working overtly together – or even acknowledging each other's existence. Current committees in this category are the Joint Committee on Consolidation Bills, the Joint Committee on Human Rights, and the Joint Committee on Statutory Instruments.

Whereas in the House of Commons only a small proportion of the most important select committee reports (chosen by the Liaison Committee) are debated, in the House of Lords all of them are. As with the Commons the government has undertaken to publish a response to all House of Lords select committee reports – usually within two months.

For the lobbyist the House of Lords select committees offer an opportunity to give evidence (or for their clients to give evidence) in a very civilised and non-confrontational environment. It should be noted, however, that the members of House of Lords select committees can be world experts in their fields, and any evidence (written or oral) has to be of the very highest standard.

Author's top tip

Other than their role as detailed scrutinisers of legislation, the House of Lords regards its select committees as the jewels in its crown. Their reports do help to shape government policy, and they often receive widespread media coverage – because of the many experts who sit in the Upper House and who make up the membership of its select committees.

4.4.6 Oral questions

Oral questions in the House of Lords are known as starred questions. This is because they appear in the Lords Minute and the Lords Order Paper with an asterisk against them – indicating that they are for oral (as opposed to written) answer.

There are up to four Starred Questions per sitting day, although (as with the Commons) if there is a Friday sitting oral questions are dispensed with. They are chosen by ballot, and then the name of the peers asking the questions and the text of the actual question are published in the Lords Minute up to a month ahead. These questions are taken at the start of business (after prayers), and questions are asked of Her Majesty's Government (HMG) as opposed to being asked of a particular departmental secretary of state, as is the case in the House of Commons.

In theory each of the four questions receives equal time for responses. In practice, if peers are obviously very interested in a particular question, exchanges can go on longer. Question time is in theory just half an hour – but again can over-run if one of the questions has attracted a lot of interest. The question is asked as it appears in the Order Paper, and is answered by a minister or Whip. The original asker then has a supplementary question (as in the House of Commons), and then other peers are free to join in. If questions and answers are kept short then as many as six – or even eight – other frontbench and backbench peers will have a chance to join in the exchanges.

The main difference in oral questions between the Commons and the Lords (apart from the nomenclature) is that it is generally not that difficult in the Upper House to get an oral question tabled, or for a peer to join the exchanges if he or she wishes to do so. Those wishing to table a starred question simply have to enter a ballot, and if they fail just re-enter until they succeed. Discourse tends to be much calmer in the Lords – exchanges are never heated, and party political point scoring is kept to a minimum.

Unlike in the Commons, government frontbenchers in the Lords are not afraid to admit they do not know the answer to a question. They merely apologise for the gap in their knowledge and the shortcoming of their brief, and promise to get back to the questioner. That is partly because of the less partisan atmosphere in the Lords, and partly because government frontbenchers have to cover so many departments and subject areas that it would be unreasonable to expect them to know everything about their wide-ranging briefs.

Anecdote

So inexperienced and inexpert are some government ministers or Whips in the Lords that it is not unknown for them to carry on reading out the wrong pre-prepared brief for several minutes without realising it. Sometimes it takes a jocular intervention from the opposition front bench to point the fact out!

4.4.7 Written questions

As with starred questions, questions for written answer in the Lords are addressed to HMG rather than a particular secretary of state or department. Written answers in the House of Lords are printed in the Lords *Hansard*, immediately after Written Ministerial Statements (which are copied from the Commons). The convention is that questions for written answer are responded to within a working week.

The main difference between questions for written answers in the Lords as compared with the Commons is simply one of numbers. Whereas it would be perfectly normal to have 300 written answers printed in the Commons *Hansard*, a more typical figure in the Lords would be 30. This is partly because peers tend to be part-time, and partly because they do not have the secretarial and research staff which MPs enjoy. Peers also eschew the kind of "round robin" questions which are routine in the Commons (asking every government department an identical question).

4.4.8 Debates

Apart from oral questions (dealt with above) and legislative debates (dealt with below) there are a wide range of types of debates in the House of Lords:

- Government motions: The government regularly initiates debates in the House of Lords on "take note" motions. These debates are usually on matters of topical domestic public policy or on foreign affairs. They often mirror similar debates which have been held in the Commons, so that the government can gauge opinion in both Houses. Sometimes these government inspired debates are tabled as motions for resolution and a vote is called.

- Opposition debates: These are normally held on a Thursday, when they are the main item of business. Generally these debates are not time limited – although on occasion the Leader of the House will announce a limitation, and the Lords have a convention that they rise at 10pm in any event.

- Backbench debates: Up until the spring recess there is a ballot for two 90 minute debates a month. Only backbenchers and crossbenchers enter the ballot.

- Select committees: There is an understanding in the Upper House that all House of Lords select committee reports should be debated. However, debates are often called at short notice, and may be of short duration.

- Unstarred questions: Unlike starred questions, these are short debates of one hour or 90 minutes. They are chosen by ballot, and take place either at the end of business (similar to a Commons adjournment debate) or during "pleasure" at 8pm (when most peers depart to have their dinner).

Debates in the House of Lords tend to be leisurely, scholarly and infinitely polite. Their main value is that the participants are very often experts in their fields. Although a substantial proportion of life peers are ex-MPs, many others are distinguished doctors, lawyers, academics and military men and women. Throw in a smattering of retired spooks, garnish with a few business tycoons and you have the makings of a very heavyweight discourse.

Author's top tip

Peers who wish to speak in a debate put their name forward and lists are compiled by the Whips Office. It is possible to obtain this speaking list from the Whips Office, the Lords Information Office or from the House of Lords website. This means that you can focus your lobbying efforts on those peers who are actually going to attend and speak.

4.4.9 Legislation

Legislation in the House of Lords has to go through exactly the same stages as it does in the Commons. The way in which some stages are treated, however, can be radically different. Before any bill can receive the Royal Assent and become an Act of Parliament it has to go through all of its stages in both Houses.

Contributor's top tip

The best way to get an amendment passed to a government bill is to forget about the House of Commons. In that House most of the time and on most issues there is a Government majority which tends to be wielded in an uncompromising way. However, in the Lords no party has a majority. This means that deal making and "horse-trading" is often the order of the day. On very controversial issues a Government of any party will want its way and may use its Commons majority with "ping pong" – or on rare occasions – the Parliament Act to force its legislation through. However, on many issues which do not involve matters of high principle the Government will prefer to compromise rather than use its parliamentary time fighting needless battles. The crucial way to convince the Government to do so is to ensure any amendment utilises what aficionados of the Lords call the "magic formula". That is, the amendment should be signed and supported by peers of all three major parties as well as by an influential crossbencher. Formal whipping is much less cohesive in the Lords and such a coalition will ensure that the government will listen, and very often concede an amendment without a vote.

Robert Khan, Head of Parliamentary and Public Affairs, Commission for Social Care Inspection

The House of Lords spends between 50-60% of its time scrutinising legislation. It tends to look at legislation in a technocratic – rather than political – way. The objective is usually simply to improve bills so that they make better Acts of Parliament. On fairly regular occasions, however, the Lords do try and make political points by amending and delaying legislation. During the 2001-2005 the government was defeated in the House of Lords on 245 occasions.

Here are the stages of legislation as they are undertaken in the upper House:

- First reading: A formality – as with the Commons

- Second reading: A wide-ranging debate on the general principles of the bill – identical to Commons procedure. Two weekends must have elapsed between first and second reading.

- Committee stage: This is the stage with the most radically different procedure. In the Lords most bills are taken in the Chamber and all peers may table amendments, speak, and vote. Since 1995 some less controversial bills are taken in Grand Committee in the Moses Room. Any peer may attend, table amendments and speak – but there are no facilities for voting divisions in the Moses Room (hence the reason that mainly uncontroversial bills are sent there). At least two weekends must have elapsed between second reading and committee stage.

- Report stage: Another chance for any peer who was not able to attend the committee stage (either in the Chamber or in the Moses Room) to table amendments. Again, at least two weekends should have elapsed between committee stage and report stage.

- Third reading: Unlike in the Commons, amendments can be tabled at this stage. However, they cannot be amendments which have been previously voted on. Third reading can follow immediately after report stage.

- Ping pong: Almost all bills are amended – sometimes substantially – by the House other than the one in which it originated. In theory a bill belongs to the House in which it started its progress, and that House has to agree to any amendments which the other house has made. Quite often there is no initial agreement, and amendments go backwards and forwards between the two Houses in a procedure which is colloquially known as "ping pong". Usually after two bouts of going backwards and forwards the Lords concede the point – three times indicates that the situation is serious. However, in 2005, on a matter of principle and constitutional importance (detention without trial) amendments went backwards and forwards between the two Houses a record seven times before the Lords finally relented and conceded.

The other big difference between the Commons and the Lords is that as well as all amendments being called and debated, there is no guillotine procedure or timetable motion in the Upper House and bills are not programmed. In theory this leaves bills vulnerable to filibustering, but this is frowned on in the Lords, and any peer trying to filibuster would undoubtedly be called to order by fellow peers.

As with non-legislative debates peers put their names down with the Whips Office to indicate that they wish to speak during the process of scrutinising legislation. Peers who do not put their names down can still speak – but only after named peers have had their say. If a very large number of peers put their names down to speak at a particular stage of a bill the time set aside for it is often extended.

As has been stated earlier the primacy of the House of Commons over the House of Lords was established early in the twentieth century – despite the latter being known as the Upper House. This legislative superiority was reinforced by the two Parliament Acts of 1911 and 1949. These prohibited the Lords from dealing in any meaningful way with money bills. These are bills (such as the Finance Bill) which deal primarily with financial matters. If the Lords do not – without having submitted them to any meaningful scrutiny – pass such bills within one month, they can receive Royal Assent without their approval.

The other main provisions of the two Parliament Acts are that the Lords are effectively barred from defeating government legislation. They can, of course, amend government bills – but as we have seen the Commons (where the government will nearly always have a majority) can insist on having its way. If, however, the Lords were to defeat a government bill, and refuse to back down, then under the terms of the Parliament Acts the government can re-introduce the same bill in the next session of parliament and, once passed again by the Commons, it will receive Royal Assent whether the Lords approve it or not. This, in effect, gives the Lords the ability to delay legislation, but not to veto it. The only proviso is that there has to be a period of at least twelve months between the initial second reading in the Commons and the third reading second time around.

The only exemption from the two Parliament Acts would be a bill to extend the life of a parliament beyond the maximum five years. This would need the agreement of both Houses (and the monarch), otherwise a government with a majority in the Commons could maintain an effective dictatorship.

The Lords are well aware that they have no electoral mandate, and that the will of the Commons should – in all normal circumstances – prevail. If nothing else, any thwarted government could simply nominate hundreds of new life peers and swamp the Upper House. This acknowledgement of the primacy of the Commons gave birth to the Salisbury Convention in 1945. It was brokered by the Conservative leader in the Upper House at the time (Lord Salisbury) when the Labour Party had just won the general election and there were concerns that the Conservatives would use their majority in the Upper House to thwart their manifesto. Under the Salisbury Convention, peers are committed not to vote against a government bill at the crucial second reading stage – provided that the bill in question reflects a manifesto commitment.

From a lobbyist's point of view it is often far easier to get a bill amended in the Lords than it is in the Commons. This is partly because procedures are more relaxed, but also because no party has an overall majority. Opposition frontbenchers are also severely under-resourced, and that usually means that they welcome briefings from lobbyists representing external interested parties.

Author's top tip

Backbench peers often table amendments at committee stage, but withdraw them before a vote is moved. This is partly to spare peers (who are often elderly) from voting frequently, and partly because they only tabled the amendment to "test the water". Sometimes, however, it is because they want to re-table the amendment at report stage or third reading – and could not do so if it had already been voted on at committee stage.

Contributor's top tip

Public affairs professionals would be wise to take the House of Lords seriously and regard its members as important target audiences for well-researched, properly thought-through briefing activity. With no party or grouping having more than 30 per cent of the membership, and much more relaxed systems of whipping, it is possible to win not just the debate, but also the vote in the House of Lords, particularly at the report stage of bills (divisions on second reading are unknown, and in committee increasingly rare). Half the government defeats tend to be reversed in the Commons, but with the remainder the government will often modify its legislation to take account of the Lords' concerns.

Do not forget, however, that under the present arrangements, the Lords accept that the Commons have the last word. Do not lose sight of the need to win the argument there too. Issues which the Lords take particularly seriously are civil and human rights matters (detention without trial, trial by jury etc) and issues where the Commons did not have the opportunity or the inclination to discuss them thoroughly. The Lords' membership is drawn from the highest echelons of public life – senior civil servants, the military, university vice-chancellors, heads of

Royal Colleges etc – so there are likely to be experts in most fields of activity. They are the ones who are listened to most. Above all, be selective in the choice of peers to contact – scatter-gun email distribution or mass mailings are most unproductive.

Lord Faulkner of Worcester

Contributor's top tip

- Do not forget the Lords is different. You can win votes. Bills are debated at length, but build your case on evidence and logic, not emotion.

- Decide on the key objectives first. Do you want clarification, a ministerial assurance, a new provision or an amendment?

- Then decide on the best way of delivering it and adjust your tactics accordingly.

- Remember that the Lords is populated by former regulators, senior civil service, top of their career legal and accountancy professionals, scientists, academics etc. Make sure you both recognise and mobilise that specialist knowledge.

- It may be the soft way – relying on the art of persuasion and ministerial openness to argument by asking a crossbencher or Labour backbencher with expertise and credibility to put the argument/put down amendments.

- Or the hard way: a campaign by Tory or Lib Dem frontbenchers which starts with questioning but becomes increasingly threatening as the bill moves from speeches at second reading through debates at committee stage to votes at report and third reading.

- Or a mixture of these at different stages of the bill.

- Make sure that key peers share your desire to achieve these objectives by building enthusiasm well before the bill gets to the Lords.

- Work with allies where you can, especially where they have strong existing relationships.

Lord Clement-Jones, DLA Piper Government Relations

Contributor's top tip

I always advised clients (when I had a real job, outside the Palace of Westminster) of three golden rules of effective political influence:

1. Any MP who has time for lunch is not worth spending time and effort on, let alone a good lunch.

2. Any communication – however inadequately argued, designed or timed – which comes from a constituency address will always get preferential attention compared with even the glossiest nationally-produced publication.

3. Every single peer has more influence as an individual than the average backbench MP. Because no Government will ever again have a built-in majority in the Upper House, even when we achieve democratic reform, ministers here have to listen to each and every member. Every peer can participate in every stage of legislation, so it follows that there are many more opportunities to influence decisions with non-partisan, well-informed contributions. That is certainly not the case in most bill committee stages in the House of Commons.

Lord Tyler

Part Five –
Lobbying Other UK
Institutions

5.1 Scottish Parliament

When the Labour Party won the 1997 general election the newly-elected prime minister Tony Blair immediately began the process of implementing manifesto commitments to introduce devolution in Scotland and Wales.

The original pledge to set up a Scottish Parliament and Welsh Assembly had been made by Tony Blair's predecessor, John Smith. Smith was a Scot who represented a Scottish seat in Monklands East. He led the Labour Party from Neil Kinnock's resignation in 1992 up until his premature death of a heart attack in 1994. He was succeeded by Tony Blair, who – although born and educated in Scotland – represented Sedgefield in the north east of England.

Tony Blair's landslide victory in 1997 gave him the mandate and the impetus to introduce constitutional change. This was strongly reaffirmed in a referendum held in the same year. Almost three-quarters of those who voted did so in favour of devolution. The 1998 Scotland Act led to the formation of the Scottish Parliament – or rather its reintroduction, as there had been a Scottish Parliament up until the time of the Act of Union in 1707.

Under the provisions of the 1998 Scotland Act the new Scottish Parliament had 129 members. Of these, 73 represented constituencies, whilst another 56 were elected through the medium of a regional list. List Members of the Scottish Parliament (MSPs) were elected under the additional member system (AMS) of proportional representation on regions based on European Parliament constituencies. If a constituency vacancy occurs, it is filled by means of a by-election. If a regional seat vacancy arises, it is filled by the highest placed, non-elected person on that party's list who is willing to serve.

The main difference between the Holyrood and Westminster is that the former is unicameral – that is to say there is no second chamber in Holyrood. Another significant difference is that the terms of the Scottish Parliament are fixed at four years. In highly exceptional circumstances, the monarch can accede to a request for a dissolution and an emergency general election has to be held. In both of the first two elections in 1999 and 2003 the result was a Labour and Lib Dem coalition, with Labour the largest party on both occasions. In 2007 the SNP emerged as the largest party (albeit by just one seat) and its leader Alex Salmond decided to form a minority administration.

Warning!

From the time that the SNP formed its minority administration in 2007 the Scottish Executive started to become known as the Scottish Government. The new first minister, Mr Alex Salmond, was of the opinion that the term Scottish Executive did not convey sufficient authority, and he let it be known that henceforward his administration should be referred to as the Scottish Government. The Scottish Executive still has legal standing under the 1998 Act, and MSPs still (for instance) table questions to the Scottish Executive, but the term Scottish Government is now almost universally used elsewhere.

Author's top tip

Because regional list MSPs do not have constituency casework to contend with they are likely to be less busy than those who are elected for constituencies. They are also accustomed to having their efficacy and legitimacy unfavourably compared with those MSPs who are directly elected to constituencies. If you lobby them and persuade them to take up your case, they are likely to have more time and enthusiasm to pursue it energetically.

Contributor's top tip

Westminster is great, but do not forget the rest of the country!

Too many lobbyists think that you can be effective in the Westminster bubble without ever leaving it.

It is sometimes fashionable to dismiss the politics of nations, regions and constituencies as "small fry", which leads lobbyists to fear ever leaving SW1. Well, get over it!

Devolved and local governments do not just matter because of the decisions that they can take in their own patches. They can be the best allies a lobbyist could ever have for the decisions you are pressing for at a national level.

If you are lobbying on a policy area that has national or regional implications (and let's face it, almost every one does) then think about the parts of the country that will benefit, or may be damaged. And then get out there and talk to them! Find the articulate local politicians and officials and involve them in your campaign.

More often than not you will be helping them to be seen fighting for their local interests, and meanwhile your campaign gains an authority and legitimacy that is simply priceless.

Sacha Deshmukh, Chief Executive, Mandate Communications

5.1.1 Powers

The powers devolved to the Scottish Parliament are granted specifically within the terms of the Scotland Act 1998. In theory that Act could be revoked and those powers withdrawn – although it is very hard to envisage the circumstances under which that might occur. The main features to distinguish a Parliament from an Assembly are the right to initiate primary legislation, and the right to raise revenue. The Scottish Parliament has both of these powers – but the degree to which they can be applied is constrained.

Warning!

Very early on after the re-formation of the Scottish Parliament and the setting up of the Scottish Executive, Scotland suffered its first lobbying scandal. Employees of an Edinburgh public relations firm were taped by an *Observer* journalist (who was posing as a potential client) boasting of their close contacts with the Labour Party and the Scottish Executive. The firm claimed to be able to access and change the diaries of ministers. This led to a string of related stories and the setting up of an official inquiry. As a result, Holyrood has been slightly wary of lobbyists ever since.

Under the provisions of the Scotland Act large areas of competency are reserved for the Westminster Parliament. The Act sets out specifically what Scotland cannot do, listing what is reserved, and operating on the basis that what is not reserved is devolved. Reserved powers mainly relate to UK-wide policy areas, or to those which stray in to the international arena. Specifically excluded matters include:

- Foreign policy
- Defence and national security
- Economic and monetary affairs
- Large scale energy projects
- Constitutional matters
- Immigration and nationality

Equally, there are policy areas which are specifically devolved to the Scottish Parliament and the Scottish Government. These include:

- Health and social services
- Education and training
- Local government and the environment
- Housing and planning
- Legal system, police and prisons
- Tourism, sports and the arts
- Economic development

There are inevitably occasions where the devolved competence and legislative competence of the Scottish Parliament and the Scottish Executive are not clear-cut. Examples include energy (reserved) and renewable energy and climate change (devolved). You can have a policy to build more power stations (reserved) but you may not get them built as planning is devolved. Under those circumstances there are mechanisms for resolving disputes. Generally discussions between the secretary of state for Scotland and the first minister result in issues being quietly resolved. There are also concordats between Whitehall departments and their Edinburgh equivalents demarking areas of responsibility where disputes have arisen or where it has been perceived that they might arise.

The advent of Sewel Motions have shown that Westminster and Whitehall are reluctant to get into a turf war with Holyrood. Under the Sewel Convention

Westminster ministers undertook not to legislate on devolved matters without the prior agreement of the Scottish Parliament. Under a process known as "executive devolution" the Westminster Parliament can devolve specific functions which are technically reserved competencies to the Scottish Parliament.

If necessary, ultimate arbitration in any disputes which cannot be resolved through routine channels lies with the two bodies' respective law officers, and ultimately with the Privy Council.

Contributor's top tip

Get the Language right.

MSPs are quick to highlight cases where lobbyists use Westminster terminology – or simply get the names wrong. It is the quickest way to appear an outsider – and end up lampooned in *The Scotsman* diary.

The biggest offence is to refer to the Scottish Parliament as an Assembly. The Scottish Parliament is very conscious of its elevated legislative status over its Welsh and Northern Ireland counterparts.

The second common error is to confuse the Scottish Parliament and the Scottish Government (the Scottish Executive as was). It is surprising how often this happens.

If you are referring to a UK minister, committee or organisation you should always make this clear. Just referring to the "health secretary" when you mean the UK secretary of state will not win friends. Members of the Scottish cabinet are called cabinet secretaries, by the way.

Similarly make sure that you are clear about the names and responsibilities of the wide range of Scottish agencies and NDPBS – and do not assume that the writ of their English equivalents runs in Scotland.

Ian Coldwell, Managing Director, Pagoda Public Relations

5.1.2 First Minister

The office of first minister is the Scottish equivalent of prime minister. He (and so far there has been no female first minister) must be appointed within 14 days of a Scottish general election, or of a vacancy occurring.

In order to become first minister an individual has to win a vote in the Scottish Parliament. The first minister will, therefore, generally be drawn from the largest party. The Presiding Officer will recommend the appointment, which is technically sanctioned by the sovereign. Under exceptional circumstances the 14 day limit can be stretched beyond that period, but if it goes beyond 28 days then a new general election has to be held.

The first minister represents Scotland in negotiations with the United Kingdom government. He also represents Scotland in the European Union (though his ministers must seek the agreement of their UK counterparts before they can hold discussions on EU policies such as fishing), and in meetings with non UK and non EU governments and bodies. However, as has already been stated, foreign relations is one of the key policy areas reserved to Westminster.

The main function of the first minister is to appoint cabinet ministers and deputy ministers. Together, the first minister, cabinet secretaries and deputy ministers make up what is officially termed, under the provisions of the Scotland Act, the Scottish Executive. The Scottish Executive is, in turn, accountable to the Scottish Parliament.

Contributor's top tip

Scotland is a small country and the typical key influencers are pretty much known to each other. In this atmosphere advocacy is a very powerful tool. To get traction on an issue you need a coalition of activists who are prepared to talk about your issue or idea. By mobilising advocates you can create an unstoppable momentum. In a minority Parliament such as we have now, it is crucial to get the whole spectrum of public policy organisations involved.

Helping MSPs do their jobs better is always a good way to get your point across. Make sure you send them briefings in advance of relevant debates – make it clear and easy to lift the information into speech notes. Networking is crucial. Through involvement in policy, business and political networks you will build an understanding of how the various strands of Scottish public life come together. If you are involved in that then it becomes much easier to identify and influence your advocates.

Moray Macdonald, Deputy Managing Director, Weber Shandwick

5.1.3 Cabinet

The Scottish cabinet is much smaller than its Westminster counterpart. This is mainly because the Scottish Parliament is so much smaller than Westminster – with less than a fifth of the number of Members. It is also because, as has been seen, significant areas of policy are still reserved to the United Kingdom Parliament.

The current minority SNP administration was elected with just 47 MSPs in total – including both constituency and regional list members. This means that it does not have a large talent pool from which to draw its cabinet secretaries from. The current cabinet consists of just:

- First minister
- Deputy first minister and cabinet secretary for health and wellbeing
- Cabinet secretary for finance and sustainable growth
- Cabinet secretary for education and lifelong learning
- Cabinet secretary for justice
- Cabinet secretary for rural affairs and the environment

Contributor's top tip

Devolution in the late 1990s transformed the political landscape of the UK, forcing organisations and lobbyists to review their approach to influencing public policy and the legislative process. The Scottish Executive and Parliament, and Welsh Government and Assembly initially went through a rather insular phase in which they shunned anyone with an 0207 number, and attempting to influence the devolved legislatures from London was difficult and somewhat futile.

Despite this initial hostility, recent years have seen the Celtic legislatures mature in their outlook with decision-makers and political-influencers adopting a more pragmatic approach. It is now possible to make significant progress in Holyrood, the Senedd and Stormont – everyone seems more accessible, and they are interested in what you have to offer, regardless of where you are based. A "one-size fits all" approach won't work and you have to be clever to ensure your campaign has traction and your messages resonate. It's not as simple as taking your

---

policy blueprint and adding a tartan flourish to the front cover – we need to be mindful that structures and policies are very different. Lobbyists are increasingly targeting the devolved regions and we need to continue chasing the decision-makers, wherever they may be.

John Lehal, Managing Director, Insight Public Affairs

5.1.4 Legislation

There are a number of similarities and differences between the legislative processes in Holyrood and Westminster.

Although each parliament is formally opened by the sovereign, the legislative programme for each session in Holyrood is outlined in the first minister's legislative programme speech.

As with Westminster, there are several different types of bills. The main types of public bills are:

- Executive bills: These are Scottish Executive bills introduced by the governing party, coalition or minority government.

- Committee bills: Unlike in Westminster, committees of the Scottish Parliament can actually propose bills. However, they have to be agreed by the Parliament and taken up by the Executive.

- Members' bills: These are bills introduced by backbench MSPs. Any MSPs may introduce up to two bills in any one session. In order to progress, however, such bills must have the support of at least 11 other MSPs.

Other types of public bill are:

- Emergency bill: These can only be introduced by the Executive and can – in theory – go through all the required stages in a single day.

- Budget Bills: These are bills to amend a previous Budget Act, or to authorise payments out of the Scottish Consolidated Fund, or to authorise direct payments of funds which would normally be paid into the Scottish Consolidated Fund.

- Consolidation bills, statute law revision bills, repeal bills: These are generally just procedural and housekeeping exercises ensuring that the Statute Book does not get clogged up with redundant pieces of legislation.

Before a bill is introduced the Presiding Officer must certify that it falls within the competence of the Scottish Parliament. It must also be accompanied by a financial memorandum detailing the potential costs associated with the bill. Finally, all bills must be accompanied by a memorandum which sets out in layman's terms:

- Its policy objectives

- What consideration has been given to any alternatives

- Details of all consultations which have been undertaken

- Assessments of its likely impact on human rights, equal opportunities, sustainable development and any stakeholder bodies (local authorities etc)

Author's top tip

If the memorandum accompanying a bill suggests that wide consultation has not been undertaken it can be challenged on that basis – either in the Scottish Parliament or in the courts.

If a bill is voted down it is obviously defeated. However, it also falls if at any division less than 25% of MSPs participate. If it is not passed by the end of a session, it equally falls. Because the Scottish Parliament is unicameral, there is no doubling-up of the process as occurs when the House of Commons and the House of Lords both consider a bill at Westminster.

The stages of a public bill in the Scottish Parliament are:

- Introduction: Purely formal.

- Printing: The bill and all accompanying documents are printed and published.

- Stage one: The parliamentary bureau refers the bill to a lead committee. Other committees may also consider the bill, but they are not required to do so. The lead committee then considers the general principles of the bill, and refers it back to a plenary session for agreement in principle.

- Stage two: This is where the bill is considered in detail. It can be taken as a committee of the whole Parliament, referred back to the original lead committee, referred to another committee, or split between two or more committees. Amendments are then tabled and considered. If the bill is amended, it is reprinted at the end of this stage.

- Stage three: This stage takes place with Parliament in plenary session. Amendments are tabled and decided upon. A bill can be sent back to committee for re-consideration, but generally once amendments have been processed the bill as it now stands is debated, and a vote is taken as to whether or not it should be passed.

- Royal Assent: As with the Westminster Parliament, all bills must receive the Royal Assent before becoming Acts of the Scottish Parliament.

There are also two different types of private bills:

- Local bills

- Personal bills

These types of bill can only be introduced on specified days in March and November and must be introduced by outside interests known as promoters. They are initially referred to a private bills committee before being referred back to Parliament in plenary session. They then go through the same stages as public bills.

The Scottish Parliament also deals with subordinate legislation – similar in principle to Statutory Instruments at Westminster. There are two basic procedures for dealing with this type of secondary legislation:

- Negative procedure: Any Member can propose a motion to the lead committee that a Statutory Instrument should not make further progress. This must be done within 40 days of it being introduced. The lead committee can then endorse this proposal and report it to Parliament in plenary session. If no such motion is received and endorsed then the instrument automatically comes into force after 40 days.

- Positive procedure: Under this procedure Parliament must actively consider and endorse an instrument before it can be brought into force. Again the time limit within which this has to occur is 40 days.

Where Scotland is different is that the lead committee can scrutinise subordinate legislation placed before it and can call witnesses where they believe the legislation is controversial or departs from the general approach of the primary legislation concerned.

Contributor's top tip

Invest in a little local knowledge to understand the differences and adapt to them. It will be appreciated and the return of goodwill on this investment will give you an advantage.

In 1999 many firms came north to impose a London PA business model on an emerging Edinburgh market. This failed in most cases, as did the journalists and PR firms who "changed codes" in search of some easy pickings, because the margins and market simply couldn't sustain them.

Those who have survived and flourished understand the nature of this still-emerging market. They have adapted to suit this, and they have also been prepared to give their clients the advice that the old Westminster conventions simply do not hold true here.

Don't talk about select committees, private members' bills or EDMs in the Scottish context as you'll simply show your ignorance. Invest in someone who knows the scene and heed their advice.

Alastair Ross, Director of Public Policy, McGrigors LLP

5.1.5 Committees

As has been seen committees in the Scottish Parliament play a central role in scrutinising legislation.

As well as this legislative role, however, they also mirror the roles of select committees in the Westminster Parliament. They hold inquiries, shadow Scottish Government ministers and departments, and interrogate witnesses. As with their Westminster counterparts the committees of the Scottish Parliament mirror the responsibilities of the cabinet ministers they shadow:

- Economy, Energy and Tourism
- Education, Lifelong Learning and Culture
- Health and Sport
- Justice
- Local Government and Communities

- Rural Affairs and the Environment
- Transport, Infrastructure and Climate Change

These committees meet weekly or fortnightly, usually on a Tuesday or a Wednesday morning. Their meetings are usually open to the public, and they are normally held in the committee rooms at Holyrood. They do, however, occasionally go on tour and hold meetings outside of Edinburgh. Each committee has a convener and deputy convener. Around 30 inquiries are held every session.

As well as these subject committees there are also a range of mandatory committees. The need for these was established with the original Scotland Act, and motions to set them up are passed at the beginning of each parliament.

The mandatory committees are:

- Audit
- Equal Opportunities
- European and External Affairs
- Finance
- Public Petitions
- Standards, Procedure and Public Appointments
- Subordinate Legislation

Author's top tip

Committees of the Scottish Parliament combine the functions of both select and standing committees in the House of Commons. They shadow government departments and scrutinise legislation. It is therefore doubly worthwhile cultivating relevant committees and establishing good working relations with their members.

5.1.6 Oral questions

MSPs must "lodge" questions with the Chamber Desk either in person or by email. If they are lodged by email the email address must be the MSP's accredited email address. If lodged before 4.30pm questions are printed in the following day's Business Bulletin.

Questions must be addressed either to the Scottish Executive (as the Scottish Government is still referred to in this context), or to the Scottish Parliamentary Corporate Body. Oral Questions are answered on just one day a week, when parliament is in session. They are lodged to be answered at either general question time, or themed question time, or first minister's question time. Question time is normally held on a Thursday, with general question time taking place between 11.40am-12pm, first minister's question time taking place between 12pm-12.30pm, and themed question time taking place between 2.15-2.55pm.

Questions to the Scottish Parliamentary Corporate Body are only answered three times a year. Very occasionally an emergency oral question to the Scottish Executive will be allowed. If it is allowed it is lodged and answered on the same day.

In terms of admissibility, the first requirement is that questions should relate to policy areas for which the Scottish Executive has responsibility. Questions should also be concise and clear, and not replicate a question which has already been asked in the last six months. Questions should also be just that – they should be seeking information, and not just making a statement dressed up as a question.

Questions for oral answer have to be lodged in a window between two and three weeks prior to the relevant question time. They are then subject to a random electronic shuffle, and the first ten names selected are printed in the Business Bulletin. Three lists are printed, with MSPs asking general questions, themed questions, and questions to the first minister. Once an MSP has been selected to ask a question he or she is automatically excluded from asking another oral question on that day.

Unlike in the Westminster Parliament MSPs asking an oral question must read out the full text of the question. Once that initial question has been answered, the original questioner is entitled to at least one supplementary question. On occasion, at the discretion of the Presiding Officer, the original questioner can even ask a further supplementary question. Other MSPs are then allowed to ask supplementary questions, provided that they are on the same theme.

There are different rules for the lodging of questions to the first minister. They too can be tabled immediately after the previous question and answer session. However, in order to ensure that there is more topicality with these questions, they can also be lodged as close as three days before first minister's question time.

All exchanges during oral question sessions are printed in full in the Official Report. Any questions for oral answer which are not reached receive a written answer. They are then published in the Written Answers Report.

As with the Westminster Parliament oral question time does represent one of the best opportunities for MSPs to not just question the first minister and cabinet ministers, but to press them hard. For the lobbyist, the same applies. If you can get an MSP to table a question, and he or she is lucky in the shuffle, you can get your issue raised at peak parliamentary time. The minister has to answer the question and defend his or her position, and the response is very much on the record.

5.1.7 Written questions

There are no limits to the number of questions for written answer which an MSP can lodge. The convention is that all such questions should be answered within ten counting days (days when the Chamber Desk is open).

Ministers can send Members holding answers, promising to answer as soon as possible. All answers are sent direct to the MSP who asked the question, and also to the Chamber Desk so that they can be incorporated into the Written Answers Report. They are also posted on the Scottish Parliament's website.

Questions are normally lodged for written answer because they are seeking information. So if an MSP is seeking detailed information or statistics, he or she would not waste a precious slot tabling a question for oral answer. Lobbyists seeking the kind of information which the Scottish Executive will almost certainly have – but has not necessarily published – can try and find a sympathetic MSP to ask the question for them.

5.1.8 Motions

Motions in the Scottish Parliament are similar to Early Day Motions (EDMs) in the Westminster Parliament. An MSP will table a Motion, and other MSPs can either add their names – or table an amendment. Whenever new names are added or an amendment is made the Motion is reprinted. As at Westminster, the subjects can be as trivial as the success of a local football team, or as vital as the financial predicament of cancer sufferers.

There is, however, one big difference between a Scottish Parliament Motion and a Westminster Parliament EDM. Whereas an EDM is never debated at Westminster, a Scottish Parliament Motion can be eligible for consideration to be debated if the MSP tabling it signals at the start that it is potentially a Motion for debate as Member's Business. Cross-party support is however always required for this.

As at Westminster Motions are an extremely valuable lobbying tool. They enable lobbyists to gauge support for (and opposition to) a particular cause, and they highlight that cause to the Scottish Executive. They have the added bonus that – provided they get widespread support – they can actually be debated.

5.1.9 Petitions

From its initial formation the Scottish Parliament instituted a system for receiving and examining public petitions.

Any Scot (other than MSPs themselves) can petition the Parliament on any subject which is within its competence. Most petitions urge the Parliament to use its influence to persuade the Scottish Government to change its policies – or to apply them in a different way. Petitions must not relate to issues which are within the remit of the Westminster Parliament, or the courts. They must also not relate to commercial issues.

As with motions, some petitions deal with very local issues, whilst others deal with issues which have a national impact. Petitions remain open for as long as the committee feels it has not completed its consideration of them. There are some open petitions that are more than six months old, while others are closed much more quickly. The Public Petitions Committee meets once a fortnight, and examines around half a dozen petitions per meeting. The main petitioners are sometimes actually invited to appear before the committee – which is a great opportunity to make their case in person. Otherwise they can be invited to submit written evidence in support of their petition. The committee can also seek written submissions from other interested parties, call the relevant minister to give evidence or pass it to another committee for consideration and a report back.

There is also a facility on the Scottish Parliament website for the setting up of electronic petitions. Although less formal than traditional hard-copy petitions, these can attract many more signatories, as viral e-marketing can significantly boost take-up.

The Scottish Parliament itself describes the petitioning process as a means by which the Scottish public can directly influence MSPs – and the legislative process. This also applies, of course, to lobbies. Starting a petition, building up the signatory list, and aiming to get it examined by the Public Petitions Committee, is a very worthwhile – if somewhat protracted – lobbying exercise.

Contributor's top tip

If you are going to engage with Scottish politicians then you need to recognise the differences between Edinburgh and Westminster. It is all too easy to spot a lobbyist or consultant with scant knowledge of the Scottish system when they use the wrong terms, do not know the names of key players or are unaware of what is happening on the ground.

It is also obvious when organisations have come to Edinburgh and expect to "do Scotland in day" before travelling back to their HQ. We're not saying we should be your most important audience always, but put the preparation in and make sure you are not completing a tick-box exercise otherwise you will probably do your reputation more harm than good.

Get used to a whole new way of doing politics – a four party system, a nationalist government, a minority government and fluid parliamentary coalitions. It all gives plenty of scope for an organisation to get its point across as long as you do your homework before you get here.

Shirley-Anne Somerville – MSP for Lothians

5.2 Scottish Government

Under the terms of the 1998 Act, the Scottish Executive is the official term applied to the first minister, deputy first minister, five cabinet secretaries, ten ministers and two law officers operating within the Scottish Parliament.

Since the SNP won the most seats in the 2007 election, and formed a minority administration, the term Scottish Government has been in more widespread use. First Minister Alex Salmond was of the opinion that the term "Executive" was derogatory, and did not convey the full powers and status of the body.

In a coalition – which is what occurred when the first two Scottish Executives were formed – the first minister could be expected to be from the party with the largest number of seats in the Scottish Parliament, with the second placed party being given the chance to nominate the deputy first minister. Currently, the deputy first minister is also a cabinet secretary with responsibility for a department in the Scottish Government.

As is the case in Westminster and Whitehall, cabinet secretaries in Holyrood are assisted by politically attuned advisers. Their titles vary, but they are known as Political Advisers, Senior Special Advisers and Special Advisers. Some of these will have expertise in specific policy areas, whilst others will simply be close to the cabinet secretary they advise – both politically and personally. The first minister also has an adviser whose specific task it is to ensure that his media appearances proceed smoothly and show him in a favourable light – although his official spokesperson is a senior civil service media officer.

Author's top tip

As with Westminster and Whitehall, Special Advisers in Edinburgh play a vital role as ministerial sounding-boards and gatekeepers. They are also generally happy to meet with lobbyists, and to hold discussions off the record.

After devolution the former departments of the Scottish Office were reorganised and placed under the authority of the Scottish Executive under the supervision of the Scottish Parliament. As with Whitehall, departments within what is now known as the Scottish Government can be reorganised in order to reflect the priorities of the first minister.

The main departments within the Scottish Government under the current SNP minority administration are:

- Finance and Sustainable Growth

- Education and Lifelong Learning

- Health and Well-being

- Justice

- Rural Affairs and the Environment

Under the cabinet secretaries there are ministers responsible for more specific policy areas. Again, under the current SNP administration these are:

- Minister for parliamentary business

- Minister for Europe, external affairs and culture

- Minister for enterprise, energy and tourism

- Minister for transport, infrastructure and climate change

- Minister for children and early years

- Minister for schools and skills

- Minister for public health

- Minister for communities and sport

- Minister for community safety

- Minister for environment

Additionally, there are two law officers. Their titles are:

- Lord Advocate

- Solicitor General

The job of the Scottish Government is to effectively manage the policy areas devolved to it. But it is also to manage the income which is remitted to Scotland by the Westminster government. As has been pointed out the Scottish Parliament has a theoretical ability to raise revenue itself. The original Scotland Act gave it the power to vary the basic rate of income tax by plus or minus three percent. In fact, this power has never been exercised – either way.

So in fact, without exercising that variance power, revenue to the Scottish Government is restricted mainly to that remitted to it by Westminster. In common with other devolved administrations, this is decided by a formula named after then Treasury minister Joel Barnett – now Lord Barnett. This Barnett Formula aligns revenue to Scotland, Wales and Northern Ireland roughly with that in England. However, traditionally, there has always been a small (but over time significant) uplift to Scotland, Wales and Northern Ireland in order to take account of certain regional and social challenges.

The main power of the devolved Scottish Government is to decide how that block grant is allocated within Scotland. In rough terms two thirds of public expenditure in Scotland is dispensed by the Scottish Government. Decisions on expenditure naturally reflect the Scottish Government's political priorities as outlined in its manifesto. Inevitably, there is also always half an eye kept on developing and implementing priorities which will maximise their chances of getting re-elected at the next general election.

Over the years this freedom to dispense the block grant allocated from Westminster has enabled successive administrations in Scotland to develop and implement policies which are significantly at variance with those of the government in Westminster. As a result, Scottish university students do not have to pay tuition fees as do their English counterparts. The social care packages for the elderly and infirm in Scotland are far more generous than they are in England, with free personal care available. Prescription charges have also been cut, and the plan is to phase them out by 2011.

In summary the main functions of the Scottish Government can be seen as:

- Implementing the policy priorities of the first minister and his cabinet

- Dispensing expenditure from the Scottish Consolidated Fund – currently some £30bn

- Administering policy in all areas devolved to Scotland under the 1998 Scotland Act – such as health, education, transport, rural affairs and justice

Contributor's top tip

Using the Media to Influence Holyrood

There are more newspapers per capita in Scotland than anywhere else in the world. And yet we are a small country, albeit a great one. Despite the proliferation of papers, within the political and media spheres everyone knows everyone else and you need only look at the backgrounds of our MSPs to see that the worlds of media and politics, and actually public affairs too, overlap considerably.

To be effective, lobbying in Scotland has to be part of an integrated campaign (given the "puddle sized" society in which we live). This does not mean, however, that the public affairs world is unsophisticated – far from it. We have seen powerful campaigns since 1999, and Scotland has been ahead of the UK on some significant pieces of legislation. When putting together any campaign, media must be the first port of call, and giving a brief to a leading column writer on *The Scotsman* can often have more influence overall than getting your point into a high profile committee report. Although doing both is not a bad idea!

Angela Casey, Managing Director, CM Porter Novelli

5.3 Scotland Office

Despite devolution, and the setting up of a Scottish Parliament and Scottish Executive, the role of secretary of state for Scotland still exists. It is, however, a much diminished role, and it has become the practice that the secretary of state for Scotland role is a bolt-on to the day job of a member of the cabinet.

The role of the secretary of state for Scotland can be summarised as:

- Maintaining a good working relationship with the first minister, his cabinet and ministers, and the Scottish Parliament.

- Representing the interests of Scotland in cabinet.

- Representing Scotland in the EU and overseas in areas which are outside of the competence of the Scottish Government and Parliament.

- Answering oral questions on non-devolved Scottish matters once a month in the House of Commons.

- Acting as the guardian of the devolution settlement.

Politically, the secretary of state for Scotland (who is always likely to be a Scot) is also expected to keep the prime minister, the cabinet and the Whips informed as to sentiment north of the border. The Labour Party has traditionally been very well represented amongst MPs sitting for Scottish seats, and they make up a vital component of that party's majority. For the Conservatives, relations with Scotland have been troubled since the days of Margaret Thatcher. When the Conservatives do return to power the role of secretary of state for Scotland will be a vital – and difficult – one.

5.4 Scottish Affairs Select Committee

Westminster's Scottish Affairs Select Committee is made up of 11 MPs. Like all select committees, its make-up broadly reflects the political complexion of the House of Commons. Most of its members either represent a Scottish seat, or they are themselves Scots, or have a Scottish heritage.

The primary remit of the Scottish Affairs Select Committee is to shadow the Scotland Office. It monitors the expenditure, policies and administration of the Scotland Office – including its relations with the Scottish Parliament and the Scottish Government.

The committee is careful not to transgress into the remit of the Scottish Parliament. Recent reports have dealt with issues such as fisheries, the oil industry and child poverty.

5.5 Scottish Grand Committee

The Scottish Grand Committee is made up of all 59 Scottish MPs. It can meet in Westminster, or anywhere in Scotland.

In the past the Scottish Grand Committee has met to consider Scottish bills which have been referred to it at the second reading – general principle – stage. However, since the formation of the Scottish Parliament, the Grand Committee has met less and less frequently, and in recent years it has not met at all.

Author's top tip

The 59 Westminster MPs representing Scottish seats are comparatively under-employed. Scottish debates and oral question sessions are rare, and only a small proportion of these MPs can sit on the Scottish Affairs Select Committee. This means that they have time to take up causes and issues, and it makes them well worthwhile lobbying – on both Scottish and UK-wide issues.

Contributor's top tip

When dealing with Government make sure what you are suggesting fits in with one of the Scottish Government's 5 strategic objectives, which are for a:

1. Wealthier and fairer Scotland

2. Healthier Scotland

3. Safer and stronger Scotland

4. Smarter Scotland

5. Greener Scotland

It also helps if you are from one of their priority sectors: life sciences, financial services and renewable energy.

Beyond that, be clear in your own mind what is devolved to Scotland and what is reserved to Westminster. You lose arguments quickly if you start talking about English/Welsh influence on health, education or environment policy, or any of the bodies running them in Whitehall, as ministers would like to think that their policies in these devolved areas are entirely different to those elsewhere.

Also, remember that Scottish civil servants are not allowed to talk to their Whitehall counterparts without seeking permission – so do not assume they know what is going on south of the other side of the border!

John Macgill, Director, Morhamburn

5.6 National Assembly For Wales

The National Assembly for Wales (or Welsh Assembly as it is more commonly referred to) was set up at the same time and under similar proceedings as those which led to the setting up of the Scottish Parliament.

A referendum was held and – as in Scotland – the devolution proposal was carried. Unlike in Scotland, however, the majority in Wales was wafer-thin. Just 50.3% of those eligible to vote actually did so, and the majority across the whole of Wales was just 6721. Nevertheless, there was no requirement for anything other than a simple majority, and the government proceeded to introduce and pass the Government of Wales Act 1998.

As was stated in the previous section, the main difference between a Parliament and an Assembly is that the latter has no powers to initiate primary legislation, and no tax raising powers. Under the 1998 Government of Wales Act neither of these powers were granted to the Welsh Assembly.

Under the terms of the 1998 Act 60 Assembly Members (AMs) were elected. Forty of these were constituency Members, and a further 20 were elected under the additional member system (AMS) of proportional representation. As in Scotland, these regional list areas are based on European Parliament constituencies. As is also the case in Scotland vacancies in constituency seats are filled by means of by-elections, whilst vacancies amongst regional list Members are filled by the next person on the list who is willing to serve.

Like the Scottish Parliament the Welsh Assembly is unicameral – there is no second chamber. Unlike the Scottish Parliament, however, the Welsh Assembly is fully bilingual. The Scottish Parliament permits the use of Scots Gaelic, but the language does not have equal status with English. In the Welsh Assembly the Welsh language has equal status with English.

Since the Welsh Assembly was set up three elections have been held. In the first election in 1999 the Labour Party won the largest number of seats, but did not have an overall majority. In that instance Labour formed a minority administration initially, although it later formed a coalition with the Lib Dems. In the second election in 2003 Labour did win an outright majority. In the most recent election in 2007 Labour (with 26 seats) formed a coalition administration with Plaid Cymru (with 14 seats).

5.6.1 Powers

The Government of Wales Act 1998 spelt out the policy areas which would be devolved to the Welsh Assembly, and also specified those areas of competency which would be reserved to the Westminster Parliament. The devolved policy areas which were transferred to the Welsh Assembly were:

- Agriculture

- Heritage, tourism, culture and sport

- Economic development and industry

- Education and training

- Health and social services

- Transport and highways

- Local government and planning

- Water and flood defence

- Welsh language

Areas of competency which were specifically reserved to the Westminster Parliament were:

- Defence and foreign affairs

- Energy projects (large scale)

- Treasury and finance

- Criminal law, prisons, asylum and immigration

- Constitutional matters

Under the terms of the original 1998 Act, the Welsh Assembly had no powers to enact primary legislation. The Assembly could develop policy in areas covered by its devolution remit, but it had to ask the secretary of state for Wales to take any required legislation through the Westminster Parliament. Equally, if the secretary of state for Wales decided to initiate primary legislation in Westminster, he would consult with the Welsh Assembly.

In 2004 the Welsh Assembly set up a Commission under Lord Richard to investigate how its powers might be extended. The result was the 2006 Government of Wales Act, which substantially enhanced the powers and status of the Assembly. The main provisions of the Act were:

- Electoral Changes: Under the 1998 Act candidates could stand for both constituencies and a regional list. Under the 2006 Government of Wales Act they have to choose one or the other.

- Separation: Under the 1998 Act the Welsh Assembly was set up as a single corporate body, with 60 Members. Under the 2006 Act there is a formal separation between the 60 seat Assembly and the Welsh Assembly Government (the Executive) which consists of the first minister, Welsh ministers, deputy Welsh ministers and the Counsel General. The first minister is appointed by the Assembly, and in turn appoints 12 ministers and deputy ministers. With the first minister and Counsel General this makes the maximum size of the Welsh Assembly Government (WAG) 14.

- Measures: Under the provisions of the 2006 Act the Welsh Assembly can seek competence from the Westminster Parliament to make a new category of legislation called Measures of the National Assembly of Wales (or Assembly Measures). The Assembly can only apply for competence to pass Measures in areas specified as being within its devolved competence, but over time it will undoubtedly accrue more power to legislate in these areas.

- Acts: Also contained in the 2006 Act is provision for the Assembly to acquire powers to make Acts of the National Assembly for Wales. However, these powers will only come into force if a two-thirds majority of the Assembly vote for a referendum to approve them. The secretary of state for Wales then has to agree, and the Westminster Parliament has to vote in favour.

- Finance: The Government of Wales Act established the Welsh Consolidated Fund to receive monies allocated to Wales by HM Treasury under the Barnett Formula. Welsh ministers can lay Budget motions before the Assembly. If approved by the Assembly, the Auditor General for Wales will approve payment, which can then be allocated according to the policy priorities of the Welsh Assembly Government.

5.6.2 First minister

When the Welsh Assembly was established in 1999 Alun Michael was appointed First Secretary. Rhodri Morgan took over the post in February 2000. In October 2000 the title of the position was changed to first minister. Rhodri Morgan has held that title since its inception, and still does at the time of writing

The first minister has wide-ranging powers and responsibilities. They include:

- Relationships with UK government, the EU, and the rest of the world
- Policy development and co-ordination of policy
- Oversight of the civil service
- Overall responsibility for public appointments
- Overall responsibility for Welsh Assembly Government
- Appointment of cabinet

As with any coalition government there are constraints on the powers of the first minister, and he (and so far there have only been a male first minister) cannot act without consulting and having due regard for the policies and priorities of coalition partners. Nevertheless, the position remains a powerful one.

5.6.3 Cabinet

As has been stated the first minister appoints the cabinet. However, since at the time of writing there is a coalition government in Wales, the post of deputy first minister is allocated to a Plaid Cymru Assembly Member, as are two other key cabinet posts. Cabinet normally meets every Monday, when the Assembly is in session.

The current cabinet consists of:

- First minister
- Deputy first minister and minister for the economy and transport
- Minister for environment, sustainability and housing
- Minister for finance and public service delivery
- Minister for social justice and local government
- Minister for health and social services
- Minister for children, education, lifelong learning and skills
- Minister for rural affairs
- Minister for heritage
- Counsel General and Leader of the House

The Chief Whip also attends cabinet meetings.

As well as cabinet itself there is also provision for the setting up of cabinet subcommittees. Whilst cabinet itself makes decisions, cabinet subcommittees are able to deal with cross-cutting issues, and are able to draw in a range of outside bodies so as to broaden the consultation process. Currently cabinet subcommittees are in operation covering the areas of:

- Children and Young People
- Public Service Delivery

Author's top tip

The formation of a cabinet subcommittee is an indication that the Welsh Assembly Government is concerned about an issue, and is looking for policy input from external organisations. If you or your clients have an interest in the area, and policy ideas to share, this is an open invitation to lobby.

Once cabinet has met and discussed and agreed policy on an issue, it issues cabinet statements – initially to the Welsh Assembly. There are two types of cabinet statement:

Oral cabinet statements: These are made to the Assembly on one of its plenary days – usually Tuesday or Wednesday. The cabinet minister making the oral statement is then cross-questioned by Assembly Members.

Written cabinet statements: Again these cabinet statements are made to Assembly Members first. They can be issued at any time, but there is no opportunity for the cabinet minister making the statement to be cross-questioned.

As well as cabinet ministers there are currently four deputy ministers. One of these deputy ministers is from the minority coalition party, Plaid Cymru. Their responsibilities are:

- Deputy minister for regeneration
- Deputy minister for housing
- Deputy minister for skills
- Deputy minister for social services

Author's top tip

The Welsh Assembly Government has demonstrated a real commitment to open government. Consequently the agendas and minutes of cabinet meetings are published on the website – with only confidential and commercially confidential information withheld.

5.6.4 Departments

Post-devolution the Welsh Assembly took over the powers and responsibilities which the former Welsh Office formerly exercised. The civil service in Wales is – like its Whitehall equivalent – broken down into departments. Each is headed up by a cabinet minister or a deputy minister.

Current departments within the Welsh Assembly Government are:

- Children, Education, Lifelong Learning and Skills
- Corporate Information and Services
- Economy and Transport
- Environment, Sustainability and Housing
- Finance
- Health and Social Services
- Heritage
- Human Resources
- Legal Services
- Public Health and Health Professions
- Public Services and Performances
- Rural Affairs
- Social Justice and Local Government

5.6.5 Finances

Neither the 1998 nor the 2006 Government of Wales Acts gave the Welsh Assembly tax raising powers. What the Welsh Assembly Government does have, however, is considerable flexibility as to how it dispenses the money allocated to it by the United Kingdom government.

As with Scotland, Wales is the beneficiary of the Barnett Formula. This allocates resources to Wales on a similar basis to allocations in England, but with a small uplift to take account of regional and social challenges. In theory the Whitehall spending round is fixed for three years under the Comprehensive Spending Review – although it is reviewed in the second and third years. Currently, the allocation which is made available to the Welsh Assembly Government by the UK government is £14.5 billion.

The Welsh Assembly Government publishes its Draft Budget in the autumn. This is debated by the Welsh Assembly, and there is also widespread consultation with external stakeholders. The Final Budget is introduced in the spring, and takes account of technical changes, representations and submissions made by the Assembly and external organisations.

Within the Final Budget allocations are made to the Main Expenditure Groups (MEGs) which reflect the priorities of the National Assembly for Wales and the Welsh Assembly Government. Currently the MEGs are made up of:

- Health and Social Services
- Social Justice and Local Government
- Environment, Sustainability and Housing
- Rural Affairs
- Economy and Transport
- Children, Education, Lifelong Learning and Skills
- Heritage
- Central Administration
- Other Ministerial Services
- Central Matching Fund
- Public Services and Performance.

Within the Final Budget and the strategic allocation to MEGs there is considerably more detail. Financial allocations are made not just to MEGs, but also to Spending Programme Areas (SPAs) and all the way down to Budget Expenditure Lines (BELs). It is at this level of detail that lobbying can be effective. Only lobbying of the UK government by the Welsh Assembly Government can hope to alter Wales's settlement under the Comprehensive Spending Review, and discussions within cabinet will decide on allocation to the MEGs. However, Assembly Members and external lobbyists are likely to have much more success in trying to increase allocations at the SPA and BEL level.

Author's top tip

The Welsh Assembly has considerable flexibility in the way in which it spends the money allocated to it under the Barnett Formula. If you or your client need funds for a project – or need extra funds for an already funded project – lobby for it in the period between when the Draft Budget becomes the Final Budget.

5.6.6 Legislation

As has already been stated, under the Government of Wales Act 2006 a mechanism was created whereby the Welsh Assembly could apply to Westminster for "Legislative Competence" to makes its own laws in areas which had been devolved to it under the original 1998 Act. Under that original Act areas which were devolved to the Welsh Assembly were categorised under "fields" and "matters":

- A "field" is a broad subject area, such as health or housing
- A "matter" is a more defined subject area within a "field"

The process of applying for this legislative competence is through a Legislative Competency Order (LCO). An LCO can be proposed by the Welsh Assembly Government, by an Assembly committee, or by an individual Assembly Member. The proposed LCO then goes before a Draft LCO committee of the Welsh Assembly (a bit like a standing committee in the Westminster Parliament), before being considered by the Welsh Assembly in plenary session. If approved by the Welsh Assembly, it then has to be sent to the secretary of state for Wales, and then has to be approved by both Houses of Parliament in Westminster.

Once Legislative Competence has been approved, and once the legislation has been introduced and passed by the Welsh Assembly, it becomes known as an Assembly Measure.

As well as this extended (but still limited) power to initiate and ultimately enact primary legislation, the Welsh Assembly also has powers to pass secondary legislation:

- Statutory Instruments: As with the Westminster Parliament, these flow from primary legislation. They are usually local in nature.

- Non-statutory instruments: These are subordinate Assembly legislation which are not required to be made by Statutory Instrument because they do not draw from primary legislation.

Under the original 1998 Act the National Assembly of Wales – unlike the Scottish Parliament – was granted limited powers. It was considered that there was less of an appetite for devolution in Wales than in Scotland – and the wide variation in the results of the two referendums bore this out. One of the main differences between an Assembly and a Parliament is that the latter has primary legislative powers. As the Welsh people grow to trust the Welsh Assembly more as a forum and as a secondary legislative body, and as it accrues more competences to itself under the terms of the 2006 Act, this distinction will undoubtedly become blurred. In time we could well see the Welsh Assembly translate itself into a Welsh Parliament.

Author's top tip

Welsh Assembly Members actually have live computer screens on their desks in the chamber. That means that you can email them during debates, and lobby in real time!

5.6.7 Debates

The Welsh Assembly meets in plenary session every Tuesday and Wednesday.

All Legislative Competence Orders and all Assembly Measures have to be debated and approved in plenary session. There is also, however, an opportunity for members to enter a ballot for a short debate. The ballot is overseen by the Presiding Officer, and the successful Member is allowed to introduce a short debate at the end of the Wednesday plenary session. A cabinet minister or deputy minister will answer the short debate. This is very similar to the adjournment debates which are held at the end of every sitting day in the House of Commons.

These short debates are perhaps the best opportunity for backbench Assembly Members to raise an issue at some length with a member of the Welsh Assembly Government. Equally, of course, they are an opportunity for lobbyists (with the assistance of a sympathetic Member) to get an issue highlighted, and to gauge the attitude of the Welsh Assembly Government towards it.

5.6.8 Committees

As with the committees of the Scottish Parliament, those of the National Assembly for Wales perform a dual role – they both scrutinise legislation, and shadow the ministers and departments of the Welsh Assembly Government. As with the Scottish and Westminster Parliaments, committees in the Welsh Assembly broadly reflect the political make-up of the Assembly as a whole.

There are four main types of committee within the Welsh Assembly:

1. Legislative committees: As the name implies, these are set up as and when needed. Their main function is scrutinising Legislative Competence Orders and Assembly measures.

2. Scrutiny committees: These committees shadow ministers and departments of the Welsh Assembly Government, and their associated bodies and agencies. However, they tend to be cross-departmental, rather than exactly matching WAG departments. Like the Westminster select committees, they have the right to examine documents and call witnesses.

3. Regional committees: These are – in UK terms – unique to the Welsh Assembly. They can cover any region in Wales, but they are only set up by the Welsh Assembly in response to a specific perceived need.

4. Mandatory committees: These cover administrative issues such as audit, broadcasting, business of the Assembly, petitions and standards.

Because the Welsh Assembly only meets in plenary session on two days a week, the work of its committees assumes a greater importance than they otherwise might. They are also very open to the public, and receptive to approaches from lobbyists.

5.6.9 Questions

The first minister answers oral questions for 45 minutes every Tuesday. As is the case with the Westminster and Scottish Parliaments, the member who asks a question is permitted to ask a supplementary question. Other members can then ask their own supplementary questions, provided that they are relevant to the original question. Depending on the length of the questions – and answers – up to ten questions can be reached during the course of the 45 minute slot.

After oral questions to the first minister there is then a half hour given over to the Business Statement and Announcement. As with the House of Commons, this is also an opportunity for the opposition frontbench to press the government for more time to discuss issues which they regard as important. It is also an opportunity for backbench members to raise their own priority issues and to press for debating time.

After the Business Statement ministers may take the opportunity to make an oral statement. They can be cross-questioned on this by the opposition front bench and backbenchers, but the time allocated to oral statements is just half an hour, so the scope for debate is limited.

Whilst the first minister has to answer oral questions for 45 minutes once a week (at least whilst the Assembly is in session), other ministers and deputy ministers have to answer oral questions relating to their areas of responsibility for 30 minutes every four weeks. These oral question sessions take place on a Wednesday. Ministers representing two different departments answer questions, with 30 minutes allocated to each. Again, the member who asks the original question is entitled to ask a supplementary question, and other members can join in – provided they stick to the broad theme of the original question.

Any oral question (whether to the first minister or to a departmental minister) which does not receive an oral answer because of lack of time receives a written answer. Questions can also be tabled specifically for written answer. Questions for written answer are tabled either to a Welsh minister representing a specific department, or to the Counsel General, or to the Assembly Commission. Questions can be tabled in English or Welsh, and answers are published (in the official report and on the website) in both languages. Questions for written answer are tabled at the discretion of the Presiding Officer, and they are ideally supposed to be answered within five working days – although it can take a great deal longer than this.

As is the case with both the Westminster and Scottish Parliaments there is a distinct difference in the rationale behind tabling questions for written or oral answer. The former usually simply seeks to elicit information. The latter is often used to press the first minister or a minister, to seek clarification, and perhaps to trap the minister into making a concession, or expressing some sympathy towards a cause.

5.6.10 Petitions

As with the Scottish Parliament the Welsh Assembly has set up a committee specifically to receive and process petitions.

The Petitions Committee meets every Thursday, and aims to deal with about ten petitions at every sitting. It only deals with petitions which have been referred to it by the Presiding Officer. Petitioners may be invited to appear in person to talk to their petition, or to supply written evidence to back it up.

Since May 2008 the Welsh Assembly has set up a facility on its website for e-petitions. The format of the petitions, and the issues they can relate to, are strictly prescribed. As with hard copy petitions, they must relate to subject areas over which the Welsh Assembly has competence.

Both forms of petition present opportunities for lobbyists. The Welsh Assembly was originally set up to provide a forum for discussion of specifically Welsh issues, and the Assembly has always shown itself to be open to outside opinions and influences. Petitions are an excellent way of giving those opinions physical manifestation.

5.7 Wales Office

As with the Scotland Office, the Wales Office is a much scaled-down version of its pre-devolution predecessor, the Welsh Office.

The Wales Office has twin bases, in Whitehall and in Cardiff Bay close to the National Assembly. It is one of Whitehall's smallest departments. It performs the twin functions of representing Wales to the UK government, and representing the UK government in Wales.

The Wales Office is the guardian of the Devolution Settlement for Wales. Unlike his Scottish equivalent, the secretary of state for Wales retains responsibility for guiding Welsh legislation through the Westminster Parliament. This includes the Orders in Council which are needed to enhance the legislative competencies of the Welsh Assembly. He is also responsible for the reserved functions which are not subject to the devolutionary process, and for overseeing the financial arrangements transferring monies from HM Treasury to the Welsh Assembly Government.

Although the powers and responsibilities of the secretary of state for Wales and the Wales Office are much diminished, it is still in many ways a more significant role than that of secretary of state for Scotland – where the Scottish Parliament has acquired substantially more direct powers.

5.8 Welsh Affairs Select Committee

The House of Commons Welsh Affairs Select Committee consists of 11 MPs. As with other select committees the membership is drawn up in rough proportion to the party make-up of the House of Commons, which means that there is only room for one Plaid Cymru MP. However, all of the members do at least represent Welsh seats.

The remit of the Welsh Affairs Select Committee is to "examine matters which are within the responsibility of the secretary of state for Wales". However, added to this fairly narrow remit is the opportunity to examine issues which affect relations with the National Assembly for Wales. So, in one way or another the committee can hold inquiries into almost any Welsh issue which it wishes to.

5.9 Welsh Grand Committee

Like the Scottish Grand Committee, the Welsh Grand Committee is made up of all of the 40 MPs who represent Welsh seats. However, unlike the Scottish Grand Committee, MPs from outside of Wales can be added to the Welsh Grand Committee. As with the Scottish and Northern Ireland Grand Committee, the Welsh Grand Committee can meet outside of Westminster.

The Welsh Grand Committee has met infrequently since the 1998 Government of Wales Act. However, there are now signs that it intends to meet more regularly.

Contributor's top tip

Know your audience is one of the key mantras of lobbying, and nowhere more so than in Wales.

The National Assembly for Wales is a comparatively young institution – still less than ten years old. Until recently, it has had fairly limited legislative powers, confined to certain devolved areas of responsibility, and even in these areas it often has had to wait for enabling legislation from Westminster before policies could be introduced in Wales. As a result, Assembly Members have not had the opportunity to become experienced legislators. However, change is on the way.

Under the provisions of the Government of Wales Act 2006, the third National Assembly, which began its term in May 2007, now has the powers to introduce legislation for Wales. A number of new policies are now being introduced, and Assembly Members are taking on more of a scrutiny role and developing the skills that come with this new responsibility.

Some Assembly Members have now sat in Cardiff Bay for nine years, while others have just begun their term of office in the past year. Most of them come from public or voluntary sector backgrounds, a very few come from a business background and three have experience as public affairs consultants. Be aware of this when crafting and targeting messages, tailor your approach accordingly and remember translation into Welsh for some material is advisable.

Finally, be aware of the time pressures under which Assembly Members operate. Leaving those who are members of the cabinet or junior ministers to one side, there are just over 40 Members to deliver on the new scrutiny role that the Assembly now has, and to hold the Government to account through the cross-departmental committees structure, and to attend to plenary and constituency business. Time is precious.

Choose your targets carefully and ensure your briefing is appropriate, bearing in mind the AM's relevant experience and knowledge of your issue. As always, do your preparation carefully and know your audience.

Rosemary Grogan – Public affairs consultant

Contributor's top tip

When lobbying in Wales always remember that policy divergence from England is an opportunity not a problem. Building on this, do not automatically imagine that any part of the UK gets everything right. In my experience, every nation has policy delivery success as well as failure. And do not assume the attitudes of the same political party are identical in different parts of the UK, or that the same philosophy is underpinning policy in all areas. Labour government in the Assembly is a different brand from Labour government in Westminster. Indeed, in many respects, this divergence is key to understanding why we needed devolution in the first place.

Where possible, you should also base any case evidence on specifically Welsh statistics. Do your research into policy and structures before, not after, you start working on any client account for Wales. There's nothing worse than someone lobbying on Welsh health policy talking about PCTs and Foundation Trusts. That sort of sloppiness gives the lobbyist and the profession a bad name.

Daran Hill, Positif Politics

Contributor's top tip

If you give just a "Welsh wash" to campaigns that are researched, designed and largely executed outside the country (please do not call us the principality), no matter how red your paint is, you will risk depriving your clients of credibility, access and opportunities.

The Welsh Assembly Government (WAG) and the four main Assembly parties are actively looking for "Made in Wales" analyses, proposals and case-making – they pay respect to campaigns or issues that show Welsh roots, alliances and policy awareness. WAG ministers have a pair of Welsh archer's fingers each and have been known to wave them.

For instance, public affairs in Wales is bilingual and commissioning a few hasty translations won't do the trick (shoddy texts are often "put in the stocks" on blogs and web forums). In fact, the Welsh language broadcast media and networks are essential channels to opinion leaders of all ages. We do not talk Welsh just when you walk into the pub, but if you order a round of Brains Dark or The Reverend James then you are talking our language!

Marc Evans, Civitas Cymru

5.10 Northern Ireland Assembly

Devolved government in Northern Ireland has a much longer – and a much more chequered – history than its equivalents in Scotland and Wales. As far back as 1920 the Government of Ireland Act equipped Northern Ireland with its own Executive (a prime minister with his own cabinet) and a bicameral (two chamber) Parliament.

These arrangements were suspended in 1972 with the outbreak of violent clashes between the Catholic and Protestant communities. British troops had to be drafted in to keep the peace, and relations between the two communities broke down almost completely. In 1973 devolution was brought to an end, and the Westminster Parliament re-asserted its legislative supremacy.

Successive British prime ministers, working sometimes closely with their Dublin counterpart (the *Taoiseach*) tried hard to bring the two communities closer together, and to restore at least a semblance of devolved government. Ted Heath, Harold Wilson, Margaret Thatcher, John Major and Tony Blair all spent a substantial part of their premierships trying to bring about a restoration of devolution. Abortive restorations occurred in 1973 and 1982, but came to nothing in the end.

The Northern Ireland Act of 1998 was passed at the same time as the Scotland Act and the Government of Wales Act. This allowed for a 108 member unicameral Northern Ireland Assembly, with six Assembly Members (known as MLAs) elected for each of the 18 Westminster constituencies under the complex d'Hondt method (named after the nineteenth century Belgian lawyer who invented it). The system was designed to force the two main communities – the Loyalists and the Nationalists – to work together.

Anecdote

The same joke is told about the d'Hondt method of PR as used to be told about the Schleswig-Holstein question. This obscure province had been the source of a long-running conflict between Denmark and Prussia in the nineteenth century. British Premier Lord Palmerston supported the Danish position, but joked that only three people had ever really understood the issue – the Prince Consort (who was dead), a clerk at the Foreign Office (who had gone mad) and he himself, (but he had long forgotten).

The 1998 Act did not bring about the end of the troubles, but it did perhaps signal the beginning of the end. The Northern Ireland Assembly was suspended in February 2000, and again in October 2002, before being dissolved in April 2003. Fresh elections in May 2003 were delayed until November 2003, but the results showed no lessening of the polarisation of the two communities. In April 2006 Tony Blair and Bertie Ahern met and announced that the Assembly would be recalled in May with a view to an Executive being re-established before the end of November. In fact it was not until elections were held on 7 March 2007 that devolution was fully restored (on 8 May 2007).

5.10.1 Powers

Because of the history of inter-community strife in Northern Ireland, a slightly more complex arrangement for the transfer of powers was put in to place. Instead of just two sets of areas of responsibility – those which would and would not be transferred – three sets were drawn up for Northern Ireland:

- Transferred matters: The Assembly was given legislative and executive powers over most day-to-day issues affecting Northern Ireland including agriculture, culture, the environment, education, enterprise, health, inward investment, rural development, social services, and training.

- Excepted matters: These areas are very similar to those which were not devolved to the Scottish Parliament and Welsh Assembly – including the constitution, defence, foreign affairs, nationality and immigration, political parties, and taxation.

- Reserved matters: These were matters which were neither excepted, nor initially transferred. They were matters which could be transferred in time once devolution proved to be working well. They included policing and criminal law, public order, civil defence, courts, consumer safety, telecommunications, financial services and competition policy.

Gradually, as devolved government becomes more established, and as sectarian violence hopefully becomes increasingly rare, more and more areas of competence will undoubtedly be moved from being reserved matters to being transferred matters.

5.10.2 First minister and deputy first minister

Under the terms of the 1998 Northern Ireland Act candidates for the post of first minister and deputy first minister must stand for office jointly, and they must receive cross-party support from within the Northern Ireland Assembly.

Following the restoration of the Assembly in 2007 veteran DUP leader the Rev Ian Paisley became first minister, with Sinn Fein's Martin McGuinness as his deputy first minister. Despite many years of fierce rivalry between the two parties, and the long history of sectarian violence, the Reverend Paisley and Mr McGuinness not only worked well together, but seemed to get along on a personal level. In June 2008 Mr Paisley stood down as leader of the DUP and first minister, and was replaced by Peter Robinson.

5.10.3 Executive Committee

The Executive Committee of the Northern Ireland Assembly (the equivalent of a cabinet) is made up of the first minister, the deputy first minister, and ten ministers – all drawn from the 108 seat Assembly. Ministers are appointed to the Executive Committee on a party basis, in proportion to the parties' standing in the Assembly. Two junior ministers, who effectively run the Office of the First Minister and Deputy First Minister (OFMDFM), also attend meetings of the Executive but do not have a vote.

The Executive Committee is responsible for initiating most of the legislation in the Northern Ireland Assembly. It sets out its legislative plans in the form of a Programme for Government, announced in the Assembly at the start of each legislative year. Legislation takes the form of Executive bills, which must be passed by the Assembly.

The Northern Ireland Assembly delegates its executive powers to the Executive Committee. This is exercised through the ten government departments which make up the civil service component of the Northern Ireland Executive.

5.10.4 Legislation

As has been stated the Northern Ireland Assembly has the power to introduce primary legislation in areas where competence has been transferred. As with the Westminster Parliament, legislation starts out as a bill, and (if successful) becomes an Act of the Northern Ireland Assembly. Acts have to be approved by the secretary of state for Northern Ireland, and they also have to receive Royal Assent.

All bills have to be accompanied by an explanatory and financial memorandum. This must explain the financial implications of any proposals contained within the bill. It must also explain the issues which the bill aims to address, and the consultation process which has taken place in advance of its publication. This consultation phase is a crucial one for lobbyists – both in-house and consultancy based.

Most legislation is initiated by the Executive Committee and is outlined in the Programme for Government at the start of each session. However, as with the Scottish Parliament and the Welsh Assembly, legislation can also be initiated by committees and by backbench MLAs. The stages of a bill going through the Northern Ireland Assembly are:

- Prior clearance: All bills must be submitted to the Speaker, who will assert that its provisions fall within the competence of the Northern Ireland Assembly. The consent of the secretary of state for Northern Ireland is also required before a bill can proceed.

- First stage: The clerk reads out the title of the bill and it is ordered to be printed and added to the list of forthcoming business.

- Second stage : As is the case in the Westminster Parliament, this is a general debate on the principles of the bill, followed by a vote if requested.

- Committee stage: The bill is referred to the appropriate statutory committee for detailed investigation. The relevant statutory committee has 30 days to consider the bill, take evidence from outside persons, and produce a report.

- Consideration stage: The bill returns to a plenary session of the Assembly for its consideration. MLAs may vote on the bill as it stands, or on amendments as proposed.

- Further consideration stage: Further consideration by the Assembly in plenary session with opportunities for further amendments and votes.

- Final stage: A final debate on the principle of the bill as it now stands, with no further amendments possible. The bill must be passed or rejected.

- Royal Assent: As with the Westminster Parliament, this stage is a formality.

The Westminster Parliament retains powers to legislate on any issues, whether devolved or not. However, the convention has been established that it will not do so without the consent of the Assembly. This consent is given through the mechanism of a Legislative Consent Motion – or LCM.

5.10.5 Finance

Like the Scottish Parliament and the Welsh Assembly, financial grants for Northern Ireland are decided by the Westminster Parliament under the Comprehensive Spending Review (CSR) programme. As with the other two devolved bodies, the final allocation of funds for Northern Ireland is arrived at under the Barnett Formula (which was described earlier).

The Northern Ireland Executive has no control over the level of financial allocation which the province receives under the block grant which is paid in to the Consolidated Fund for Northern Ireland. However, the minister of finance and personnel (the Northern Ireland version of the chancellor of the exchequer) can introduce proposals for raising duties and taxes – although any such proposal must have cross-party support. The Northern Ireland Executive also has considerable discretion as to how the money which is paid into the Consolidated Fund under the terms of the Barnett Formula is allocated.

The minister of finance and personnel is required to lay before the Assembly a draft Budget setting out the programme of expenditure proposals which have been agreed by the Executive. This draft Budget must be presented to the Assembly before the end of the financial year – 31 March.

A Budget Bill is then introduced, which must pass through all of the stages outlined above for normal bills. The Budget Bill authorises payments out of the Northern Ireland Consolidated Fund to government departments and other public bodies. The resources allocated under the remit of the Budget Bill include both operating accruing resources (running expenses) and non-operating accruing resources (capital expenditure).

The first Budget Bill introduced in the new Northern Ireland Assembly covered the years 2008-2011. The provisions contained within the bill had been put out to widespread consultation, and the Executive stated that it had taken account of the responses to the consultation process when allocating funds.

The finances of the Northern Ireland Executive are subject to similar scrutiny processes as those which apply in mainland Britain. There is a Comptroller and Auditor General for Northern Ireland, and the Northern Ireland Assembly operates a Public Accounts Committee which directs its work.

5.10.6 Debates

The Speaker on the Northern Ireland Assembly has considerable powers over the rules of debate. No minister or backbencher can speak without being called by the Speaker, and unless proposing an amendment no MLA can speak more than once in any debate. The Speaker also decides on the allocated speaking time per MLA in every debate.

The Northern Ireland Assembly generally meets in plenary session on just two days a week – Mondays and Tuesday. The types of debate which take place in the Northern Ireland Assembly are:

- Legislation debates: The second stage, consideration stage, and final stage debates of a bill take place in the Chamber.

- Motion debates: Any MLA can seek to introduce a motion, but cannot actually do so unless given permission by the Speaker.

- Adjournment debates: These take place every Tuesday between 3-6pm.

For the lobbyist all three of these types of debate offer substantial scope for intervention. MLAs can be briefed about concerns over certain bills, or over certain clauses within them. They can also be urged to try and raise an issue through either a motion debate or an adjournment debate.

5.10.7 Committees

The committee system in the Northern Ireland Assembly is well established and plays a vital role in its proceedings. The composition of the committees – and the selection of chairs – is broadly reflective of the proportion of votes which the various parties received at the last elections. Each party which secured representation in the Assembly should be represented on each committee. The rules also state that the chair and deputy chair of committees should not be from the same political party as the departmental minister which it is shadowing.

There are three types of committee set up within the Northern Ireland Assembly:

1. Statutory committees: There are ten statutory committees, each shadowing a member of the Executive and a Northern Ireland Government department. They can call for papers and summons witnesses. They can examine and debate the activities of their relevant departments, and recommend changes. They can look at the finances allocated to the government departments, and recommend changes in the way in which they are allocated. They can both initiate legislation, and examine legislation which has been initiated by the Executive or backbench MLAs.

2. Standing committees: These are established at the start of each session. They are established to assist the Assembly with largely procedural matters. Current standing committees deal with the Assembly and Executive Review, Audit, Business of the Assembly, Procedures, Public Accounts and Standards and Privileges. There is also a Standing Committee of the Centre, which shadows the work of the Office of the First Minister and the Deputy First Minister.

3. Ad Hoc committees: As the name implies these committees are set up as and when needed, and disbanded when their work is complete. They look at either draft orders (recent examples include Draft Order on Sexual Offences and on Life Sentences), or consultations (recent examples include children's rights, local postal services, and migration).

5.10.8 Questions

The first minister and deputy first minister, and departmental ministers, are required to answer oral questions during Assembly question time. Questions to the first minister and the deputy first minister come first, and then ministers representing Northern Ireland Government departments answer questions according to a rota. Oral questions are known as Assembly question oral – or AQO.

Questions for oral answer are taken between 2.30-4pm on Mondays. Northern Ireland Government departments take it in turn to answer oral questions. Ministers representing three government departments answer questions at any one Assembly Question Time. Questions are chosen at random by means of a computer sift. The questions and answers are published in the Official Report.

Questions for written answer are known as Assembly questions written or AQW. They can be addressed to the first or deputy first minister, or to any minister representing a government department. They are normally answered within ten days. Answers are published once a week in the Written Answers Bulletin. A list of all unanswered questions is carried in the Consolidated List.

From the lobbyist's point of view questions in the Northern Ireland Assembly offer the same opportunities as they do in all of the other legislatures we have examined. If an MLA can be persuaded to table questions for written answer, then that is a very good way of getting factual information out of the Northern Ireland Government and civil service. A question for oral answer, however, is much better for pressing a minister and trying to secure concessions, or clarifications, on the executive's policy in a particular area.

5.10.9 Petitions

The Northern Ireland Assembly does not give as high a priority to petitions as the Scottish Parliament and Welsh Assembly do.

No petition can be presented to the Assembly without the permission of the Clerk to the Business Committee. The MLA presenting a petition can only state who the petition is from, how many signatories it has attracted, and the broad outline of the allegations or requests contained in the petition.

Petitions in the Northern Ireland Assembly therefore offer limited opportunities for lobbyists trying to highlight an issue.

5.11 Northern Ireland Executive Departments

Each of the ministers within the Executive Committee heads up a department within the Northern Ireland Executive. There is also a department specifically tasked with supporting the first and deputy first ministers – the rough equivalent of the Cabinet Office in Whitehall.

The departments of the Northern Ireland civil service are:

- Office of the First Minister and Deputy First Minister

- Department of Agriculture and Rural Development

- Department of Culture, Arts and Leisure

- Department of Education

- Department of Employment and Learning

- Department of Enterprise, Trade and Investment

- Department of the Environment

- Department of Finance and Personnel

- Department of Health, Social Services and Public Safety

- Department of Regional Development

- Department of Social Development

The responsibilities of the individual departments are obvious from their titles. However, the Office of the First Minister and Deputy First Minister (OFMDFM) has a wide, complex and powerful role. The OFMDFM is responsible for:

- Supporting the first minister and deputy first minister and the institutions of government

- Servicing the machinery of government and implementing the modernising government programme

- Promoting better community relations

- Targeting social deprivation and promoting social inclusion

- Overseeing the implementation of Public Service Agreements across all of the Northern Ireland Executive departments

There are three other bodies which the Northern Ireland Assembly and the Northern Ireland Executive have to take note of when developing policies and initiating legislation. They are:

- The British Irish Council: This is made up of representatives from the British and Irish governments, and also the devolved institutions of Scotland, Wales, Northern Ireland, the Isle of Man and the Channel Islands. It is tasked with developing harmonious relationships between the various bodies, but also with developing policies to deal with cross-border issues such as drug smuggling and tourism.

- The North/South Ministerial Council: This is composed of members of the Irish Government and those with executive responsibility for the government of Northern Ireland. It meets to discuss issues of concern to the whole island of Ireland.

- The British-Irish Intergovernmental Conference: This is made up of senior representatives from the UK and Irish governments and discusses bilateral collaboration on all matters of mutual interest.

Contributor's top tip

Innovation is key to creating the atmosphere for influence and change, and think carefully about how you make your approach.

- Seize the moment with care and delicacy, outside the office back door, in the car park, after mass or church, in the supermarket, but then avoid overkill.

- Lodge your presence and message with rapier-like accuracy.

- Do not ask the question until you know the answer – it's much harder to reverse a "No".

- Persistence, short of stalking, is essential – lobbying is a competitive activity. Some even call it a blood sport.

- Never say never – you may not win this time, but you may have planted the seed that will fruit next time around.

- Use humour – short of humiliation. Ali G without the cudgel.

- Be imaginative – a picture is worth more than 1000 words, the colourful banner draws the eye towards it and the single word placard is better noticed than the treatise.

- You need the eye of the photo editor, the nose of the news hound.

- Like the knight on the chess board, you must creep up silently, jump over obstacles, use reverse gear and move in unexpected directions.

- Make your own luck, do not expect it to come to you!

Quintin Oliver, Director, Stratagem

5.12 Northern Ireland Office

As is the case with the Scotland Office and the Wales Office, a small Northern Ireland Office remains in Westminster, based at Millbank.

The principal role of the Northern Ireland Office is to support the secretary of state for Northern Ireland. As no bill can progress to become an Act without the approval of the secretary of state for Northern Ireland, the post retains a direct legislative role. The secretary of state for Northern Ireland also has a similar ambassadorial role to the secretaries of state for Scotland and Wales, in so far as he or she represents Northern Ireland in cabinet, and represent the UK government in Northern Ireland.

As is also the case with the other two secretaries of state he or she represents Northern Ireland at the European Union and abroad. Unlike his or her other two cabinet colleagues, however, the Northern Ireland secretary of state also has to deal regularly with the Irish government on what are still often sensitive issues, and to sit on some of the cross-border bodies.

5.13 Northern Ireland Affairs Select Committee

The role of the Northern Ireland Affairs Select Committee is to "examine the expenditure, administration and policy of the Northern Ireland Office". It does not involve itself or concern itself with matters which are devolved to the Northern Ireland Executive or Assembly. Recent reports have dealt with the prison system, the criminal justice system, and political developments in the province.

There are 13 members on the select committee, but only four of them represent Northern Ireland constituencies. These are from the Social Democratic & Labour Party (SDLP), Ulster Unionist Party (UUP) and Democratic Unionist Party (DUP). Other members are drawn from Scotland and England, although some were originally from Northern Ireland.

5.14 Northern Ireland Grand Committee

The Northern Ireland Grand Committee is made up of all of the 18 MPs from the province, plus a further 21 from England, Scotland and Wales.

Whilst devolution was suspended the Grand Committee played a key role. It considered bills and delegated legislation, held debates, and had oral question sessions. Now that devolution has been restored the Grand Committee rarely meets, and it has a much diminished role.

As with the other two Grand Committee this committee can, with the permission of the House of Commons, meet outside of Westminster. Generally, however, it meets in the Grand Committee room off of Westminster Hall. Its role now that the new Northern Ireland Assembly is up and running is to meet occasionally, to debate, and to produce reports on non-devolved matters. Should devolution ever again be suspended, the Grand Committee would resume its former pivotal role.

Contributor's top tip

My top-tip on lobbying would be: if you want to get someone's support for your cause, make sure it becomes their cause as well, even if you have to play the long game and predict the future for them. A good example of this at Bowel Cancer UK is our gaining MPs' support for the bowel cancer screening programme. This was vital when screening was under threat and remains so as it rolls out across the country. One by one, each MP – and MSP and MLA and AM – is engaging with screening as it begins to affect them and their constituents. Also, be generous with ownership of ideas and credit others wherever possible. If you are seen as egotistical and grasping, other people will wonder why they're supporting you. As the man said – always leave something for the next guy, and that includes lobbying. No one has ever lost face by being gracious, and it is disarming and effective when you are.

Ian Beaumont, Bowel Cancer UK

Contributor's top tip

The Northern Ireland Executive has made it through a surprisingly straightforward first year. However, there have been recent signs of a snarl up within the Executive with rumours of frequently cancelled meetings and a backlog of legislation.

Therein lies my first top tip for lobbying here – do not overstep the line between getting the job done and being overly pushy, because there are still difficulties being hammered out and delays are to be expected. Presenting oneself as an aid, as a resource to MLAs and ministers, is much more likely to yield a result than pushing too hard for one.

The next top tip is this – be thorough. Because there are so many departments, responsibility for major areas of policy, such as tackling problems within the planning system, can often be spread over several departments, making achieving a result very difficult. Therefore, all bases need to be covered, with the lobbyist sometimes finding themselves in the strange position of fostering dialogue between departments as well as between clients and government.

Barry Turley, ASITIS Consulting

Contributor's top tip

Northern Ireland has a tortured political history, but largely the fundamentals of public affairs and lobbying are unaffected. Just as anywhere else the focus is on individual relationships and the need to maintain a broad range of contacts among politicians, civil servants and other stakeholders.

One does, however, have to remember two key distinguishing elements that mark Northern Ireland out from the norm. The political parties are largely single issue groups – they are either unionist (ie, pro the Union with GB) or they are nationalist (ie, in favour of a united Ireland). The affect of this is that on most policy issues the main parties contain hugely contrasting views within their own ranks. In effect, although the parties are important on many instances you are faced with 108 individual views among the 108 MLAs who make up the Assembly.

Secondly, the unusual system of government which means that all four main parties are, of right, in the Executive, means that to achieve anything in the Northern Ireland Assembly requires you to always treat all four parties equally and to build cross party support. Although ministers have considerable discretion within their own departments there is a strong emphasis on achieving consensus. In addition, with effectively eleven departments, issues often cross departmental boundaries and hence you will need to get agreement from the ministers of rival parties.

Keep focused on individual relationships and it is not as complicated as it sounds!

Neil Johnston, Chambre Public Affairs

5.15 Greater London Authority

During the 1980s the Conservatives under Margaret Thatcher dominated UK politics. However, the Greater London Council (GLC) was controlled by the left, and under its leader Ken Livingstone it was a constant thorn in the side of the Tory government. From its base at County Hall, just the other side of Westminster Bridge, the GLC raised a succession of banners taunting the Conservative government and mocking its attachment to market forces. Margaret Thatcher's response was typically bold and ruthless: she abolished the GLC.

When Labour returned to power under Tony Blair in 1997 it did so on the back of a manifesto which committed it to devolution in Scotland and Wales, and the restoration of devolution in Northern Ireland. It also promised to hold a referendum on the establishment of a strategic authority for London, with a directly elected Mayor and Assembly.

The referendum was held in May 1998, and the vote was three to one in favour of the devolution proposals. The Greater London Authority Act was duly introduced, and received Royal Assent in 1999. The Act contained provision for the direct election of a Mayor, but also for a London Assembly. This would consist of 25 members – 14 representing giant constituencies (made up of five or six Westminster constituencies), and 11 list members elected under a system of proportional representation. The Act also allowed the new GLA to absorb the London Planning Advisory Committee, the London Research Centre and the London Ecology Unit.

The London Mayor commands the third largest electoral mandate in Europe – after the French and Portuguese presidencies. The first elections took place in May 2000. The former GLC leader Ken Livingstone, standing as an independent, was elected Mayor under the Single Transferable Vote (STV) system. Standing again in 2004 – this time as the official Labour Party candidate – Mr Livingstone was again successful. However, at the most recent elections in May 2008, he was defeated by the Conservative Boris Johnson.

Anecdote

It was agreed during the passage of the GLA Bill that the position of Lord Mayor of the City of London, elected by the Aldermen of the City of London for one year, would continue. The Lord Mayor is frequently confused with the Mayor of London who represents all 32 London Boroughs and the City of London. Perhaps the most famous such occasion was when the Speaker of the House of Commons referred to Boris Johnson in his last speech in Parliament on 4 June 2008 as 'Lord Mayor'. Hansard spared his blushes and recorded that he said 'the Mayor'.

Chris Kelsey, Associate Partner, Finsbury Group

The Greater London Authority (GLA) consists of the directly elected Mayor and the 25 Assembly Members elected by a combination of first-past-the-post and proportional representation. The GLA is supported by some 600 full-time staff.

The main areas of responsibility of the GLA are:

- Transport
- Policing
- Fire and emergency planning
- Economic development
- Planning
- Culture
- Environment
- Waste
- Health

The original Greater London Authority Act of 1999 provided for a clear separation of powers between the Mayor and the Assembly.

5.15.1 Mayor of London

Perhaps the primary responsibility of the London Mayor is to act as a spokesman for the capital city. He (and to date there has been no female Mayor) represents London in its dealings with Westminster and the 32 London boroughs (plus the City of London Corporation). The Mayor also represents London abroad, and acts as a cheerleader for London when foreign delegations visit.

The Mayor also has a clear executive role. He is tasked with consulting, developing and publishing strategies for several key policy areas which have a huge impact on the capital and its inhabitants. Areas which he is charged with developing strategies on include:

- Transport
- Spatial development
- Environment

The Mayor also sets budgets for the :

- Greater London Authority (GLA)
- Transport for London (TfL)
- Metropolitan Police Authority (MPA)
- London Fire & Emergency Planning Authority (LFEPA)
- London Waste and Recycling Board (LWaRB)
- London Development Agency (LDA)

Under the terms of the 1999 Greater London Authority Act the Mayor can make up to 12 personal appointments. He has the power to appoint deputy Mayors with specific areas of responsibility. They can be drawn from the ranks of the London Assembly, or from outside of it. Under the terms of the original legislation, however, there is officially only one Deputy Mayor – and he or she must be a Member of the London Assembly.

The Mayor is supported by the Mayor's Office, which consists of some 30 staff who report directly to him. There is also a pool of permanent staff some 600 strong which supports the Mayor and the Assembly, and which is headed up by a chief executive.

Warning!

The London Mayor has been granted new powers to oversee planning and housing. He now has responsibility for London's housing budget (in excess of £1 billion), which is designed to boost the supply of affordable housing. He also has powers to call in major planning applications where London Boroughs fail to have due regard to the London Plan, or where they unreasonably delay planning decisions.

5.15.2 London Assembly

The main role of the 25 members of the London Assembly is to scrutinise the actions and expenditure of the Mayor, and to hold him to account.

The London Assembly holds the Mayor to account in several ways:

- Questions: The Mayor must attend 10 London Assembly question sessions a year.

- Scrutiny: The Assembly scrutinises the Mayor's proposals and can suggest alternatives.

- Inquiries: The Assembly can initiate its own inquiries and publish the results. It can summon the Mayor or any body in a contractual relationship with the London Assembly or in receipt of an Assembly grant.

- Budget: The Assembly can reject or amend the Mayor's Budget – but only with a two-thirds majority.

- Appointments: The Assembly appoints the chief executive, the monitoring officer, and the chief finance officer.

- Deputy Mayor: The official deputy Mayor must be a Member of the London Assembly.

- Membership: The London Assembly provides members to serve on the Metropolitan Police Authority, the London Fire & Emergency Planning Authority, and the London Development Agency.

In order to undertake its scrutiny role the London Assembly has set up a wide range of committees, all of which are served by a professional secretariat. Current committees are:

- Audit Panel
- Budget Committee
- Budget Monitoring Subcommittee
- Business Management and Administration Committee (formerly the Business Management and Appointments Committee)
- Confirmation Hearings Committee
- Economic Development, Culture, Sport and Tourism Committee
- Elections Review Committee
- Environment Committee

- Health and Public Services Committee
- Planning and Spatial Development Committee
- Standards Committee
- Transport Committee

5.15.3 Finances

As has already been stated the London Assembly plays a key role in scrutinising the Mayor's Budget. It does this in plenary session, and also through the Budget Committee and the Budget Monitoring Sub-committee. The Assembly can also amend or reject the Mayor's Budget, but only if it can muster a two-thirds majority in favour of such a move.

Mayor Ken Livingstone's final Budget was approved by the London Assembly in February 2008. It set the Budget for 2008-9 at £3148.6m. In order to reach this figure, an average Council Tax Precept in Band D was increased by some 2% – or 11p a week. Overall, the bodies controlled or overseen by the London Mayor command a budget in excess of £11 billion.

As well as the Mayor's precept which is levied on Council Tax payers, the Mayor is also allowed to raise money through charges. Currently the Congestion Charge raises the bulk of the money raised through charges, and Mayor Livingstone devoted most of the receipts to boosting the bus fleet deployed by TfL. In 2006 the Congestion Charge raised over £250m in revenue – although more than half of this was eaten up with administration costs.

The Mayor is also obliged, under the terms of the 1999 Greater London Authority Act, to prepare a capital spending plan for :

- Metropolitan Police Authority (MPA)
- Transport for London (TfL)
- London Development Agency (LDA)
- London Fire & Emergency Planning Authority (LFEPA)

The Mayor must also provide in his Budget for the running costs of the Greater London Authority. This includes his own salary, the salaries of Assembly Members, and of all civil servants and support staff – as well as the running costs of City Hall. This currently amounts to some £50m a year.

Contributor's top tip

"All roads lead to the Mayor". The power of the GLA is centralised within the Mayor's office. Get to know the relevant advisers they are key – even more than 10 Downing Street Policy Unit in my experience.

The Assembly does not have much power. To steal Austin Mitchell MP's famous quote about the role of HM opposition, 'The Assembly can only heckle the steamroller [the Mayor]'. It votes on the Mayor's Budget and can cross examine the Mayor with questions, compile reports and write to him/her and release such reports/letters to the media to raise issues and exert political influence but that is about it.

But AMs are still useful. They are engaging and from my experience listen to briefings and act upon them. They can be dogged campaigners.

Don't forget the boroughs and London Councils. The boroughs retain power over certain roads and planning issues, and they can influence the Mayor.

Chris Kelsey, Associate Partner, Finsbury Group

Contributor's top tip

If I could make one plea it would be "keep it relevant". Politicians receive piles of mail every day but most of it isn't constituency business – it is unsolicited briefings, reports, press statements and conference invitations. My in box is full of emails which have been sent to every opinion former on a long list with no thought for my constituency, portfolio or actual responsibilities.

They do not get read.

So the message is do your research first. Identify a small number of people with a real responsibility or a genuine interest in what you have to say. Make it concise, preferably get it all on one page because busy people do not read worthy reports or attend all-day conferences. With a small number you can follow up with a phone call and perhaps a meeting.

"Shotgun lobbying" is disrespectful to your target audience and to your clients.

Roger Evans, GLA Member

Contributor's top tip

Many people have no idea what the GLA is or does and sadly that includes many lobbyists. If you want help from an Assembly Member remember they have no power (except those of us who now hold office in the Boris Administration), but do have some influence. Make sure you have a clear idea of the functions of the Mayor, Assembly and Mayoral Advisors before you approach any of them. I have spent far too many meetings explaining the workings of the London Government Act to lobbyists who think we are a metropolitan version of the Welsh Assembly. My second piece of advise is if your client wants to build a tall building anywhere in London do not bother lobbying because the answer is no!

Brian Coleman, GLA Member

5.16 Local Government

Successive governments have tinkered with the structure, electoral systems and finances of local authorities to create the rather chaotic and patchwork system which we have today.

No incoming government seems capable of resisting renewing the process of upheaval – either in order to right some perceived wrong, fulfil a manifesto commitment, or gain some kind of electoral advantage. Local authorities – because they receive most of their funding direct from Whitehall – do not seem to have the will to resist this constant tinkering. Occasionally, however, resistance from the local population does make central government back away from yet another re-organisation.

Although local authorities command big budgets and have considerable power at a local level, it remains the case that the really big decisions are taken at Westminster and Whitehall – local authorities are more about implementation than decision-making.

5.16.1 Structure

In broad terms there are three basic structures for local government in the United Kingdom:

- *Unitary authorities*: As the name implies, these authorities are responsible for delivering the full range of local services – although some (such as fire and police) may be co-ordinated across boundaries. All local authorities in Scotland and Wales are unitary. So too are authorities in London and the English metropolitan areas (Tyne & Wear, Greater Manchester, Merseyside, West Midlands, South Yorkshire and West Yorkshire). Some other parts of England have also successfully applied for unitary status. In Northern Ireland all local authorities are unitary, but some of their powers currently reside with the Northern Ireland Assembly.

- *Two tier authorities*: In those parts of England which are not metropolitan boroughs, or which have not successfully applied for unitary status, there is a two tier system of local government. County councils deal with issues such as roads, traffic, social services, education, libraries, refuse disposal and consumer protection. The more numerous and smaller district councils deal with local planning, housing, leisure and tourism, environmental health, refuse collection, and electoral registration. Some areas of activity are shared, such as economic development, voluntary sector groups, and fire and emergency planning.

- *Parish councils*: In England and Wales (where they are known as community councils) there are about 10,000 parish council representing another tier of local authority. They have limited powers over environment and recreation issues (village halls, greens, car parks, playing fields, allotments, street signs and lighting) but they must be consulted on local planning applications.

Just to add to the complexity caused by the various structures, there are also a number of different structures for local authority elections:

- *Whole council first-past-the-post (FPTP)*: Most councils in England and Wales have elections every four years where all the council seats are up for election on an FPTP basis. This is known as the "all in, all out" system.

- *Whole council proportional representation (PR)*: In Scotland, a system of PR has been introduced for local authority elections. PR has been used in local elections in Northern Ireland since 1973.

- *Part council by thirds or halves:* In some English local authorities either a third or a half of council seats are up for election each time.

Just to add a further level of complexity to the local government model in the UK the Local Government Act of 2000 made provision for directly elected Mayors. These were to be distinct from the creation of the post of London Mayor, which as we have seen was introduced with the Greater London Authority Act 1999. Currently there are directly elected mayors in:

- Bedford
- Doncaster
- Hackney
- Hartlepool
- Lewisham
- Mansfield
- Middlesbrough
- Newham
- North Tyneside
- Stoke-on-Trent
- Torbay
- Watford

In total there are 468 local authorities in the United Kingdom. The number of local authorities in each country within the UK are:

- England – 388
- Scotland – 32
- Northern Ireland – 26
- Wales – 22

Warning!

Councils in Northern Ireland currently have very few powers. However, with the restoration of devolution to Stormont, the whole structure of local government is likely to be reviewed, and they are likely to be granted similar powers to those wielded by local authorities on the mainland.

In the past local authorities have generally been controlled through a system of full council meetings and committee meetings. Increasingly, however, local authorities are moving towards a more streamlined system of control with a cabinet made up of up to ten councillors. Committees still meet, and full council is still sovereign, but cabinet makes most of the decisions.

Councillors are not paid a salary as such. Every councillor, however, receives an allowance. This allowance is considerably enhanced if the councillor is also a committee chair or a member of the cabinet.

The key personnel when dealing with local authorities are:

- Chief executive: He or she is like a cross between a Whitehall permanent secretary and a company CEO. They are highly experienced – and highly paid – individuals. They report to the majority group leader, but have responsibilities to all councillors, and wide-ranging legal responsibilities laid down by statute. The chief executive is also often the monitoring officer. This is a position introduced in the Local Government and Housing Act 1989. It carries extensive responsibilities for ensuring that the local authority conforms to all relevant laws and regulations.

- Chief officer: Sometimes called a director, or given the title "Head of". This individual runs a department within a local authority. Depending on the size of the local authority there can be upwards of a dozen individuals holding these posts. Nearly every local authority would have a Chief Officer for Finance, Planning, Housing, Education, Social Services, Environment and Leisure. Sometimes roles are combined – eg, Director of Housing and Planning.

- Planning officers: For the lobbyist this is often the key department. Planning Officers have considerable latitude when dealing with residential applications, but anything large-scale enough to involve lobbyists would go to the Chief Planning Officer, the Planning Committee, or even full council. However, cabinet and councillors are guided by officers – and very often heed their advice. It is well worthwhile meeting planning officers (and the chief planning officer) in order to make sure that they are well acquainted with the benefits of any scheme you are proposing.

- Committee clerks: Every Planning Committee has a clerk. Whilst the clerk does not take any part in making decisions, they can often advise you on matters such as the timing of the cycles of Planning Committee meetings, and what scale of representation is permitted and encouraged.

As has already been stated although officials run councils on a day-to-day basis, and have some leeway for making routine decisions, ultimately it is elected councillors who must make – or endorse – all of the major decisions. The key elected personnel are:

- Leader: The leader will be elected by the majority group at its AGM – usually held in May each year.

- Deputy leader: As the name implies this person covers for the leader when he or she is not available. If it is a hung council, with no overall control, the deputy leader may be from the minority coalition party.

- Cabinet: Most local authorities are now run by cabinets consisting of the Leader and up to nine other senior councillors. The cabinet makes many of the most important decisions facing a council, but on the advice of the officers and subject to ratification by full council.

- Committee chair: Usually from the majority group, these individuals have considerable influence over the agendas and decisions of their committees. This goes for the Planning Committee as much as any other committee.

- Chief Whip: This individual will be the councillor within the majority group charged with maximising attendance at full council and committee meetings. The Chief Whip also has a strong influence in deciding who within the group gets promoted (or demoted), and is often the "fixer" behind the scenes who makes sure that deals are done and followed through.

- Opposition spokespersons: It is usually best to deal with the ruling majority group. If, however, that group is hostile to your point of view, you may have to turn to the opposition in order to get them aired. In a hung council the views of opposition spokespersons are obviously particularly crucial.

- Ward councillors: These individuals play a key role in advising and lobbying within the council. No leader who wanted to survive the next AGM makes any decisions without consulting the ward councillors. If the leader decides to go against the advice of the ward councillors they are usually allowed to speak and vote with their electors rather than the group whip. Bear in mind that ward councillors might also be members of the cabinet or sit on relevant committees.

- Political adviser: Many groups have a political adviser. A bit like a Special Adviser in Westminster, they advise the group leader about the political implications of any decisions. Like the Special Adviser, they are a useful sounding board, and a good conduit for setting up deals.

All local authorities now have comprehensive websites which provide details of all elected councillors, and also all senior officers. The *Municipal Journal* (MJ) is the hard copy "bible". It lists all of the elected councillors throughout the country (some 25,000 of them) plus all chief executives and chief officers.

Lobbying councillors and local authority officers involves very similar techniques to lobbying MPs and Whitehall civil servants. The key is always to inform them in order to influence them. Most decisions at a local level have a political and legal – as well as an administrative – background. The rules as to how you can make formal representations to council and to committees varies from one local authority to another. They are, however, generally spelt out in the council's standing orders. If in doubt, consult the office of the chief executive.

The best way to inform and influence councillors and officers are:

- Letters (or emails): The contact details of both councillors and officers are on council websites and listed in the MJ. Write to councillors if your proposal affects their ward or if they have relevant cabinet or committee responsibilities. Write to the chief officer of the relevant department, and he or she will pass on your correspondence to the responsible official.

- Meetings: Once you have written to the relevant councillors and officials seek a face-to-face meeting. In the case of councillors – because they may have day jobs – this will often be in the evenings or at weekends. In the case of officers, it will almost certainly be in office hours. In either case make sure that you have a memorandum, proposal or brochure detailing your case to leave with them.

- Site visits: These can be appropriate for planning or licensing issues. Again, they must be arranged at a time which is convenient to the councillors or officials, and again it is best to have some literature to hand out which they take away with them.

- Surgeries: Most councillors have weekly, fortnightly or monthly surgeries. These are usually held at the town hall, local library or at the local party headquarters. If you have experienced problems arranging a meeting with a councillor turning up at their surgery may be your only option.

- Local press: Both councillors and officers are avid readers of the local newspapers – both paid for and free. If you can arrange a meeting with the editors – or reporters – and get them on your side, it is a great way to influence the local authority. Equally, if the local press is hostile, you should try and meet them and get them to soften their line.

- Petitions: Many councillors are elected with tiny majorities – in single figures, dozens, or a few hundred at most. A petition with even a relatively small number of signatories can have a big effect on their thinking.

- Opinion polls : Again, a positive poll taken from even a relatively small sample of the local population can have a disproportionate effect on the thinking of councillors and officers.

- Local MP: Technically there is no formal relationship between the local MP and the local authority. In practice, however, MPs tend to have a fair amount of sway over officers and councillors – especially if they are from the same party as the ruling group. Many MPs started out their careers as councillors – either for the seat they represent or elsewhere – so they know the system and how to influence it.

Contributor's top tip

Councillors' home addresses are a matter of public record. Some councils list them on their website, but some others release them only when asked. If you are lobbying councillors, do not write to them at the council offices, where mail will often go unopened for weeks. Instead, spend a little time researching addresses, and then write to them at home. That way, you are much more likely to have your letter read rather than ignored, or indeed binned unopened.

Francis Ingham, former Councillor

Other groups worth engaging with are:

- Local authority organisations: Bodies such as the Local Government Association (LGA), Convention of Scottish Local Authorities (COSLA), the Welsh Local Government Association (WLGA), the Northern Ireland Local Government Association (NILGA) and London Councils play a key role. They lobby central government on behalf of their members. They also collect and disseminate best practice in policy areas which fall within the remit of local authorities. Investigating their policies, and enlisting their support, can often be worthwhile.

- Regional Development Agencies: There are eight Regional Development Agencies in England, plus the LDA in London. Their role is to "act as strategic drivers of regional economic development in their region". They have both big budgets and a lot of influence at both national and local levels.

- Local party: Councillors maintain strong formal and informal links with their local associations and parties. They are dependant on them for being re-selected and re-elected. It is worth engaging with the parties at local level in order to get to know the key players, and to try and convince them that your proposal will be beneficial to the local area.

- Residents' associations: Residents' associations, residents' groups and preservation societies are often extremely influential. Being an established part of the local scene they will have built up strong relationships with the local councillors, the local MP, and the local press. If you can get them on your side that is often half the battle. If they oppose your project, you can find yourself struggling.

Author's top tip

The letters page of local newspapers are more widely read than any other section. They are read not just by the local electorate, but also by councillors and council officers. They are, therefore, a very good place to get your views across. By the same token, if a letter appears which contradicts your case, you might well be advised to write a letter in response.

5.16.2 Planning

Most of the situations where a professional lobbyist (as opposed to local campaigner) lobbies local authorities are planning related. Councils at every level – from unitary to county to district to parish – have either a decision-making or an advisory role in planning decisions.

The majority of planning applications which come before local authorities relate to domestic properties. They can be applications for a loft conversion, for an extension, or to add or convert a garage. Local businesses also approach the local authority on a regular basis to apply for permission to extend their premises. Generally all such small-scale applications – residential or commercial – are promoted either by the applicant themselves, by an architect, or by a local firm which specialises in planning issues.

Commercial lobbyists generally get involved on much larger scale projects. Examples might include building a new supermarket, converting a football ground into shops or flats, or building an entire housing estate in the grounds of a hospital which has been closed down. Sometimes applications can be hugely controversial – as is almost invariably the case when any application is made to undertake any sort of development (even recreational or educational) on the green belt. This is where the advocacy and communication skills of the lobbyist can come into play.

As with most other areas of local authority activity, the basic rules for planning are laid down in legislation passed in Westminster and applied through Whitehall. The current Whitehall department which oversees local government is the Department of Communities and Local Government (DCLG). Under a succession of Acts of Parliament local authorities are obliged to construct and publish plans which provide a template for development in their areas.

Under the provisions of the Planning and Compulsory Purchase Act 2004 local authorities became obliged to produce strategic plans. These are modelled on the London Plan, which was initiated by the Greater London Authority Act of 1999. Previously local authorities had to prepare a local plan – Development Plans in the case of District Councils, Structure Plans in the case of County Councils, and Unitary Development Plans (a combination of the two) in the case of Unitary Authorities. Each local authority has to prepare a Local Development Framework (LDF) which details its policies regarding development and land use. Under the same Act, county Structure Plans were scrapped and replaced with Regional Spatial Strategies, which are formulated by a Regional Planning Body. These are indirectly elected bodies which were supposed to be the precursor's for regional government in England – a move stalled by failed referendums in the North East and North West.

When compiling their plans, local authorities must take note not just of legislation, but also of guidance issued by the DCLG. Current guidance takes the form of:

- Planning policy guidance

- Planning policy statements

- Regional planning guidance

Within these constraints, local authorities do have considerable leeway in the way in which they deal with planning applications. As has already been stated, local councillors receive an allowance and not a salary – and that means that most of them are part-time. The initial port of call in anybody dealing with local authorities is, therefore, often an officer. The relationship is similar to Whitehall and Westminster which was dealt with earlier in the book. You start off dealing with the civil servant (or in this case local authority officer), and generally only go over their heads to the elected politician if you do not succeed with this initial approach.

Planning Committees are not supposed to be whipped, and they are not supposed to vote along party lines. In practice, however, there are sometimes informal discussions ahead of Planning Committee meetings, and votes are often cast along broadly party lines. However, when making representations to Planning Committees – either in person or by way of a written submission – it is vital to avoid the slightest hint of either party bias or special pleading along party lines. Planning decisions are supposed to be based on two criteria – the law as laid down by the Westminster Parliament and as interpreted by the courts, and the wishes and needs of the local population. Councillors may have more regard for the latter than the former, but officers will ensure that they pay due regard to the former.

Contributor's top tip

Undertaking the public affairs work securing planning consent for a scheme, be it a large multi-billion pound 70 storey tower or a small block of flats, I always observe the following:

- I treat everything like a campaign, measuring everything I do against the ultimate objective of securing consent.

- I ensure my client speaks to stakeholders early, and that together we target any leading activists to brief them in a friendly environment.

- I ensure we always have full knowledge of the issues, both about the area of development and the person with whom we are liaising.

- I treat my fellow colleagues, be they architects or planning consultants, with absolute respect, and expect the same respect to be shown to my profession. I focus on the decision – and securing a positive outcome. I know, and so does the client, that I and my team are only as good as our last decision. That's why we have an outstanding record of success.

Richard Patient, Managing Director, Indigo Public Affairs

If a planning application does not go your way it is not necessarily the end of the story. You have other avenues which you could explore:

- Resubmission: You can re-submit your application, but with amendments which take account of the committee's objections.

- Appeal: Local authorities must make an appeal procedure available and must offer guidance as to how it can be accessed.

- Planning gain: Local authorities will often soften their opposition to a planning application – or even remove it altogether – if incentives termed "planning gain" are offered. Under these developers may offer to build a local facility (a school or a library for instance) at no cost to local residents in return for permission to proceed with a development. These are often referred to as Section 106 Agreements.

- Courts: If you feel that proper procedures have not been followed, that the council has not acted in conformity with its own standing orders, or that the council or the Planning Committee has not acted in accordance with the law, you can go to court. Many councils will seek a compromise when faced with the prospect of legal action, as the costs can be exorbitant, and the council tax payer will not necessarily thank them for spending money on legal fees as opposed to local services. There is also sometimes the option of reporting a local authority to the Commissioner for Local Administration (the ombudsman), or to the Audit Commission.

- Calling-in: The secretary of state for Communities and Local Government can call in any planning application. In practice they only tend to do this where major planning applications are concerned – but they can be encouraged to do so. Again, the threat of this can have a salutary effect on the thinking of local authorities. The London Mayor also has powers to call in planning applications – and to influence schemes even before formal applications have been made.

Contributor's top tip

Lobbying in relation to planning applications.

The uncertainty brought about in the minds of residents when they are informed of a proposal to develop close to where they live can be disturbing. However hard local authorities try, it is a challenge to fully engage residents in a debate about the Local Plan, or Local Development Framework, as it is now called. Yet it is the policies set out in this framework, which is tested through public consultation and a public inquiry, against which planning applications are assessed.

So when a local authority has to decide whether or not to grant permission, it has to look at the policies in the Development Plan first. The views of local residents are a material consideration but can not override the policies of the plan. It is, therefore, important for residents who wish to lobby against a planning application to carry out the following:

- Read up the policies set out in the Development Plan – the Council website will allow access to this information.

- Seek to establish which policies are appropriate to consideration of the application especially those policies which assist in opposing the application

- Compose an informed letter to the local authority based on the policies and on fact. Simply opposing is not good enough. The grounds for objection must be planning based and not other issues such as covenants.

- Contact your local ward councillors, speak to them, send them copies of your letters.

- Send copies of your letter to all members of the Planning Committee.

- Enlist the assistance of the local Civic Society or residents' association.

- Ask to speak at the Planning Committee, and be concise and cogent.

If you are a developer making an application life is more difficult in that, following the Nolan Committee, every local authority is signed up to a code of conduct for councillors. This can preclude any lobbying by applicants for planning permission direct to councillors. If councillors are approached by applicants, they have to declare it if they are members of the Planning Committee and, would normally, not be allowed to speak or vote on that application. Tactics have to be different. If it is a large development, ask if you can give a presentation to members of the planning committee outside of the normal committee process. Prepare information leaflets describing factually what the application is about for circulation to councillors. Above all, before the application is submitted, talk to the local residents and amenity groups. Involve them in commenting on the scheme and make changes in the light of the comments received. Trying to negotiate out objections beforehand can pay substantial dividends.

Martin Jewell, Planning Consultant and former Head of Planning for a London borough

5.16.3 Licensing

Under the provisions of the Licensing Act 2003 (which came into force in November 2005) responsibility for licensing was transferred from magistrates' courts to local authorities – who officially became the Licensing Authorities.

The 2003 Act stipulated that not just landlords but also premises had to be licensed. It also allowed local authorities to exercise considerable discretion when granting – or refusing – licences. The Act applies not just to public houses, but also to nightclubs and private members' clubs. Licensing policy is considered by the Licensing Committee, whilst individual applications are dealt with by the Licensing Sub-committee.

In theory the new arrangements introduced a strong element of local accountability to the licensing process. Local councillors would make the decisions – and be held accountable for them by the local population. In practise, most local councillors will privately admit that the acquisition of the powers granted under the 2003 Act have brought them many headaches. Although central government was happy to devolve the authority to local councils, it did not – in the opinion of many councillors – devolve sufficient funding to deal with the amount of administration involved. In addition, many of the decisions taken inevitably offend one section of the population or another – with different positions being pressed on them by local residents on the one hand, and licensees, pub-goers and clubbers on the other.

Problems with licences have been exacerbated by the increasing trend for pubs to be set up in high street locations. Other shopkeepers sometimes find that pubs make uncomfortable neighbours. Many of the shops also have flats above them and the owners or tenants are often unhappy with the noise which is often associated with modern pubs – with music and widescreen TVs almost omnipresent. The nuisance to neighbours and local residents has been made considerably worse by the introduction of smoking bans across the UK. The effect of the bans has been to push large numbers of drinkers outdoors at all hours and in all seasons, causing noise and litter nuisance.

What the Licensing Act 2003 has done is to open up a new revenue stream for lobbyists. Pubs and clubs can be big business – whether they are part of a chain or independently owned. There is a great deal of money at stake for licensed premises to keep or extend their licences. Licensing Committees and Sub-committees, like Planning Committees, sit in a quasi-judicial capacity. They are influenced primarily by the law and by facts. However, they also have to take account of all sides of an argument, and can be swayed by a skilful presentation. As with planning, there is definitely scope for lobbyists to offer their advocacy skills in this area, and to help to formulate the case for licence acquisition, retention or extension.

Contributor's top tip

If you want a licence till 3am apply for one until 4am. If you want to have 250 people in the place apply for 350. Don't agree with any of the conditions requested by Health and Safety, the police or Trading Standards until just before the licensing hearing, otherwise they will dream up new ones.

Anonymous, Councillor serving on Licensing Committee

Contributor's top tip

My top tip for licence applications would be: eliminate all opposition from neighbours and residents in advance as far as possible. Keep them on side because councillors do listen to them. Be reasonable, if you have a block of flats with several hundred residents 20 yards from your back door, you are not going to get a licence into the small hours of the morning. Prove that your intentions are sincere. If you are aiming for a younger market, do not pretend it will be a place for quiet, mature customers.

Cllr Henry Lamprecht, London Borough of Enfield

5.16.4 Procurement

Local authorities are obliged by law to provide certain services and amenities to local residents. They are not, however, necessarily obliged to provide those services and amenities themselves. Some are provided by council employees or their Direct Labour Organisations. Others, however, are supplied by either companies or charities and not-for-profit groups.

Overall local authorities account for almost a quarter of all government spending in the UK. This will amount to around £150bn in 2008. Much of that goes on wages and pensions, and mandatory areas of ring-fenced expenditure such as education and social services. A substantial proportion of that money, however, goes on services and capital expenditure which can be contracted out.

Under the previous Conservative government all local authority contracts of any size had to be put out to Compulsory Competitive Tendering (CCT). That meant that a specification was drawn up, a tender document issued, and whoever came in with the lowest bid won the contract. Services such as refuse collection, catering, street lighting and maintenance are now routinely contracted out.

Under the current Labour administration, however, CCT was replaced by "Best Value". This meant that cost – although the single most important factor – was not the sole arbiter. Contracts did not have to be awarded to the lowest bidder, but other factors could be taken into account in deciding which tender offered best value overall.

Under this concept of Best Value councils must produce annual performance plans. These set out both their achievements, and future targets. They must also set out a schedule for which services are to be reviewed. Suppliers are rated not just on cost efficiency, but also on customer satisfaction and public perceptions.

For the lobbyist, Best Value provides more opportunities than CCT. Under the latter, only accountants and lawyers were needed when preparing a bid. Under Best Value, lobbyists can help to prepare a case for a company or organisation which goes beyond the simple figures. A proposal can draw on client recommendations, and surveys, and market research. It can also be framed in a way which most closely meets the priorities of the council issuing the tender. Lobbyists can play a role both in securing an initial contract, and in ensuring that it is renewed.

Author's top tip

Before launching a public affairs programme in a locality try and attend a full council meeting and at least one relevant committee meeting. It will give you a good feel for who are the key players, how the parties inter-react and how decisions are taken.

5.17 Parliamentary Commissioner For Administration (The Ombudsman)

Before proceeding to the cost of applying to the courts there is one almost cost free quasi-judicial route which the lobbyists can recommend that their clients should consider pursuing.

The Parliamentary Commissioner for Administration – more commonly referred to as the ombudsman – has wide discretion to investigate (and rule on) cases of alleged maladministration by the government or its agents. The Westminster ombudsman also covers Wales (where he or she reports to the Welsh Assembly) and is also the health commissioner for England and Wales. There is a Scottish equivalent reporting to the Scottish Parliament, and the same in Northern Ireland, reporting to the Assembly.

Since 1994 the ombudsman has also been given responsibility for overseeing the code on open government. This means that if a government department is unreasonably withholding information which should be available under the Freedom of Information Act, the help of the ombudsman can be solicited in forcing them to do so – without going through the courts.

The ombudsman can only investigate complaints referred by an MP. This is where a lobbyist's skills can come in to play, by helping to identify an MP who would be willing to pursue a complaint. The ombudsman now has a staff of 230 to help to investigate complaints. The staff have unparalleled access to government records, and it is this access – and the standing and status of the ombudsman – which creates fear amongst government agencies.

If the ombudsman finds in favour of the complainant he or she can make recommendations that the grievance be addressed. No actual power to enforce her findings is granted, but there is a strong imperative for government's to accept the recommendations. This is especially the case as the press often seize on the ombudsman's findings, making it even harder for the government to ignore them. A good example was the case of the collapsed financial institution Barlow Clowes. The government rejected the ombudsman's findings but after a media outcry made an *ex gratia* payment of £150m to the victims of the collapsed fund. Since then the ombudsman has also urged the government to compensate victims of the Equitable Life collapse.

5.18 The Judiciary

Unlike most countries the UK has no formal written constitution. One of the effects of this is that there are fewer opportunities for the courts to rule on political issues, and there are fewer clashes between the judiciary and the government. In countries with a formal written constitution – such as the United States – courts are regularly asked to rule on the legality of legislation, measured against the written constitutions. In the US the Supreme Court over-rules acts passed on Capitol Hill on the basis that they are incompatible with one or another of the articles of the US constitution.

That is not to say that British courts have not ruled against governments – they have certainly done so. What is more, several developments have made it more likely that this will become an increasingly frequent occurrence. These developments include the landmark Pepper v Hart ruling, and the passing of the Human Rights Act and the Freedom of Information Act (see below for more details). These provide the lobbyist with opportunities to open up a new front, where standard public affairs techniques have failed to achieve the desired objective.

From the perspective of the lobbyists, "going legal" is very much a last resort – the public affairs equivalent of going nuclear. This route should not be considered until all other options – including using the media – have been tried. Going to the courts is costly, and it is hard to predict the outcome. Having once resorted to the courts, and failed, it is very hard to see how any subsequent concessions could be wrung from the government. Perhaps the best example is the pro-hunting lobby led by the Countryside Alliance. Having vigorously lobbied Whitehall and Westminster from Green Paper to Royal Assent, and having enlisted the support of large sections of the media and organised a huge protest march of 400,000 people in central London, they ultimately resorted to the courts, but still failed.

5.18.1 Pepper v Hart

In a landmark case in 1993 the High Court ruled that if the language of an Act of Parliament is ambiguous or obscure the courts could refer back to the speeches made by ministers when guiding the bill through its parliamentary stages in order to construe and clarify meaning. Until this ruling, any attempt to quote *Hansard* in support of a case was regarded as a breech of parliamentary privilege.

The case arose when the Inland Revenue (in the form of one Inspector Pepper) attempted to pursue a school-master (Mr Hart) for the cash equivalent of the concessionary education which his children received as a result of his employment as a teacher at a private school. The dispute was over the meaning of the term cash equivalent. This could be interpreted as the difference between the full fees and the concessionary fees, or it could be interpreted as the marginal cost to the school of providing a subsidised place to Mr Hart's children – especially where there were vacant places available. Although the actual wording in the Finance Act was ambiguous, a comment by the financial secretary to the Treasury during the committee stage of the bill clearly indicated that it was the intention for the marginal benefit to be taxed.

This judgement created two precedents. Firstly, that *Hansard* could be quoted in the courts without issues of privilege being raised. And secondly, that where the meaning of a provision within an act was uncertain, any statement made by a minister promoting the bill could be used to clarify and interpret the legal position.

For the lobbyist, this ruling has two potential benefits. Firstly, if during any stage of a bill a minister can be pushed into making – or even implying – a concession it could have force of law. Secondly, it is the ultimate rationale for monitoring the proceedings of a bill carefully. If a minister strays from his or her brief, and introduces an element of confusion into the proceedings, then subsequent legal recourse becomes a realistic prospect.

5.18.2 Judicial Review

Applications for Judicial Review are fairly frequent, with some 2000 applications being made each year. This is despite the potentially substantial costs of the process – £50,000 is widely regarded as the starting point. What is more, only about one-third of applications actually succeed.

The procedure for applying for a Judicial Review is laid down in Order 53 of the Rules of the Supreme Court. It is a two stage process, with an applicant initially seeking leave to apply, and then (if successful) moving onto an actual hearing. There are five remedies available under the Judicial Review process:

- *Certiorari*: This quashes a decision which has already been made, and deprives it of legal effect.

- *Prohibition*: This prevents a proposed decision from actually being put into effect.

- *Mandamus*: This is used to force a public body to do something, or to exercise its discretion in a particular way.

- *Declaration*: This sets out the legal position in areas where there is a dispute.

- *Injunction*: This is used to restrain illegal actions, and to put a hold on a situation pending an application for prohibition (see above).

The Judicial Review procedure can be used against central government, local government, or any of their agencies or bodies. The only stipulation is that the applicant must have *locus standi* – that is to say a direct interest in the case. Applications for Judicial Review often involve routine cases – such as immigration appeals, or disputes over access to benefits or housing. Obviously the cost of Judicial Review is almost invariably beyond the means of such complainants, but charities and pressure groups fund such applications where they consider a great injustice is being perpetrated, or where they are seeking to establish a legal precedent.

It should be noted that the Judicial Review process cannot be used to challenge primary legislation. The use of the process is restricted to the challenging of delegated or secondary legislation. Judicial Review can also be used to challenge the way in which ministers give effect to primary legislation, or to any guidelines they issue which flows from primary legislation. Three of the remedies available under Judicial Review (*Ceriorari*, Prohibition and *Mandamus*) are not applicable to government. Applicants must seek either Declaration (clarifying the legal position) or Injunction (restraining illegal action).

Landmark Judicial Reviews over the years have included:

- Coal mine closures: In 1992 the National Union of Mineworkers successfully challenged the decision of the then president of the Board of Trade, Michael Heseltine, to shut 31 coal mines without consultation.

- Victims of crime: In 1994 the Home Secretary Michael Howard was ruled to have acted illegally when he cut compensation to victims of violent crime.

- False passports: In 1999 Home Secretary Jack Straw was judged to have acted illegally over the prosecution and imprisonment of refugees who had travelled using false passports.

- NHS care for asylum seekers: In 2008 Health Secretary Alan Johnson was ruled to have acted illegally in refusing to provide free NHS treatment to asylum seekers who had not been ordered to leave the UK.

5.18.3 Human Rights Act

The Human Rights Act received Royal Assent in 1998 and came into force in October 2000. It makes the provisions of the European Convention on Human Rights directly enforceable in the UK, without requiring recourse to the European Court of Human Rights in Strasbourg.

The main provisions of the European Convention on Human Rights are:

- Article 2: The right to life.
- Article 3: Prohibition of torture.
- Article 4: Prohibition of slavery and forced labour
- Article 5: Right to liberty and security
- Article 6: Right to a fair trial
- Article 7: Right to immunity from retrospective legislation
- Article 8: Right to respect for family and private life
- Article 9: Right to freedom of thought, conscience and religion
- Article 10: Right to freedom of expression
- Article 11: Right to freedom of assembly and association
- Article 12: Right to marry
- Article 14: Right not to suffer discrimination

The Human Rights Act has been widely and repeatedly used in the UK since it came into force in October 2000. Examples of cases which have been brought include:

- Prevention of the deportation of illegal immigrants where they might be tortured if returned to their countries of origin.
- Refusal to admit holders of UK passports.
- Over-turning the ban on homosexuals serving in the armed forces.

- Sex discrimination cases relating to equal pay.

- Restrictions on political activity of charities.

The government has accepted that it has an obligation not just to refrain from activities which breach the European Convention on Human Rights, but also a positive duty to ensure that its provisions are given effect. Whenever ministers introduce new legislation – in the Westminster Parliament or the devolved bodies – they are now obliged to append a statement confirming that the proposed legislation is compatible with the Convention.

For the lobbyist, the Convention offers the opportunity to challenge legislation when it is introduced, where there is doubt over the ministerial statement of compatibility. Retrospectively, it is possible to apply to the High Court for a declaration of incompatibility with the Convention. This has the effect of forcing the government to introduce fast-track legislation removing any such compatibility. Should they fail to do so, an application can be made to the Court to force them to take remedial action.

Although there has not been the tidal wave of court cases citing the Human Rights Act and the Convention which many had predicted, there has been a steady stream of cases – some of them establishing significant precedent. It has also heralded another substantial blurring of the boundaries between the judiciary and the body politic, and introduced another avenue of opportunity for the lobbyist seeking to over-turn or head off the effects of government legislation.

5.18.4 European Court of Justice

It is often stated that the House of Lords is the highest court in the land. Whilst this is technically – and geographically – correct, since the European Communities Act of 1972 EU legislation has had primacy over UK legislation. This in effect makes the European Court of Justice in Luxembourg the ultimate court of appeal.

The primacy of EU legislation was underlined in the 1991 *Factortame* case. In this case the High Court ruled that the 1988 Merchant Shipping Act had no effect, because it contravened EU law. This vividly demonstrated that all UK legislation must be drafted – and applied – with the primacy of EU legislation in mind.

Just as lobbyists can use Judicial Review or have recourse to the Human Rights Act to seek to influence government policy or overturn government decisions through the British judicial system, they can equally look to Europe for ultimate redress. The European Court of Justice (and its offshoot the Court of First Instance) rules on domestic matters in all EU member states. The only problem with the European Court of Justice is that it can take several years to arrive at a judgement, and in the meantime legal fees can rise alarmingly. For a lobbyist, recourse to the European Court of Justice really is the last resort.

In this section of the book we have discussed how lobbyists can use the legal system if all other avenues of advocacy be blocked. In the next part of the book we will see how the European Union has a direct and pervasive influence on all legislation and government decisions in the UK, and therefore cannot be ignored by UK organisations or lobbyists.

Part Six – Lobbying The European Union

6.1 History And Background

The roots of the European Union can possibly be traced as far back as the Franco-Prussian war of 1870. As Germany emerged as a powerful nation state, it regularly found itself in conflict with its longer-established neighbour. The comparatively small-scale wars of the nineteenth century gave way to the world wars of the twentieth century, and France found herself not just defeated, but also occupied.

The first world war was supposed to be the war that ended all wars. Yet it was followed by the second world war, which was truly global in scale and which resulted in the death of more than 40m civilians and military personnel. It was from the rubble of a devastated France and Germany that the idea of – and the imperative for – some kind of a united Europe was born. Ironically, it may well have been the pro-American British patriot and statesman Winston Churchill who first mooted the idea of a United States of Europe in a speech delivered to the House of Commons in the middle of the second world war in 1942. He fleshed out his ideas in a speech given at Zurich University in 1946, in which he said:

> 'Our constant aim must be to build and fortify the strength of the United Nations organisation. Under and within that world concept we must recreate the European family in a regional structure called – it may be – the United States of Europe and the first practical step will be to form a Council of Europe.'

However, Churchill's speeches and ideas are largely ignored by most writers and historians when the genesis of the European Union is chronicled. Conventional wisdom has French foreign minister Robert Schuman, along with his compatriot Jean Monnet, as the godfather of the EU. Schuman's memory is kept alive with a number of streets and buildings in France and Belgium – and a metro station in Brussels – named after him.

Here is a brief chronology charting the major developments affecting what is now the European Union:

- 1950: French foreign minister Robert Schuman announced plans for the creation of the European Coal and Steel Community. In the Schuman Declaration he proposed that Europe should move towards greater integration through the formation of a body which would aim for constant evolution and the gradual expansion of power and territory. He was inspired to make the speech by the French entrepreneur and post-war planner Jean Monnet.

- 1950: First Inter-Governmental Conference, chaired by Jean Monnet.
- 1951: Treaty of Paris lays foundations for the setting up of the European Coal and Steel Community (ECSC).
- 1952: The European Coal and Steel Community is founded, with France, West Germany, Italy, Belgium, Holland and Luxembourg as the founder members and Jean Monnet as the first president of its High Authority.
- 1952: The Messina Resolution called for the creation of a united Europe and a common market.
- 1955: Second Inter-Governmental Conference, paving the way for the Treaty of Rome.
- 1955: Formation of the Western European Union (WEU).
- 1957: Treaty of Rome is signed as a precursor to the setting up of the European Economic Community (EEC) and the European Atomic Energy Community (Euratom).
- 1958: The EEC is set up, with the same six members as the European Coal and Steel Community. Its main aim was the establishment of a customs union with a common external tariff for all goods entering the EEC.
- 1960: The Stockholm Convention is signed by Austria, Denmark, Norway, Portugal, Sweden, Switzerland and the United Kingdom. It sets up the European Free Trade Area (EFTA).
- 1961: The United Kingdom applies for EEC membership.
- 1963: France, under President de Gaulle, vetoes the UK's EEC membership application.
- 1965: Merger Treaty bringing together the EEC, ECSC and Euratom.
- 1966: UK, Ireland and Denmark apply to join EEC for the second time.
- 1966: UK application is again vetoed by President de Gaulle.
- 1968: Agreement is reached on the formation of the Common Agricultural Policy.
- 1970: Membership applications by the United Kingdom, Denmark, Norway and Ireland are accepted.
- 1972: Norwegian referendum on EEC membership is voted down and its application is withdrawn.

- 1973: The first enlargement, with the accession of Denmark, Ireland and the United Kingdom.

- 1975: Referendum to confirm UK membership of the EEC.

- 1975: Greece applied to join the EEC.

- 1977: Portugal and Spain apply to join the EEC.

- 1979: The European Monetary System (EMS) starts to operate using the Exchange Rate Mechanism (ERM).

- 1979: First direct elections for the European Parliament are held.

- 1981: Second enlargement with Greece acceding.

- 1982: Greenland withdraws from EEC.

- 1984: The "Esprit" programme for research and development in information technology is adopted.

- 1984: EEC and EFTA agree to free trade.

- 1985: The Schengen Agreement on the elimination of border checks is signed by France, Germany, Belgium, Holland and Luxembourg.

- 1985: European Council agrees to the drawing up of the Single European Act.

- 1986: Third enlargement with the accession of Portugal and Spain.

- 1986: Single market comes into force with the signing of the Single European Act.

- 1986: European Economic Community (EEC) becomes European Community (EC).

- 1987: Turkey applies to join the EEC.

- 1989: Austria applies to join the EEC.

- 1990: Accession of the five German Lander which were previously part of East Germany.

- 1990: Agreement establishing the European Bank for Reconstruction and Development (EBRD) is signed.

- 1990: Cyprus and Malta apply to join the EEC.

- 1991: The Treaty of Maastricht is signed. It introduces two new "pillars" (justice and home affairs and defence and security) to the EEC's competence, paves the way for the single currency, and transforms the EC in to the European Union (EU).

- 1991: Agreement creating a European Economic Area (EEA) is signed by the EU and EFTA.

- 1991: Two Inter-Governmental Conferences are held to discuss monetary union and political union.

- 1991: Sweden applies to join the EEC.

- 1992: Currency speculators force the United Kingdom to withdraw from the ERM in what became known as "Black Wednesday".

- 1992: Finland and Switzerland apply to join the EEC.

- 1992: Norway re-applies to join the EEC.

- 1992: Treaty of Maastricht signed.

- 1993: Single Market comes fully in to force.

- 1993: Treaty on European Union comes in to force – the European Community is absorbed in to the European Union.

- 1993: The Copenhagen Conditions for new countries seeking to join the EU are agreed.

- 1994: Creation of the European Economic Area.

- 1994: Hungary and Poland apply to join the EEC.

- 1994: Norwegian referendum again results in a "No" vote.

- 1995: Fourth enlargement with the accession of Austria, Finland and Sweden.

- 1995: The Schengen agreement comes into force with France, Germany, Belgium, Holland Luxembourg, Spain and Portugal opening their borders to each other.

- 1996: An Inter-Governmental Conference is held to pave the way for the Treaty of Amsterdam.

- 1996: Czech Republic and Slovenia apply to join the EU.

- 1997: Treaty of Amsterdam is signed restructuring the EU in preparation for further expansion.

- 1997: Treaty of Amsterdam comes into force.

- 1999: Launch of the euro.

- 2000: Danish referendum rejects euro.

- 2001: Treaty of Nice is signed. It allows for further EU integration, and the accession of the Eastern European states.

- 2001: Swiss referendum rejects proposal to join the EU.

- 2001: Irish voters reject Treaty of Nice in a referendum.

- 2002: Irish voters accept Treaty of Nice in second referendum after assurances protecting Ireland's neutrality.

- 2002: Convention on the Future of Europe is established with a remit of trying to make the EU more democratic and efficient.

- 2002: First euro notes and coins go in to circulation.

- 2003: Inter-Governmental Conference leads to the setting up of the Convention on the Future of Europe.

- 2003: Convention on the Future of Europe publishes its report.

- 2003: Treaty of Nice comes into force.

- 2003: Swedish referendum rejects the euro.

- 2004: Fifth enlargement with Cyprus, Czech Republic, Estonia, Hungary, Latvia, Lithuania, Malta, Poland, Slovakia and Slovenia all acceding.

- 2004: European heads of government sign the European constitution.

- 2005: EU constitution rejected by voters in referendums in France and Holland.

- 2007: Slovenia joins the euro zone.

- 2007: Inter-Governmental Conference paves way for signing of the Treaty of Lisbon.

- 2007: Sixth enlargement with Bulgaria and Romania acceding.

- 2007: Treaty of Lisbon signed by EU leaders as alternative to rejected EU constitution.

- 2008: Cyprus and Malta join the euro zone.

- 2008: In a referendum on 12 June the Irish public reject the Treaty of Lisbon.

As has been seen what is now the EU evolved steadily over the last fifty or so years. The same could also be said of its institutions.

The changes in the relative strengths and the competencies of the institutions of the EU have resulted from the provisions of successive treaties. However, they have also evolved naturally, and their relationships have changed without there necessarily having been any formal agreement that this should occur. This has come about partly as a result of external events and movements. Thus the desire for greater democracy and openness across Europe and across democracies at large has undoubtedly helped to boost the standing of the European Parliament. This, in time, led to the extension of its powers. Equally, the authority of the European Commission was undoubtedly enhanced by the long tenure and strong ambitions of Jacques Delors when he was president of the Commission from 1985-1994. A succession of less respected presidents who occupied the post for a shorter period of time saw the authority of the Commission wane.

Although the relative fortunes and authority of the three main institutions of the EU have risen and fallen, it has undoubtedly always been difficult to place them in any order of importance. This is an integrated system, with a substantial series of checks and balances, and all three institutions are intimately involved in the development of policy and the passing of legislation. There are also a host of EU and non-EU bodies advising the big three institutions, and overseeing their decisions – not least the European Court of Justice. So rather than try and put the three main institutions into any kind of order of importance, I will simply deal with them in alphabetical order.

Contributor's top tip

Transparency is key to successful lobbying in Brussels. And despite their image of smoke-filled rooms and closed doors, the Brussels institutions are surprisingly open and accessible. It is still easier to ring up officials in the Commission and request a meeting than it is to approach ministries at national level. In return, it is essential that you are transparent about who you are and whom you represent. That way you immediately generate a better level of trust, formulate arguments based on what you know (rather who you know), and have a chance to build a long-term relationship with decision-makers.

This approach has been picked up and formalised by Commissioner Kallas in his European Transparency Initiative. While many professional consultancies such as Fleishman-Hillard have been signatories to the Code of Conduct for Public Affairs practitioners since it was originally formed in 1995, the sheer explosion of lobbyists since then has meant that new parameters are required. One particular outcome of this initiative is the Commission's voluntary register for all interest representatives in Brussels which was launched in June 2008. Fleishman-Hillard, as other members of EPACA (European Public Affairs Consultancies Association), is intending to sign up to the register as long as we are satisfied that the same level of transparency is required across the board.

Caroline Wunnerlich, Managing Director, Fleishman-Hillard

6.2 Council Of Ministers

Of the three main institutions of the EU the Council of Ministers may well have the claim to being the most powerful. What it undoubtedly is, however, is the least well known of the institutions. This is partly because it is so amorphous, partly because the layman has no idea what it does, but mainly because it conducts most of its activities in private. Agendas and working papers are not always published. Television cameras are now allowed into some Council meetings, though they are rarely allowed into the ones where deals are done or key decisions are taken.

The Council of Ministers is made up of ministers from the member states meeting in one of nine Councils (or "configurations" as they are sometimes known), depending on what is the nature of the topic under discussion. The Council of Ministers is based in Brussels – partly because that is the true seat of power within the EU, partly because it is convenient from a travel point of view for most ministers and partly so that the relevant European Commissioner can also easily attend.

Although there are no official alliances amongst the member states and the ministers who represent them at the Council of Ministers, there are certain groups which have a history of close collaboration. France and Germany have long worked in tandem as the driving force of what is now the EU – although the strength of the bond does vary along with the warmth of the personal relations between their leaders. There is also often an informal alliance between the member states who are net contributors to the budget. This alliance separates Germany (a big net contributor) from France (a big net beneficiary). The Nordic countries often vote together, as do the Mediterranean countries. The smaller member states often band together for protection, and the longer-established member states are sometimes united by their frustrations at the demands of the newer entrants. These constantly shifting alliances make the work of the Permanent Representatives and the transient ministers both difficult and interesting.

The frequency of the meetings of the various configurations of the Councils of Ministers varies enormously. The most powerful Council is known by its acronym GAERC – which stands for the General Affairs and External Relations Council. This meets at least once a month, and brings together foreign affairs ministers from all the member states to deal with over-arching issues – either within the EU or outside of it. Since the launch of the Single Currency the importance of ECOFIN has also increased. The Agriculture and

Fisheries Committee is always important, since the EU spends so much of its budget subsidising farmers, and fishing disputes are always bitter. Meetings are usually over within one day, but occasionally stray into a second day where no agreement has been reached.

A full list of Councils is:

- Agriculture and Fisheries

- Competitiveness

- Economic and Financial Affairs

- Education, Youth and Culture

- Employment, Social Policy, Health and Consumer Affairs

- Environment

- General Affairs and External relations

- Justice and Home Affairs

- Transport, Telecoms and Energy

The Council is supported by a series of committees and working groups. They prepare Decisions for the main Councils, and also for any *ad hoc* Councils which are set up. They also follow up on any decisions which are taken. The committees are made up of representatives from the member states, plus one member of the Commission. Working groups can be set up to deal with a transient dossier. They also do preparatory work for COREPER – see below.

The contact details for the General Secretariat of the Council of Ministers are:

✉   Rue de la Loi 175
    1048 Brussels
    Belgium

☎   00 322 285 61 11

@   public.relations@consilium.eu.int

6.2.1 Presidency

Currently the presidency rotates on a six monthly basis. The original idea of this was to give every member state the chance to run the Council (and in the early days that effectively meant the whole EEC/EC/EU), and to prioritise issues which were uppermost in their domestic agenda.

Originally the presidency rotated on an alphabetical basis, based on how each member state referred to itself. Thus Spain came under Espana, not Spain. This system was modified so that the presidency alternated between large and small member states. The current projected presidencies consist of:

- 2008 First Half: Slovenia

- 2008 Second Half: France

- 2009 First Half: Czech Republic

- 2009 Second Half: Sweden

- 2010 First Half: Spain

- 2010 Second Half: Belgium

- 2011 First Half: Hungary

- 2011 Second Half: Poland

- 2012 First Half: Denmark

- 2012 Second Half: Cyprus

- 2013 First Half: Ireland

- 2013 Second Half: Lithuania

- 2014 First Half: Greece

- 2014 Second Half: Italy

The problems of the "stop-start" natures of the rotating presidency were recognised well ahead of the abortive EU constitution and the proposed replacement Treaty of Lisbon. That is why the Council of Ministers operates the concept of the troika. Under this system, liaison and collaboration takes place on a rolling basis between the current presidency, its immediate predecessor, and its successor.

The powers and roles of the presidency are considerable. The member state holding the presidency has the opportunity to:

- Set the agenda for the Council (and to an extent for the whole EU) for six months. This gives the member states the opportunity to highlight – and perhaps solve – any vital issues which are at the forefront of its domestic policy agenda.

- Chair meetings of the Council of Ministers.

- Set the agenda for meetings of the Council of Ministers.

- Promote co-operation amongst member states, and broker "presidency compromises" where policies or legislation have become log-jammed.

- Represent the EU on the world stage. This can involve bilateral meetings with other countries, or meetings with institutions such as the G8.

- Chair at least one meeting of the European Council. This is the gathering of heads of government which takes place at least once in every six month period. It is often known as an EU Summit. These meetings give the ultimate power brokers the opportunity to resolve any issues which have not been resolved at Council of Ministers level.

Because the Council of Ministers is made up of serving politicians, it is often the arena for a great deal of horse trading – or *proposer monnaie d'echange*, as the French would refer to the process. The aim is always to reach agreement through negotiation, compromise, bargaining and diplomacy. This can hold dangers for the lobbyist, who may have been given cast iron assurances that a position will be held, only to find it bargained away because an issue of more vital national importance is in the balance.

Where the Council of Ministers fails to reach agreement through the aforementioned discussions and bargaining, there is a complicated system for voting which varies according to the nature of the issues being decided. The three methods of voting are:

- Unanimity: This method of voting and agreement was once in fairly common usage – and was often referred to in the UK press as the veto or the British veto. Under successive treaties the situations where unanimity is required have been gradually whittled away. Unanimity is now required only where the Council wants to change a Commission proposal without the agreement of the Commission, or where an issue is if of constitutional importance – or is a matter of very great political sensitivity. This last definition is obviously extremely vague, but if member states feel that they are going to be denied the opportunity to veto a policy which is anathema to them, they can threaten to not turn up and leave an empty chair – a tactic used by President de Gaulle which nearly brought the EEC to a grinding halt.

- Simple majority: Again, this used to be a common method of voting. However, successive treaties have introduced more and more occasions where an alternative method of voting is used.

- Qualified majority voting (QMV): This is now the most commonly used method of voting. Where no agreement has been brokered, and no consensus reached, QMV is used to decide the issue. Countries are allocated votes roughly in proportion to their size (see below), and a vote under QMV must achieve a triple majority. First, a proposal must receive just under three quarters of the vote – at least 255. Secondly, it must receive a majority of the member states voting for it – and in some instances a two-thirds majority. Finally, the member states voting in favour of a proposal must represent 62% of the population of the EU.

The number of votes allocated to each member state for deployment in votes taken under the QMV system are:

- 29 votes: France, Germany, Italy, UK

- 27 votes: Poland, Spain

- 14 votes: Romania

- 12 votes: Belgium, Czech Republic, Hungary, Portugal

- 10 votes: Austria, Bulgaria, Sweden

- 7 votes: Denmark, Finland, Ireland, Lithuania, Slovakia

- 4 votes: Cyprus, Estonia, Latvia, Luxembourg, Slovenia

- 3 votes: Malta

It should be noted that if the provisions of the Lisbon Treaty are ever accepted and implemented, the post of president of the European Council would cease to rotate on a six monthly basis. Instead, a president would be chosen for a two and a half year period of office – renewable once. The president would be chosen by qualified majority vote of the member states. The chair of the Council meeting in specialist configuration (GAERC, ECOFIN etc) would still rotate on a six-monthly basis.

Contributor's top tip

Good European Union lobbying is essentially the same as good UK Government lobbying. Ignore those who would have you believe that Brussels is a mysterious place that plays by different rules. Of course, the institutional framework is different (the European Commission proposes, and national governments and the European Parliament decide) and different national cultures and sensitivities need to be taken into account. But it is more important to appreciate that all the common sense rules that work in London (get in early, keep it simple, listen etc) apply just as well in Brussels and Strasbourg. The key is to lobby all three institutions (and influencing stakeholders) and to remember that the Council (the national governments) is best lobbied at home by locals (British industry talking to British politicians and officials in London etc). Remember that the currency of Brussels is gossip, rumour and intelligence and that UKREP and the other permanent representations can help you to understand what is really going on and who thinks what.

Michael Burrell, Vice Chairman Europe, Edelman

6.2.2 Comitology

This obscure system arose out of the Council of Minister's reluctance to accept the primacy of the Commission in formulating and implementing legislation. Under the *comitology* system a further layer of scrutiny is applied to delegated legislation, and this scrutiny is transparent to the Commission, the Council, the Parliament, and to external bodies and organisations.

The system of *comitology* was originally established by the Council of Ministers in a Council Decision in 1987, modified in 1999. This in turn was replaced by a new Council Decision in July 2006. Under the modified 2006 Council Decision, there are four procedures for implementing *comitology*:

- Procedure I – Advisory committees: The Commission consults the advisory committees, and then makes a decision having taken the committees' opinions into account.

- Procedure II – Management committees: If a management committee disagrees with the position of the Commission, the Commission must refer it to the Council. If the Council of Ministers votes opposing the Commission position using QMV then the Commission must delay application of its decision for up to three months.

- Procedure III – Regulatory committees: If regulatory committees disagree with the Commission's proposals, then they must be referred to the Council of Ministers and to the Parliament. The Council must agree or introduce an amendment within three months – otherwise the Commission can implement the proposals.

- Procedure IIIB – Regulatory committee with scrutiny: Under this procedure both the Council of Ministers and the European Parliament can undertake prior scrutiny of a proposal before its adoption by co-decision. If either the Council or the Parliament opposes the measure, the Commission may not proceed, although it can submit an amended proposal.

6.2.3 COREPER

The Committee of Permanent Representatives (known as COREPER) was set up by Article 207 of the Merger Treaty which effectively established the European Community. COREPER is made up of the ambassadors to the European Union of the member states. Its meetings are chaired by the ambassador of the member state which holds the rotating presidency.

The role of COREPER is to prepare the work of the Council, and to carry out tasks assigned to it by the Council. In practice, COREPER makes many of the decisions for the EU – decisions which are then rubber stamped by ministers flying in from the member states. COREPER provides a forum for dialogue between the member states. It also provides an element of political control – overseeing the work of the expert groups which advise the Council of Ministers.

Ahead of each meeting of the Council of Ministers COREPER scrutinises all of the dossiers which are to be presented to the meeting. These mainly consist of proposals and draft legislation being put forward by the Commission. COREPER seeks to reach agreement on them ahead of the meetings. If it fails to reach agreement, it will still produce options and suggested solutions which are very often taken up by the Council of Ministers.

Broadly speaking the agendas for Council Meetings are dictated by the progress – or lack of progress – which has taken place in COREPER meetings. Council agendas are divided in two. The first part consists of items which simply require confirmation – without discussion – of matters which have been agreed by COREPER. The second part consists of items which require discussion – either because COREPER has failed to agree, or because they are important enough to require ministerial level approval.

Author's top tip

If, as a lobbyist, you can persuade the UK representative on COREPER – UKREP – to refuse to agree to a proposal, it will be relegated to the second part of the Council of Ministers' agenda – and may be delayed. This will give you the opportunity to continue lobbying at all levels across all of the institutions.

COREPER functions in two distinct configurations:

- COREPER I: This is made up of deputy permanent representatives, and deals mainly with technical issues.

- COREPER II: This is made up of full ambassadors, and deals with more important commercial, economic, institutional or political matters.

COREPER deals with all policy areas except agriculture. Dossiers for the Agriculture Council are prepared by the Special Committee on Agriculture. This again illustrates the special role which agriculture has always played throughout the history of what is now the EU.

6.2.4 UKREP

Each member state has its own permanent representation in Brussels which inputs into COREPER. The United Kingdom's permanent representation in Brussels goes by the acronym of UKREP.

Technically UKREP is run by the Foreign and Commonwealth Office (FCO). In practice it is made up of permanent civil servants seconded from a range of Whitehall departments. This gives them the subject expertise – and the contacts back in Whitehall – to be able to deal with often highly technical topics effectively.

UKREP secondees are allocated to a particular subject desk – in the old Foreign and Commonwealth Office model. They play an absolutely crucial role in liaising and negotiating with other member states' permanent representatives in Brussels. They also promote the UK view within the Council of Ministers and to the Commission. Finally, they play a vital role in feeding back intelligence and advice to their home Whitehall Departments.

UKREP representatives also sit alongside or behind ministers at European Council and Council of Minister meetings. Ministers may arrive at meetings poorly briefed, late, tired and flustered. However, UKREP will always be there to assist them. No minister should ever be allowed to commit a major *faux pas* or to cede a major concession whilst a UKREP official is on hand to guide them.

Another crucial function of UKREP is to co-ordinate the work of the UK national civil servants who sit on the Working Parties of the Council of Ministers. Again, they seek to maintain a consistent policy line, and to facilitate the transmission of intelligence and information in both directions.

Finally, a regular function of UKREP is to reach a compromise with other permanent representatives. In an EU of 27 members no individual member state is going to get its way all of the time. UKREP has to have an eye for the priority policy issues of the UK, and to use its skills and experience to reach compromises on issues which are of secondary importance.

Warning!

UKREP should be the first port of call for any lobbyist with a fresh issue or who is new to Brussels. UKREP secondees are extremely knowledgeable, and extremely helpful. Bear in mind, however, that they will readily sell you and your issue down the river if it enables them to get their way on a matter of priority concern.

⊠   UKREP
      Avenue d'Audergham 10
      1040 Brussels
☎   00 322 287 82 11
@   ukrep@fco.gov.uk

Contributor's top tip

Whilst lobbying in the EU is rightly focussed on the Commission and Parliament in Brussels, too many forget the power of the Council of Ministers. The Council is still the ultimate authority on most EU issues and you forget it at your peril.

It is of course possible to lobby the permanent representations of the member states, but the officials in Brussels are often representatives rather than decision makers, so I advise clients to make their case in the national capitals as well.

Having to make the case in the national capitals forces you to take account of each county's individual needs and interests, a discipline which will stand you in good stead when making arguments to the Commission and MEPs.

Lobbying in a number of member states will help ease the creation of an alliance of member states, which is key to driving policy through the Council.

Simon Gentry, Campbell Gentry

6.3 European Commission

The European Commission is often described as the civil service of the EU – and there is some validity in that description. However, the Commission, whilst performing all of the functions of a civil service, also has several other key roles. These include extensive powers of initiative for legislation, and very real decision-making powers on a wide range of delegated matters.

6.3.1 Powers

The European Commission can trace its roots back to the High Authority of the European Coal and Steel Community, set up in 1952. Certainly the Commission pre-dates the European Parliament, which was only established as an elected body in 1979. For the first couple of decades of the EEC, EC and EU, the Commission was pre-eminent.

At some 24,000 (and with many of them translators and interpreters) the staff of the European Commission is quite small by the standard of European member states. Commission officials are generally known by the French term of *fonctionnaire*, or (somewhat unkindly) eurocrats. However, in EU terms, its staffing levels dwarf those of the other institutions. It also absorbs some 3% of the EU budget for its administration – some 3.4m Euros.

Although the Council of Ministers has always had the final say in EU matters, and the Parliament has acquired more authority over the years, the Commission still retains many powers and a great deal of influence. In summary these can be listed as:

- Legislation – initiation: The European Commission still holds the sole right to initiate legislation. It might do so at the behest of the European Council, the European Parliament, the European Court of Justice, member state governments or even external pressure groups or companies, but the power of initiation is the Commission's alone.

- Legislation – progress: Having initiated legislation (either at its own behest or that of another EU or external body) and sent it to the European Parliament and the Council of Ministers for scrutiny and final decision, the Commission is still closely involved at every stage of its progress. Commission officials meet constantly with officials from other EU institutions in a process known as *engrenage*.

- Implementation: Once a piece of legislation or a policy has been adopted, the European Commission is responsible for ensuring that it is implemented. It does so by working through the member states, or (where necessary) through the European Court of Justice – but the responsibility belongs to the Commission alone.

- Finances: The European Commission plays a key role in drafting the annual budget and steering it through the Council of Ministers and the European Parliament. It also ensures that EU revenues are collected, and it administers EU spending.

- External relations: The European Commission is charged with representing the EU in its relations with other international bodies such as the United Nations and the World Trade Organisation. It also handles relations with national governments. Some 150 nations maintain embassies in Brussels, and the Commission has opened around 130 offices around the world which facilitate relations between those nations and the EU.

- Policy initiatives: The European Commission is the main driving force behind major EU policy initiatives, such as the single market, the single currency, and enlargement.

- Guardian of the treaties: The European Commission acts as the conscience of the EU, trying to ensure that all policies and legislation are in keeping with the treaties, and that nation states pay due regard to their obligations under those treaties.

Contributor's top tip

Lobbying in the EU is changing. We face a period of enormous potential change and ongoing uncertainty: the Irish "No", a new Commission and new European Parliament in mid-2009. Global energy, food, environmental and security issues are challenging Europe's ability to set its own course without reference to the wider world. The pace of technology means that new business models are outstripping the powers of comprehension, the speed of adaptation of regulators and the policy framework alike. Against this background the staple diet of traditional consensus building of EU public affairs professionals looks strained and limited in its effectiveness.

Effective and representative interest groups are still needed, but those who wish to become successful advocates in the EU environment now need to build new types of inclusive partnerships with stakeholders across the whole "policy value chain" – think customer to supplier – rather than segment by producer or retailer etc. Segmentation should instead focus on the audience where much more varied interests abound than ever before. These need to be catered to in a far more individualistic way in order to join the policy dots and create a coherent policy picture.

There are now much greater opportunities for businesses which lead their sector to be involved earlier in debate on an individual basis, and to act as catalysts for policy makers in setting the EU agenda.

Julia Harrison, Managing Partner, Blueprint Partners

6.3.2 President

The position of president of the European Commission has always been a key post. Consequently, there is always a great deal of angst – and many negotiations behind the scenes – when the time comes to replace the incumbent. There have been frequent rows amongst the member states, and several firm favourites have been vetoed over the years. The United Kingdom, under Conservative governments, vetoed a succession of candidates because they were regarded as being too federalist.

In the early days of what is now the EU, the candidate for the Commission Presidency would be decided behind closed doors after extensive negotiations between the larger member states. The 1991 Treaty of Maastricht introduced some changes – and some improvements – to the system. The term of the Commission president was extended from four years to five years, so as to coincide with the term of the European Parliament. The issue of who should be the next Commission president is now routinely discussed at the June European Council of Heads of State, well ahead of the expiry date of the incumbent's term of office. Crucially, under Article 214 of the Treaty of Maastricht, there is now a requirement for the candidate for the post to be acceptable not just to the Council of Ministers, but also to the European Parliament.

The president of the European Commission has several key responsibilities and roles:

- Figurehead: Until such time as there is a president of Europe, the president of the European Commission is the nearest thing that there is to being a figurehead for the EU.

- Appointments: The president (or incoming president) plays a key role in agreeing to the member states' candidates for the post of European Commission, and in allocating the roles of Commissioner and directorates-general once they are appointed. He can also hold reshuffles mid-term and redistribute portfolios. The president also appoints five vice presidents, who hold notional seniority within the College of Commissioners.

- Chair: The president of the European Commission chairs the crucial weekly meeting of Commissioners which decides on much of the business of the EU.

- Representative: The Commission president represents the Commission in its dealings with other EU institutions and national governments.

In order to help him with these responsibilities the Commission president has his own Office of the Presidency of the European Commission. It is quite small, but is staffed by high-flying *fonctionnaires,* external administrators and policy experts drafted in at the president's personal behest.

Some Commission presidents have become household names across Europe, either because of their longevity, or because of their energetic pursuit of a particular agenda. Here is a list of the presidents to date:

- 1958-67: Walter Hallstein, West Germany, Christian Democrat
- 1967-70: Jean Re, Belgium, Centrist
- 1970-72: Franco Maria Malfatti, Italy, Christian Democrat
- 1972: Sicco Mansholt, Holland, Centrist
- 1973-76: Francois-Xavier Ortoli, France, Gaullist
- 1977-80: Roy Jenkins, UK, Labour
- 1981-84: Gaston Thorn, Luxembourg, Socialist
- 1985-94: Jacques Delors, France, Socialist
- 1995-99: Jacques Santer, Luxembourg, Christian Democrat
- 1999: Manuel Marin, Spain, Socialist
- 1999-04: Romano Prodi, Italy, Socialist
- 2004-: Jose Manuel Barroso, Portugal, Social Democrat

6.3.3 College of Commissioners

There are currently 27 Commissioners – one from each member state. Before recent enlargements the larger states (France, Germany, Italy and the UK) used to have two Commissioners each. If the provisions of the ill-fated EU constitution come into effect through the medium of the Lisbon Treaty, the number of Commissioners will actually be reduced. The proposal is that there should be no more Commissioners than the number which represents two-thirds of the member states. With the current figure of 27 member states, that would equate to 18 Commissioners.

The Commission is largely based in Brussels – the true centre of power of the EU. However, for historical reasons, part of the Commission bureaucracy is based in Luxembourg. Commissioners serve five year terms, renewable once. Until the Treaty of Maastricht changed the terms of the Commission president and the Commissioners, they served four year terms. Commissioners are chosen from nominees put forward by the member state governments. The Commission president has a strong say in deciding who should be successful, and the whole Commission is then subject to acceptance or veto by the European Parliament. The Parliament cannot in theory veto an individual nominee, but if it expresses a strong antipathy towards an individual candidate this can result in the member state withdrawing its nomination.

Once approved Commissioners are supposed to forswear any allegiance to their member state, and to resist any pressure from their national government. In practice most Commissioners still see themselves as, to some degree at least, representing their country of origin, and they do frequently exert discreet pressure on behalf of their national government – especially if they qualify for re-nomination. Those Commissioners who are regarded as having "gone native" are unlikely to secure re-nomination from their national government. A change in the political complexion of the national government also normally dooms a Commissioner to a single term. Most Commissioners retain close links with their former political parties.

Like the UK cabinet, the Commission is supposed to accept the convention of collective responsibility. This is often regarded as a theoretical exercise, with ambition and national prejudice over-riding corporate loyalty. A great deal depends on the character of the Commission president, and whether he is able to lay down a clear vision and strategy and to see it through. All 27 Commissioners come together once a week for a meeting (chaired by the Commission president) where they are collectively known as the College of Commissioners.

Dealing with Commissioners is a bit like playing three dimensional chess. In theory the correct point of contact is the Commissioner whose portfolio covers your area of interest. In practice, the Commissioners nationality – and national interest – is always a factor. So too is their political party and what part of the political spectrum they represent. Some issues are anathema to centre left Commissioners, and others to centre right Commissioners. Despite their high office, Commissioners are both human beings and politicians, and it is sometimes possible to approach them for assistance or advice outside of their narrow portfolio policy areas.

Every Commissioner has his or her own *cabinet* (pronounced the French way – phonetically cab-i-nay). This is the equivalent of a UK minister's private office. It is made up of high-flying Commission *fonctionnaires*, and partly of secondees from the Commissioner's home civil service. It is headed up by a *Chef de cabinet*, who is usually from the Commissioner's home nation.

Author's top tip

Chefs de cabinet are the equivalent of UK principal private secretaries – and more. They are the principal adviser to their Commissioner, and also his or her gatekeeper. The chefs de cabinet come together for a weekly meeting to make many of the decisions which do not even surface at the weekly Commissioner's meeting.

Within each Commissioner's cabinet there will be at least one political appointee who is the equivalent of the Whitehall Special Adviser. He or she will be an expert in the policy field covered by the Commissioners' portfolio, but will also have acute political antennae. He or she will nearly always come from the Commissioner's home nation, and will also have responsibility for liaising with the extensive network of working groups which the Commission sponsors.

Author's top tip

Most Commissioners make frequent trips back to their home countries. During that time they are anxious to maintain their relationships with their political parties, and to prepare for life after Brussels. It is often possible to get them to attend lunches or dinners, and to speak at events. They are also very approachable – and fairly open – when shorn of their protective screen of fonctionnaires and advisers.

6.3.4 Directorates-General

Each Directorate-General (DG) has a clearly defined portfolio of policy areas for which it is responsible. The DGs are in many respects the equivalent of the main Whitehall departments in the UK. Each one has a commissioner (and sometimes two commissioners) who heads it up (the equivalent of a secretary of state), and also a Director General (the equivalent of a Permanent Secretary). Beneath the Director General are a number of directors, and beneath them are section heads and then desk officers. As with the UK civil service, lobbyists should aim to deal at section head and desk officer level – only going over their heads when necessary.

Advising the DGs and the Commissioners is a huge network of several hundred regulatory, management and advisory committees. These are made up of government officials from the member states, in a system known as *comitology*. There is also a network of expert committees which are made up of national civil servants, national government appointees, and external experts from the corporate world and from interest groups.

Subject to time constraints DG officials are very open to approaches from external bodies – including lobbyists. They regard it as being a key part of their job to consult widely. Like Whitehall, the DGs often produce Green Papers and then White Papers in order to make the consultation process as open and wide-ranging as possible.

The address and telephone number of the European Commission are:

✉   B-1049 Brussels
     Belgium
☎   00 322 299 11 11

Bear in mind that this is a postal address. Commission and DG buildings are scattered throughout Brussels, and you should double check the address before you set off for a meeting.

Author's top tip

Where any proposal for legislation is put forward which is likely to pose a substantial regulatory burden on business the Commission is supposed to produce an assessment of the potential burden in the form of a fiche d'impact. Should they fail to do so, they can be challenged, and the process delayed until one has been produced.

It is fairly easy to enter in to correspondence with Commission officials (by letter or, increasingly, by email), and to talk to them on the phone. Subject to time constraints they are also very open to meeting with external bodies and lobbyists. Whatever the form of your communication with these *fonctionnaires*, it is important to realise that you may have to find a language which you have in common. Fortunately, most speak English, and if they do not then they are likely to speak French. The Brussels lobbyist is well advised to learn to communicate in more than one language.

DG officials are also nearly always happy to share draft documents with interested parties – either in hard copy form or PDF. Again, the rationale is that their job is to produce the best possible policy and the best possible legislation – and the best way to do that is to circulate papers widely.

Having stressed how open DG officials are, there are certain circumstances where they might be less helpful. The first has already been mentioned – if the lobbyist makes no effort to find a common language, and is resolutely "monoglot", he or she might be rebuffed. The other circumstance where doors might not open quite so easily is where the external body or lobbyist is seen as representing just one member state. Priority will always be given to federations or confederations which represent more than one member state. The ideal – often hard to achieve – is to put together a lobby which has support from every member state.

Finally, it is important to realise that your issue may transcend a single DG. This can work in your favour. If the lead DG is proving to be unsympathetic, you can sometimes enlist the support of one or two other DGs. If, however, you fail to realise that your issue is of concern to more than one DG, and you have not approached and briefed the other relevant DGs, then your case can be lost before you even realise it.

As has been said earlier, all of the EU bodies are in a constant state of evolution. As has also been said, the Commission president allocates portfolios amongst Commissioners at the start of each term, and also has the power to initiate mid-term reshuffles. These, however, are the Directorates-General at the time of writing:

- Administrative Affairs, Audit and Anti-Fraud
- Agriculture and Rural Development
- Budget
- Communication
- Competition
- Development
- Economic and Financial Affairs
- Education and Culture
- Employment, Social Affairs and Equal Opportunities
- Energy and Transport
- Enlargement
- Enterprise and Industry
- Environment
- External Relations
- Health and Consumers
- Humanitarian Aid
- Information Society and Media
- Internal Market and Services
- Justice, Freedom and Security
- Maritime Affairs and Fisheries
- Regional Policy
- Research

- Taxation and Customs Union

- Trade

There are also a number of internal service Directorates dealing with essential administrative areas. These include:

- Budget

- European Anti-Fraud Office

- Interpretation

- Legal Service

- Personnel and Administration

Author's top tip

Although all of the DGs have websites, they are not necessarily as detailed or as up-to-date as they could be. Internally many fonctionnaires rely on a DG's "organigramme" and "Guide de Services" – both of which are sometimes obtainable through a friendly contact.

6.3.5 UK offices

The European Commission maintains a network of offices throughout the European Union which facilitate liaison with the national governments, and provide information and advice to interested parties. They also host weekly press conferences where journalists from the national media can question Commission officials.

When high-ranking representatives from the Commission visit the member states, these offices also act as a base from which they can work. They frequently organise special press conferences for the visitors to answer questions from the local press, and organise social functions so that they can meet local politicians and other stakeholders.

These offices can be a very useful first port of call for lobbyists based in the member states. They can provide documents, and also guidance as to procedure. They can also put lobbyists in touch with the correct *fonctionnaire* in Brussels.

The UK offices representing the Commission are currently based at the following addresses:

✉   European Commission Office
    Jean Monnet House
    8 Storey's Gate
    London
    SW1P 3AT
☎   020 7973 1992

✉   European Commission Office
    9 Alva Street
    Edinburgh
    EH2 4PH
☎   0131 225 2058

✉   European Commission Office
    2 Caspian Point
    Caspian Way
    Cardiff
    CF10 4QQ
☎   029 2089 5020

✉   European Commission Office
    Windsor House
    9/15 Bedford Street
    Belfast
    BT2 7EG
☎   028 9024 0708

Somewhat ironically the European Commission is in negotiation with the Conservative Party to purchase their former headquarters at 32 Smith Square. This was where Margaret Thatcher's three general election victories were celebrated – and where much plotting to thwart the ambitions of Jacques Delors went on.

Contributor's top tip

Commission officials appreciate people coming over to Brussels and engaging constructively.

Good lobbying in Brussels involves understanding what politicians appreciate from us and what we appreciate from them.

If a lobbyist has been available to provide trustworthy industry insight even before the legislative process has started, their views will have more weight than those of a lobbyist who appears belatedly half way through the process.

Lobbying is not always a simple task – it takes years to build a reputation for honesty and reliability, but only seconds to destroy it.

Nick Lansman, Political Intelligence

6.4 European Parliament

The European Parliament is unique in that it is the only directly elected international legislature in the world. It is a unicameral institution with 785 members elected from 27 different nation states and speaking 23 different languages. The total population of the member states is 492m. MEPs are elected by a variety of different versions of Proportional Representation (PR). The first direct elections were held in 1979, and they have taken place at five year intervals ever since.

Somewhat bizarrely, the European Parliament is based in three different cities. Plenary sessions are held in Strasbourg for three or four days every month – except August. The Parliament's administrative headquarters are in Luxembourg, whilst committee meetings are held in Brussels for two or three weeks of every month. The Parliament also holds additional plenary sessions in Brussels each month. For most MEPs – and therefore most lobbyists – Brussels is very much the centre they are drawn to. Despite the ambience and facilities in Strasbourg, politicians, *fonctionnaires,* journalists and lobbyists all quietly resent this monthly pilgrimage to Strasbourg simply to please the French government. The French have vehemently resisted any attempts to move plenary sessions away from Strasbourg, citing the historical significance of a city which France and Germany fought over for several generations.

The European Parliament has gradually acquired more powers and responsibilities for itself as the EU has developed. The European project's biggest weakness has always been the "democratic deficit". This is code for the lack of direct accountability to the population at large, and the absence of any real affection for the EU amongst the populace at large. The European Parliament's position as the only elected body within the EU has put it in a powerful position to seek and gain further powers. With each successive treaty it has gradually built itself up to the point where it can now claim to be an equal partner (a co-legislator) with the Council of Ministers – a watchdog for the European Commission, and a conscience for the EU as a whole.

The European Parliament has always been the most open and accessible institution within the EU. All plenary sessions are open to the public – as are most committee meetings. Commissioners are obliged to answer both oral and written questions from MEPs, and all debates, questions and statements are published in the *Official Journal.*

For the lobbyist, the Parliament has always been the favoured point of access into the machinery of the EU. It is made up of elected MEPs, who need to get re-elected, and who need to stay in touch with grass roots opinion at home. They also – despite the generous office and staff allowances they are paid – often lack the resources with which to take on the Commission and the Council. This means that they welcome the attention of lobbyists, who can supply them with both facts and arguments. As we have seen in the section of this book which deals with ethics, the Parliament has always operated an open door policy for lobbyists – provided they play by the rules.

Contributor's top tip

How best to lobby the European Parliament?

Too many public affairs practitioners in Brussels have a vested interest in prolonging disputes. To justify their jobs, Commission bureaucrats and corporate bureaucrats spend unnecessary time arguing for arguments sake.

Good lobbying in Europe means finding the right doors to knock on, not knocking on the doors of the softest targets. I have the least respect for consultants who traipse in with client after client to see their MEP and Commission "friends", or who impress clients with the number of meetings they arrange with MEPs and officials. All too often these meetings are not followed up by the lobbyist, demonstrating a lack of commitment to the issue.

Winning in Brussels is not a numbers game. It is about identifying the right people (such as the person who sets the Whip on an issue) and persuading them by constructing a rational and realistic case which shows politicians how they can achieve their objectives.

Syed Kamall MEP

6.4.1 President

Like both the Commission and the Council of Ministers, the European Parliament has a president.

The president is elected by MEPs in a secret ballot. If no candidate can obtain an absolute majority after three ballots, the fourth ballot decides the issue by simple majority. The president's term of office is two and a half years

– half a parliamentary term – but it is renewable. In practice the president is chosen by behind the scenes negotiations between the larger political groups.

The position of president of the European Parliament is an important one. He or she directs the activities of the Parliament. The president also allocates proposals to one committee or another. When Parliament sits in plenary session, the president is in the chair. The president also represents the Parliament in its negotiations with other EU institutions, and in its dealings with the outside world.

To help the president perform these duties there is a president's *cabinet*. This is headed by a *chef de cabinet* (who also has a deputy), and is composed of some 20 advisers and speechwriters. A fair proportion of the members of the president's *cabinet* generally come from his or her home state, but others are drawn from across the EU.

The president is assisted by a number of vice presidents and *Quaestors* – who are again elected by MEPs. They perform a wide range of administrative tasks within the Parliament, and oversee sensitive areas such as MEP expenses and the allocation of security passes.

Finally, the president also chairs the Conference of Presidents. This consists of all of the leaders of the Party groups, and many of the key decisions relating to the agenda, priorities and functions of the European Parliament are decided at these meetings.

6.4.2 Members of the European Parliament

As has been said there are 785 MEPs elected from 27 member states by a variety of forms of PR. Election is by universal suffrage, with EU citizens residing in EU countries other than their own still entitled to vote.

From the 2009 elections onward the number of MEPs will actually be reduced from 785 to 736. The number of MEPs will also be capped at that figure, so that if the EU enlarges further and there are more accession states, existing member states will have to sacrifice more of their MEPs to make room for them. This is partly for reasons of practicality (there is not physically room for any more MEPs), and partly for external PR reasons (that is public relations not proportional representation). MEPs are well aware of the public perception that Brussels is a gravy train, and in response they are cutting back on their own numbers – and their perks.

> ## Warning!
>
> Although the dates of elections for the European Parliament are fixed, MEPs can – and do – resign at any time. This is often because they have been offered a better political job back home. Because they are all elected by one form of PR or another, the job simply goes to the next person on the list. This constant change of characters can however, make life challenging for lobbyists.

Seats within the European Parliament are allocated roughly in proportion to the population size of the member state. The current line-up and the post 2009 line-ups are:

- 99 seats (staying the same): Germany
- 78 seats (reducing to 72 seats): France, Italy, United Kingdom
- 54 seats (reducing to 50 seats): Poland, Spain
- 35 seats (reducing to 33 seats): Romania
- 27 seats (reducing to 25 seats): Holland
- 24 seats (reducing to 22 seats): Belgium, Czech Republic, Greece, Hungary, Portugal
- 19 seats (reducing to 18 seats): Sweden
- 18 seats (reducing to 17 seats): Austria, Bulgaria
- 14 seats (reducing to 13 seats): Denmark, Finland, Slovakia
- 13 seats (reducing to 12 seats): Ireland, Lithuania
- 9 seats (reducing to 8 seats): Latvia
- 7 seats (staying the same): Slovenia
- 6 seats (staying the same): Cyprus, Estonia, Luxembourg
- 5 seats (staying the same): Malta

These allocations are roughly proportionate. However, the smaller counties have fought very hard to boost and then maintain their allocations. The effect of this is that the big four member states (France, Germany, Italy, UK) have roughly one MEP per 800,000 citizens, whilst the smallest countries (Luxembourg and Malta) have one MEP per 80,000 citizens.

As with any Parliament or Assembly the European Parliament is organised into Party groups. This is because its many rules are complex, and there is a need – as with any legislature – for some kind of party structure and discipline to make sure that these powers are utilised efficiently, and that legislation is scrutinised effectively. See below for more details on Party groups.

Warning!

MEPs receive huge numbers of invitations and are often double or triple booked for a lunch, dinner or reception. They – or their staff – have a habit of simply accepting all invitations, and then deciding when the time comes where they will actually turn up. If you are organising an event for a client, warn them of this phenomenon.

6.4.3 Powers

Although for a long time regarded as the junior partner in the big three EU institutions, the European Parliament can today at least lay claim to a degree of equality.

This gradual accretion of competencies and power has been based on the Parliament's status as the only democratically elected body within the EU. The Parliament has skilfully used its claim to be the only body capable of rectifying the democratic deficit to reach its current position of relevance and authority.

The powers of the European Parliament can be summarised as:

- Legislation: The European Parliament is now a co-legislator with the Council of Ministers under the co-decision procedure. Parliament can also now initiate legislation by requiring the European Commission to submit an appropriate proposal. The Parliament's role in legislation will be dealt with more fully later on.

- Budget: The Parliament has the sole right to accept – or reject – the EU's annual Budget. It also has oversight – through its Budgets Committee – of the way in which EU resources are allocated and spent. Parliament also has the sole right to discharge (ie, sign off) previous year's Budgets. In 1998 the Parliament's refusal to discharge the Budget led to the Commission having to resign en masse.

- Supervision: The Parliament has supervisory powers over the other main EU institutions. It debates the annual programme of the Commission, and questions Commissioners. It has to approve the appointment of the College of Commissioners and can dismiss it (see below). It can also block the appointment of an individual Commissioner by threatening to veto the entire College, and it can refuse to endorse the portfolio allocation mooted by the president of the European Commission. Parliament can also put questions to the Council of Ministers, and thereby exercises a degree of supervision over that body.

- Dismissal: With a two-thirds majority vote the European Parliament can dismiss the College of Commissioners. This has never happened, but the threat of a motion of no confidence forced the resignation of Jacques Santer's Commission in 1999.

- Judicial: The Parliament has acquired the right to bring actions before the European Court of Justice.

6.4.4 Parties and political groups

Within the European Parliament national political parties are not irrelevant, and they do not cease to operate. However, they are subsumed within political groups.

The political groups control much of the agenda of the Parliament through the Conference of Presidents. This is made up of the leaders of each political group, plus the president of the European Parliament. Without being a member of one of the political groups it is very hard for independent MEPs to get speaking time in debates, to get onto key committees or to become *rapporteurs*.

The rules state that European Parliament groups must have at least 20 members drawn from at least six nations. This stipulation tends to lead to broad coalitions covering fairly wide political spectrums. Political groups do come and go – splitting up and re-forming – but there has always been at least one left of centre group, a right of centre group and a centrist group.

At the time of writing the main political groups within the Parliament with their current memberships are:

- 227 members: Group of the European People's Party (Christian Democrats and European Democrats)

- 217 members: Socialist Group of the European Parliament

- 106 members: Group of the Alliance of Liberals and Democrats for Europe

- 44 members: Union for Europe of the Nations Group

- 42 members: Group of the Greens/European Free Alliance

- 41 members: Confederal Group of the European United Left – Nordic Green Left

- 23 members: Independence/Democracy Group

- 20 members: Identity, Transition and Sovereignty Group

No political group has ever had a majority in the European Parliament. This means that there are constant alliances and accommodations being formed as groups coalesce around particular issues and then split apart over others.

As well as having a president (who attends the crucial Conference of Presidents meetings) each political group also appoints spokesmen and coordinators for each policy subject area. Lobbyists need to keep abreast of who holds which role within the major groups, and to cultivate a relationship with them. As with any Parliament there are reshuffles and individuals change portfolio – but then you just have to start all over again. Relationships built up relating to a particular portfolio are never wasted in any event.

Finally, the larger political groups also have national sections made up of members from a particular nation state. These delegations also have their own leaders and officers. Members of these national sections can be a good initial point of contact for lobbyists. Although they do not have much power in terms of voting numbers, they do have influence and they will be able to tell you what deals are being done behind the scenes.

Author's top tip

The political groups have their own secretariats. They also have desk officers covering the main subject areas. Getting to know the desk officers covering your particular area of interest – especially in the larger political groups – is a big priority. Ask a supportive MEP who is a member of the group in question to give you the contact details.

6.4.5 Committees of the European Parliament

As most new MEPs, journalists and lobbyists soon discover, much of the real work of the European Parliament is done in committee.

Committees are set up at the beginning and mid-way through the five year parliamentary term. Membership varies from just 22 members up to 84 – plus substitutes. Subcommittees can also be set up, as can temporary *ad hoc* committees – which are set up for a renewable 12 month term. Committees of inquiry are set up from time to time in order to investigate allegations of maladministration, or possible infringements of EU law.

The committees vary in terms of their importance and prestige. The more important committees – such as the Foreign Affairs, Budget Committee and the Agriculture Committee – tend to have the largest number of members. MEPs are allocated to committees partly on the basis of their seniority, partly on the basis of their membership of a political group and partly on the basis of their nationality. Thus Irish MEPs might have a strong interest in being on the Agriculture Committee, whilst UK MEPs might be more interested in the Internal Market Committee. Scandinavian MEPs tend to be keen to serve on the Human Rights Committee, whilst MEPs who come from member states which are big net contributors to the EU might try to get a place on the Budgets Committee.

As has been said the number and nature of committees can change from one parliament to the next – or from one half parliament to the next. Obviously certain Committees – such as Budgets – will always be in existence. Here is a list of Committees in existence at the time of writing – with acronyms and numbers of members:

- Agriculture and Rural Development – AGRI – 47 members
- Budgetary Control – CONT – 33 members
- Budgets – BUDG – 52 members
- Civil Liberties, Justice and Home Affairs – LIBE – 58 members
- Constitutional Affairs AFCO – 29 members
- Culture and Education – CLT – 37 members
- Development – DEVE – 34 members
- Economic and Monetary Affairs – ECON – 51 members
- Employment and Social Affairs – EMPL – 51 members

- Environment, Public Health and Food Safety – ENVI – 67 members
- Fisheries – PECH – 33 members
- Foreign Affairs – AFET – 84 members
- Human Rights – DROI – 32 members
- Industry, Research and Energy – ITRE – 53 members
- Internal Market and Consumer Protection – IMCO – 43 members
- International Trade – INTA – 33 members
- Legal Affairs – JURI – 27 members
- Petitions – PETI 25 members
- Regional Development – REGI – 57 members
- Security and Defence – SEDE – 29 members
- Transport and Tourism – TRAN – 53 members
- Women's Rights and Gender Equality – FEMM – 35 members

The main functions of these committees are :

- Approval: European Parliament committees hold hearings to assess the suitability of the commissioners-designate in their own specialist field.

- Inquiries: Ad hoc committees of inquiry can be set up to examine specific issues – such as BSE and climate change.

- Legislation: Committees play a key role in initiating and scrutinising legislation on behalf of the Parliament.

As can be seen there are enough places on committees to accommodate all those MEPs who want to serve on them. They occupy more of an MEP's time than any other function, and they play a crucial role in the work of the Parliament. The central role which Parliament committees play in the legislative process will be fully dealt with later in this section.

Author's top tip

Because European Parliament committees meet for two or three weeks a month in Brussels, and they only go to Strasbourg for plenary sessions for three or four days a month, the best place to arrange a meeting with them is almost always in Brussels.

Contributor's top tip

Focus on the rapporteurs

There are 785 MEPs. An influencing strategy would have to be incredibly well resourced to work in any meaningful way on all those elected by the 27 member states. In my experience, however, there are too many in the lobby business who fail to identify serious targets – this wastes your time and resources and irritates the MEPs who can be politely puzzled by the approach. So who should you see? I would focus on the rapporteurs – the MEPs tasked with producing the reports and leading the discussion.

There will be a rapporteur for each piece of legislation going through, allocated to the political groups in proportion to the election results. There will also be shadow rapporteurs for the other groups. Rapporteurships are prized by parties and by MEPs. People work hard on the roles and become personally committed to the result. Their assistants will be the gate keepers and you should get to know them and their information needs. One thing is certain – if you are not talking to them others will be, including national governments.

Ian Twinn, Director of Public Affairs, Incorporated Society of British Advertisers (and former MEP)

Contributor's top tip

Lobbyists are an important part of the political process. They must inform elected politicians at all levels about the issues of concern to them. Information should be concise, intelligible, useful and relevant to the receivers – and backed up by a friendly, but not too close, personal relationship with the key figures. Lobbyists need to target their messages both in terms of content and the people they send it to. All other relevant organisations need to be lobbied if the lobbying is to be truly effective and efficient. Lobbyists must find out and fully understand the inter-relationships between the Council, the Commission and the European Parliament. They must also understand how the national Parliaments fit into the picture. They need to find out which Intergroups are applicable to their work and join in their activities as appropriate. They need detailed and updated listings of all the committee appointments and interests of the politicians they will be dealing with.

Den Dover MEP

6.4.6 Intergroups

These are informal groups formed outside of the main structure of the Parliament. They are very similar in format and intent to Westminster All-Party Parliamentary Groups.

Like Westminster APPGs, Intergroups tend to be transient. Some come and go as an issue rises of prominence and then fades away. Others survive because the issues they relate to are perennial. Also like Westminster APPGs, Intergroups can involve outside bodies. The most famous Intergroup was the "Kangaroo" group set up shortly after the first direct elections to the European Parliament in 1979. This group aimed to create a situation where trade barriers could be "hopped over" – hence the name. It played a significant role in securing the establishment of the Single Market in 1992.

Many Intergroups relate to countries – and often involve fact finding trips for MEPs. Others deal with serious subjects of interest to MEPs' constituents. Some examples are:

- Ageing
- Animal Welfare
- Anti-Racism
- Complementary Medicine
- Disabled
- Food Policy
- Gay and Lesbian Rights
- Law Enforcement
- Local Government
- Maritime Affairs
- Regional Languages
- Sports

At any one time there are probably in excess of 50 Intergroups. Some of the larger ones have their own secretariat, and organise monthly meetings. They try to influence policy, contribute to debates at plenary sessions, and when there is legislation affecting their area of interest they sometimes try to secure the *rapporteurship* for one of their members.

As well as these subject-orientated Intergroups there are also a large number of Inter-Parliamentary Delegations, which link up with countries from Afghanistan to the United States. There is also a (smaller) group of joint Parliamentary Committee Delegations, which foster relations with countries (many of whom are applicant states).

Warning!

As with Westminster APPGs lobbyists can get involved in the running of Intergroups. They can be extremely useful in promoting a cause, and in getting a lobby's point of view across to MEPs and officials. However, Parliament presidents in the past have warned that Intergroups should not try to imply that they have official status, and lobbyists should strictly comply with all of the rules associated with the setting up and running of these groups.

6.4.7 Questions

Because of the sheer size of the European Parliament, the number of languages spoken, and the infrequency in which it meets in plenary session, questions are not as useful – for either MEPs or lobbyists – as they are in most national legislatures. Nevertheless, questions do play a role in the work of the Parliament and its efforts to scrutinise the work of the Commission and the Council of Ministers.

As has been said, Parliament only meets in full plenary session for three or four days once a month in Strasbourg. At these sessions there is a monthly oral question time, when the Commission can be pressed on the issues of the day. Answers are, however, pre-prepared – and are simply published if there is no time for an oral answer. Also, many MEPs try and avoid the monthly round trip to Strasbourg, and if they are not in their place then they will not receive an oral answer to their question.

Questions to the Council of Ministers often do not produce a meaningful answer. They are answered by the Council president – usually the foreign secretary of whichever member state currently holds the rotating presidency. However, unless the Council of Ministers has had the opportunity to agree a position on the issues in question, there is not much that the Council president can tell the MEP who has tabled the question.

Because of the lack of time available for oral questions, most questions to both the Commission and the Council of Ministers have to be tabled for written answer. The answers are published in the *Official Report*. Unfortunately, however, it can take weeks – or even months – for questions to be answered, and the answers are not always as detailed or enlightening as they might be.

6.4.8 Resolutions

MEPs can table Resolutions calling for an action to be taken or a situation to be investigated. These are generally referred to the relevant committee, where they may on occasion form the basis for a future report.

There is, however, a procedure for tabling a Resolution which is open for other MEPs to add their name. This is a similar device to the Early Day Motion (EDM) in the House of Commons. It also serves the same purpose – to raise the profile of an issue, and to gauge the level of support. As such it is a useful lobbying tool.

6.4.9 Petitions

Under articles 21 and 24 of the treaty establishing the original European Community, any citizen living in, or conducting business in, the EU has a right to petition Parliament. Petitions must state the name, occupation, nationality and address of every petitioner. All petitions do, however, have to be on a subject on which the European Parliament has some competence.

Unlike petitions delivered to the Westminster Parliament, petitions delivered to the European Parliament can have some effect. They are initially referred to the Parliament's own Petitions Committee, which can be dealing with up to a thousand petitions at any one time. In order to help the Parliament's officials to deal with this volume of work, officials are seconded from the Commission.

Petitioning the European Parliament does frequently result in the Commission acting on the issue which is the subject of the petition. Some UK environmental groups have used this almost cost-free procedure to force the UK government to produce environmental impact assessments for major infrastructure projects.

If the Petitions Committee considers that a petition falls within its competence, and has validity, it can pursue three different courses of action. First, it can ask the Commission to look at the complaint and to report back. Alternatively, it can refer the complaint to the ombudsman. It can even, if it considers the subject warrants such attention, refer the petition for adoption at a full plenary session – whereupon it might be referred to the relevant committee for investigation.

6.4.10 Ombudsman

The post of ombudsman was established by the Treaty of Maastricht in 1992. The ombudsman is appointed for a five year term to run concurrently with that of the European Parliament. The ombudsman can mount an investigation either on his or her own initiative, or because a complaint has been referred to him or her.

The ombudsman's remit does cover all of the institutions of the EU. He or she does, however, tend to work most closely with the European Parliament, simply because most complaints and petitions are channelled through the Parliament and its Petitions Committee.

Where the ombudsman discovers that a complaint appears to have validity, he or she can refer it to the EU institution concerned, in which case a response must be forthcoming within three months. Alternatively, he or she can conduct an independent investigation, and submit suggestions for the resolution of the complaint. If there is no agreement on the complaint or on a suggested solution, the ombudsman may refer the matter to the European Parliament for resolution.

Every year the ombudsman must give a report of his or her activities to the European Parliament. The report is published and made available on the Europa website.

6.4.11 UK offices

As with the European Commission the European Parliament maintains a network of information offices in the member states.

There are two such offices in the United Kingdom. The main office is in London, with a subsidiary office in Edinburgh

Again, just like the European Commission offices in the UK, they are a valuable source of information and advice for the public – and for lobbyists.

The contact details of the two UK offices are:

⊠   European Parliament Office
       2 Queen Anne's Gate
       London
       SW1H 9AA
☎   020 7277 4300

@   eplondon@europarl.europa.eu

⊠   European Parliament Office
       The Tun
       4 Jackson's Entry
       Holyrood Road
       Edinburgh
       EH8 8PJ
☎   0131 557 7866

@   epedinburgh@europarl.europa.eu

Contributor's top tip

- Set clear corporate goals

- Cultivate a sympathetic political climate (long-term effort)

- Positive and detailed arguments: present what you want rather than what you do not want

- Integration between EU and national level activities

- Be able to move easily between institutions – value of information, monitoring, recognise the "institutional" identity of different target audiences

- Recognition of importance of understanding procedural opportunities, especially in Parliament, Council and in comitology

- Intelligent use of trade associations in the European context

- Role of consultants as facilitators rather than representatives

- Do not underestimate the complexities introduced by differences of language, nationality, philosophy and religion

- Beware of political will – it can alter both the content and timing at short notice

Tom Spencer, Executive Director of the European Centre for Public Affairs

6.5 Policy Formulation

Policy formulation in any democratic society is a complicated and convoluted process. In the case of the European Union that complexity is multiplied exponentially by the fact that there are 27 member states, 23 official languages, and at least three major institutions having a direct input in to policy formulation.

6.5.1 Drivers

There are always a large range of drivers feeding into any system designed to facilitate policy formulation. In the case of the EU, the range of factors is probably wider than with any other comparable institution – not that there is any comparable institution.

The drivers which lead to policy formulation within the EU are:

- Treaties: Under the terms of the original founding treaties, and all subsequent treaties, the roles of EU institutions are defined, as are broad outlines for future policy developments.

- Member states: Most member states have their own pet projects and policy priorities which they promote. If they are one of the larger member states there is a good chance that they will eventually push their priorities to the top of the agenda. Member states also have the opportunity to promote their policy priorities when they hold the six month rotating Presidency.

- External: Pressures from outside the EU can lead to a requirement to formulate an effective policy to deal with external situations. The EU has dealings with individual nations, and also with international bodies (UN, World Trade Organisation etc). The EU also has the power to sign treaties, which can impose internal obligations on member states.

- Internal: There is continual pressure to harmonise within the EU. This is partly a matter of treaty obligations, but is more about the fact that EU officials possess and exhibit a strong centralising and co-ordinating ethos.

- Voters: Both the directly elected European Parliament and the Council of Ministers (mainly consisting of elected ministers) are subject to pressures from the voting public.

- Pressure groups: Literally thousands of pressure groups engage with the EU and seek to influence its policy agenda. These range from multi-national trade bodies to NGOs and charities.

- Lobbyists: Again there are thousands of lobbyists in Brussels – all trying to promote the policy agenda of their clients.

Author's top tip

Member state governments are not above promoting policy initiatives which will disproportionately benefit their own industries. Thus the free trading British were at the forefront of single market initiatives, the German government promoted the mandatory adoption of catalytic converters because it knew it would benefit its technologically-advanced automotive industry, and the French government is famously keen to defend and extend EU agriculture policy – and was at the forefront of the bio fuels initiative.

Contributor's top tip

It is a commonplace assumption that European lobbying is a many-splendoured thing, but that is a limited insight. The good EU lobbyist should identify and agree the core message, then involve the company or client in a "deep dive" of message development to develop the most appropriate variations of the message so that they are effective to each of the particular and distinct audiences. I use the acronym "STEEPLE" in team work to ensure a comprehensive differentiation of the basic core message. Such an exercise creates well-targeted and often unique lobbying messages through applying the seven filters of uniquely social, technical, economic, environmental, popular, legal and ethical perspectives. The approach attunes the message accurately to different targets with varying interests and creates the basis of a well-tailored communications programme – variations on a theme. It also meets the need to "listen before you talk", a relatively under-explored precept of good lobbying.

Lionel Stanbrook, Head of Global Issues Management, Syngenta International AG

6.5.2 Policy areas

The policy areas over which the EU has direct and indirect power have been laid down by successive treaties. They are also, however, always being extended into new areas. The EU seeks to expand its areas of competency by agreement between the member states, by precedent, and by extending the scope of existing competencies. It also seeks to do so by using the European Court of Justice to rule that policy areas which were previously the sole responsibility of member state governments are not insulated from related policy areas where the EU has competence.

The notion of subsidiarity was never fully embraced by the EU institutions, and has therefore rarely been applied. Where member states do secure opt-outs from particular initiatives the Commission and the Court often find ways of extending existing competencies so as to encroach into that previously immune area. A good example was the initial UK initial opt-out from the social chapter, which was considerably undermined by the Commission's tactic of using health and safety legislation to enforce compliance.

Here are the areas where the EU has considerable or partial competence and where it (at least for the moment) has none:

- Policy areas where the EU is paramount: Agriculture, competition, employment conditions, fisheries, internal market, trade.

- Policy areas where responsibility is shared: Broadcasting, culture, energy, environment, foreign affairs, overseas aid, postal services, regional development, social policy, training, transport.

- Policy areas where member states are paramount: Citizenship, criminal justice, defence, education, elections, health, tax, welfare.

Author's top tip

Regulators from the member states have regular meetings in order to exchange information and share best practice. If you can persuade your national regulator to adopt a policy which is favourable to you or your client they might also be persuaded to feed this into one of these trans-national meetings.

6.5.3 Roles of the institutions

All three of the main EU institutions – the Commission, the Council of Ministers and the Parliament – have some say in policy initiation and formulation. They also all have some say in how that policy is translated into legislation, and how that legislation is applied.

The role of the main EU institutions in the policy field can be summarised as:

- European Council: Although the heads of government of the member states only generally meet twice a year, they do dictate the strategic policy priorities for the EU.

- Council of Ministers: These member state ministers dictate the strategic policy priorities for their own particular areas – agriculture, transport etc.

- European Commission: The Commission is the main driver for EU policy initiation, formulation, and implementation.

- European Parliament: The Parliament – and its various committees – uses its democratic mandate to persuade the Commission to adopt its policy initiatives.

Other EU institutions which have a strong influence on the policy agenda are:

- COREPER: The Committee of Permanent Representatives does a great deal of the preparatory work ahead of Council of Minister meetings – and a great deal of this often involves early-stage policy work.

- European Court of Justice: The ECJ has, as part of its remit, a duty to ensure that all policies are compatible with the EU's *acquis communnautaire* and the treaties.

   Working groups and advisory committees: The groups and committees set up under the comitology system advise all of the EU institutions, and have a strong input in to the policy-making process.

6.5.4 Documents

The various EU institutions produce a plethora of policy documents of one kind or another. The two best known are:

- Green Papers: These are produced by the European Commission and represent the very earliest stage of the consultation process. All interested parties are invited to respond, and a Green Paper on a key area can elicit several hundred responses.

- White Papers: A White Paper generally follows on from a Green Paper. It indicates that after the initial consultation, the Commission is convinced of the need for specific action or legislation. It also outlines the form which the Commission envisages that the action or legislation will take. The Council of Ministers will have to approve a Green Paper before it is progressed to White Paper stage.

However, there are a number of other types of policy documents which are technically internal and which are not as well known outside of the EU institutions. They include:

- Commission situation papers or position papers: These are technically internal documents for *fonctionnaires* only. They are, however, made available to some external bodies which have a particularly strong relationship with the Commission, or a particularly strong interest in the policy area under review.

- Directive preliminary drafts: Again, these are technically internal working documents – but they are shown to a select few in order that they can be reality checked before wider publication.

- *Draft proposals:* These appear initially as com.doc and are more widely circulated. They are not, however, published in the *Official Journal* for some time.

- Framework documents: The Commission constructs and implements framework programmes for all key policy areas which run for six years. Once published they are fairly set in stone – but drafts do circulate well in advance of publication.

Author's top tip

There are a phenomenal number of draft policy proposals in circulation in Brussels. Generally speaking, if you know about their existence, the Commission will be prepared to let you have sight of – or a copy of – the proposals. Failing that, MEPs on the relevant European Parliament committee will almost certainly either have – or be able to obtain – access to the proposal. As a last resort quote transparency and freedom of information and threaten to go to the European Court of Justice.

6.6 Legislative Process

There are a large number of differences between the legislative process in the EU and the legislative process in Westminster – or any of the devolved bodies.

Perhaps the biggest difference is the gestation period. A proposal for legislation can be around for years – or even a decade or more – before it finally becomes part of the *acquis communautaire*. This is partly because of the extremely thorough consultation process – and partly because of the hugely convoluted legislation process. The other factor, of course, is that in the EU there is no set time limit. In Westminster most legislation has to get through in one parliamentary session. On occasion, it may be carried through to a second session. In the EU, legislation can meander along in a leisurely fashion until it finally manages to clamber over all of the multiple hurdles which are placed in its way.

Author's top tip

Legislation never really gets killed off in the EU. Many member states – and many lobbyists – have thought that they have finally seen off a proposal – only to see it picked up, dusted down, and re-introduced by the Commission with the support of a new presidency.

When a new piece of legislation is being prepared a drafts team is set up within the Commission. This is similar to the bill team which a Whitehall department would set up. There is inter-service dialogue between the drafts team and officials from other Directorates-General with an interest in the policy area concerned. This team will follow the legislation through all of its multiple stages, and if you can identify the *fonctionnaires* working on that team you may have a better chance of helping to shape the legislation as it progresses.

Every year the European Commission has to set out its annual Work Programme in the form of a com.doc. The Work Programme is sent to the Council of Ministers, the European Parliament, the European Economic and Social Committee, and the Committee of the Regions. The Commission president also makes an oral statement in the Parliament.

Ahead of the publication of the Work Programme there will have been a great deal of discussion with the various other institutions. As with the Queen's

Speech in Westminster, the Commission also reserves the right to introduce legislation not outlined in the Work Programme should the need arise.

6.6.1 European Union law – types

The foundation of all EU laws is provided by the succession of treaties which stretch back to the 1957 Treaty of Rome. Technically this means that all other EU law is secondary legislation, since it is the treaties which provide it with a legal base. There is also case law, which consists of the accumulated rulings of the European Court of Justice. Together these three strands make up the *acquis communautaire*. As has already been noted, EU law has primacy over the legislation of member states.

As with any type of legislation EU law falls in to several categories. In order of their importance these are:

- *Regulations:* These are the most powerful forms of EU legislation. They are directly applicable in all member states, and do not need to be transposed into law by the national legislatures of the member states. They are binding and come in to immediate effect (unless they contain provision for coming into effect at some specified future date).

- *Directives:* Unlike regulations, directives do need to be transposed in to national law by the legislatures of the member states. They state an objective and a required outcome ("binding as to the result to be achieved") but it is up to the member states how they bring the objectives of directives into force. However, there is usually a deadline by which this must have taken place, and member states are obliged to keep the Commission informed as to their progress.

- *Decisions*: Like regulations, decisions are binding. However, they are generally not aimed at member states *en masse*, but usually at an individual member state (or groups of member states), or at institutions, companies or even individuals. Decisions are often used where the European Commission has to mediate in disputes between member states.

- *Recommendations and opinions*: As the name implies these are not mandatory. They are often used to provide interpretation of regulations, directives and decisions.

The number of laws which the EU passes has fallen from about 7000 a year at its peak in the 1990s to under 2000 a year today. This is partly because in the 1990s a raft of measures had to be passed to bring the single market into effect. However, it is also undoubtedly the case that since the Delors era the Commission has accepted the opinion of the public and the Council of Ministers that it should try to do less, but more effectively. The procedure for passing laws has also, as we shall see, become much more complicated.

6.6.2 European Union law – procedures

The procedure for making EU law has been continuously modified under successive treaties. The general trend has been for the European Parliament to acquire more influence over amending and passing legislation. The European Commission retains the sole right to initiate legislation, but it can now be prompted to do so by the European Council, the Council of Ministers, or the European Parliament.

The procedures which are used for processing Commission legislative proposals fall in to three main categories:

- *Consultation procedure*: This procedure was established under the Treaty of Rome. Under this procedure the Parliament gives its opinion on a Commission proposal. The Commission then revises its proposal in the light of the Parliament's opinion before passing it on to the Council of Ministers. The Council has to have regard for the Parliament's opinion, but is not bound by it. This procedure is now largely obsolete.

- *Cooperation procedure*: This procedure was introduced under the provisions of the 1987 Single European Act (SEA). Under cooperation procedure the Parliament gives Commission proposals a second reading. Once the Parliament's original opinion has been considered by the Commission, the Council of Ministers has to adopt a common position. The Parliament then looks at the Council's common position and also (crucially) can propose further amendments. The Council still has the final say – but if Parliament rejects the Council's common position then the Council can only adopt the measure by unanimity.

- *Assent procedure*: This was also introduced under the Single European Act. It gives the Parliament the chance to signify its approval or disapproval of some Council decisions – but not to seek to amend them. It is effectively a

345

right of veto for the Parliament by simple majority. It mainly applies to constitutional proposals for changing the structure of the EU, treaties with external nations or bodies, or changes to the workings of key bodies such as The European Central Bank. It also crucially covers the accession of new member states.

• *Co-decision procedure*: This procedure came about through the provisions of the Treaty of Maastricht and was extended to new policy areas under the Treaty of Amsterdam. This procedure considerably enhances the powers of the Parliament by giving it the right to third readings. Under this procedure if the Parliament is minded to reject a common position then a Conciliation Committee of the Parliament and the Council is convened. If it reaches agreement on a proposal, it still has to be approved by both bodies. If it fails to reach agreement, then the Council can still proceed with the measure, but the Parliament can reject it with a simple majority vote.

As we have seen the passage of EU legislation can be a long and complicated process. There are, in theory at least, up to seven hurdles which legislation must clear before becoming enacted. They are:

• Stage one: The Commission produces a draft legislative text which will have been produced by one Directorate General, but will have been circulated to other DGs for comment in a process known as inter-service consultation. Once agreed by the DGs, the draft is adopted by the College of Commissioners and sent to the European Parliament.

• Stage two: In the Parliament one committee (known as the lead committee) will be put in overall charge of the Commission proposal – although other committees (know as opinion giving committees) will be consulted. By agreement between the groups one MEP will be appointed as *rapporteur*. The lead committee discusses the proposal and sets a deadline for amendments. It then debates the amendments, and votes on them. Once this has occurred, and the opinions of the opinion giving committees have been received, the lead committee adopts its report and sends it to the Parliament. The amendments adopted by the lead committee are voted on by all MEPs in plenary session on a simple majority basis – that is to say a majority of MEPs taking part in the vote have to be in favour. Further amendments can be tabled at plenary either by them being supported by a block of 40 MEPs, or by their being supported by one of the political groups.

• Stage three: The Council of Ministers then considers any amendments which the Parliament has made to the proposal. If the Council has

Commission support it can agree to Parliament amendments by qualified majority voting (QMV) – otherwise it has to do so by unanimity – and that is the end of the process. If the Council does not agree with the Parliament's amendments, the Council amends them and produces a common position which is arrived at by negotiation between a Council working group and COREPER.

- Stage four: Once the common position is sent to the Parliament it then has three months (four months if holidays intervene) to give it a second reading. If this deadline is missed, then the common position is automatically adopted. Otherwise the process in the lead committee is the same, but no other committees are consulted. The lead committee amendments are voted on by the Parliament, and further amendments can be introduced as per stage three.

- Stage five: Amendments at second reading have to be accepted by a vote equal to a majority of all MEPs – not just those who are participating in that particular vote. Therefore, amendments are much less likely to be carried at this Stage. However, if this does occur, and the Council rejects the amendments, then the conciliation procedure is invoked.

- Stage six: Under the conciliation procedure 27 MEPs and representatives from all 27 member states meet to try and reach a compromise. The procedure is supervised by the European Commission. If a compromise is reached, it is sent back to the Parliament for a final vote. If no compromise is reached, the proposal is abandoned.

- Stage seven: MEPs then vote on the compromise arrived at under the conciliation procedure. As all of the main groups are represented in the Conciliation Committee, it is unusual for legislative proposals to be voted down at this stage.

Author's top tip

If you are asking a rapporteur, a group or an MEP to table an amendment for you, it is always a good idea to have a pre-prepared text ready to give to them.

Since the procedure for EU legislation is so convoluted there are many opportunities for lobbyists to try and seek to secure amendments. The main access and pressure points are:

- Rapporteurs: As has been said these individuals play a key role both in committee and in plenary session.

- Opinion-giving committees: MEPs on these committees can be useful for suggesting amendments to the lead committee – and for telling you what is likely to happen to a proposal.

- Directorates-General: It is not just the lead DG on a legislative proposal which is important – under the inter-service consultation procedure other DGs have a say and can have influence. If you are not making progress with the lead DG, try going in sideways through one of the others.

- Political groups: The political groups decide on who the rapporteur should be. Political groups can also table amendments when a proposal goes from committee to plenary. They are also represented on the Conciliation Committee. If you can get one of the main groups on your side, you have a good chance of achieving a result.

- Member states: If the Council does not have Commission support for an amendment put forward by the Parliament then unanimity is required, so any member state can veto it.

Author's top tip

As has been said regulations are directly applied in the member states, but the directives have to be transposed and applied. Some legislatures take the opportunity presented by directives to tack on all sorts of ancillary provisions not covered by the original directive. This is known as "gold plating" – and the UK is particularly prone to this practice. Even if you have not got your way amending or seeking to derail a directive, you should at least try and ensure that your member state government does not try to use it as an excuse to introduce a range of related provisions.

6.7 Finances

Budgets are all about how much money is raised, where it is raised from, and where it is spent. This is true of any legislature, but as ever with the EU its multi-institutional and multi-national nature adds several layers of complexity to the process.

The Budget for the EU in 2007 was 130 billion euros. This represented just over 1.2% of the GDP of the member states – and the Budget is not allowed to exceed 1.24%. The controversy arises because some states are net contributors, and some are net beneficiaries. The disparities between the sums paid in and the sums taken out can be quite substantial.

The EU is not allowed to borrow money in order to meet any shortfalls, so the Budget itself (and budgetary control) is crucial. There are three basic principles controlling the setting of the Budget:

- Unity: All revenue and expenditure has to be brought together in a single Budget document.

- Annuality: All revenue and expenditure has to relate to a given year.

- Balance: Because the EU cannot borrow money expenditure must not exceed revenue.

Responsibility for the Budget is shared between the three main institutions of the EU:

- European Commission: The Commission has responsibility for producing the preliminary Draft Budget, guiding it through the Council and Parliament, and administering all expenditure.

- Council of Ministers: The Council and the European Parliament share budgetary authority. Where expenditure is compulsory the Council has the final say. The Council and the European Parliament employ the Conciliation Procedure to resolve any differences over the Budget. The Council and the Parliament meet twice a year to discuss the Budget.

- European Parliament: The Parliament shares budgetary authority with the Council of Ministers. Where expenditure is discretionary the Parliament has the final say. The Parliament can adopt the Budget, or (with a two-thirds majority) reject it. It also has the power to decide whether or not previous years' Budgets should be discharged.

Author's top tip

The European Parliament Budgets Committee can make remarks against any Budget line suggesting how expenditure can be allocated. The Budget can also create a pour memoire line without a sum attached to it. This is a heavy hint to the Commission to make provision for expenditure in a given area in the future.

In terms of revenue raising in rough terms the EU Budget is funded by:

- National contributions: Approximately 70% of revenue is raised from national contributions based roughly on the GDP of the member states.

- Value Added Tax: Approximately 15% of the revenue is raised from VAT.

- Customs duties: Another approximately 15% of revenue is raised from customs duties from goods imported from non-member states.

In terms of expenditure the EU Budget is roughly allocated as follows:

- Cohesion Policy: Approximately 36% of expenditure goes on policies designed to harmonise the standards of living within the EU – mainly through the European Social Fund. This area of expenditure has grown in recent years.

- Agriculture and Fisheries: About 34% of expenditure goes towards subsidising farmers and fishermen – and towards rural development. This area of expenditure has shrunk in recent years.

- Administration: Approximately 5% of expenditure goes towards the administration of the institutions of the EU.

- Miscellaneous: Whatever is left over is spent on a variety of other policy areas, such as research and development, transport, energy, the environment and foreign policy initiatives.

Over the years there have been strong moves to stabilise the EU's Budget. The European Council tries to decide on a global Budget figure stretching several years ahead. The Commission, Council of Ministers and European Parliament meet to discuss financial perspectives, which seek to agree on spending priorities several years ahead. This can be adjusted by the Commission to take into account inflation and any unexpected increases in the GDP of the member states. To date the agreed financial perspectives have covered the periods:

- 1988-1992

- 1993-1999

- 2000-2006

- 2007-2013

Within the global ceiling set by these six year financial perspectives there is considerable flexibility on where the money is spent. As ever with the EU, this is the subject of considerable debate and negotiation between the member states, the institutions, and the political groups.

6.8 Other European Union Institutions

Throughout this section I have referred to the big three institutions of the EU. In fact there are a number of other bodies which are central to the way in which the EU – and its main institutions – works. Here is a brief round-up of what they are and what they do

6.8.1 European Court of Justice

The European Court of Justice (or ECJ) is often ranked amongst the main institutions of the EU. It is based in Luxembourg, and is made up of the same number of judges as there are member states of the EU. Its main function is to uphold EU law as laid down by the treaties, and to interpret EU legislation as it has been built up in to the *acquis communautaire*. It only deals with subject areas where the EU has competence. The rules of procedure of the ECJ can now be voted on by the Council of Ministers using QMV.

Judges are appointed for a six year renewable term. They elect one of their number to be the president of the Court, for a renewable three year term. Partial replacement of judges takes place every three years. The judges are assisted by eight advocates-general, who are appointed for an eight year term. Cases can be referred to the ECJ by courts in member states, by other EU institutions, or by individuals or organisations living or working in the EU.

In practice the ECJ deals with two broad types of case:

- Infringement proceedings: Ensuring that the instruments of other EU institutions are compatible with the treaties.

- Rulings: Providing national courts with definitive rulings on the validity and legal base of provisions contained within EU law.

The ECJ can sit in Full Court (involving all of the judges), as a Grand Chamber (involving 13 judges), or in Chambers (involving three to five judges). In 1989 the Court of First Instance (CFI) was set up, in order to take some of the burden off of the ECJ and to relieve some of the backlog of cases. Under the Treaty of Nice the ECJ can similarly set up specialist tribunals in order to deal with cases such as those brought by employees of EU institutions. As with the ECJ the CFI has 27 members, and votes to appoint a president for a renewable three year term.

Cases can be referred to the ECJ or the CFI by:

- Other EU institutions (Commission, Council, Parliament etc)

- Member states

- National courts of member states

- EU citizens

- Companies or organisations operating in the EU

Author's top tip

Controversially, judges at the ECJ are political appointments, and appointees do not even need to have judicial experience – they just need to be "legally competent". This has led to some strange rulings, not unmotivated by political considerations. Referring a case to the ECJ really is the last throw of the die. It is expensive, slow, and the end result does not always seem to be based on sound legal principles.

6.8.2 European Court of Auditors

Like the ECJ the European Court of Auditors was set up in 1975 and is based in Luxembourg. Also like the ECJ it has one appointee from each member state, appointed for a six year renewable term. Once appointed by the Council of Ministers – in consultation with the European Parliament – the Court of Auditors acts with complete independence.

The role of the Court of Auditors is to oversee the revenue and expenditure of the EU and all of its institutions and agencies. It is responsible for checking all expenditure for regularity, and also for ensuring that the institutions and agencies of the EU adopt sound management practices. It is charged with providing the Parliament and the Council with a statement of assurance on the reliability of the Commission's accounts, and it publishes an annual report at the end of each budgetary year.

The Court of Auditors has the power to report any irregularities to the Parliament and the Council – but it has no power to impose any penalties.

6.8.3 European Economic and Social Committee

The European Economic and Social Committee (EESC – also known as ECOSOC) was set up in 1957. This was well before the advent of elected MEPs, so the EESC was set up as an advisory body which the Council and the Commission could consult. It had – and has – some influence, but no power.

The EESC meets in Brussels. It consists of 344 members (24 from the UK) nominated by member state government for renewable four year periods. Its members fall in to three distinct categories:

- Employers: Representatives of industry and commerce.

- Employees: Representatives of the trades unions.

- Other: Representatives of the professions, consumers, the social economy and the voluntary sector.

The EESC has specialist sections covering all of the main areas of EU competence. When a proposal is referred to the EESC by the Commission, the Council or the Parliament a "study group" is formed to consider it. This is very similar to the committee system of the European Parliament – and as with the Parliament a *rapporteur* is appointed to coordinate the response. Once the study group has produced its report, it is considered at section level, before being passed onto one of the EESC's monthly plenary sessions for debate and agreement. The EESC is only an advisory body, but it is approachable, and very accessible for lobbyists.

Author's top tip

Officials from the lead DG associated with any proposal attend EESC study groups and section meetings. For the lobbyists, this is a great opportunity to identify the fonctionnaires dealing with a proposal, and to approach them and get to know them.

6.8.4 Committee of the Regions

The Committee of the Regions was created in 1992 by the Treaty of Maastricht, and came in to being in 1994.

Like the EESC it is an advisory body with 344 members appointed by the member states for a four year term. Whereas EESC members represent employers, employees and other groups, members of the Committee of the Regions represent local and regional authorities from the member states.

The Committee of the Regions is consulted by the Commission, the Council and the Parliament. It must be consulted on any proposal which affects its members – which is usually reckoned to be about three quarters of all proposals. Areas where the Committee of the Regions must be consulted include:

- Economic policy
- Education policy
- Employment policy
- Energy policy
- Environment policy
- Social Policy
- Telecommunications policy
- Training policy
- Transport policy
- Youth policy

Author's top tip

Members of the Committee of the Regions are made up of locally elected politicians and they are organised into political groups. They are open to approaches by lobbyists on that basis.

6.8.5 European Central Bank

The European Central Bank (ECB) was founded in 1998 and established in Frankfurt. It has a governing council consisting of the central bankers from each member state participating in the single currency. There is also an executive board which has six members serving eight year non-renewable terms. The ECB's activities are directed by a president appointed by the

European Council – at the time of writing this is the Frenchman Jean Claude Trichet.

Representatives of member states who are not members of the euro zone sit on the ECB's General Council – including the Governor of the Bank of England. Although since 1999 the main function of the ECB has been to maintain price stability in the euro zone by setting interest rates, it does have other important functions. These include preparing member states who wish to join the euro zone, conducting exchange operations, and managing the foreign reserves.

The ECB sets interest rates for the euro zone on a monthly basis, and other central bankers watch its actions and listen to its comments carefully. The ECB also publishes a very detailed *Monthly Bulletin*, which is again analysed carefully by central bankers and the financial markets.

The ECB has shown itself to be able to resist pressures from the EU institutions and the member states. There are indications, however, that it is becoming more susceptible to public opinion, as expressed through the media.

6.8.6 European Investment Bank

The European Investment Bank (EIB) was set up under the provisions of the Treaty of Rome. It is based in Luxembourg and is the financial institution of the EU. The EIB is owned by the member states of the EU, and its board of governors consists of the finance ministers of the member states.

The task of the EIB is to enhance the economic, social and territorial cohesion of the EU. It invests about 2 billion euros a year by way of long-term finance for projects which have been vetted for their environmental, social and financial viability. Many projects in which the EIB invests are in the education, energy, training, telecommunications and water sectors.

Following the 2000 Lisbon summit the EIB was mandated to expand its operations in order to assist small and medium-sized enterprises (SMEs). The result was the creation of the European Investment Fund (EIF), which supports SMEs by providing medium-term loans and guaranteeing bank loans.

The EIB also has a role outside of the EU's boundaries. It supports and advises pre-accession states and candidate countries to help prepare their economies for accession. It also has a role in assisting non-European states who are part of the African, Caribbean and Pacific (ACP) group of states which the EU supports under a variety of initiatives.

> ### Author's top tip
>
> The EIB – and the EIF – have very substantial funds to invest, and a very wide remit. Preparing bids for EIB support is a specialist undertaking which must involve substantial financial expertise. However, lobbyists can contribute to the process by emphasising the political advantages of any proposal, and the beneficial PR which could accrue to the EU as a result of acceptance.

6.8.7 European Union agencies

As the EU has expanded, and as successive treaties have broadened and deepened its remit, it has set up a large number of agencies to fulfil the requirements of its enhanced role. Unlike the main institutions of the EU these tend not to be based in Brussels, Luxembourg or Strasbourg.

The EU agencies are:

- Community Fisheries Control Agency (CFCA), Vigo
- Community Plant Variety Office (CPVO), Angers
- European Agency for Safety and Health at Work (EU-OSHA), Bilbao
- European Agency for the Management of Operational Cooperation at the External Borders of the Member States of the European Union (FRONTEX), Warsaw
- European Aviation Safety Agency (EASA), Cologne
- European Environment Agency (EEA), Copenhagen
- European Centre for Disease Prevention and Control (ECDC), Stockholm
- European Centre for the Development of Vocational Training (Cedefop), Thessaloniki
- European Chemicals Agency (ECHA), Helsinki
- European Food Safety Authority (EFSA) Palma

- European Foundation for the Improvement of Living and Working Conditions (Eurofound), Dublin

- European Fundamental Rights Agency (EFRA), Vienna

- European Global Navigation Satellite System Supervisory Authority (GNSS), Brussels

- European Maritime Safety Agency (EMSA), Lisbon

- European Medicines Agency (EMEA), London

- European Monitoring Centre for Drugs and Drug Addiction (EMCDDA), Lisbon

- European Network and Information Security Agency (ENISA), Heraklion

- European Railway Agency (ERA), Valenciennes and Lille

- European Agency for Reconstruction (EAR), Thessaloniki

- European Training Foundation (ETF), Turin

- Office for Harmonisation in the Internal Market (Trade Marks and Designs) (OHIM), Alicante

- Translation Centre for the Bodies of the European Union (CdT), Luxembourg

6.9 Other European Institutions

Whilst what is now the European Union is by far the biggest and most important organisation in Europe, there are other bodies which do have influence and which all lobbyists ought to be aware of.

6.9.1 Council of Europe

The Council of Europe (not to be confused with the European Council) was set up in Strasbourg in 1949. It precedes the formation of the European Coal and Steel Community, and the Schuman Declaration. Its creation was closely linked to Winston Churchill's Zurich University speech in 1946 in which he specifically called for the formation of a Council of Europe. Its remit is to defend human rights, parliamentary democracy and the rule of law.

The Council of Europe has a secretariat of nearly 2000 people drawn from all of the member states. It is headed by a secretary general – currently the UK's Terry Davis. The UK contributes over £20m a year to help to fund the work of the Council of Europe.

Not only is the Council of Europe older than the EU and its antecedents, it is also much larger. The Council of Europe has 47 member states, stretching from Iceland to Turkey. Following the collapse of the Soviet Union nearly all of the newly-independent states joined the Council of Europe. The only European country not a member is Belarus, and it too has applied to join. The US, Canada, Japan and several other nations have observer status.

The Council of Europe has a Committee of Ministers made up of the foreign ministers of every member state. There is also a Parliamentary Assembly, consisting of nominated delegations from each member parliament. There is also a third tier made up of representatives of local and regional government.

Although the Council of Europe has very little actual power, it is influential. To date it has brokered 160 conventions which member states have signed up to and agreed to be bound by. Many of these relate to human rights, and they include a ban on torture and the right to take part in peaceful demonstrations. There are also conventions on medical standards and animal testing.

In 1950 the Council of Europe adopted the European Convention on Human Rights. This is designed to entrench fundamental human rights across the whole continent of Europe. This convention established the European Court of Human Rights.

6.9.2 European Court of Human Rights

As has been said the European Court of Human Rights (not to be confused with the European Court of Justice) or ECHR was set up through the Council of Europe's adoption of the European Convention of Human Rights in 1950. This in turn had drawn inspiration from the UN Universal Declaration of Human Rights.

Any person or organisation can access the European Court of Human Rights if they feel that a member state government which is a signatory to the Convention has not upheld its principles, or acted in accordance with its provisions. However, the complainant must have first pursued appropriate remedies through the institutions of their member state. If an application is deemed admissible (and many are not), the European Court of Human Rights will approach the member state concerned and ask it to respond. It will then seek to resolve the situation by arbitration, only proceeding to make a judgement when all other avenues have been exhausted.

Obviously cases which the European Court of Human Rights has passed judgement on all concern one aspect of human rights or another. High profile cases it has ruled on include:

- Use of corporal punishment in schools
- Immigration and deportation
- Detention without charge
- Rights of prisoners
- Equality for homosexuals

In an effort to stop the succession of high profile cases taken to the European Court of Human Rights by British citizens, the UK government passed the Human Rights Act in 1998. This enshrined the rights and obligations of the Convention into UK law. The effect of this has been to stem the flow of cases brought by UK citizens in the European Court of Human Rights, as they now have redress under UK law.

Contributor's top tip

At first sight the European Institutions appear remote and full of needless complexity, despite the constant expenditure upon information and public relations exercises across the now 27 national states.

But that first impression is deceptive.

Yes, there are a whole range of bureaucratic monoliths headquartered not just in Brussels but across the rest of Europe, each with their own cultures and ways of operating (to say nothing of a European Parliament that bridges a veritable potpourri of political cultures and a vibrant layer of NGOs at the European level) but the key difference in the EU as opposed to Westminster is ease of access.

Underneath all the remote complexity is actually a system ready to engage with policy and political necessities, to meet to discuss issues, and often to offer personal attention to the detail and to maintaining contact.

The real and effective world of European Union public affairs is personal, direct and often discussed over food. The key need is to identify your influencers and build that relationship.

Dr Richard Margrave, Managing Director, Margrave Communications

Contributor's top tip

Be part of the thinking process: As well as getting to the decision maker when an issue is first appearing, establish processes to identify issues which will arise in future which might require decision-makers to act.

Strategise – and move with history: Some battles in the EU are "un-winnable" head-on. Identify the direction of change and when necessary adapt to change and influence its direction, rather than trying to stop it.

Think politically: Identify the focus of the political argument, the values and interests involved, and the potential basis for consensus.

In Brussels, Europeanising the message is important, and frequently it needs politicising too: Defending purely national interests in Brussels is difficult and often counter-productive – although a national argument may be appropriate with some MEPs or permanent representation.

Communications: Recognise – and utilise – the imperfect communications which are endemic between and within EU institutions.

Be transparent: Today's political orthodoxy requires all interest to have the right to be heard – so do not be afraid to be totally open about who you represent, or surprised about others being heard too. The EU institutions are more transparent than most national administrations.

Allies, partners and coalitions: Search for allies, and build coalitions whenever possible. Ad hoc and temporary issue specific coalitions can be just as influential as long-standing partnerships.

Recognise that sound science on its own is a poor lobbying message: Support it with reference to the social and political choices decision makers must necessarily make.

Understand the policy-process-strategy interconnection: In Brussels institutions and processes make a difference. Understand the relationship between process and policy outcome. Timing is crucial too, as is targeting the right people in the right way with appropriate briefing materials for the different types of audience (official and politician).

Empower Brussels advocates: Get beyond "fly in and fly out" lobbying. The speed and constancy of EU decision making, and the compromises necessary, make it impossible for outsiders to influence EU decision making effectively. Be there on the ground.

Diversity: Recognise and respect Europe's diversity in culture, language, and thought, and where possible use it to your advantage.

Be creative: S/he who crafts the compromise will often win in Brussels.

David Earnshaw, Chairman, Burson-Marsteller Brussels

Part Seven –
Lobbying In The United
States Of America

The United States of America (USA) is important for this book and its readers for two reasons. As was stated in the introduction, professional political lobbying was effectively invented in the US, and most people would agree that lobbying in Washington is on a higher level than that in London or Brussels – in terms of both scale and professionalism. Also, of course, the US is the world's only military super-power, and – for the moment at least – far and away the world's biggest economy.

7.1 The Constitution

The current political and legislative structure in the US is still broadly similar to that outlined in the constitution drawn up in 1787 and ratified in 1789. This made provision for a system whereby the power of the president was held in check by Congress – and the whole system was overseen by the judiciary. Bearing in mind that Congress is itself divided into a Senate and a House of Representatives, and that the two main parties (the Republicans and the Democrats) usually control one or the other of them – or hold the Presidency – then you have a very elaborate series of checks and balances. It is also worth constantly bearing in mind that many powers are reserved for state legislatures in what is a truly federal structure.

The constitution sets out in great detail the respective roles of the institutions. Its main articles are:

- Article one – Legislative branch: The roles, membership and election procedures for the Senate and the House of Representatives were spelt out, and the legislative process outlined.

- Article two – Executive branch: The procedure for electing the president was set out, along with details of the president's executive powers and relationship with Congress.

- Article three – judicial branch: The powers of the Supreme Court were spelt out, and provision made for the appointment of inferior courts. The right to trial by jury was guaranteed, and the circumstances under which charges of treason could be laid were specified.

- Article four – states: The roles and responsibilities of individual states – to each other and to the federal government – were detailed. The procedure for the setting up of new states was laid down, and all states were guaranteed a republican form of government.

- Article five – amendments: The procedure for amending the constitution was specified. Two-thirds of both Houses of Congress have to be in favour, as would two-thirds of all states, before the constitution could be amended.

- Article six – debts, supremacy and oaths: This article confirmed that the new United States would honour all debts, that all treaties entered into and laws passed by Congress would have supremacy over state law, and that all those elected at Congressional and state level – and all judges – should swear an oath of allegiance to the constitution.

- Article seven – ratification: This declared that ratification of Conventions by the states was sufficient authority to bring the constitution into force.

The first ten amendments to the constitution – all ratified in 1791 – are known as the Bill of Rights. The provisions of the Bill of Rights are:

- Amendment one: Freedom to practice any religion, freedom of speech, freedom of the press and freedom to petition Congress.

- Amendment two: Right to bear arms. This amendment is used by the pro-gun lobby in the US to underpin its case.

- Amendment three: Quartering of soldiers. This was highly relevant at the time – one of the biggest grievances against the British was that they habitually quartered their soldiers with US citizens – often without compensation.

- Amendment four: Search and seizure. Again, this largely harks back to the British tactic of searching homes without warning and taking what they wanted – often without compensation. Still relevant today however – an American's home is still his castle.

- Amendment five: Trial and punishment, compensation and takings. This established the principle of double jeopardy – which said that nobody could be tried twice for the same offence – and stipulated that nobody could be required to give evidence which might convict themselves.

- Amendment six: Right to speedy trial and confrontation of witness. This stipulates that trials should be conducted locally with juries drawn from the local population, unless the crime was of federal nature.

- Amendment seven: Right to trial by jury in civil cases. This right is still sacrosanct in the US, whilst it is under pressure in the UK.

- Amendment eight: Right not be subjected to cruel and unusual punishment. This amendment has been quoted in extraordinary rendition cases and by inmates at Guantanamo Bay, where there have been numerous allegations of torture.

- Amendment nine: Construction of constitution – the powers authorised by the constitution should not be used to deny other rights which citizens enjoy. This is a guarantee against the slow accretion of power by Washington.

- Amendment ten: Powers of the states and people – those powers not specifically allocated by the constitution to Congress should be reserved to the states and the people. As with amendment nine, this seeks to prevent Congress from gradually acquiring more powers which were previously exercised at state level.

The US constitution and Bill of Rights are not just historic or academic documents – they have as much validity today as they did when framed in the eighteenth century. The separation of powers between the executive, the legislature and the judiciary is still very much in place. Within the Bill of Rights, the first amendment is crucial to all US lobbyists. It guarantees not just freedom of religion, but also freedom of the press, freedom of speech and the right to petition Congress. This is, in effect, a lobbyists' charter.

7.2 The President

The president of the United States is frequently referred to as the most powerful man in the world. This is partly because of the US's pre-eminent global position following the collapse of the Soviet Union, and partly because the US president has considerable executive power. To an almost unparalleled extent – at least in a democracy – the US president is also regarded as the figure-head of the nation.

The powers of the president can be summarised as follows:

- Commander in chief: The US president is commander in chief of what are undoubtedly the world's most powerful armed forces.

- Cabinet: The president appoints his own cabinet made up of individuals who are very often not even politicians. These cabinet members head up the 13 main administrative departments of the federal government.

- Supreme Court: The president has the power to appoint the Chief Justice and the eight associate judges who make up the Supreme Court. These are lifelong appointments with no mandatory retirement age.

- Federal agencies: The president appoints the heads of federal agencies, and has wide powers of patronage over senior and middle-ranking positions.

- Foreign policy: The president has a very large say over how the foreign policy of the US is conducted. He (and at the time of writing all presidents have been male) also represents the US at summits, and negotiates treaties with foreign nations. Additionally, he appoints US Ambassadors and some lower ranking diplomatic posts. He can also enter executive agreements with foreign powers which are not subject to Congressional scrutiny or approval.

- Legislation – initiation: As the chief formulator of public policy, the president is a major initiator of legislation. The president delivers his State of the Union address to Congress, outlining his legislative priorities. He also sends an annual message to Congress as well as special messages.

- Legislation – veto: The president can veto any Act of Congress.

- Budget: The president is responsible for the preparation of the Budget through the Office of Management and Budget.

- Executive Orders: The president can issue some regulations and instructions to federal agencies which do not require Congressional approval.

- Party politics: Finally, of course, the president has always in modern times been the head of one of the two main political parties – and this gives him varying degrees of power in both Houses and in the country at large.

Having gone to war in order to rid themselves of what they regarded as the tyrannical depredations of a British monarch, the framers of the constitution were determined to ensure that under the US constitution the president could never assume similarly dictatorial powers. The powers of the US president are, therefore, constrained by a series of checks and balances:

- Commander in chief: The president must have the approval of Congress to go to war – and he must ask Congress to pay for any conflict.

- Appointments: All cabinet appointments (along with appointments of sub-cabinet, senior military officers, senior diplomats and senior judges) are subject to ratification by the Senate. When the opposition party controls the Senate, the president has to propose appointees acceptable to them or risk rejection.

- Federal agencies: All senior appointments are subject to ratification by the Senate.

- Foreign policy: No treaties signed by the president can come in to effect until endorsed by two thirds of the Senate.

- Legislation: The president's veto can be over-ruled by a two thirds majority in both Houses. If the president does not veto a bill within ten days it automatically becomes law.

- Budget: Congress can substantially alter the president's Budget and refuse to approve it unless its amendments are accepted.

- Party politics: If the president finds that his party is in a minority in both Houses then he is very much at the mercy of Congress when it comes to getting his appointments confirmed, legislation passed and his Budget approved. If his party controls just one House then he may be less constrained. Even if his party controls both Houses, the president is not guaranteed his legislation or his Budget.

Apart from the legal and constitutional niceties it is undoubtedly the case that a president's popularity ratings have a direct affect on his relations with Congress. If a president is popular and has high opinion poll ratings, it is much less likely that Congress will behave in an overtly obstructionist manner. However, given that the constitution (since the days when Franklin D Roosevelt served four terms) now forbids a president to run for a third term, there is no doubt that a president starts to lose authority at some point in the second half of his second term. He becomes what is known as a lame-duck president.

Every president has a vice president. Various vice presidents over the years have gone to great lengths to downplay the importance of the role. It does, however, carry with it various important responsibilities:

- *Replacing the president*: If the president were to be impeached, to resign, to be assassinated, to become incapable or to die of natural causes the vice president would immediately assume the role of president. In the twentieth century, five vice presidents replaced the president – Theodore Roosevelt, Calvin Coolidge, Harry S Truman, Lyndon B Johnson and Gerald Ford. The first four succeeded because of the death of the president, the fifth because of his resignation.

- *Deputising for the president*: The vice president can represent the president at functions and events – ceremonial and functional – in the US and abroad.

- *Succeeding the president*: Some vice presidents go on to secure election as president in their own right. In the twentieth century only Richard Nixon and George H W Bush were elected president having first served as vice president, and there have been none so far in the twenty-first century.

- *Chairing the Senate*: The vice president of the US serves as president of the Senate. He presides over some of its meetings, and has a casting vote. In recent years the Senate has on occasion been tied and the vice president's casting vote has been crucial.

Author's top tip

Unless you are the CEO of a major US corporation or a senior diplomatic or political figure the US president is pretty well impossible to lobby. However, in recent years US presidents have set up Congressional Liaison Offices, whose job it is to try and ensure that the president's policy priorities are enacted. This office (along with the Congressional Relations Office in each major federal agency) is approachable and they are there to do deals. If they think you have a block of votes you can deliver in either House they will be happy to listen to your proposal.

7.3 The Senate

As we have seen the drafters of the US constitution opted for a bicameral legislature, with both an upper and a lower chamber.

There is no doubt that the upper House in the US – the Senate – has considerably more prestige than the lower House – the House of Representatives. Apart from anything else there are only 100 Senators, and this gives them a certain aura of exclusivity denied to their colleagues in the lower House.

There are two Senators elected from each one of the 50 states. Candidates must be more than 30 years old, must have been US citizen for at last nine years, and must reside in the state which they aim to represent. They are elected for six year terms, with one third of Senators coming up for re-election every two years. No two Senators for the same state are ever up for re-election to full six year terms on the same year. However, sometimes two Senators are on the same ballot when one has just been appointed to a vacancy caused by a death or resignation. In cases such as these the appointed Senator must run at the next election for the remaining two or four year term.

7.3.1 Senior positions

At the beginning of each session the Senate meets to approve appointments to various senior positions:

- President: As has been seen the vice president of the US serves as president of the Senate and chairs its meetings.
- President pro tempore: A Senator (usually the most senior member of the majority party) is elected to act as chairman of the Senate when the vice president is unavailable. In fact Senators (usually junior) often act as Presiding Officer for a portion of a sitting day.
- Majority Leader: As the name implies this is the leader of the party with the most seats in the Senate. He or she has considerable power over appointments and legislation, but because there is no time limit on debates in the Senate, he or she must rely on the co-operation and goodwill of Senators from both parties in order to function effectively.
- Majority Whip: This post is also elected. The Majority Whip must try to maximise attendance, and try to persuade Senators to toe the party line.

- Minority Leader: This person liaises with the majority leader to ensure that the interests of the minority party are not ignored. If the president's party is in a minority in the Senate the minority leader also acts as his spokesperson in this chamber.
- Minority Whip: Again this post is elected by Senators from the minority party. The Minority Whip liaises with the Majority Whip to ensure that the proceedings of the Senate run smoothly – the US version of the UK's usual channels.

There are several other party bodies within the Senate which have a strong influence on its proceedings:

- Conferences: Both the Democrats and the Republicans in the Senate call their caucus a conference. These conferences are composed of all of the Senators from the party in question. They elect the leaders, approve committee assignments, set party rules and adopt strategies for dealing with legislation.
- Policy committees: Both parties have policy committees which both formulate policy and coordinate responses to existing policy initiatives.
- Senate Democratic Steering Committee: Proposes which Democratic Senators should sit on which committee.
- Senate Republican Committee on Committees: Proposes which Republican Senators should sit on which committee.

Warning!

Party caucus conferences should not be confused with the conference committees which are created when differing versions of bills pass the two Houses. When this happens, each House sends a number of conferees to a joint conference committee to resolve the disputed points in conference – both Houses can then agree a joint version.

Author's top tip

Senators are very open-minded and are frequently prepared to vote against the party line. The best way to approach them is through their constituents, but otherwise policy committees on occasion accept offers from external organisations to provide a verbal or written briefing – usually to the research staffers.

7.4 House Of Representatives

There are 435 members of the House of Representatives. Whereas in the Senate every state gets two seats regardless of its size and population, the seats which a state has in the House of Representatives are allocated according to population size. This is based on censuses which are held every ten years. Every state is, however, entitled under the constitution to at least one Representative, no matter how small it is. Thus currently New York has 34 Representatives, but Delaware has just one. There are also non-voting delegates from the District of Columbia, the Virgin Islands, Guam and American Samoa, plus a non-voting Commissioner from Puerto Rica.

Officially members of the House of Representatives are called Members of Congress. This is obviously confusing, as both Houses together are know as Congress. Therefore they are more commonly referred to as Representatives, or Congressmen and Congresswomen. Whereas Senators are elected for a six year term, Representatives are elected for just two years at a time. They must be at least 25 years old on the date of election, have been a US citizen for at least seven years, and be resident in the state they wish to represent.

7.4.1 Senior positions

As with the Senate there are a number of senior positions in the House of Representatives which are decided by votes of the party caucuses at the beginning of every new Congress. They are:

- Speaker: The Speaker, as the Presiding Officer, has enormous influence over the proceedings of the House of Representatives:

    - He or she rules on points of order, and calls Representatives to speak.

    - He or she allocates bills to the appropriate committee.

    - He or she has a strong say in the appointment of Chairs and members of committees.

    - He or she can become a national figure, and go on to higher office.

    - The Speaker has a vote, but generally only uses it to break a tie.

- House Majority Leader: This person is the majority party's chief spokesperson and advocate. He or she coordinates the party's legislative programme with the Speaker, and liaises with the minority party Leader.

- House Majority Whip: As with the Senate Whips, the function of the House Majority Whip is to ensure that the party's majority is translated into votes and the legislative programme is steered through the lower House.

- House Minority Leader: The House Minority Leader generally seeks to have good relations with his or her majority counterpart. This is because US politics is largely consensual at a senior level, but also because the positions could be reversed in a short period of time.

- House Minority Whip: Again, the Minority Whip seeks to have a good working relationship with his or her majority counterpart. When relations between the parties break down in one Congress the ill feeling can be carried into the next.

As with the Senate there are a number of important bodies which help to ensure that the House of Representatives runs smoothly.

- Democratic caucus: This is made up of all Democratic Representatives and elects the Leader and Chief Whip – and also the Speaker when the Democrats are the majority party. It also works out the party's floor strategy and considers the party's line on particular legislative proposals.

- Republican conference: This is the Republican version of the Democratic caucus, and it performs an identical function.

- Policy committees: Both parties have a policy committee which initiates and reviews policy.

- Steering committees: These assign Representatives to particular committees subject to the approval of the caucus or the conference.

Author's top tip

As with the Senate, the best way to get to a Representative is through their constituents – especially bearing in mind that they have to be re-elected every two years. The policy committees, however, can provide a viable alternative route.

7.5 Committees

Both Houses of Congress have strong committee structures. The chairmanship – and membership – of committees is much sought after. Proceedings of committees are widely reported and televised, and viewing figures can be high. This is especially the case where a high-profile presidential appointment candidate is being cross-examined as part of the Congressional ratification process.

Committees set their own timetables and adopt their own rules of procedure. There are rules governing how many committees a Senator or Representative can sit on. These are laid down both by the Chamber and by the political parties. As with the Westminster Parliament (and many other legislatures) representation on committees is roughly in proportion to membership of the parent Chamber.

Committees can also set up their own subcommittees. These subcommittees – and their chairs – have considerable autonomy and are not totally beholden to their parent committee. They also adopt their own procedures and timetables, and appoint their own staffers. Subcommittees can even block legislation referred to them by the parent committee by not acting on it – in which case the legislation automatically falls.

Author's top tip

The committees of both Houses play a crucial role in scrutinising legislation, formulating policy and vetting appointments. Establishing relationships with relevant committees is vital – whether that be with the chair, with ordinary members, with the clerks or with researchers. Watch out for any opportunity which may arise for you or your client to give expert evidence.

7.5.1 Senate committees

In the Senate both parties rank the committees in order of importance from A to C. Senators can serve on a maximum of two category A committees, and one category B committee. They may, however, also serve on one category C committee.

The category A committees are:

- Agriculture
- Appropriations
- Authorization
- Armed Services
- Commerce, Science and Transportation
- Energy and Natural Resources
- Government Affairs
- Foreign Relations
- Health, Education, Labor and Pensions
- Small Business

The category B committees are:

- Ageing
- Budget
- Rules and Administration

The category C committees are:

- Ethics
- Indian Affairs
- Intelligence

In the Senate the chairs of subcommittees are not elected. They emerge after discussion between the majority group chair of the parent committee and the other majority group members. Allocating the chair of a subcommittee to a relative novice is regarded as a way of helping them to gain political experience quickly, and as a way to rapidly progress the career of a newcomer who is regarded as having a great deal of potential.

7.5.2 House of Representatives committees

In the House there is much more competition to serve on committees and subcommittees – simply because there are 435 Representatives as against just

100 Senators. Because of this, some committees are designated as Exclusive committees – meaning if a Representative is assigned to any one of them he or she cannot serve on any other committee. If a Representative is not assigned to an exclusive committee he or she can serve on one major committee and also on one non-major committee.

The committee structure is very similar to the Senate, with the committees at the time of writing being:

- Agriculture
- Appropriations
- Armed Services
- Budget
- Education and Labor
- Energy and Commerce
- Financial Services
- Foreign Affairs
- Homeland Security
- House Administration
- Intelligence
- Judiciary
- Natural Resources
- Oversight and Government Reform
- Rules
- Science and Technology
- Small Business
- Standards and Official Conduct
- Transportation and Infrastructure
- Veterans' Affairs
- Ways and Means

In the House of Representatives the chairs of subcommittees are elected by a vote of all of the majority party members of the parent committee. They also have the power to decide how many subcommittees there will be and what subject areas they will cover.

7.5.3 Joint committees

Again as with the Westminster Parliament the Senate and the House of Representatives form joint committees to cover key policy areas. Examples include:

- Joint Committee on Taxation
- Joint Economic Committee

Although these committees meet in order to try and arrive at a consensus over key policy areas – such as the economy and taxation – they have no power to actually approve expenditure or to pass legislation.

7.6 Legislation

As we saw earlier, article one of the US constitution vested Congress (the Senate and the House of Representatives) with all legislative powers. Both have equal powers to initiate and pass legislation, other than revenue bills designed to raise money. As is the case at Westminster only the lower House – the House of Representatives – has the power to initiate bills with a revenue-raising purpose.

Author's top tip

Although the House of Representatives has the sole power to initiate revenue-raising bills, the Senate can amend such bills. This means that in effect they have the power to raise revenue for specific projects simply by tacking an amendment onto a House of Representatives bill.

It should be noted that although Congress was given unique authority over legislation by the constitution, the impetus for legislation originates from a wide variety of sources. The president – through his position as leader of one of the main parties – obviously has the ability to ensure that legislation which he desires or requires is introduced. Some proposals also come from the executive branch of government – including departments and agencies. As has been noted the president makes his State of the Union address in which he outlines his proposals for legislation. These suggestions are then picked up by Senators or Representatives who are member of the president's political party. When this occurs, the legislation is said to have been introduced by request.

There are, however, many other sources of ideas for legislation. These include the states, think tanks, corporations, pressure groups, Congressional staffers, and lobbyists. The number of bills introduced into both Houses during the course of a year can be very large – but only about 10% actually pass through all of the required stages and become law.

As has been said legislation can be introduced into either House. Every bill is given a designation made up of letters showing where it originated (S for Senate and HR for House of Representatives) and a number (so it could be S99 or HR 101). The types of legislation are:

- Private bills: These relate to a grievance which a private citizen may have with the government which is not able to be resolved by the courts. As with any other bill they have to be introduced by a Senator or Representative. They are extremely rare.

- Public bills: This is the category into which the vast majority of legislation falls. Unlike at Westminster there are no government bills or private members' bills, but bills obviously have a much better chance or progressing if they have majority group support.

As well as private bills and public bills there are also resolutions. There are three types of resolution:

- Joint resolution: These have their own designation – HJRs and SJRs. Like a bill these need to be passed by both Houses and to be approved by the president. They are generally used to authorise specific payments out of federal funds, or even to propose an amendment to the constitution – in which case they need a two thirds majority in both Houses.

- Concurrent resolution: Again, these have their own designation – HConRes and SConRes. These are generally used to express sentiment – they do not go to the president and they do not have the force of law. However, they do need to be passed by both Houses.

- Simple resolutions: The designations for these are HRs or SRs. As with concurrent resolutions they are used to express sentiment – but in his case of one House or the other.

Author's top tip

Although concurrent resolutions and simple resolutions do not have the force of law they can be used to constrain Congressional action. Thus concurrent resolutions are used to restrict Congress to budget limitations and simple resolutions are used to adopt debate limitations on bills.

As with most legislatures, there is a long and complicated process which all legislation must go through in Congress before it goes up to the president to be signed into law. Here are the legislative stages which bills have to go through in two Houses of Congress:

- Stage one: A bill is introduced into either the Senate or the House of Representatives by a Member of Congress. It is then referred to the appropriate committee. If the committee does not act on it, then the bill dies. This is what happens to most bills.

- Stage two: If the committee decides that it will be progressing the bill, it schedules hearings, which are open to the public. Witnesses are called, including from departments or agencies representing the executive branch. The committee may then choose to make amendments (known as mark-ups), before approving it.

- Stage three: The bill – as originally introduced or as amended by the committee – is then debated and voted on the floor.

- Stage four: If approved, it is then passed onto the other House (ie, the House other than the one it was introduced into originally).

- Stage five: The bill then gets referred to the relevant committee in that House. Again, it can either be approved or amended with mark-ups.

- Stage six: It then gets debated and voted on the floor. Again, amendments can be tabled and voted on.

- Stage seven: If there have been any amendments carried in the second House to which the bill has been referred then a conference committee made up of members of both Houses is convened to resolve any differences and to report a final version back to both Houses.

- Stage eight: Both Houses must then vote on and approve the bill in full plenary session on the floor.

- Stage nine: If approved by both Houses the bill then goes up to the president to approve, or veto.

- Stage ten: If the president approves the bill, it becomes an Act and comes in to force either immediately or at a specified date. If the president vetoes the bill, his veto can be over-turned by a two-thirds majority of both Houses. If he does nothing, the bill automatically becomes an Act after ten days.

Author's top tip

Members of Congress often add 'riders' to bills. These are amendments which do not need to have any relevance to the bill in question. They can be an attempt to sneak in a legislative change without introducing a whole new bill – or they can be an attempt to get funding for a pet project (often referred to as "pork barrel" politics). Alternatively, however, they can be an attempt to wreck a bill – by introducing a rider which is unacceptable to the majority of Senators or Members of the House of Representatives.

Contributor's top tip

Pay attention to the House Rules Committee. The members of Congress who sit on this committee have the power to establish which bills are debated, to allocate (and restrict) debating time and to determine which types of amendments will be allowed.

Get constituents to back your bill. The best lobbyists know that members of Congress will meet with their voters and respond to the ideas and concerns coming from their district.

The best way to get an amendment to a bill is through the committee mark-up process. That's where the bills really get written because floor debate is often limited.

Deborah Rozansky, Principal, OPM, Former Presidential Management Intern

7.7 Finances

As we have seen under the US constitution Congress has the power of the purse. However, in practice responsibility for the Budget is shared between the executive (the president) and the legislature (Congress). This interplay between the president and the two Houses of Congress is in this context known as the Budget process.

Expenditure is split between discretionary and mandatory spending. Generally speaking discretionary expenditure is only authorised for a short period (usually a year), and has to be authorised by an Appropriations Bill passed by the Appropriations Committee of both Houses. Mandatory expenditure is longer term and has already been authorised by previous legislation. Medical assistance for the poor and social security fall in to this category.

The Budget process is a complicated one, involving as it does both Houses of Congress, the president, and a number of other offices and agencies. Here is a brief summary of the process:

- Stage one: As per the Congressional Budget and Impoundment Act the president presents his proposed Budget to Congress on or before the first Monday in February. This contains his estimates – based on inputs from the federal Agencies – for expenditure and revenue needs in the fiscal year ahead.

- Stage two: Both Houses of Congress are obliged to agree on identical Budget Resolutions. This outlines Congress's expenditure and revenue proposals for the next fiscal year, and for the next five fiscal years. The Budget Committees of both Houses hold hearings and call as witnesses Administration officials, Members of Congress and external experts. Based on these sessions and their own deliberations the Budget Committees produce Budget Resolutions with their own mark-ups. They must report their final Budget Resolutions to their respective Houses by 1 April.

- Stage three: Both Houses of Congress now have the opportunity to debate the Budget Resolutions, and to amend them.

- Stage four: Both Houses then jointly appoint Members to the conference committee which meets in order to resolve any differences, and can therefore be in a position to agree a unified version of the Budget Resolution by 15 April.

- Stage five: By 15 April both Houses must have approved the Conference Committee's unified Budget Resolution by majority vote. This Budget Resolution must agree spending allocations (or spending limits) on all discretionary programmes for the coming year and the next five years. Discretionary spending accounts for approximately one-third of the federal budget, and does not include uncontrollable factors, such as the payment of interest on the national debt. These allocations cannot be exceeded.

- Stage six: The Appropriations Committees then take these spending allocations and divide them in to 13 sub allocations. These are made up of:

    - Agriculture, Rural Development, Food and Drug Administration and related agencies

    - Departments of Commerce, Justice, and State – the judiciary and related departments

    - Department of Defense

    - Operations of the government of the District of Columbia

    - Energy and water resources development

    - Foreign Operations, export financing, and related programmes

    - Homeland Security

    - Department of the Interior and related agencies

    - Departments of Labor, Health and Human Services, Education and related agencies

    - Legislative Branch

    - Military construction, family housing, and base realignment and closure for the Department of Defense

    - Department of Transportation, Treasury, the United States Postal Service, the Executive Office of the President, and certain Independent Agencies.

    - Veterans' Affairs and Housing and Urban Development, and for sundry independent agencies, boards, commissions, corporations and offices

The Appropriations Committees have from 15 May until 10 June to finalise their 13 spending bills and forward them to their respective Houses. The 13 spending bills may be consolidated into one omnibus Reconciliation Bill.

- Stage seven: By 10 June both Houses have to begin consideration of the 13 spending bills. These bills have to follow the same legislative procedure as other bills, although there are some special rules of debate to prevent filibustering.

- Stage eight: The Spending bills are debated and amended on the floor of both Houses. They therefore have to go through the same conference committee procedure as the Budget Resolution in order that a single version of each bill is reached. This can then be agreed by both Houses.

- Stage nine: Once the conference committees report their agreed spending bills to the Houses. They must agree them by majority vote by 30 June.

- Stage ten: The president then has ten days to decide what he will do with each of the 13 spending bills. He can sign them to signify his approval, veto them, or deliberately miss the deadline so that they become law – but without his express approval. If he does veto any bill, his veto can be overturned by a two-thirds majority vote in both Houses.

If Congress cannot agree and pass the Appropriations Bill before the start of the fiscal year (which begins on 1 October) it is able to pass continuing resolutions in order to ensure that the federal government continues to function. The president can also request that Congress pass supplemental appropriations bills or emergency supplemental appropriations bills.

Author's top tip

Congress has a system known as "earmarking" whereby Senators or Representatives can try to get specified sums of money allocated to a particular organisation or project. So-called "soft earmarks" (usually to be found in committee reports) do not have the force of law, but are often put into effect, whilst "hard earmarks" or "hard marks" do have the effect of law and must be allocated as directed. Lobbyists often collaborate with Members of Congress to get such "earmarks" inserted.

Contributor's top tip

Money. Money. Money.

Other factors differentiate lobbying in Washington from elsewhere – separation of powers, the patchwork quilt of federal, state and local competencies, the absence of a national print media – but none more so than the transactional dynamic which defines lobbyists' relationships with elected politicians and their campaigns. In my 20 plus years in UK public affairs I have never witnessed an equivalent dynamic.

Every election cycle K Street pumps millions of its clients dollars into candidates campaign coffers through political action committees, party fundraising efforts and other "non-partisan" mechanisms. Many a lobbyists' evening is spent sipping mediocre sauvignon blanc or chewing rubbery chicken cordon bleu at a $2000 a head fundraiser for Gubernatorial, Senate, Congressional and – every four years – presidential - hopefuls or actual nominees.

Establishing oneself as a prodigious fundraiser is a sure way to get noticed on staff radar screens and is the first big step towards winning friends and then – most importantly – gaining access. Decision makers will always deny any direct relationship between the largesse some lobbyists provide for their electoral efforts and positions they adopt on policies of interest to said lobbyists clients. The record speaks for itself.

Nick DeLuca, Chairman, Open Road

7.8 Judiciary

The judiciary is the third leg of the stool constructed by the US constitution. It is the main guardian of the constitution, and the upholder of the constitutional rights of US citizens. It is also regularly called in to mediate and rule on disputes between the executive branch (the president) and the legislative branch (Congress).

As with any other nation there is a hierarchy of courts within the US judicial system. Ranked in terms of importance and authority they are:

7.8.1 Supreme Court

The Supreme Court is the highest court in the US federal court system – and therefore the highest court in the US. As we have seen the Chief Judge of the Supreme Court (formally the Chief Justice of the United States) and the eight Associate Judges (formally Associate Judges of the Supreme Court) are all appointed by the president – although his appointments have to be ratified by the Senate. Judges are appointed for life.

The principle role of the Supreme Court is that of being the guardian and the interpreter of the US constitution, and all of the amendments which have been passed since its adoption. This includes the first ten amendments which make up the Bill of Rights. The Supreme Court has the power to declare any piece of legislation unconstitutional, in which case it immediately ceases to have effect. It can also declare any action by the president or the executive branch to be unconstitutional – in which case it is has to be immediately reversed. Any ruling in this respect by the Supreme Court creates a precedent that can subsequently be applied to similar pieces of legislation or similar executive actions.

The Supreme Court also has the function of dealing with disputes between states. Again, its rulings in this respect are deemed to create precedent, and have a bearing on any similar cases brought at a future date. The final role of the Supreme Court is in ruling on any disputes relating to treaties with foreign nations or multinational organisations. Again, the Supreme Court uses the constitution as the sole guide to its deliberations with respect to both state disputes and disputes over treaties.

7.8.2 Other courts

There are a number of other levels of court in the US – created either by the constitution or by Congress. They are:

- *Courts of Appeal*: These are second in seniority only to the Supreme Court. There are 13 of them in total.

- *District Courts*: The first Congress divided the US in to judicial districts and set up federal courts in each of them. There are 94 of them in total. These are the general trial courts for federal law, dealing with federal offences such as counterfeiting, terrorism, kidnapping etc. They also deal with civil actions.

- *State Supreme Courts*: These courts are the final authority within their states. They cannot be over-ruled by the US Supreme Court unless it can be shown that the case has a federal dimension.

- *State courts – other*: Below the State Supreme Courts are Courts of Appeal and municipal courts.

- *Speciality courts*: These are courts set up to deal with specific areas of law – such as tax courts and bankruptcy courts.

7.9 The States

The individual states of the United States of America retain a substantial degree of autonomy. The US is a very good example of a truly federal system of government.

The individual states have a great deal of freedom of action – provided their actions do not contravene the US constitution. As we have seen the US Supreme Court rules in all cases where there is an implication that the states have strayed in to areas of responsibility which are the preserve of the federal system.

Examples of things which the states cannot do are:

- Have their own currency.

- Have their own armed forces (other than the National Guard – which has the president as its Commander in Chief).

- Make treaties with foreign powers.

Author's top tip

Quite often Congress will pass legislation pre-empting the rights of the states to take action. Frequently these pre-emptive moves relate to commercial issues such as product regulation.

There are 50 states in all – although four of them prefer to be known as commonwealths. The commonwealth states are Kentucky, Massachusetts, Pennsylvania and Virginia – although there is no practical difference between these and the other 46 states. There is nothing to prevent US citizens from moving from one state to another, unless they are ex-prisoners on parole (in which case inter-state movement can be prohibited).

The laws between states can vary enormously. The most prominent examples are laws relating to speed limits and driving age, and the ownership of firearms. There are also some variations on when and where alcohol can be sold – with some states prohibiting sales on a Sunday. Judges in State Supreme Courts and lower courts are elected in some states, appointed in others.

The states also have the same three tier structure as the federal United States. Every state has a Senate and a House of Representatives. The exception which proves this rule is Nebraska. It is unicameral, and it is also unique in refusing to recognise political parties.

The executive role of the president is replaced by that of the governor. The senior posts in the executive branch of state government are variously elected and appointed. A typical state (not that there is such a thing) might have:

- Governor

- Lieutenant governor

- Attorney General (the head lawyer for the state government)

- Secretary of state (usually the top election official)

- Treasurer

- Auditor

- Superintendent of ...(Education, Transportation etc)

The constitutions of states can be changed if both Houses vote by a two-thirds majority for the amendment. In some states the constitution can also be changed by popular initiative (ie, by an amendment proposed by petitions bearing a required number of signatures). Alternatively, constitutions can be changed where the legislature refers the amendment to a state-wide referendum. All states must recognise the laws of other states.

Author's top tip

As well as the huge lobbying industry in Washington, every state capital has its own cadre of public affairs consultants. This will vary according to the size of the state in question. However, as every state has the right to pass its own laws – and to set its own budgets – there is plenty of work for lobbyists at state capital level in the US.

Contributor's top tip

Access to lawmakers, their staffs and government officials representing Executive Branch Departments is key to effective lobbying and is typically obtained by one of three distinct approaches:

- Access through relationships
- Access through political and/or financial support
- Access through expert public policy guidance

Lobbying in the U.S. routinely includes the following activities:

- Direct advocacy before a legislative committee or government regulatory body at the federal, state or local levels
- Issues management, legislative and regulatory monitoring at the federal, state and local levels of government
- Legislative and political assessments at the federal, state and local level
- Grassroots and Grasstops mobilization and e-advocacy services
- Crisis management and messaging

David McCloud, Managing Director, The Advocacy Group Inc.

7.10 Ultimate Lobbying

Lobbying in the US – as we saw in the History section of this book – can be traced back to 1792, when William Hull was retained by Virginian veterans of the Continental Army to lobby for increased compensation for their war efforts. What is more, the right to lobby is enshrined in the US constitution. The first amendment guarantees US citizens not just freedom of religion, but also freedom of speech, a free press and the right to petition (ie, lobby) Congress.

Author's top tip

Anybody wanting to get a feel for the legislative, political and lobbying scenes in the US should spend some time going through journals such as the Congressional Quarterly, Roll Call, The Hill, and Politico.

From these early roots lobbying in the US has developed enormously in scale and sophistication. According to the Center for Public Integrity in Washington DC alone there are now in excess of 35,000 paid advocates lobbying the federal government. The development of the lobbying industry has been aided by the fact that getting elected (and re-elected) in the United States is an enormously expensive business. This is especially the case in the House of Representatives, where Congressmen and Congresswomen serve two year terms. This means that the minute they are elected, they have to start thinking about getting re-elected in just two years time. Given that in the US candidates are allowed to run advertisements on radio and TV, this is a hugely expensive business. In rough terms a candidate for the Senate must raise and spend upwards of $10m, and a candidate for the House of Representatives about $2m. Candidates for the Presidency, of course, have to raise substantially more money – figures of up to $300m have been quoted.

Unless candidates are personally wealthy – and many of them are – this means that they have to raise money from pretty well any source they can. Individual party members are able to donate – as are the public at large – but it takes a great many $10 cheques to hit that $2m or that $10m mark. This means that large donations have to be sought – and they often come with a price tag. Lobbyists help Senators and Representatives – and candidates – in a number of ways:

- By forming Political Action Committees – which are able to donate $5000 in each electoral cycle if multi-candidate or $2300 if single candidate.

- By contributing to party committees – Democratic and Republican, National and State Committees, House and Senate, Democratic and Republican, campaign committees etc.

- By attending fund-raising breakfasts, lunches and dinners – where prices of $2000 a head are not uncommon.

- By setting up Independent Expenditure Committees (also known as "527" committees after the tax code number). Technically these groups function totally separately from the candidate and the parties, and cannot even contact the candidate's campaign. However, they have a strong indirect influence, and business, the unions and special interest groups spend hundreds of millions of dollars using them to try and influence the results of elections.

- By supporting 'non partisan' voter registration and turn-out groups. By concentrating on carefully selected areas, these 'non partisan' groups can have a significant impact on the outcome of elections.

- By providing experienced and motivated activists and political campaigners on the ground during election times.

Warning!

Federal law limits the contribution of any one individual to any one candidate's election campaign to $2300 – adjusted for inflation every two years. However, primary and general elections are treated separately, so if a candidate has both the donation can be $4600 (although general election money cannot be spent on a primary). Married couples are treated separately so both can donate in their own right.

As well as the hard (ie, strictly controlled) money donated by Political Action Committees, soft money is also contributed. This can be channelled through so-called "527 groups", which do not directly advocate the election of a particular party or group, but whose activities broadly favour one party or another or one candidate or another. "Bundling" is another uniquely US phenomenon, whereby one person gathers in donations from a range of individuals and organisations, and acts as the conduit for a one-off donation.

This technique is frowned upon but is not against the rules, and it has on occasion been used by lobbies to disguise the true origin of donations.

Of course the resources which lobbyists – in house and in-consultancy – have at their disposal varies enormously. Probably the best funded and best organised lobby in the US is the National Rifle Association (NRA). This was set up to defend the second amendment – the right to bear arms. Its annual lobbying budget across the US is rumoured to be in the region of $100m. Perhaps just as importantly, the NRA is organised in every state in the US, with election volunteer coordinators appointed and ready to get to work when the electoral cycle begins. They make sure that activists set up telephone call centres, distribute posters, leaflets and bumper stickers, and send their activists out with walk lists to knock up their supporters and get out their vote. The NRA ranks every Member of Congress from 1 to 10, with strong supporters receiving financial and electoral help, neutrals being lobbied and leaned on, and opponents being targeted.

Another factor which perhaps contributes to the strength of lobbying in the US is the two party system. Occasionally there is an independent candidate (such as Ralph Nader or Ross Perot) running for the presidency, but basically the race for the White House, the Senate, and the House of Representatives is a two horse race between the Democrats and the Republicans. This does make life simpler for the lobbyist, and in most seats it is easy to spot – and back – the winner.

The US system is also good for the lobbyist because once elected both Senators and Representatives are generally prepared to vote against the party line. They do this either because of constituency and electoral imperatives, for reasons of conscience, or simply because they have been persuaded by a skilful lobby. This is probably the biggest difference between the UK and US systems – in the United States constituency interests trump party loyalty every time. This obviously assists the efforts of lobbyists.

Warning!

Although independent and third party candidates cannot themselves win, they can have a dramatic effect on the outcome of elections by siphoning off votes from a candidate who would otherwise have won. An example is Ralph Nader taking enough votes in Florida to deprive Al Gore of victory in that state, which in turn cost him the Presidency. The same could be said for Ross Perot and George Bush senior in 1992.

Another reason why lobbying thrives in the US is the vast amount of money which government in Washington (and in the individual states) has to disburse. In the financial year 2007-8, the total US federal Budget was $2.66 trillion. Add to that enormous figure the spending by individual states – some of which have economies the size of large European countries – and you have a truly staggering amount of money up for grabs. Traditionally, Members of Congress from both Houses have used a process known as "ear marking" to get federal funds allocated to specific projects in their districts. Quite often these "ear marked" funds represent their condition for supporting a specific bill. For the lobbyist, the "ear marking" process provides them with a very direct way of earning their fees and demonstrating their worth.

In the US, as in most other developed democracies, the media has a strong impact on the thinking of politicians and is therefore used by lobbyists to reinforce their case. Every Member of Congress, from either House, reads his or her local papers assiduously. Every Member of Congress – plus the president and his cabinet – reads the US national press, the *Washington Post*, *The New York Times* and the *Wall Street Journal*. They also channel-hop the TV news programmes, with particular attention being paid to ABC, CBS, CNN, MSNBC, NBC and Fox News. New media (blogs and websites) also have a strong influence on the thinking of legislators.

Many lobbying techniques in the US are identical to those used in the EU and Europe – indeed many of the techniques used in Westminster and Brussels originated in Washington. Opinion polls are regularly used as part of the lobbyists' armoury on both sides of the Atlantic. The difference, perhaps, is that lobbyists in the US will commission polls at a much more local level in order to demonstrate to an individual Member of Congress why he or she should vote a particular way or support a particular campaign.

Coalitions are also very much a feature of the US lobbying system – as they are in the EU. The Coalition to Stop Gun Violence was set up in order to take on the lobbying leviathan which is the National Rifle Association. It brings together medics, teachers, social workers and parents in a broad coalition with one main aim in mind – to restrict the ownership of guns. On particular bills one-off coalitions are formed – in favour or against. Both US politicians and US lobbyists are totally at ease with the concept of coalitions of convenience – where a pressure group can be your ally on one bill in the Senate whilst being your opponent on another in the House. Sometimes this can even be the case when the bills are going through simultaneously.

Websites are also probably used more in the US than in the UK and EU. Because lobbying campaigns are generally better funded in the US, lobbyists will think nothing of commissioning a fully-fledged and fully functional website for a single issue campaign. These websites can be used to gather signatures for a petition, and to send targeted emails to Senators and Representatives. Blogs are also used widely, to broadcast a message and to stimulate debate.

One peculiarly American technique is the "fly-in". This is a tactic whereby a trade association or pressure group will get all of its members from all over the US to literally fly in for a day, and demand to see their Senator or Representative. Sometimes these fly-ins are timed to coincide with a crucial stage of a bill which the organisers are either vehemently opposed to or strongly in favour of. Volunteers are supplied with "lobbying kits" with details and contact numbers of their Members of Congress, key messages to be put across, and a score card to record where their Representatives are (on a scale of 1 to 10) on their issue.

Lobbyists in the US have always used grassroots campaigning to put pressure on Members of Congress. As the late Speaker of the House of Representatives Tip O'Neill very truthfully – if ungrammatically – once said, "all politics is local". Both Senators and Representatives have to be re-elected – every two years in the case of the latter. They therefore keep their ears very close to the ground, and stirring up an issue in their backyards can produce a swift and positive response.

As well as being avid users of grassroots campaigns, US lobbyists have also pioneered "grass tops" campaigns. With this technique lobbyists meticulously research who it is who has the ear of Members of Congress. It could be their family, community leaders, their priest, their doctor or their dentist. Once those individuals have been identified, they are lobbied so that they in turn can lobby the Members of Congress who value their opinions.

One of the reasons why American lobbyists have to use such a variety of techniques is just to cut through the "fog of war". Senators and Representatives receive such vast volumes of communications of all forms that – even with their large staffs – they struggle to assimilate all of the information which is sent to them. By way of illustration, postal mail is delivered to Congressional offices five times a day six days a week. Around about 1000 items of post hit each office every day – from letters and postcards, to circulars, newspapers and magazines. Throw in the faxes and emails, plus the 30m phone calls which Congress receives every year, and you really do have to do something a bit different to get yourself heard above the cacophony.

Lobbying is a huge business in the US. As we saw in the section on ethics, there have been problems associated with lobbying in Washington and in the states. There are, therefore, strong controls on what lobbyists can do and what they can give. The Public Affairs Council of America, which was founded in 1954, has done much to professionalise – and regularise – lobbying in the US. It has some 5000 member organisations, corporations, associations and consultancies. Full-on face-to-face lobbyists now have to sign a register and record their dealings with Members of Congress, and around 35,000 have done so. They in turn are probably supported by at least twice as many support staff, who do the research, monitoring and preparation, but do not undertake advocacy work.

Overall the Washington lobbying scene is in a league of its own in size, sophistication and status. European lobbyists can learn a great deal by studying their techniques, many of which are transferable.

Contributor's top tip

Although yet to be adapted/utilized effectively in most other democracies, the single most powerful lobbying tool to emerge in the last three decades in Washington is the mobilization of large numbers of voters/constituents (grassroots) and an array of important stakeholders/community leaders ("grass tops").

In a democracy, the ultimate power/incentive/threat is the ability to assure or deny re-election. That power can be exercised through mail and email, blogs and advertising, news and editorial copy, endorsements and rallies, petitions and phone calls, alliances and coalitions, contributions and volunteers. To be credible it must be genuine, focused, compelling, and sustained over time.

In the US, established political parties are useless.

Most industry organizations are useless. This power is most effectively exercised by a single company, prepared to step out from/in front of its industry and actually DO something – letting public officials know there are both rewards and reprisals for how well they represent their constituents' interests.

John Ashford, Chairman & CEO, The Hawthorn Group

Part Eight –
Lobbying In Asia

The public affairs industry in Asia is very distinct and in many ways very different from that in the UK, the EU and the US. There are huge disparities between the cultural norms of the West and the East, and there are distinct differences in the political scenes within the huge continent of Asia. But Asia is well worth studying and engaging with. Lobbying in Asia is a fast-growing industry – and it is worth bearing in mind that Asia is home to both the world's largest democracy (India) and the world's most populous state (China).

Having talked about the disparities within the region there are common themes which do recur throughout, especially in the Association of Southeast Asian Nations (ASEAN) countries (Brunei, Cambodia, Indonesia, Laos, Malaysia, Myanmar, Philippines, Singapore, Thailand and Vietnam), Japan, India and China. Most public affairs practitioners agree that the term lobbying is not the best terminology to use in Asia. The term carries a negative connotation and is viewed with suspicion by those who would be the target of the lobbyist. For this section of the book we will therefore largely eschew the latter term in favour of the former.

Public affairs is practised at national and local level throughout Asia, with many Western professionals applying skills they honed in the US and Europe and adapting them to an Asian context. Categorising those who practice public affairs can be more difficult, but those who are engaged in the process of influencing government or regulatory outcomes range from corporate communications directors, to public affairs managers, to chief financial officers. The phenomenon of corporate social responsibility (CSR) in Asia in general, and China in particular, is very significant and a source of a great deal of business for the Western public affairs and public relations companies in the region. While CSR may give way to the next corporate buzzword in the West, it appears set to become an ever-more ingrained aspect of corporate strategy in Asia, and is already being termed as "sustainability" among senior corporate figures in Asia.

Contributor's top tip

The issue of "face" in Asia remains important. So are networks. The Chinese use the term Guanxi to describe basic personalised networks of influence. They are a central concept in Chinese society and play an important part in the decision making process. However the downside to a system based on networks is the presence of corruption, side deals and the "Mr 5%" phenomenon – which for companies governed by Sarbanes Oxley strictures makes Asia a complex arena in which to practice.

The principle of saving face also means that effective public affairs in Asia requires patience and expectation management when reporting back to senior colleagues in the West. A polite yes can actually mean no, so expecting the unexpected, even from senior politicians and officials, is important. One senior lobbyist cites the case of a senior Vietnamese minister giving a cast iron assurance on the derogation of a new tax, only for it to be almost immediately implemented without any period of derogation.

Craig Hoy, PublicAffairsAsia

Conducting public affairs in Asia is almost certain to become even more complex than it is today. As a result of the huge transfusion of investment from East to West and West to East, Asian governments (partly at the request of Western corporations) are passing legislation at a pace not seen before. China, for example, has passed 12 major pieces of corporate and tax legislation in recent years. However, in Asia legislation is often written in terms of general principle – which means the subsequent interpretation can be potentially difficult. The lawyer advising a client on compliance regarding a law which is drafted in a vague fashion may be more in the business of risk assessment than anything else. Cast iron advice and assurances are hard to come by.

The general absence of Western style liberal democracy, plus the presence of large-scale coalition governments, also means that Western style lobbying may not be directly applicable. India, for example, has experienced a coalition composed of 18 parties. Even if the current prime minister – Manmohan Singh – supports measures to liberalise markets where the licensed Raj exists, no amount of lobbying will necessarily achieve such an outcome overnight.

The role of the courts and the issue of post-legislative or reputation defending litigation also adds a confusing dimension when looking at lobbying in Asia. In Europe and the US effective lobbying can continue beyond the passing of an Act of Parliament. In the area of home affairs in the UK, for example, the courts regularly strike down laws passed by Parliament. In Asia, however, it can be a foolish move for a Western company to refer disputes with the government to the courts of that country. In Thailand in mid-2008 Tesco was engaged in three defamation suits relating to its Tesco Lotus company. It accused columnist and academic Kamol Kamoltrakul and former Thai National Legislative Assembly (NLA) member Jit Siratranont of defamation and sought to sue them for 100m baht and 1 billion baht (US$3.3m and US$33m) after they were critical of the company's expansion strategies. The legal challenge resulted in the Southeast Asian Press Alliance (SEAPA) accusing the company of intimidation against its critics, describing the move as a challenge to a free press.

The public affairs industry in Asia is itself a less transparent industry than its equivalents in Europe or North America. There is no push, demand or recognition of a need for a register of lobbying professionals - although the PR industries have adopted codes of conduct similar to those applied by their Western counterparts. APCO, for example, says on its own Chinese website that "much of ACPO's work is confidential in nature". The company does, however, offer an insight into its work by revealing case studies from clients ranging from ASEAN to Microsoft and Mercedes-Benz.

The politics and economics of Asia also make the public affairs arena interesting and dynamic. The Chinese government is coming under pressure from its own people regarding the recent liberalisation of its markets. A feeling that Asia has "given too much away" to Western conglomerates means that increased resistance to further Western "investment" (at a time when Asian governments are sitting on massive cash surpluses) will require multinationals to rethink both their market entry and expansion strategies in Asia. This change in mood was exemplified during the Szechuan earthquake, when the users of chat rooms on Chinese websites began criticising Western companies for their initially lackadaisical response to the aid effort.

The respective state of the economies of Europe, the US and Asia also opens up a new lobbying arena – the East on West lobbying offensive. Sovereign Wealth Funds (SWFs) are now encountering significant issues in the US, the EU and Australia. Questions about their motives, transparency and future strategies are being asked at a time when large stakes in European companies are being traded at values significantly lower than they would have been five years ago. In one sense the West now wants to know whether Asia is seeking to replicate the West, or to dominate it.

It is no surprise, therefore, that the Western "lobby shops" in countries such as India and China appear interested in using their offices as conduits for new business related to Brussels rather than Beijing or Bangalore. It also seems to be the case that for Asian companies not well versed in the subtleties of the softer side of lobbying in Europe or America, interesting lessons are already being learned. Money talks in Asia, but no amount of money assist a Chinese company seeking to buy a regional airport in the UK if the local population or the local media are resolutely opposed to the move.

Warning!

No honest account of lobbying in Asia could pass by the issues of corruption. In a region where laws are sometimes written deliberately to create a grey area the benefits of officialdom can be fertile ground for those who control decision making processes. The scale of corruption can be eye-watering, although the crackdowns appear more frequent and the punishment more severe. In 2008 former Shanghai Communist Party chief Chen Liangyu was jailed for 18 months on graft charges involving £2.5 billion in misappropriated funds, and earlier in the same year Thailand's police chief was sacked by prime minister Samak following allegations of corruption.

The essence of decision making in Asia is also a more complex affair than in the West. The Chinese, for example, are astute negotiators – even negotiating after the contract has been signed. The process of negotiation may look chaotic – the Chinese will jump from one issue to the next specifically to throw their counterpart off their course. The thread of an argument may appear weak and the approach may look amateur to an evidence-based Western lobbyist, but this can be a tactic specifically designed to give the Asian negotiator the upper hand. Following a meeting if you cannot clearly report what has been agreed – and what is not agreed – then the Chinese official has scope to change the terms of the agreement at a later date.

Contributor's top tip

Getting to know your suitor or your prospective partner is important – this process takes longer in Asia, and despite the rapid growth of the region's economies, Western lobbyists operating in Asia can falter by trying to go too far too quickly. They can also make the mistake of seeking to make too much of a relationship which is not yet strong enough to withstand the level of commitment being requested.

Mark O'Brien, PublicAffairsAsia

Trying to understand the geo-political mindset of those who you are trying to influence is vital. Thailand's politicians are suspicious of inward investing business (particularly where it originates from China) in what remains a nationalistic country. However, they appear to be comfortable with having closer links to American business interests than they do with European corporations. A certain cadre of Chinese officialdom may insist they are learning how to legislate from Europe – a coded way of displaying anti-American sentiments. Therefore, identifying where someone stands on an issue – be it Taiwan, Kashmir, pro-Thaksin or anti Tibetan independence – and making their view your view (providing it does not generate a conflict of loyalty or present other problems elsewhere) can aid your lobbying efforts and your influence.

Contributor's top tip

First, relationships are key. It is essential to invest time to develop personal relationships with decision-makers. They will not do business with you (and you should not try to do business with them) until a relationship and a level of trust has been established.

Second, with few exceptions (eg, Japan and India), many countries in Asia are either young developing democracies or not democracies at all. This means that unlike in the West, decision-making processes are often not transparent and there are rarely open opportunities for consultation or advocacy. Having said that, all government systems have a decision-making process and it's important to get to understand where the pressure points are, however complex or Byzantine. Don't expect to write letters and send position papers and get well reasoned replies clearly stating policy. It rarely happens like that. It is useful to submit your views on paper (preferably in local languages) but seek meetings for reactions rather than expect formal replies.

Mark Leverton, Diageo

To illustrate the terrain of Asian public affairs – even if not considered frontline lobbying in an Asian sense – it is useful to examine China (one-party state), India (multi-party democracy), Thailand (constitutional monarchy), Vietnam (one-party Socialist Republic), and Japan (constitutional monarchy). It is also well worthwhile examining Hong Kong (special administrative region of China) which bridges the gap between its mainland links and its colonial Western past.

8.1 China

Whilst China is not a liberal democracy in the Western sense, it does not mean the country exists in a political vacuum. It has a clear structure of government, which appears to function relatively smoothly in a cycle unencumbered by the distraction of an electorate or rival political leaders. Those looking for a guide to the individuals who occupy the key positions of government should seek out the China Government guide produced by the English-language *China Daily* newspaper.

Since 1948 China has been a one party government but not a one party state. The Communist Party runs the People's Republic in a manner which can be described as authoritarian and socialist. The Communist Party of China (CPC) is in control of the government and that control is guaranteed by the constitution. Whilst there is no wholesale move towards democratisation, the decision-making process is more transparent than 30 years ago, and the closed door of the late 1970s is now ajar in certain important respects.

The constitution of the People's Republic of China is the country's rulebook. It divides power among three bodies, whose senior ranks are exclusively occupied by senior representatives of the CPC. The CPC itself is controlled by the small and immensely powerful Politburo Standing Committee. Like Russian dolls, the three branches which control China are all essentially the same – the Party. They can, however, be viewed as three distinct sub-branches – the Party itself, the State and Central People's Government, and the People's Liberation Army (PLA). We look at each of these interlinked bodies in turn.

8.1.1 The Communist Party of China (CPC)

Under the constitution, the power to run China's economy, law-making process, governance and military rests with the Communist Party of China. Other parties do exist in China but they cannot be part of the government under the strictures of the constitution. In this sense China can accurately be described as a one-party state.

8.1.2 The State and Central People's Government

The State and Central People's Government effectively discharges the functions of government and selects those who will run the country's vast network of central and provincial governments. The distinct branches are:

8.1.3 National People's Congress (NPC)

The National People's Congress is the primary state body and the only legislative chamber in China. Its membership is largely decided by the CPC and the body now debates and determines outcomes – rather than simply assenting to the wishes of the country's leadership. Defeats for government proposals are very rare, but they do occur. The NPC is also a forum where disputes between different strands of the party can be addressed through reasoned dialogue.

The NPC also takes the key decision on the appointment of the country's political leadership. Both the president, who is head of state, and the vice president are elected by the NPC once every five years. To date this process has been determined by a single candidate election, reflecting the fact that the party's high command essentially controls the line of succession.

The NPC also appoints the Supreme Court, which is the judicial branch of China. Its writ does not, however, run in Hong Kong or Macau – which operate their own legal systems based on their colonial heritage.

8.1.4 State Council

The administrative central government of China is the State Council, which is appointed by the NPC. It is chaired by the Premier – rather than the president – and is comprised of a membership of around 50 administrative, departmental and agency heads.

During a period of selecting and re-ordering the State Council a hiatus occurs – not unlike the period prior to a major ministerial reshuffle or prior to a general election in the West.

8.1.5 People's Liberation Army (PLA)

Like the other branches of state and government of China, the Communist Party effectively controls the country's military – known constitutionally as the People's Liberation Army. Command and control is discharged by the Central Military Commission, which is overseen, and whose leadership is elected by, the National People's Congress. In essence, however, the CPC is in full control of the military in that the Central Military Commission of the party possesses and operates the real power.

Apart from central government, China also has a huge network of provincial and sub-provincial government. The central government appoints the provincial leadership, with the National People's Congress rubber-stamping those selections. These regional governors – who preside over both provinces and regions – have little real autonomy. Hong Kong and Macau are Special Administrative Regions and the former is dealt with under its own heading later in this chapter.

Underneath the provincial level (with some provinces having populations bigger than the largest European nations) there is a thriving sub-provincial government structure. At the last count it was assessed there were some 50 rural prefectures, 283 prefecture level cities, over 370 county level cities, over 850 county level districts, 808 urban districts and over 43,000 township level regions.

In many of these tiers of government the leadership is determined by central government, although there is an increasing trend towards direct and contested elections at the village level. These plebiscites are seen by some as the first semblance of a move towards greater democratisation. They could become more commonplace, and if they rise up through the tiers of local government this could eventually lead towards some form of democratic selection at the level of the National People's Congress.

8.1.6 The People

Assessing where the people enter into the equation is an interesting question for those studying China as it opens itself up to greater examination by the West. Moves to combat corruption, tackle rural poverty, and open up decision-making through pre-legislative consultation are a clear sign that the Communist Party of China does not govern in a vacuum. But the hard-line tactics used to shut down the Tibet protests underline the fact that the right to free speech and self determination in China are not state-sponsored entitlements as they are in the West.

Western politicians confirm that their Chinese counterparts now engage in free and open debate and discussion rather than reading prepared scripts. This view is borne out by the debate and dialogue about Chinese politics and policy which take place in the media and through the Internet.

Without wide scale democratic elections it is difficult to assess how the Chinese view their government. However, the transparent response to the earthquake revealed that China acknowledges its global responsibilities as well as its responsibilities to its own people. The media and industry are also important in China. Influencing the media, industry and the government can be indivisible at times – so comprehensive strategies which encompass a wide range of groups can be powerful.

Contributor's top tip

In a Western context, PR and government affairs can quite naturally exist in separate spheres. One characteristic unique to China, however, is the level of direct government links to industry and media. Therefore, in China, it is not only natural, it is often necessary that a corporate strategy of PR is complemented by a strategy of government affairs. We have described this complementary approach as convergence because under this rubric PR and government affairs converge to more comprehensively reach all key stakeholders. For example, PR and government affairs merge in corporate social responsibility initiatives.

Most government affairs firms in China focus on a unidirectional, top-down approach. They seek to utilise their relationships with government officials to effect legislative change. While my approach certainly calls upon an extensive network of relationships in various government ministries, convergence also emphasizes a bottom-up dynamic. Effective public affairs involves forging connections with industry associations who have interests in common. These semi-government industry organisations (for example the China Cotton Association) can play an invaluable role in educating policymakers and garnering support among grassroots Chinese companies. The work of these organizations, which we call "third party lobbyists", should be supplemented with PR media coverage.

Yuan Haiying, President of Yuan Associates

8.2 Hong Kong

Although Hong Kong acts as a hub for many professionals working in public affairs, very little in the way of public affairs or lobbying activity appears to take place (at least on the surface) in the Special Administrative Region (SAR). Since its handover, Hong Kong has operated as part of the People's Republic of China. Under terms conceded by Deng Xiaoping, the mainland must permit Hong Kong to remain sovereign on all issues except national security and foreign affairs until 2047 – 50 years after the historic handover.

Hong Kong remains a dynamic global marketplace, financial centre, and a gateway to China. Its strategic importance to the West is therefore assured, as is its importance to modern day China. In the immediate aftermath of the 1997 handover some fears were expressed that Hong Kong's global status would be eroded by a creeping tide of Chinese control. However the "one country two systems" approach has been maintained and Hong Kong is still seen alongside Singapore as a secure location for Western companies to do business.

Under a document termed "the Basic Law" the SAR's status and government structure are assured for half a century. Hong Kong therefore still operates a legal system very similar to that in the UK and its structure of government is very different to that seen in mainland China. However, that does not mean that Hong Kong resembles a modern-day democracy. Despite immense pressure from Chris Patten (the last British governor of the territory) to leave democratic structures in place, they were dismantled after the handover.

Despite the settled structures in Hong Kong, and its low-tax and pro-business approach, there is little in the way of Western style lobbying in Hong Kong. Most multi-national public affairs and public relations companies have a presence in Hong Kong. However, this is probably more to do with its status as a gateway to China than the need to effectively engage in frontline public affairs with the territory's political leadership. Strong and established chambers of commerce in Hong Kong, and the presence of active government bodies such as Invest Hong Kong, means there is regular and generally cordial dialogue between business, commerce and the decision makers.

8.2.1 Chief Executive

The Chinese operate the territory via a Chief Executive who is elected under rules laid down in the Basic Law. At the time of writing the post is held by Mr Donald Tsang.

The Chief Executive is formally appointed by the PRC, and the government of Hong Kong lists his responsibilities as "signing bills and budgets, promulgating laws, making decisions on government policies and issuing executive orders". The Chief Executive is assisted in policy making by the Executive Council.

8.2.2 Executive Council

The Executive Council is chaired and formally appointed by the Chief Executive and determines what legislation is put before the elected Legislative Council (known as LegCo).

The Executive Council is 30 strong and its membership is selected on the basis of 15 principal officials and 15 selected from non-official positions. The Executive Council in large part determines what decisions are enacted by the Legislative Council – and LegCo members can also be members of the Executive Council. There is no fixed term of office, although the membership expires at the end of the chief executive's period of office.

8.2.3 Hong Kong government

The Hong Kong government is wider than the Executive Council. The main administrative and executive functions of government are carried out by 12 policy bureaux and 61 departments and agencies. These departments are generally operated by a civil service not unlike that of the UK.

The Chief Executive is the head of the Hong Kong administration and is supported by three senior ministers – the Secretary for Justice, the Secretary for Administration and the Secretary for Finance. They in turn are supported by secretaries for areas such as food, health and home affairs.

8.2.4 Legislative Council

This 60-strong partly elected body is comprised of 30 members elected by popular vote from geographical constituencies and 30 based on their function or profession – such as financial services or transportation.

Using the language and practices of the Westminster parliamentary model a bill proceeding through the Legislative Council (LegCo) must be read three times. The first reading is procedural, with the title simply being read by a clerk at a session of the council. The second reading allows the membership to pass or reject the bill. If the bill is passed it proceeds to a committee of the full council for detailed scrutiny before being given a third reading where it is formally accepted before being signed by the chief executive. A bill cannot pass if it is rejected by the council at second reading.

In reality LegCo, because it does not generally determine which legislation it creates, acts more as a revising or monitoring chamber than an actual legislative body. However there have been high profile stand-offs with the Government, which in 2003 was forced to withdraw its anti-subversion legislation in anticipation of a defeat by LegCo.

8.2.5 The future

Pressure for further democracy in Hong Kong remains widespread, although in local elections the people of the SAR have demonstrated strong support for the Chinese Communist Party.

The withdrawal of the anti-subversion clause to "the Basic Law" was symbolic of the region's "one country, two systems" approach, although moves to give the Hong Kong people full electoral say over the entire membership of the Legislative Council have been delayed until 2020. Plans to give Hong Kong the right to elect its Chief Executive have been delayed until 2017. Lobbying for greater democracy will continue, and business will continue to press for a relaxed, pro-commerce approach by the political decision makers, both in mainland China and in the administrative region.

Contributor's top tip

A bit like Africa or Europe, only more so, there is no such thing as Asia, every country being different. However, apart from Japan (which adopts more of a Western corporate model) and of course Australia/NZ (also Western given their history), all the Asian countries rely on personal contact and often family connections to get things done, with only very limited systematic approaches to lobbying and public affairs. Nothing comes close to the formalised approaches of Washington, London, Paris or Brussels where particular norms of behaviour and processes are adopted.

Just as it is more difficult to penetrate the civil service in the West than obtain access to politicians, the same is true of democracies in Asia - Taiwan, for example, or to a limited degree Malaysia and Hong Kong. India is another case (being the largest democracy in the world) where you have access to politicians as well as to the officials. This is easier – if more chaotic – than China, where you have to assess complicated organagrams in order to work out who you need to talk or write to get something done or arrange a meeting. India is the one Asian country which truly understands the Western approaches, due to its British past. To some extent Malaysia is also like this, and Indonesia too, because of its Dutch heritage.

But with all these countries, lobbying is a matter of building relationships, having personal connections on the ground and ensuring you fully comprehend the rank and power structures of the organisations which you are dealing with. You also need to have an awareness of which countries like being given gifts and which do not, and also when it is appropriate to entertain.

In Asia lobbying takes place informally and is not as sophisticated as in the West. This does not mean that over time the West's approaches will be replicated, rather they will need to be adapted to suit local culture - this despite globalisation.

Roger Hayes, Senior Counsellor, APCO WORLDWIDE

8.3 India

As the largest democracy in the world, India represents both a huge challenge and a huge opportunity for the public affairs professional. India is currently undergoing large-scale market liberalisation and it is therefore the focus of many Western businesses. In some areas, such as brewing, banking and legal services, the barriers to trading are significant. This creates fertile territory for the Western PA practitioner seeking to assist those trying to break into those markets.

As the structures of government, the legal systems and language are in many ways replicas of the British system Western PA practitioners will find the terminology and practices familiar, although they will also find that the politics of India are far more complex. As Karan Bilimoria, the chairman of Cobra beer, and the head of the UK India Business Council, said in an interview with PublicAffairsAsia,

'The Indian relationship is founded on fundamentals we take for granted. An enduring democracy. The rule of law. The same principles, based on British law. The language of business is English. The wavelength of business is very similar, we have similar corporate governance rules, and a free and vibrant press and media.'

At the time of writing India is governed by an 18-party government coalition. The coalition is one reason why those present in India, such as Bilimoria, suggest Western companies seeking to influence issues in India must take a longer-term view. The constitution of India in part reflects the huge land mass and population of the country. It also reflects its heritage, and one of the reasons India has a parliamentary democracy similar to that of the United Kingdom is because of the long and close historical association between the two nations.

Although India has a president, power is effectively shared and discharged by a combined force of executive and legislature – operating at a national and federal level. To an extent the Indian political system can be seen as a fusion between the UK parliamentary model and the US federal system of government. At the top of the pyramid is Parliament, which is elected by the people of India. Whilst the president has a nominal power base, the real power is wielded by the prime minister and his or her cabinet. The prime minister and the cabinet are drawn from a bicameral legislature, structured into two houses – the Lok Sabha and Rajya Sabha. Lok Sabha is elected by the country's eligible voters, whilst Rajya Sabha members are elected by the state legislative assemblies using the single transferable vote (STV) version of proportional representation.

The Lok Sabha elects a Presiding Officer who is called the Speaker. He or she is assisted by a Deputy Speaker who is also elected by Lok Sabha. The conduct of business in the Lok Sabha is the responsibility of the Speaker. In the other chamber the vice president of India is the ex-officio Chairman – being elected by the members of an electoral college consisting of members of both Houses of Parliament.

As in the UK, the directly elected House has more powers. Legislation relating to India's finances – money bills – can only be introduced in Lok Sabha. The Rajya Sabha, however, has some exceptional powers to declare "that it is necessary and expedient in the national interest that Parliament may make laws with respect to a matter in the state list or to create by law one or more all-India services common to the Union and the states".

8.3.1 The legislative process

As is the case in the UK and the US, a bill is the draft form of a piece of legislation. Once a bill successfully completes all of the required legislative stages it then becomes an Act. As with the Westminster Parliament bills can be introduced either by a government minister, or by a private member. In the case of the former it is known as a government bill, in the case of the latter it is known as a private members' bill. Another similarity with the Westminster Parliament is that a bill may be introduced into either House, and must pass through identical stages in both Houses.

The stages of a bill passing through the Indian Parliament are:

- First reading: A bill can be introduced either in to either the Lok Sabha or the Rajya Sabha. The member-in-charge must ask leave to introduce the bill. If leave is given the bill receives its first reading. If the motion to introduce the bill is opposed, the Speaker may allow a brief debate between the member-in-charge and the member with the opposing view. Where the introduction of a bill is opposed on the grounds that the bill seeks to initiate legislation outside the legislative competence of the House, the Speaker may still allow a debate to take place. A vote can then be taken.

- Publication in Gazette: Once leave has been given for a bill to be introduced, it is published in the *Official Gazette*. With the permission of the Speaker a bill can be published in the *Official Gazette* even before it is formally introduced. In that circumstance, formal leave to introduce the bill is not required.

- Standing committee: After a bill has been introduced the Presiding Officer of either House can refer it to a standing committee. The standing committee looks at the general principle of the bill, but also examines it clause by clause. The committee can also call expert witnesses. Once its deliberations are completed, the standing committee reports on the bill to the House.

- Second reading – first stage: This is a general debate on the underlying principles of the bill. The House then has the option to refer the bill to a select committee, or a joint committee of the two Houses. If this occurs, the committee again examines the bill clause by clause, and amendments can be proposed. It can also summon expert witnesses, as well as other interested parties. The opinion of the governments of the states and union territories can also be sought, and their opinions are placed on the table of the House. The committee then reports to the House.

- *Second reading – second stage:* The House then considers the bill as reported by the committee. Amendments can be moved and voted on (by simple majority of those present). Amendments are considered before any clause is approved. After the amendments and clause have been considered, schedules are considered – as are the enacting formula and the long title.

- Third reading: Once these earlier stages have been successfully completed, the member-in-charge can move that the bill be passed. There is then a debate on the general principles of the bill as it now stands. Only formal, verbal or consequential amendments are allowed to be moved at this stage. For an ordinary bill, only a simple majority of those present is required. In the case of a bill to amend the constitution, however, a majority of the total membership of the House and a majority of at least two-thirds of those members actually present is required in both Houses of Parliament.

> **Author's top tip**
>
> There are many opportunities to try and get amendments to a bill
> proposed at its various stages of progress through both Houses. What
> is more, there are also good opportunities for you or your client to give
> evidence either in favour of or against the bill if it is referred to either a
> select or joint committee.

8.3.2 Finances

Another distinct similarity between the Indian Parliament and its Westminster
equivalent lies in the way in which they treat bills which are of a financial
nature. In both Parliaments, such bills can only be introduced in the lower
House – the House of Commons in the case of Westminster, and the Lok Sabha
in the case of the Indian Parliament. This restriction applies to all provisions
for raising or abolishing taxes, and the appropriation of resources. These are
known as "money bills".

The Upper House – the Raiya Sabha – does examine and debate money
bills. It cannot amend such bills, though it can make recommendations – which
the Lok Sabha is perfectly at liberty to ignore. The Raiya Sabha must return
all money bills to the Lok Sabha within 14 days.

If the Lok Sabha accepts any recommendations from the Raiya Sabha then
the money bill is deemed to have been passed. If on the other hand the Lok
Sabha does not accept any of the recommendations of Rajya Sabha, the money
bill is deemed to have been passed by both Houses in the form in which it was
passed by Lok Sabha, without any of the amendments recommended by Rajya
Sabha. If a money bill passed by Lok Sabha and transmitted to Rajya Sabha
for its recommendations is not returned to Lok Sabha within the statutory 14
day time limit, then it is deemed to have been passed by both Houses at the end
of that period in the form in which it was passed by Lok Sabha.

8.4 Japan

The Japanese legislature – the Diet – was established in 1890. It was the first parliamentary-style legislature to be established in Asia. Japan is still the world's second biggest economy.

The size of Japan's economy, and the fact that it is Asia's oldest parliamentary democracy, make it essential that it be included in this book. As China's economy continues to grow, and as Japan's once-mighty economy remains largely moribund, the struggle for leadership between these two Asian titans is likely to become ever fiercer. Both China and Japan will be looking to attract inward investment – and will be keen to ensure that Western markets remain accessible to their exports. The challenge for Western business people – and lobbyists – is to try and ensure that the accessibility is two-way.

8.4.1 The Diet

Prior to the second world war the Diet had been known as the Imperial Diet. Under the Meiji constitution it was the Emperor who exercised ultimate legislative power – albeit with the approval of the Diet.

Under the post-war 1946 constitution (adopted in 1947) the Diet became the National Diet. Article 41 established the fact that the Diet is the "sole law-making organ of the state". The Emperor was reduced to a ceremonial role, and Japan was re-invented as a modern state with a constitutional monarchy and a bicameral legislature.

The 1946 constitution saw the old House of Peers (based on the British model) abolished. The new bicameral legislature consisted of an Upper House (the House of Councillors) and a Lower House (the House of Representatives) elected by secret ballot with universal adult suffrage.

The Diet has wide-ranging powers, including:

- The sole right to initiate legislation
- The right to approve – or vote down – the annual Budget
- The right to sanction – or refuse to sanction – treaties with foreign powers
- The ability to conduct investigations in to the conduct of government
- The power to impeach judges found guilty of criminal offences

- The right to decide who should be prime minister

- The power to dissolve the government – if a motion introduced by at least 50 members of the House of Representatives is passed

- The ability to draft changes to the constitution – which must then be approved by a referendum of the Japanese people

8.4.2 House of Representatives

There are 480 Members of the Lower House – the House of Representatives. Of these, 300 are elected for constituencies under the first-past-the-post system, whilst the remaining 180 are elected for eleven super constituencies under the party list system of proportional representation. In theory Members are elected for four year terms. However, this is a maximum term – the House and the prime minister can call a general election at any time, in which case there is an immediate dissolution.

Before the 1946 constitution was introduced both Houses in the Diet had equal powers. After 1946, however, the so-called Lower House, the House of Representatives, became the dominant chamber.

If a bill is approved by the House of Representatives, but is then voted down by the House of Councillors, it still returns to the House of Representatives. If the bill is then passed again by the Lower House, with a majority greater than two thirds of those voting, it is immediately passed into law.

This procedure to establish the primacy of the House of Representatives applies to all normal bills. There is a separate procedure, however, for more important bills. These are bills to:

- Select the prime minister

- Adopt the Budget

- Approve treaties with foreign powers

In these instances, both Houses should agree. If they do not, a joint committee composed of both Houses is convened with a view to finding a compromise. If after 30 days a compromise is not reached the will of the House of Representatives prevails.

8.4.3 House of Councillors

There are 242 Members of the Upper House – the House of Councillors. Of these 146 are elected to represent 47 prefectural constituencies, whilst the other 96 are elected using the party list system of proportional representation. They are elected for six year terms, with one half up for re-election every three years. The six year term is fixed, and the House of Councillors cannot be dissolved when a general election is called (although it does go into recess during the election period).

There are two distinct types of constituency in the House of Councillors. Prefectural constituencies are represented by 13 Councillors on a super constituency basis, whilst the rest are elected by proportional representation. This PR innovation was introduced in 1982, and was the first major constitutional change to the 1946 constitution. In theory the system was introduced to stem the vast amounts of money which individuals were spending on their election (and re-election) campaigns. Many critics, however, maintained that the reform was designed to cement the stranglehold of the dominant party (the Liberal Democratic Party or LDP) and its principal rival (the Japan Socialist Party – later the Social Democratic Party of Japan).

8.4.4 The government

In theory all ministers, including the prime minister are appointed by the Emperor. However, as we have seen, since the adoption of the 1946 constitution the Emperor wields only symbolic power.

In practice the prime minister is chosen by the Diet. Both Houses are involved in the process, although ultimately the House of Representatives can over-rule the House of Councillors. There have been occasions when both Houses have put forward candidates for the post of prime minister, but the Lower House has always prevailed.

The prime minister then has the right to appoint his own cabinet. Most members are drawn from the Diet – although this is not a constitutional requirement. The main ministries are:

- Prime Minister's Office
- Ministry of Foreign Affairs
- Ministry of Finance

- Ministry of Economy, Trade and Industry
- Ministry of Health, Labour and Welfare
- Ministry of Land, Infrastructure and Transport
- Ministry of Justice
- Ministry of Agriculture, Forestry and Fisheries
- Ministry of Education, Culture, Sports, Science and Technology
- Ministry of Internal Affairs and Communications
- Ministry of Environment
- Ministry of Defence

Author's top tip

The Ministry of Economy, Trade and Industry (formerly the Ministry of International Trade and Industry) has been crucial to Japan's post-war economic revival and its emergence as the world's second largest economy. Officials in META hold huge sway over Japan's economy, and that Ministry should be your first port of call if you have a commercial issue or proposal.

8.4.5 The future

Although Japan is a modern democracy with a constitutional monarchy and a huge (if currently static) economy, it presents enormous challenges to Western lobbyists. Throughout most of the post-war period political power has rested with one political party – the LDP. Occasionally a coalition of other parties prises the LDP's fingers from the levers of power, but to a large extent Japan has been a one-party state since 1946.

In common with most Asian states personal relationships are crucial. With the Japanese propensity for elaborate courtesy and ritual such relationships can take a long time to develop. As with many other Asian cultures, it is considered very bad manners to just say "no". Lobbyists and Western businessmen must therefore develop a sense for the true meaning of the various versions of "yes" which might be proffered.

Author's top tip

Japan may be the country of elaborate ritual and courtesy – but it is also the land of karaoke and sake. If you can persuade your contacts to meet on an informal basis, and hit the town with them, then you might be able to break though the barriers and have what the Japanese refer to as "asa made nama terebi" – roughly translated as an unfettered conversation (usually alcohol fuelled) in the small hours of the morning. You might find out what is really going on – and you might forge the kind of close relationship which is essential to making progress when lobbying in Japan.

Japan has a huge and vibrant media industry. Newspaper readership is reckoned to be the highest in the world, and there are also strong radio, TV and Internet media channels. These various branches of the media do report on politics, the activities of the government, and the foibles of individual members of the Diet and the government. They are, however, constrained by membership of various press clubs. These are sponsored by government departments and agencies as well as senior politicians, and they are widely reckoned to have a negative impact on the independence of the press and its ability to expose corruption.

Apart from the strong influence of the Ministry of Economy, Trade and Industry which has already been mentioned, Japanese industry is closely tied to government through a series of elaborate networks. Chief amongst these are the Japan Federation of Economic Organisations, the Japan Committee for Economic Development, and the Japan Federation of Employers Associations. There is also the less overt – but no less powerful – informal network of the *Zaibatsu*. This informal network of giant conglomerate companies goes back to pre-war Imperial days, and still has a powerful hold over Japan's economy (and political scene) today.

The support of big business in Japan has helped the LDP maintain its tight grip on power through most of the post-war period. The aim of Japanese business has been to maintain maximum access to external markets – whilst ensuring that the barriers to imports have remained high.

Author's top tip

Lobbying in Japan is always going to be a difficult proposition involving a long-term commitment. The best way to lobby in Japan (other than through long-established relationships) can be through official agencies – the British Trade Promotion Office in Osaka, and United Kingdom Trade & Investment and British Trade International in London.

8.5 Thailand

The structure of government in Thailand is technically clear, but the application of the country's constitution – and its future governance – is far less easy to assess or predict.

Thailand is a constitutional democracy with an elected government and a monarch as head of state. In 1932 a revolution put restrictions on the role of the monarch, although Thailand's long-reigning King Bhumibol remains a powerful and revered figure in a country where the political situation is often uncertain. Whilst the King wields little in the way of actual constitutional power, his influence has been felt throughout his reign – a period in which the country has been run by a succession of elected governments, appointed leaders and military juntas.

The latest military coup in Thailand came in 2006, when the military seized office from prime minister Thaksin Shinawatra amid allegations of corruption and a political stalemate brought about by the decision of the Democrat Party not to contest the general election. For about 18 months the generals were engaged in what was widely seen as a less than successful effort to run the country.

However in 2007 Thais voted in support of a new constitution, and set their country back on a rough but ready course towards democratic politics. The focus and public face of that national democracy is the National Assembly.

8.5.1 National Assembly

The head of Thailand's government is the prime minister, who is drawn from the bicameral Parliament. Technically known as the National Assembly, the legislature is formed of a 480-strong House of Representatives and a 150 strong Senate.

In recent times political parties in Thailand have come and gone – with Thaksin Shinawatra's Thai Rak Thai (Thais Love Thais) the most notable arrival and departure. At the time of writing the government of the country is headed by prime minister Samak Sundaravej, whose People's Power Party is seen as largely sympathetic to previous Shinawatra movement. The next leading party is the Democrat Party, which is more popular among prosperous metropolitan Bangkok Thais. Other parties to contest the last general election were the Thai

Nation Party, For the Motherland, Thais United National Development Party, the Neutral Democratic Party and the Royalist People's Party.

Thailand uses a system of direct election, an element of proportional representation and a system of appointment to select its legislators. In the House of Representatives 400 members are elected using direct election, with the remaining 80 being selected on the basis of party proportionality in eight electoral districts.

The composition of the Senate, however, is different. The Senate has 76 directly elected members from each of the country's 76 districts, as well as another 74 who are selected from professions such as the law, academia, business and public service. This process of selection is overseen by a body known as the Senate Selection Committee.

The process of lobbying on individual clauses of legislation is not common practice in Thailand. Changes to the laws governing foreign ownership of companies were passed by the military government to significant (and relatively rare) criticism by *farang* business heads and diplomats. The law was passed, but it has not to date been put into practice.

Much public affairs activity also takes place around the application of existing laws, rules and regulations. The American Chamber of Commerce, for example, has been very active in trying to ensure customs matters are applied by officials in a transparent and consistent manner within the Kingdom of Thailand.

In Thailand locally appointed governors, and local provincial administrations, wield devolved and delegated powers and are often influential in issues such as planning applications, the situating of power plants and local infrastructure projects. They are therefore an additional focus for those involved with inward investment and lobbying in Thailand.

Contributor's top tip

At a time when leading companies are rapidly increasing their presence and investing vast amounts in Asia, most understand that a strong public affairs presence is invaluable. They soon realize that the rules of the game back home do not apply to the emerging market where they are about to make that big investment, and they need to get up to speed quickly.

The first key difference is that the system of lobbying, or legitimately seeking to influence government decisions that we take for granted, is often frowned upon. The first time I mentioned lobbying in India, it was misinterpreted as seeking an unethical influence over the authorities. You swiftly acquire the correct terminology.

Then one quickly realises that many Asian countries have deeply entrenched domestic economic interests that your company is seeking to compete with, and they are closely connected to the governing elites.

Ultimately, it is this pure complexity and lack of transparency in policy making that makes Asia the most challenging, yet fascinating, arena for public affairs today.

Liam Benham, Vice President of Government Relations with Ford and a Governor of the American Chamber of Commerce in Thailand

8.6 Vietnam

Vietnam is a one-party Socialist Republic run by a powerful Communist Party. Its legitimacy as effectively the sole party of the country was determined by the National Assembly through a constitution agreed after decades of political and military instability.

Despite the absence of Western-style democracy the country has secured record foreign direct investment over recent years and is now the focus of significant inward investment from Asian nations such as China, and from European and American multinational companies. The government has decreed itself committed to a political and economic renewal agenda, which is known as *doi moi* (or renovation).

The scope for the future business and PA activity is set to increase markedly following a decision by the government to begin the wholesale sell-off of the key state-owned assets. Under a complex set of rules, which determines how much foreign owned companies will pay for their stake in the new companies, the "equitization process" is being road-tested through the sale of the state owned telecommunications network. This follows the relaxation of the rules governing company ownership, and the high profile move by HSBC to acquire a 10% stake in a Vietnamese insurance company formerly owned by the state.

Despite the *doi moi* programme, some senior public affairs professionals question the wisdom of significant investment in a country where decision making is not transparent, and where power is concentrated firmly in the hands of its leadership. Two individuals in particular - the prime minister and the general secretary of the Vietnamese Communist Party – wield enormous political power.

The Republic is headed by a largely ceremonial president of state, who is elected by and from the country's National Assembly every five years. Whilst he formally enacts laws and assumes the head of state role, his powers are widely seen as titular. Elections for the National Assembly take place every five years. In the election held in 2007, candidates represented only organs of the Communist Party – often in the form of the Vietnamese Fatherland Front – or those affiliated to the party.

At the time of writing the government is headed by prime minister Nyugen Tan Dung. He is supported by a team of 25 ministers, which includes three deputy prime ministers. Based on a constitution agreed in 1992 – which vests power in the Communist Party of Vietnam (CPV) – all functions of the state are essentially run by the Party. Therefore any group contesting an election must be affiliated to the Party. After the struggles for independence from colonial power, the Communists formalised their control of the country through the constitution, which has checks and balances, most notably in the form of the elected National Assembly.

The Vietnamese Government is accountable to the National Assembly, the National Assembly's Standing Committee and the president of state. The prime minister can, technically at least, be removed by a vote in the National Assembly. The assembly meets at least twice a year, sits for five years, and only members of the Communist Party of Vietnam can contest the elections.

The CPV operates with a mission of "rich people, strong nation, equitable, democratic and civilized society". To achieve these goals, the CPV, in accordance with the principle of the people as the country's roots, has set up a wide and diversified political system. The political apparatus of Vietnam is composed of a number of bodies. They consist of the CPV, political organisations, socio-political organisations, socio-professional organisations, and mass associations. Article 4, chapter 1 of the current constitution says the role of the CPV is to be 'the leading force of the state and the society' and that the 'party's activities are governed by the constitution and laws.'

Whilst the CPV is all-powerful, in functional terms it is the National Assembly which determines legislation. Under the constitution the president of the Republic, the standing committee of the National Assembly, the Ethnic Council, the committees of the National Assembly, the Government, the Supreme People's Court, the Supreme People's Procuracy, the Vietnam Fatherland Front and its members, are all entitled to put legislation before the country's legislature. This is in addition to the Deputies of the National Assembly.

Prior to being presented to the National Assembly, bills are sent for consultation to the Ethnic Council or a relevant committee. The bills are then sent to all Deputies to the National Assembly at least 20 days before the opening of the National Assembly session. Legislation which requires public discussion is published and broadcast by the mass-media "so that the people and the state organs at all levels are able to have comment before presentation of those bills to the National Assembly".

Every piece of legislation is formally debated at the National Assembly session, initially by groups of members, and then by all the members at a plenary session. An individual piece of legislation becomes duly-adopted law when a simple majority of the Deputies to the National Assembly vote in favour of its adoption. After being adopted by the National Assembly, a bill must be signed by the president of the National Assembly. The president of the Republic then formally introduces the new law, which becomes effective (and on occasion can be made public for the first time) no later than 15 days from the date of its adoption.

Given the situation in Vietnam, most effective public affairs activity is therefore targeted at the ministerial level. However, decision making is not transparent and delegations of Western aligned interests can find that pledges given on issues such as new taxes are not necessarily followed through. Given the cost of labour and production in the country it has been the focus of significant Western interest – some in part displaced from Thailand as a result of recent political instability.

Whether those making significant investment into Vietnam will encounter longer-term issues in the country remains to be seen. The monopoly of power held by a small Communist elite, and the lack of transparency in the legislative process, might however give some Western companies – and governments – pause for thought.

8.7 Unique Challenges

The case of the amendment of foreign ownership legislation in Thailand during the military coup typifies the challenges faced by much of the public affairs industry in Asia. Where laws are written badly they may be unenforceable. They may also be difficult to interpret and therefore subject to confusion - even among those responsible for implementing them. It is also the case that even where laws are passed, they may never be enforced. In any event, it is a universal truth that business hates uncertainty and may hold off investment plans where the political scene is in a state of flux, and where laws are poorly drafted or randomly enforced.

The interpretation of laws is another problem for business, and therefore it is an area where public affairs practitioners, accountants and lawyers find themselves engaged in seeking to find solutions. One senior Chief Financial Officer in China says he makes a habit of attending official briefings on the finer points of interpreting new legislation.

Yan Jin, China CFO of US-based Eaton Fluid Power, told CFO Asia magazine 'In China, the guidance always comes out late – I'm used to it.' Jin attends – or has a staff member attend – presentations by officials who helped to write the laws, and asks them about interpretation 'My approach is to write down their name,' he says. 'I have five plants in different cities. If I have an arbitrary decision at the city level, then I show this person's name. I say, "If there's a problem, then let's go together to visit him."'

In China in particular corporate legislation is emerging at such a pace that the guidance on interpreting the new law may not be published for months after its enactment. An increasing culture of pre-legislative scrutiny does mean, however, that in China laws may be clearer and based less upon broad principles than in other parts of Asia.

In conclusion, Asia remains a challenging environment for the Western lobbyist. Whilst some maintain that lobbying is lobbying throughout the world, requiring the same skills of articulate advocacy and gentle but determined persuasion, others realise and acknowledge that the Asian scene is unique. The pace of legislation, allied to the increasing volume of inward investment, guarantees that the amount of public affairs activity can only increase.

In a recent interview Jeff Blount, a senior lawyer in Beijing, summed up what this chapter hopes to have projected - a significant growth in government relations in Asia. He said,

'You have to be able to deal with new legislation quickly, and you have to be able to work with the government when you have regulatory uncertainty. That means you've got to have a full infrastructure in this country, including in-house counsel, HR staff, and government relations personnel. It's a matter of running a fully integrated business model, not just running a manufacturing plant and sending money back to the US.'

This view underlines why there will undoubtedly be more lobbyists in Asia in the coming decades. They will not, however, be lobbying in the same manner, or using the same terminology, as they do in the West. Asia has its own distinct cultures, and Asian countries have their own unique political systems. Western lobbyists and public affairs consultancies wishing to operate successfully in Asia need to adapt their practices and their outlook accordingly.

Contributor's top tip

- Establish and cultivate both personal and institutional relationships with stakeholders and influencers. This process crucially includes developing trust and confidence between the parties concerned.

- Make use of stakeholder mapping: identify key stakeholders and influencers for each issue of concern, and develop an understanding and appreciation of the agendas and relations among stakeholder groups and individuals.

  - Classify by business impact, support/hostility, issues of shared interest, flexibility, etc.

- Develop multi-level engagement with influencers at all levels

  - Direct via meetings

  - With relevant government officials

  - Via business forums or the like

  - Through home country commercial delegations

  - Indirect through third-party advocates

- Government supported CR program

- Joint research projects, White Papers, etc.

- Trade association roundtables and other industry events

- Incorporate media relations into a public affairs strategy and program, and connect with media on different platforms and creatively

  - News releases, exclusive executive interviews, tours, roundtables/workshops

  - Informal gatherings, media lunches, teas, receptions

- Recognize and appreciate differences in cultures and practices among and within Asian countries – one size does not always fit all. But also realise that some strategies and tactics may be applied across cultures and countries: be wary of admonitions that "we can't do this in our country."

Mark Michelson, Deputy Director, Invest in Hong Kong, Vice Chairman APCO Asia

Part Nine –
Lobbying In The Middle
East

L obbying in the Middle East is not as yet well-established. This is mainly because of lack of Western style liberal democracies, which is the main environment in which commercial lobbying has traditionally flourished. With the exceptions of Israel, Kuwait and the Lebanon, fully-fledged democracy in the Western mould is largely absent – although elections do take place throughout the region. Most Middle Eastern states are, however, either one party states, theocracies, or absolute monarchies.

Another reason why commercial lobbying has yet to take off in the region is that Middle Eastern societies tend to be complex and closely-knit. Family and clan relationships can be decades or even centuries old, and even the most experienced and astute Western lobbyist might struggle to make an impact in a region where relationships are based on history and tradition, rather than the more ephemeral imperatives of commerce and democracy.

There are signs, however, that the region is – in parts at least – becoming more accessible to Western companies and Western lobbyists. Of course Western oil and defence companies have long operated in the region. Now, however, there is a move to open up markets to 'softer' industries – such as tourism, publishing and PR.

Finally, there is the 'reverse lobby' concept. With the price of commodities generally, and oil in particular, growing strongly in recent years, Middle East governments are looking to invest their vast oil revenues in the West. That means preparing the ground in order to make it acceptable for Middle Eastern Sovereign Wealth Funds to buy key Western industries and utilities. And that, in turn, means that the skills and contacts of Western lobbyists will be much in demand.

9.1 United Arab Emirates

The United Arab Emirates (UAE) has led the way in opening up its markets to Western companies, and in seeking Western investment and skills.

The UAE is a federation of independently ruled states. Seven absolute monarchies, operated by oil-rich ruling families, have joined together to create a powerful economic region which co-operates where common interests arise, but which compete where national self-interest is at play. The UAE is, in effect, the EU of the Gulf.

The seven independently ruled states are Abu Dhabi, Ajman, Dubai, Fujairah, Ras al-Khaimah, Sharjah and Umm al-Qaiwain. The Ruler of Abu Dhabi is the president of the UAE, and the Ruler of Dubai is its prime minister. These two Rulers are often cited as the two most powerful regional players.

Politics of the United Arab Emirates takes place within the framework of a federal presidential elected monarchy, which is a federation of the seven absolute monarchies. Dubai is headed by a ruling family which is headed on a day-to-day basis by His Highness Sheikh Mohammed bin Rashid Al Maktoum, vice president and prime minister of the UAE and Ruler of Dubai. In 2001 he declared his country's mission statement as: 'We must ease the lives of people and businesses interacting with the government and contribute in establishing Dubai as a leading economic hub.'

However, to say there is no lobbying or public affairs in Dubai or the UAE would be to assume a Western, democratic based definition of both practices. Where there is government – and where there is wealth – there is lobbying, and the UAE, the Gulf and the Middle East are not exceptions to this rule. As in the Far East, however, lobbying in the Middle East is a slower and perhaps more subtle version of the art which is practised in the UK, US and EU.

Rising like a beacon of capitalist development from the deserts of the Gulf, Dubai City is leading the economic and architectural transformation of the Gulf. Such a process cannot be achieved without discussion and dialogue, and the relocation of businesses from the West. As the senior members of the ruling families often have top level positions on the boards of companies (such as the region's airlines and banks) they engage in external business and political discussions around areas such as investment, mergers and acquisitions, and partnerships.

Lobbying in the sphere of oil is also present through organisations such as OPEC, and the Emirates are actively engaged in public affairs activity in Europe and the United States as a result of hugely increased activity by Middle Eastern Sovereign Wealth Funds. As with the Far East, lobbying is a two way street, and Middle Eastern interests are actively promoted in the West by public affairs professionals and consultancies.

Author's top tip

Dubai is now a regional media hub, and the centre of the communications industry in the Middle East and the Gulf. As lobbying activity takes root and continues to grow in the region, Dubai is likely to become the PA (as it already is the PR) base for multinational firms.

Bibliography

Public Affairs in Practice: A Practical Guide to Lobbying, Stuart Thomson & Steve John (Kogan Page Limited)

Lobbying in Washington, London, and Brussels: The Persuasive Communication of Political Issues, Conor McGrath (The Edwin Mellen Press Ltd.)

Politico's Guide to Political Lobbying, Charles Miller (Politico's Publishing)

Revolving Gridlock: Politics and Policy from Jimmy Carter to George W. Bush, David W.Brady & Craig Volden (Westview Press)

The Campaign Handbook, Mark Lattimer (The Directory of Social Change)

The Political Campaigning Handbook, Lionel Zetter (Harriman House)

The Politico's Guide to Local Government, Andrew Stevens (Politico's Publishing)

Vacher's Quarterly, Editor Valerie Passmore (Dods)

Words That Work, Dr. Frank Luntz (Hyperion Books)

Guide to the House of Commons 2005, Editors Tim Hames and Valerie Passmore (Times Books)

Almanac of British Politics, Robert Waller & Byron Criddle (Croom Helm Ltd.)

How Parliament Works, Robert Rogers & Rhodri Walters (Pearson Education Ltd.)

Understanding the European Union: A Concise Introduction, John McCormick (Palgrave Macmillan)

Websites

- www.parliament.uk
- www.scottish.parliament.uk
- www.new.wales.gov.uk
- www.niassembly.gov.uk
- www.labour.org.uk
- www.conservatives.com
- www.libdems.org.uk
- www.snp.org
- www.plaidcymru.org
- www.dup.org.uk
- www.sinnfeinassembly.com
- www.theyworkforyou.com
- www.work4mp.com
- www.politicalbetting.com
- www.iaindale.blogspot.com
- www.order-order.com
- www.conservativehome.blogs.com
- www.labourhome.org
- www.recessmonkey.com
- www.totalpolitics.com
- www.stephentall.org.uk
- www.libdemblogs.co.uk
- www.whatisrss.com
- www.youtube.com
- www.coe.int/T/e/Com/about_coe
- www.europa.eu/index_en

- www.ec.europa.eu
- www.ue.eu.int
- www.europarl.europa.eu
- www.ukrep.be
- www.epp-ed.eu
- www.socialistgroup.eu
- www.alde.eu
- www.house.gov
- www.senate.gov
- www.parliamentofindia.nic.in
- www.english.gov.cn
- www.gov.hk/en
- www.government.ae/gov/en/index.jsp
- www.eppo.go.th/index_thaigov.html

Index

1922 Committee 168

527 Groups 393

A

AAPPG – *see* Associate All-Party Parliamentary Groups

Abramoff, Jack 16

Acquis communnautaire 341, 344, 352

Adam Smith Institute 21, 47

Advocacy Group, The 391

AdvocacyOnline 90

Agincourt Communications 94

Ahern, Bertie 247

Airbus UK 137

al Fayed, Mohamed 8, 10

All-Party Parliamentary Groups 34, 85, 141, 166-168, 332

Allen, Woody 184

Almanac of British Politics 81, 438

Anderson, Iain 115

APCO 403, 413, 432

APPC, *see* Association of Professional Political Consultants

APPG, *see* All-Party Parliamentary Groups

ASEAN – *see* Association of Southeast Asian Nations

Ashford, John ix, 397

ASITIS Consulting 260

Associate All-Party Parliamentary Groups 167-168

Association of British Insurers 93

Association of Professional Political Consultants 4, 8, 10-12, 16, 62, 65

Association of Southeast Asian Nations xxi, 401, 403

Astley, Simon 13

Atack, Steve ix, xx, 56, 61

Atrium, The 37, 170

Attlee, Clement 7

Audit Commission 181, 279

Augure 86-87

Automobile Association 127

B

BAE Systems 13, 28

Bank of England 121, 356

Barclay, Steve 115

Barclays Bank 115

Barlow Clowes 284

Barnett Formula 222, 231, 235-236, 250

Barroso, Jose Manuel 313

Basic Law 410-412

Beaumont, Ian 259

Bell Pottinger Public Affairs 132

Bell, Kevin 162

Bellenden Public Affairs 137

BELs, *see* Budget Expenditure Lines

Bennett, Katherine 137

Betts, Barrie 87

Bhumibol, King 424

Bigg, Alex 142

Bilimoria, Karan 414

Bill Team 154, 343

Bills

    Ballot bills 177

    Consolidation bills 192, 212

    Draft bills 45, 144, 153

    Finance Bill 175, 182-185, 198

    Hybrid bills 178

    Presentation bills 178, 179

    Private bills 51, 176, 178-179, 191, 214, 379-380

    Private members' bill 72, 171, 177, 415

Bingle, Peter 132

Bircham Dyson Bell vii, 5

Birt, Lord John 125

Blair, Tony 14, 26, 45, 122-125, 128, 205, 246-247, 262

Blount, Jeff 430

Blueprint Partners 312

BMA, *see* British Medical Association

Bow Group 168

Bowel Cancer UK 259

Bracken, Jonathan vii, ix

BRAD 92

Brady, Graham 143

Brands2Life 42

Bricken, Matt 50, 89

British Medical Association 27

British Polling Council 124

British Trade International 423

British Trade Promotion Office 423

Brown, Gordon 21, 101, 122, 127-128, 144, 180-181, 184

Brunel University 54

Buckby, Simon 18

Budget

    Budget Bill 250

    Budget Bundle 181

    Budget Cycle 180-181

    Budget Expenditure Lines 236

    Budget Report 29, 181

    Budget Statement 29, 183

    Budget Submission 183-184

Bundling 393

Burnham, Andy 107

Burrell, Michael 305

Burrowes, David 152

Burson-Marsteller 362

Bush, George 122, 394

Business Bulletin 216-217

Business Questions xii, 156, 157

C

C&AG – *see* Comptroller & Auditor General

Cabinet Submission 131

Cambridge University 54

Cameron, David 44, 46, 107

Campaign Group 169

Campbell Gentry 309

Campbell, Alastair 123

Caplan, Darren 42

Carlton's Directory of Westminster and Whitehall 103

Casey, Angela 224

Cash for honours 121

Cash for questions 8

Cass 48

CBI, *see* Confederation of British Industry

CCHQ, *see* Conservative Campaign Headquarters

CCO, *see* Conservative Central Office

CCT, *see* Compulsory Competitive Tendering

Centre for Economic and Business Research 48

Centre for Policy Studies 21, 46-47

Chambre Public Affairs 261

Champollion 18

Chan, Gerald 180

Charity Commission 27, 112

Chartered Institute of Public Communist Party of China 406-408

Chartered Institute of Public Relations 4, 10-11, 16, 54, 62, 65

Chatham House 47

Chef de cabinet 315, 324

Childs, Peter 56-57

China Daily 406

Churchill, Winston v, 293, 359

Cicero Consulting 115

Cinnamon Club 37

CIPR, *see* Chartered Institute of Public Relations

Citigate Dewe Rogerson 44

City of London Corporation 185, 263

Civil Service Code 14-15, 104, 106

Civil Service Year Book 33, 103, 126

Civitas Cymru 245

Clement-Jones, Lord 200

CM Porter Novelli 224

Coalition to Stop Gun Violence 395

Coldwell, Ian 209

Coleman, Brian 268

College Public Policy 106

Comitology 305, 316, 337, 341

Commission for Social Care Inspection 196

Committee on Standards and Privileges 12

Committee stage 51, 175-176, 184, 197, 199-200, 249, 286

Commonwealth Parliamentary Association 167

Communist Party of China 406-408

Communist Party of Vietnam 427-428

Compass 47, 169

Comprehensive Spending Review 180, 235-236, 250, 401

Comptroller & Auditor General 180-181, 251

Compulsory Competitive Tendering 283

ComRes 48-49, 54, 88

Concordats 208

Confederation of British Industry 28, 122, 185

Confidence Motion 173

Congestion Charge 119, 266

Congressional Liaison Office 370

Connect Public Affairs 186

Conservative Campaign Headquarters 19, 43, 116-117, 274, 320

Conservative Central Office iii, xx

Consultation document 44

Convention of Scottish Local Authorities 275

Cornerstone Group 169

Corporate Social Responsibility 58, 186, 401, 409

Countryside Alliance 26, 285

Covington, Graham 90

Cranborne, Viscount 187

COSLA, see Convention of Scottish Local Authorities

CPC – see Communist Party of China

CPV – see Communist Party of Vietnam

CreativeBrief 63

CSR, see Comprehensive Spending Review

D

Dale, Iain 55, 75

Dalton, Hugh 182

DCT, see Disproportionate Cost Threshold

David, Miliband 107

de Gaulle, President Charles 294, 303

Debates

Adjournment Debate 134, 157-158, 173-174, 195, 251

Legislative Debates 172, 174, 194, 197

Opposition Day 173-174

Substantive Motion Debate 172-173

Westminster Hall Debate 157

DeHavilland 34, 78, 86, 103

Delegated Legislation 178-179, 259, 305

Delivery Unit 125-126

Deloitte 48

Delors, Jacques 298, 313, 320, 345

DeLuca, Nick 386

Democratic Unionist Party 258

Demos 21, 47

Deng Xiaoping 410

Deshmukh, Sacha 207

Diageo 108, 405

Diet xvii, 311, 418-420, 422

Dilnot, Judith 59

Direct Labour Organisations 282

Disproportionate Cost Threshold 165

DLA Piper Government Relations 200

Dodonline 33-34, 86, 103

Dods 33, 48, 50, 54-56, 79, 86, 89, 438

Doi moi 427

Dover, Den 332

Downing Street 75, 86, 106, 121-128, 132, 140, 158, 267

Drafts Team 343

Draper, Derek 30

DUP, see Democratic Unionist Party

E

EAPC, *see* European Association of Political Consultants

Early Day Motion 16, 72, 88, 116, 139, 154-156, 215, 218-219, 334

Earmark 16

Earnshaw, David ix, 362

ECB, *see* European Central Bank

ECGD, *see* Export Credits Guarantee Department

ECOFIN 300-304

ECSC, *see* European Coal and Steel Community

Edelman 142, 305

Eden, Anthony 122

Editors Media Directory 92

EDM, *see* Early Day Motion

EEA, *see* European Economic Area

EFTA, *see* European Free Trade Area

Elections and Referendums Act 19

Electoral Commission 20

Electus 56, 59

Elliott, Simon 142

Ellwood & Atfield 56

Ellwood, Gavin 58

EMS, *see* European Monetary System

Energy Retail Association 113

Enfield, London Borough of 282

EPACA, *see* European Public Affairs Consultancies Association

ERM, *see* Exchange Rate Mechanism

Ernst & Young 48

Erskine May 82

Euratom 294

European Association of Political Consultants 17

European Central Bank 346, 355-356

European Centre for Public Affairs 337

European Coal and Steel Community 293-294, 310, 359

European Economic Area 296

European Free Trade Area 294-296

European Monetary System 295

European Public Affairs Consultancies Association 16, 299

European Transparency Initiative 17, 299

Evans, Marc 245

Evans, Roger 267

Exchange Rate Mechanism 295-296

Executive Agency xii, 3, 73, 85, 108-109

Export Credits Guarantee Department 28-29

F

Fabian Society 47, 169

Factortame 289

Falklands War 123

Faulkner, Lord 200

Fawkes, Guido 75

Federation of Small Businesses 28

Fiche d'impact 317

Financial Secretary to the Treasury 286

Financial Services Authority 111

Financial Times 93

Finsbury Group 263, 267

First reading 175, 179, 196, 412, 415

Fleishman-Hillard 162, 299

Fonctionnaire 310, 319

Food Standards Agency 111

Ford 370, 426

Foreign and Commonwealth Office 100, 307

Foreign Policy Centre 47

Freedom of Information Act 18, 284-285

Freeman, Gidon 94

French, Jonathan 93

FSB, *see* Federation of Small Businesses

G

G8 303

GAERC 300, 304

GAG, *see* Government Affairs Group

Gallup 48

Gentry, Simon 309

George, Lloyd 180

Gifford Jeger Weeks 8

Ginger Group 60, 168-169

GJW, *see* Gifford Jeger Weeks

GLA, *see* Greater London Authority

GLC, *see* Greater London Council

Glover, Mark 137

Gold plating 51, 348

Golds, Peter 100

Gore, Al 394

Government Affairs Group iii, xx, 4, 10-11

Government of Wales Act 97, 229-231, 236, 243, 246

GovNet 55

Grant, President Ulysses S 6

Grass roots 323

Grass tops 396, 397

Greater London Authority 262-264, 266-268

Greater London Authority Act 97, 262-264, 270, 277

Greater London Council 262

Green Paper 45, 152-153, 175, 285, 342

Greer, Ian 8, 10

Grogan, John 16

Guantanamo Bay 367

Guardian Media Directory 91

Guardian, The 8, 10, 225, 241, 387

Gunner, Dan 78

H

Haiying, Yuan 409

Hallward, Madeleine 113

Hamilton, Neil 8

Hansard 31, 52, 72, 77, 100, 156, 158, 160, 178, 194, 263, 285-286

Hanson Search 56

Harrison, Julia 312

Hawkins, Andrew 49

Hawthorn Group 397

Hayes, Roger 413

Healey, Denis 98

Heath, Sir Edward (Ted) 138, 246

Henley Management College 48

Her Majesty's Stationery Office 72, 109, 182

Heseltine, Michael 128, 287

Highways Agency 110

Hill, Daran 244

Hill, Dave 123

HM Treasury, *see* Treasury

HMSO, *see* Her Majesty's Stationery Office

Holbeche, Barney 98

Hollis 62, 81, 91-92

House Magazine 55, 81

Howard, Michael 287

Hoy, Craig ix, xx, 402

HSBC 427

Human Rights Act xv, 285, 288-290, 360

I

Iaindale.blogspot.com 74, 439

Ian Greer Associates 8, 10

ICM 48

IGA, *see* Ian Greer Associates

Incorporated Society of British Advertisers 331

Indigo Public Affairs 278

Ingham, Bernard 123

Ingham, Francis ix, 12, 275

Inland Revenue 286

Insight Public Affairs 75, 212

Institute for Fiscal Studies 48

Institute for Public Policy Research 21, 46-47

Institute of Directors 28

Institute of Economic Affairs 21, 47

IoD, *see* Institute of Directors

IPPR, *see* Institute for Public Policy Research

Inter-Parliamentary Union 167

Intergroup 332

Ipsos MORI 48

J

Japan Committee for Economic Development 422

Japan Federation of Economic Organisations 422

Jewell, Martin 280

JFL 56

Jin, Yan 430

John, Steve xix, 438

Johnson, Alan 288

Johnson, Boris 119, 262-263

Johnson, Helen 36

Johnston, Keith 185

Johnston, Neil ix, 261

Joseph, Sir Keith 46

K

K Street 16, 386

Kallas, Siim 17

Kamall, Syed 323

Kelsey, Chris ix, 263, 267

Khan, Robert 196

King, Edmund 127

Kinnock, Lord Neil 205

Koder, Martin 102

KPMG 48, 120

L

Lamprecht, Henry 282

Langley, Quentin 60

Lansman, Nick 321

Lanson Communications 102

Law Officers 209, 221-222

Law Society 11, 28

LCO, *see* Legislative Competency Order

LDP, *see* Liberal Democratic Party

Lead committee 213-214, 346-348

Leeds Business School 53

Legislative Competency Order 236-237

Lehal, John 212

Leno, Jay xix

Leverton, Mark 405

Lewis Communications 76

Lewis, Chris 76

Lexington Communications 94

LFEPA, *see* London Fire and Emergency Planning Authority

LGA, *see* Local Government Association

Liaison Committee 192

Liberal Democratic Party 420-422

Licensing Act 2003 281

Livingstone, Ken 119, 262, 266

Lobbying Disclosure Act 16

Local Government Association 275

Lockwood, Keith 132

Lok Sabha 414-415, 417

London Business School 48

London Fire and Emergency Planning Authority 264-266

London Mayor 97, 119, 262-268, 270, 279

London Plan 264, 277

Lord Chancellor 129, 188

Lord Speaker 188

Lords Minute 72, 192-193

Luff, Peter 186

M

Macdonald, Moray 210

MacDuff, Robbie 72

Macgill, John ix, 228

Magna Carta v, 6, 97

Major, John 8, 10, 128, 184, 246

Majority Leader 371-372, 374

Majority Whip 371-372, 374

Mandate Communications 207

Manifesto 43-45, 50, 116-117, 144-145, 169, 198, 205, 223, 262, 269

Margrave, Dr Richard 361

Marin, Manuel 313

Mayor of London, *see* London Mayor

McCloud, David 391

McGrath, Conor xx, 438

McGrigors 215

McGuinness, Martin 248

McLeod, Jon 184

Mediadisk 92

Mediahub 92

Merchant Shipping Act 1988 289

Metropolitan Police Authority 264-266

MI5 121

MI6 121

Michael, Alun 231

Michelson, Mark 432

Miller, Charles xix, 438

Milner, Karl 4-5, 53

Ministerial Code 13-14

Minority Leader 372, 374

Minority Whip 372, 374

MJ, see Municipal Journal

Mohammed, Sheikh Mohammed bin Rashid Al Maktoum 436

Monnet, Jean 293-294, 320

Morgan, Rhodri 231

Morhamburn 228

Morris, Gill 186

MPA, see Metropolitan Police Authority

Municipal Journal 273

Murphy, Dan 46

N

Nader, Ralph 394

NAO, see National Audit Office

National Audit Office 29, 180-181, 288

National Farmers' Union 98

National Health Service 7, 29, 109

National Institute for Health and Clinical Excellence 29, 110, 112

National People's Congress xvii, 407-408

National Rifle Association 394-395

National Union of Mineworkers 287

Nayyar, Simon 44

NDPB, see Non-Departmental Public Body

Neil Stewart Associates 54

New Policy Institute 47

New York Times 395

Newsnight 26, 135

Nguyen Tan Dung 427

NHS, see National Health Service

NICE, see National Institute for Health and Clinical Excellence

NILGA, see Northern Ireland Local Government Association

No Turning Back Group 169

Nolan Committee 8, 15, 280

Non-Departmental Public Body 108-111, 209

NOP 48

Northcote-Trevelyan 99

Northern Ireland Act 1998 246, 248

Northern Ireland Assembly xiv, 84, 97, 120, 246-255, 259, 261, 269

Northern Ireland Executive 248, 250-251, 254-255, 258, 260

Northern Ireland Local Government Association 275

NPC 407

NRA, see National Rifle Association

O

O'Brien, Mark xx, 404

O'Keefe, James 54

O'Neill, Rory 32

O'Neill, Tip 396

Obama, Barack 75

Observer, The 10

Official Report 218, 239, 253, 334

Oliver, Quintin 256

Ombudsman xv, 279, 284, 335

Open Road 386

Opinion Leader Research 48

Opinion poll 49-50, 83, 124, 369

OPM 382

Order Paper 72, 154, 158-160, 163, 165, 178, 192-193

order-order.com 74, 439

Oxford University 54

P

PA Consulting Group 48

Pagoda Public Relations 209

Paisley, Rev Ian 248

Parliament Act 180, 182, 196

Parliamentary Agent 176-179

Parliamentary Commissioner for Standards 15, 166, 168

Parliamentary Labour Party 168

Parliamentary Private Secretary 100, 126, 137-138, 160, 165

Patient, Richard 278

Patten, Chris 410

People's Liberation Army 406, 408

Pepper Media 87

Pepper v Hart xv, 52, 177, 285

Pepper, Adrian 87

Perot, Ross 394

Peter Childs Associates 56, 57

Ping Pong 51, 196-197

Pinnacle PR Training 54

PLA, see People's Liberation Army

Plaid Cymru 120, 229, 232-233, 242

PLP, see Parliamentary Labour Party

PMS Guide to Interest Groups 81

PMQs, see prime minister's questions

Policy Exchange 46-47

Policy Network 47

Policy Studies Institute 47

Political Action Committee 386, 393

Political Intelligence 71, 74, 77-79, 321

Political Parties, Elections and Referendums Act 19-20

Political Research and Communications International iii, xx, 8

Political Wizard iii, 88-89

politicalbetting.com 74, 439

Poll, see opinion poll

Populus 48

Pork barrel 16, 381

Portcullis House 170

Positif Politics 244

Postcomm 111

Powell, Commander Christopher 7

PPERA, *see* Political Parties, Elections and Referendums Act

PPS, *see* Parliamentary Private Secretary

PPS Group 100

PR Newswire 92

PR Peoplebank 60

PRCA, *see* Public Relations Consultants Association

Pre-Budget Report 29, 181

Precise Public Affairs 72

Presiding Officer 188, 210, 213, 217, 237, 239-240, 371, 373, 415-416

Press Gallery 145, 157, 162, 166

PriceWaterhouseCoopers 48

Prime minister 14, 45, 101, 120-130, 137-139, 144-147, 159, 162, 163, 184, 188, 205, 209, 225, 246, 402-404, 414, 419-436

Prime minister's questions 162-163

PR+CI, *see* Political Research and Communications International

Privy Council 209

Prodi, Romano 313

Progress 27, 47, 59, 66, 72, 117, 146, 169, 172, 197, 211-214, 257, 306, 310, 344, 348, 376, 417, 422

PRWeek 81

PSAs, *see* Public Service Agreements

PubAffairs 55

Public Affairs Council of America 397

Public Affairs News 55, 81

Public Bodies Directory 109

Public Relations Consultants Association 4, 10, 12, 54, 62-65

Public Service Agreement 180, 254

PublicAffairsAsia iii, xx, 402, 404, 414

Q

QMV, *see* Qualified Majority Voting

Quaestors 17, 324

Qualified Majority Voting 304-305, 347, 352

QUANGO *see* Quasi-Autonomous Non-Governmental Organisation

Quasi-Autonomous Non-Governmental Organisation 3, 109

Queen's Speech xii, xiii, 99, 143, 144, 145, 146, 181, 190, 343

Questions

Named Day 164

Oral 16, 72, 134, 150, 157-165, 172, 185, 192-194, 216-218, 225-240, 252-259, 322, 333-343

Starred 192-195

Supplementary 159-162, 180, 184, 193, 217, 239

Unstarred 195

Written 66, 72, 150-151, 164-166, 169, 179, 185, 194, 218-219, 239-240, 274, 277, 322, 334, 372, 382, 402-40

Quirinale 37

R

Radio 4 93

Raiya Sabha 417

Randall's Parliamentary 78

Rapporteur 16, 331, 346-348, 354

Rasmussen 48

recessmonkey.com 74, 439

Red Book 181

Reform 14, 42, 47, 101, 111, 147, 169-170, 189, 191, 201, 377, 420

Register of Members' Interests 12-13, 15, 33

Reid, John 101

Remploy 46

Report stage 52, 176, 182, 184-185, 197, 199

Reporting Cycle 180-181

Reshuffle 99, 407

Richard, Lord 230

Riders 381

Robathan, Patrick 78

Robinson, Peter 248

Rogers, Bradley 79

Roosevelt, President Franklin D 369

Ross, Alastair 215

Royal Assent 178, 182, 195, 198, 214, 249-250, 262, 285, 288

Royal College of Obstetricians and Gynaecologists 180

Royal Pharmaceutical Society 141

Rozansky, Deborah 382

Rumbelow, Richard 164

Rycroft, Tim 108

S

Salisbury Convention 119, 198

Salisbury, Lord 198

Salmond, Alex 205-206, 221

Samak, Sundaravej 424

Santer, Jacques 313, 327

Sarbanes Oxley 402

Schengen 295, 296

Schuman Declaration 293, 359

Schuman, Robert 293

Scotland Act 205-210, 216, 222-223, 246

Scotland Office xiii, 225-226, 241, 257

Scotsman, The 209, 224

SDLP, *see* Social Democratic & Labour Party

SEAP, *see* Society of European Affairs Professionals

Second reading 175-179, 182, 196-200, 227, 345, 347, 412, 416

Sewel Convention 208

Sewel Motion 208

Shepherds 37

Sherlock, Neil 120

Sherman, Alf 46

Shinawatra, Thaksin 424

Singh Manmohan 402

Single Transferable Vote 262, 415

Smith Institute 21, 47

Smith, Doug ix

Smith, John 205

Smith, Tim 8

Smith, Warwick 106

Social Democratic & Labour Party 258

Social Market Foundation 47

Society of European Affairs Professionals 16-17

Society of Trust and Estate Practitioners 185

Sovereign Strategy 32

Sovereign Wealth Funds 403, 435, 437

SPADS, *see* Special Advisers

Speaker 39-40, 157-161, 175, 176, 188, 249, 251, 263, 373-374, 396, 415-416

Special Adviser 9, 14, 38, 86, 102, 106-108, 116, 125-126, 131-132, 136, 138, 149, 160, 221, 273, 315

Spencer, Tom 337

St John Stevas, Lord Norman 147

Stakeholder 32, 58, 87, 213, 431

Stanbrook, Lionel 339

Statutory Instrument 214, 237

Stratagem 256

Straw, Jack 107, 287

Stuart, Amanda 75

Sub judice 112, 154

Subsidiarity 340

Sunday Times 8, 10

Syngenta International AG 339

T

T-Mobile 164

Table Office 159

Taoiseach 246

Tesco 402

Tetra Strategy 54

Thatcher, Margaret 8, 21, 46, 99, 108, 121, 123, 128, 147, 184, 188, 225, 246, 262, 320

Think tank 21, 46-47, 50, 124, 175

Third party endorsement 45-49, 84, 183

Third reading 52, 176, 182, 197-200, 412, 416

Thomson, Stuart xix, 5, 438

Times Guide to the House of Commons 81

Times, The 10

Today Programme 93, 123, 135

Tory Reform Group 169

Total Politics 55, 75, 81

totalpolitics.com 74, 439

Traverse-Healy, Professor Tim 7

Treasury 98-100, 127, 131-132, 148, 180-185, 222, 230-231, 241, 286, 384

Treaty of Amsterdam 97, 296, 346

Treaty of Lisbon 97, 297, 302

Treaty of Maastricht 97, 295-296, 312, 314, 335, 346, 354

Treaty of Nice 297, 352

Treaty of Paris 294

Treaty of Rome 97, 294, 344-345, 356

Tribune Group 169

Tsang, Donald 411

Turley, Barry 260

Twinn, Ian 331

Tyler, Lord 201

U

UK India Business Council 414

UKREP 305, 307-308, 440

UKTI, *see* United Kingdom Trade & Investment

Ulster Unionist Party 258

UN, *see* United Nations

United Kingdom Trade & Investment 423

United Nations 101, 293, 311

Usual Channels 138, 145, 149, 190, 372

UUP, *see* Ulster Unionist Party

V

Vacher's Quarterly Companion 62, 81, 103, 126

Value Added Tax 350

VAT, *see* Value Added Tax

VMA 56

Vocus 92

W

WAG, Welsh Assembly Government 231-236, 238, 241, 245

Wall Street Journal 395

Walpole, Sir Robert 120

Washington Post 395

Watney and Powell 7

Webb, Justin 41

Weber Shandwick 184, 210

Weekly Information Bulletin 72, 81

Welsh Local Government Association 275

Western European Union 294

Westlake, Sheridan 118

Westminster Bookshop 82

Westminster Explained 54

Westminster Hall 157, 170, 172, 173, 174, 259

WEU, *see* Western European Union

Wheeler, Adrian 94

Whip 128, 138-140, 168, 187-190, 193, 233, 272-273, 371-372, 374

White Paper 145, 152-153, 175, 342

Whitehouse Consultancy 147

Whitehouse, Chris 147

Whitelaw, Lord William 188

Who's Who in Public Affairs 62, 81

Williamson, Rt Hon Lord 187

WLGA, *see* Welsh Local Government Association

Willis, Charles 141

Wilson, Tim ix, 114

WMS, *see* Written Ministerial Statement

Work4MP 439

Written Ministerial Statement 165-166

Wunnerlich Caroline 299

Y

YouGov 48

YouTube 75-76, 439

Yuan Associates 409

Z

Zaibatsu 422